Fundamentals
of Digital Switching

Applications of Communications Theory
Series Editor: R. W. Lucky, *Bell Laboratories*

INTRODUCTION TO COMMUNICATION SCIENCE AND SYSTEMS
John R. Pierce and Edward C. Posner

OPTICAL FIBER TRANSMISSION SYSTEMS
Stewart D. Personick

TELECOMMUNICATIONS SWITCHING
J. Gordon Pearce

ERROR-CORRECTION CODING FOR DIGITAL COMMUNICATIONS
George C. Clark, Jr., and J. Bibb Cain

COMPUTER NETWORK ARCHITECTURES AND PROTOCOLS
Edited by Paul E. Green, Jr.

FUNDAMENTALS OF DIGITAL SWITCHING
Edited by John C. McDonald

A Continuation Order Plan is available for this series. A continuation order will bring delivery of each new volume immediately upon publication. Volumes are billed only upon actual shipment. For further information please contact the publisher.

Fundamentals
of Digital Switching

Edited by

John C. McDonald
Continental Telecom Inc.
New York, New York

PLENUM PRESS • NEW YORK AND LONDON

Library of Congress Cataloging in Publication Data

Main entry under title:

Fundamentals of digital switching.

   (Applications of communications theory)
   Includes bibliographical references and index.
   1. Telephone switching systems, Electronic. 2. Digital electronics. I. McDonald,
John C., 1936–   . II. Series.
TK6397.F86 1983   621.3815′37   83-2143
ISBN 0-306-41224-1

© 1983 Plenum Press, New York
A Division of Plenum Publishing Corporation
233 Spring Street, New York, N.Y. 10013

Printed in the United States of America

Contributors

D. H. Carbaugh ● Western Electric, Lisle, Illinois

A. E. Joel, Jr. ● Bell Telephone Laboratories, Holmdel, New Jersey

John C. McDonald ● MBX Inc., New Canaan, Connecticut

N. L. Marselos ● Western Electric, Lisle, Illinois

David G. Messerschmitt ● University of California, Berkeley, California

Sushil G. Munshi ● United Telecommunications Inc., Kansas City, Missouri

Myron J. Ross ● GTE Products Corporation, Sylvania Systems Group, Needham Heights, Massachusetts

Matthew F. Slana ● Bell Telephone Laboratories, Naperville, Illinois

Preface

The development of low-cost digital integrated circuits has brought digital switching from a concept to an economic reality. Digital switching systems have now found worldwide acceptance and there are very few new switching systems being considered either for design or application which are not digital. Digital technology has created new opportunities for innovation including the integration of digital transmission and switching, the combination of voice and data services in one switching entity, and the design of switching systems which are economical over a broad range of sizes.

In the strict sense, the term "digital switching" refers to a system which establishes a message channel between two terminations where information is represented in digital form. In more common usage, a digital switch usually contains a time-divided network composed of logic gates and digital memory to accomplish the switching function.

The intent of this book is to provide an introductory level explanation of the principles of digital switching. These principles apply to both public and PABX switching. The book is aimed at those who apply, design, maintain, or simply wish to understand digital switching techniques. An electrical engineering degree is definitely not required for comprehension. We have concentrated on explaining digital switching techniques without the use of detailed mathematics. However, each chapter contains a comprehensive list of references which will lead the reader to sources for a more in-depth study of the many subjects covered. Also, a glossary of digital switching terms is located at the end of the book for easy reference. Since digital switching is international in scope, the impact of international standards is referenced throughout the book.

There are many technologies involved in digital switching and one individual can rarely master them all. Therefore, this book has many authors who are experts in various digital switching specialties. A sincere attempt has been made to minimize any subject overlap in the various chapters without detracting from the benefits a reader might derive from multiauthor views.

Material for the book comes from a course on digital switching which has been presented over the past four years at the University of California at Los Angeles and at the University of Maryland. The authors have all lectured in this course and have received valuable suggestions from the students regarding organization and presentation of the material.

The book is organized as follows. Chapters 1 through 4 contain material on circuit switching fundamentals, traffic theory, stored program control, and software. These subjects are not unique to digital switching and apply equally to analog switching. The balance of the book is unique to digital switching. Chapters 5 and 6 discuss the time-divided network for both circuit switching and packet switching. Analog and digital information interfaces to a digital switch are discussed in Chapters 7 and 8. Digital switching architectures are presented in Chapter 9, and the book concludes with a discussion of networks containing digital switches in Chapter 10.

This book is organized around a historical approach to the subject with Chapter 1 covering the basics of circuit switching and subsequent chapters proceeding more deeply into digital switching. However, each chapter stands alone and it is not necessary for the reader to begin at Chapter 1 and proceed to Chapter 10. Each author has referenced other chapters in his text so readers can begin with their favorite subject and proceed on. The "meat" of digital switching begins in Chapter 5.

Finally, on behalf of the authors, I wish to acknowledge the support and assistance of their companies. In alphabetical order they are:

Bell Laboratories, Inc.
Continental Telecom, Inc.
General Telephone and Electronics, Inc.
MBX, Inc.
TRW, Inc.
United Telecommunications, Inc.
University of California
Western Electric, Inc.

A final acknowledgment goes to the hundreds of students who have stimulated us to write this book and who have helped us to more completely understand this powerful technology.

New Canaan, Connecticut   Jack McDonald

Contents

3. Switching System Controls

A. E. Joel, Jr.

4. Switching System Software

D. H. Carbaugh and N. L. Marselos

5. Time-Division Networks

Matthew F. Slana

6. Circuit versus Packet Switching
Myron J. Ross

7. The Analog Termination
John C. McDonald

10. Digital Networks
John C. McDonald

Circuit-Switching Fundamentals

A. E. Joel, Jr.

1. Introduction

There are three major elements in a multiuser telecommunication system. These are the station or terminal equipment, the transmission media and repeaters, and the centralized or distributed switching entities including the signaling required for them to function.

There are several forms of switching, the most widely known being circuit, packet, and store and forward. Considerations in the design and deployment of all switching systems have much in common. This chapter will describe the various types of switching with most emphasis on circuit switching. Circuit switching is delineated from packet switching in Chapter 6 of this volume.

Emphasis in this chapter will be on switching principles, definitions, and environmental and operational aspects of the best-known, most common and universally available form of switching. *Circuit switching* is defined as switching that provides for the establishment of dedicated paths for the passage of messages, one way or conversational (duplex) such as for voice and telex, between two or more terminals, known in telephony as "stations." Circuit switching is for instantaneous communications where the switching process introduces no perceptible and variable delay between the receipt and delivery of a message or any portion thereof. The public telephone network is an example of a circuit-switching application where the investment is divided approximately as follows: switching equipment (25%),

A. E. Joel, Jr. • Bell Telephone Laboratories Holmdel, New Jersey outside cables and plant (29%), stations (20%), transmission terminal equipment (15%), and building, land, and miscellaneous (11%). These economic ratios reflect many years of development and growth of public telecommunication, with switching slowly increasing its share of the total. The reasons will be given later in this chapter.

This chapter is divided into three major sections. Section 2 emphasizes the networking aspects of circuit switching including the trades between transmission and switching and signaling between nodes of the network. Section 3 illuminates the general factors and functions in the design of circuit-switching systems. Both the system environment in a network or the marketplace and the internal system architecture objectives affect the design parameters. The principal unique function of a circuit switch is the interconnection switching network. The design principles of these networks as well as other internal system connectives are covered in this section. Section 4 introduces by definitions the subject of digital switching.

2. Circuit-Switched Networks

2.1. Relations between Transmission and Switching

Economic tradeoffs between transmission facilities and switching systems have been recognized since the earliest days of telephony. Originally, *transmission facilities,* pairs of wires known as *lines,* connected each station with the others where users had a "community of interest". As shown in Fig. 1, while there appeared to be no switching used in this primitive system, there was indeed a switching system at each station (see Fig. 2). This type of arrangement is well known today as used in small business systems, known as *key systems.* Generically these are known as *station* switching systems where each system serves the needs of only one station. Note that switching for N stations required $(N - 1)N$ switches or crosspoints and $N(N - 1)/2$ two-way lines. This noncentral form of switching system provides and delineates the following service attributes: (1) selection, (2) alerting (ringing), (3) privacy, (4) call attempt, (5) the two-way message (conversation), and (6) the two-way line (same line used for originating and receiving calls).

By centralizing switching for stations at a node (Fig. 3), the number of transmission lines required is reduced by a factor of $(N - 1)/2$ and the number of crosspoints by a factor of 2. The array of crosspoints is shown as a triangle (see Section 3.3) and provides for $N/2$ simultaneous connections that each station can be connected to some other station if it is not busy. The great advantage of centralized station (local) switching is that since the

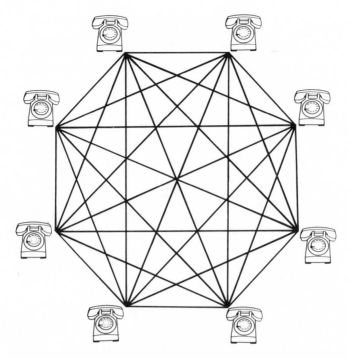

Fig. 1. Need for switching. (From *IEEE Proceedings*, September 1977.)

number of simultaneous connections expected in normal usage, even at the busiest time, lies in the range $0.1N$ to $0.2N$, the number of crosspoints may be reduced further. If more call attempts are made than can be accommodated, then the concept of *blocking* is introduced. The number of crosspoints may be reduced as shown in Fig. 4. In this figure connections are established over *links* designated L. The crosspoints of the calling and called stations are simultaneously operated to connect to a particular link. The total crosspoints are LN. If $L = 0.2N$ the required crosspoints would be $0.2N^2$ for a reduction of approximately 60%. As N becomes larger the increase in crosspoints opens up the subject of switching network topology covered in Section 3.3. The probability of a call attempt being blocked is a function of the number of links provided and the average expected call attempts. Blocking is given as a decimal representing the average chance, P, of no link being available. As shown in Fig. 5, the larger the number of links L (group size) the larger the average number of simultaneous calls that can be carried with the same chance of blocking.

Locating the switching function at a node defines a two-way line per station which on the average is longer than the more direct routes of the lines shown in Fig. 1. Also defined are the initiating and detecting of service

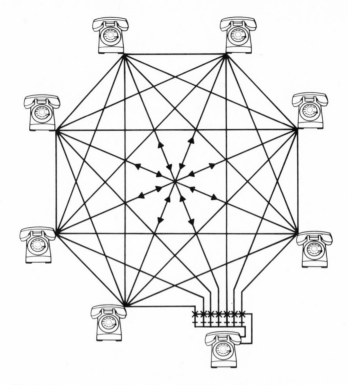

Fig. 2.   Noncentral switching. (From *IEEE Proceedings*, September 1977.)

requests (known as *attending*) and the remote control of crosspoint operations that must accompany the centralization of switching. The concept of
blocking introduces the entire field of traffic theory and engineering that is
covered in more detail in Chapter 2 of this volume. Traffic engineering
takes into account such items as probability of blocking, sometimes known
as *loss* or *grade of service*. While this may be measured in most situations it
is desirable to predict loss based on assumptions of traffic offered. Offered
traffic is measured by the sum of the length, in time, of the offered messages
or calls, known as the *holding time*. While theoretical assumptions may be
made about the arrival and departure of calls, the specific conditions such
as coincidence, time of day (and year), and community of interest among
the users may require the application of different engineering criteria.

The central node is located at a wire center that includes power
equipment, cable vaults, and termination or distribution frames where internal and external cables are joined and where transmission multiplex and
signaling terminals are located in addition to switching entities. Figure 6
shows other techniques that are being employed to refine the advantages of
trading transmission for centralized switching. Years ago, when lines were a

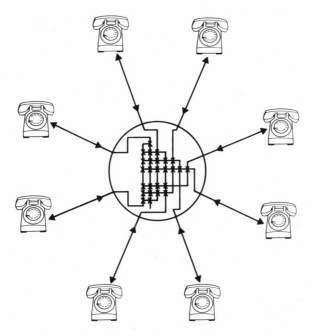

Fig. 3. Central switching (nonblocking).

larger part of the cost of providing telephone service, switching system terminations were arranged to serve lines with more than one station. This was known as *party-line* service and is shown at the top center of the figure.[1] Transmission multiplexing (carrier), particularly using the more recent development of low-cost semiconductor repeaters and terminations, has made possible a reduction in the cost of longer lines where the lines become channels of a carrier system (designated T in the figure).[2]

Another trade is possible by providing some simple switching functions at a point closer to a small group of lines. The links of the switch, being fewer than the number of lines, are brought to the wire center as *trunks*. These are defined as common arteries for traffic. This function is known as *remote line concentration* and a remote line concentrator (RLC) is a particular type of switching entity. Blocking is introduced as close to the group of stations as economically possible.

To avoid the need for using two trunks on an intraconcentrator call, some remote concentrators and even some line carrier systems include capabilities for intraline calling. Some remote units are even capable of limited intraline call processing independent of the node. In this case the RLC is known as a *remote switching system or unit* (RSS) or (RSU).[3] (These are generally known as *units* or *modules* rather than "systems" since they are highly dependent upon the interchange of information with a "host"

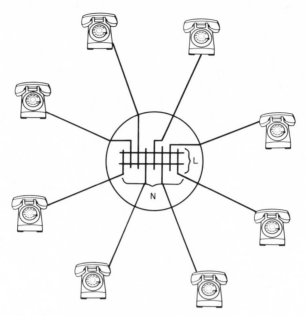

Fig. 4.   Central switching (blocking).

switching entity.) In general the wide scale use of RLCs and RSUs is referred to as *distributed switching*. (Of late, it has been known also as *clustering*.) The use of carrier transmission integrated into the design of the RLC or RSU, shown as T/S, further reduces the cost of providing access to stations from wire center nodes providing many opportunities to trade between the cost of switching and transmission.[4]

These arrangements for distributing switching have been part of the switching art almost since its beginning. Remote-controlled automatic devices were used as one of the early opportunities to extend manual service. This idea was tried with frequency multiplex, but it has no advan-

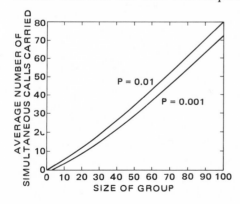

Fig. 5.   Group traffic efficiency at different blocking percentages.

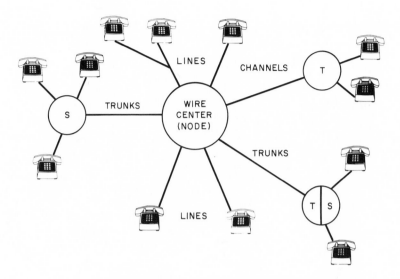

Fig. 6. Switching and transmission trades to reach wire center node.

tage over more conventional switching (see Section 3.3). However, with the advent of digital multiplex (carrier) transmission, a synergy exists between the switching of these signals in their multiplex form without returning them to baseband.

The basic advantage of distributed switching is economic. If station usage is high or if there is an insufficient number of stations to provide high usage on the serving trunks, then the decentralization of switching does not provide the optimum trade with transmission.

To cover very large geographical areas a trade between switching and transmission is possible by dividing the area with switching entities serving each subarea. Trunks are common arteries that carry traffic between switching nodes. A network of offices is formed by interconnecting nodes with one or a group of trunks. Centralized switching entities may be added to serve other switching entities. In a network of switching offices there may be more than one level of centralization. In this manner networks (of distributed offices) are formed.

Pursuing further the trades between transmission and switching, *private branch exchanges* (PBXs) are a form of RSU that usually has independent controls. However, for large groups of PBX lines close to the wire center it may be more economical to serve them directly on the same switching entity that serves the lines of other customers. This is one characteristic that defines *CENTREX CO* (central office) service.[5]

Digital telephony is characterized by conversion of the vocal variations into electrical signals that are transmitted as a series of on and off (digital) pulses. When these pulse streams are switched without reconversion to analog voice signals, then "digital switching" is being employed.

Since most data are initiated as digital signals they may be and generally are transmitted over the same digital multiplex transmission facilities as digital voice signals. Since the digital signals for both uses may arrive at the wire center multiplexed, there is an incentive, if economically feasible, to serve both voice and data with the same centralized switching.

Switching for two-way conversation requires a path that is instantaneously available. A dedicated path or circuit is established for the duration of the call, and therefore, the term "circuit switching."

Telephone service generally uses two-way voice messages in a conversational mode with instantaneous response an important characteristic. *Time assignment speech interpolation* (TASI) takes advantage of the fact that conversational speech is not continuous and it is unlikely that the two directions of transmission are used simultaneously.[6] Switching is used to insert speech spurts of other sources on channels where silent intervals are detected. By this technique the capacity of a transmission facility may be increased by as much as 50%. This kind of switching has been costly. It is therefore applied only to long transmission facilities, such as ocean cables and satellites. It should be noted that this is a form of time division circuit switching where the samples are not restricted in length and the time slots may appear in any of a number of parallel channels. It is one form of "virtual circuit switching" where a path or circuit is assigned only when the message is transmitted. Otherwise it is available for other messages. In a sense networks employing time division multiple access satellites are used in a virtual circuit configuration.[7]

Messages need not be conversational. One-way messages have different characteristics. The factor of "delay" or "storage" may be introduced into the transmission of messages. Storage may be from a fraction of a second to hours depending upon the availability of transmission facilities. Storage requires memory and memory is a switching function. Memory is involved in input-to-output connection relationships (see Section 3.3).

New trades between transmission and switching are possible with the introduction of the delay factor. The degree of delay utilized here is at least an order of magnitude greater than transmission propagation delay which is at its worst in satellite transmission. By storing messages from a number of sources, transmission facilities may be used more efficiently. Lines may transmit messages to a switching node where they are received and stored for later transmission. Figure 7 shows that for low blocking probabilities the occupancy of a trunk cannot exceed about 78% or 0.78 erlangs and then only when it is part of a large group. By delaying rather than blocking (turning back) messages, occupancies of as high as 100% may be obtained if delays in the order of 10 message lengths (or holding times) are tolerable

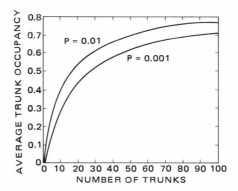

Fig. 7. Average trunk occupancy at different blocking percentages.

(see further discussion in Section 1.2.3. Providing for delay at the switching system is generally known as *store and forward switching*. Packet switching, discussed in Chapter 6 of this volume, is a form of store and forward switching.

Storage of data messages may occur at the station or terminal. By limiting the length of the transmitted message to a fixed format and length with each message preceded by an address, a form of switching knows as *packet switching* may be introduced at the node. Here the amount of storage at the node is reduced and each packet may be switched independent of the other packets that form the complete message. Packets may therefore take different routes to arrive at their destinations. This form of service is most suited to short messages since the overhead and station storage requirements might otherwise make it uneconomical. Chapter 6 of this volume covers these differences in greater detail. *Integrated services digital networks* (ISDN) might involve combinations of circuit and store and forward switching. Packet switching is a particular form of store and forward switching and involves networking as well as station storage considerations. Virtual circuit switching has found application in packet message service.

2.2. Networking

Wire centers and the geographical areas served by them are convenient elements by which service characteristics and their serving vehicles may be delineated. In the United States these geographical areas are known as *exchanges*. In particular there is a *community of interest* among users served within an exchange as compared to the calls they direct outside of the exchange. Generally the rates charged for calls to and from all lines in an exchange are the same since the costs of serving can generally be averaged based upon the community of interest.

Frequently remote switch units serve distinct exchanges separate from the exchange of the host wire center. This gives rise to a need to allow for the possibility of different charges for originating calls. To account for charges on calls terminating at the remote unit, a different central office code is generally required so that this fact may be distinguished by billing or accounting equipment for calls originating outside of the exchange.

Some areas are large enough to require more than one wire center to serve all stations within the exchange boundary. Not only is this usually the result of a good trade between transmission and switching, but it may also be required because of electrical limits on loop length. To tie together exchange areas or wire centers within an area, the same considerations as for individual stations become obvious. Each wire center must be able to reach every other wire center. The nodes would appear as the stations in Fig. 1. Furthermore, a group of trunks rather than a single channel is usually required between nodes. Between contiguous wire centers or exchanges these channels usually handle traffic in only one direction (calls may originate from only one end of the trunk) so two groups are required, one from *A* to *B* and one from *B* to *A*. On longer trunk groups, particularly where they terminate in different time zones, two-way operation (calls originate from either end) is encountered most frequently. One-way trunk groups are also used to distinguish different classes of traffic.

To provide most economically for internodal circuits, one or more levels of intermediate switching are needed. Intermediate offices are known as "tandem" or "transit" offices. Depending upon the degree of telecommunication development several levels of intermediate switching might

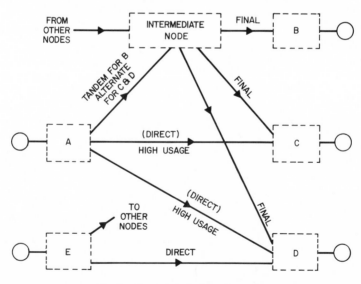

Fig. 8.   Tandem and alternate routing.

prove economically advantageous. Within an exchange with multiple wire centers, local tandem offices are found.

Where the amount of traffic justifies them, it has been the practice for trunk groups to directly connect end offices or terminating nodes as shown by *A* to *C*, *A* to *D*, and *E* to *D* in Fig. 8. However, since the intermediate node generally reaches many end offices it may be more economical to provide a smaller direct trunk group, called *high usage*, and to carry the remaining or overflow traffic over the tandem trunk group. This is known as *alternate routing*. The tandem trunk group is engineered to carry most economically the overflow traffic to all end offices reached via the intermediate office as well as the traffic to end offices that can only be reached in this manner.[8] Since the traffic offered to this group from various sources may peak at different times, this method of providing service becomes quite economical. Traffic that terminates in an end office or other office from which traffic cannot be alternate routed is carried by a trunk group that is engineered for low blocking. The larger the intermediate switch the fewer nodes are required. Trunk groups become more efficient and fewer trunks are required.

In the dominant public network in the United States there are five levels in a hierarchical toll network configuration as shown in Fig. 9.[9] Each level is given a name of "center" but it should be emphasized that these are switching function classes. A given switching entity may act in combination for several functional classes. Also as modern technology is

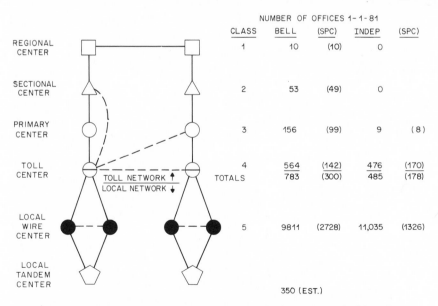

| | NUMBER OF OFFICES 1-1-81 | | | |
	CLASS	BELL	(SPC)	INDEP	(SPC)
REGIONAL CENTER	1	10	(10)	0	
SECTIONAL CENTER	2	53	(49)	0	
PRIMARY CENTER	3	156	(99)	9	(8)
TOLL CENTER	4	564	(142)	476	(170)
TOTALS		783	(300)	485	(178)
LOCAL WIRE CENTER	5	9811	(2728)	11,035	(1326)
LOCAL TANDEM CENTER		350 (EST.)			

TOLL NETWORK ↑
LOCAL NETWORK ↓

Fig. 9.   Bell system and independent telephone switching nodes (United States).

finding greater application in the United States, combining the local end office function with the toll center function is occurring more frequently. Generally less traffic flows upward between levels since high-usage groups, shown dashed in the figure, carry most of the traffic. Multiple alternate routes in a fixed order are permitted.

Star networks are the most familiar form of centralized switching. Star or hierarchical networks are found in most public telecommunications applications. They are distributed networks in their most sophisticated application. Other topologies for interconnecting nodes as well as stations have been postulated. Most prominent among these are the grid, the ring, and the bus (see Fig. 10). The *grid* is generally used to provide a greater degree of alternate routing without calls passing through additional nodes. The *ring* requires more switching and less transmission facilities. The *bus* serves in the same manner as the ring without the advantage of redundancy that occurs with some rings should they be cut accidentally. The ring and bus are particularly useful as noncentral adjuncts to an end office as a means to concentrate and to switch intraconcentrator or RSU traffic. Rings with the ultimate of a distributed switch per station are known as *local area networks.*[10]

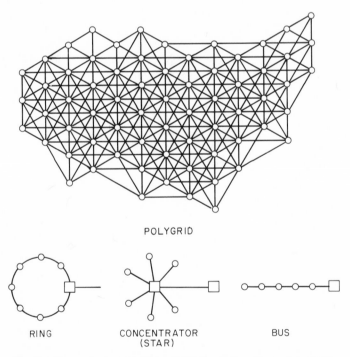

POLYGRID

RING   CONCENTRATOR   BUS
              (STAR)

Fig. 10.   Types of networks. (From *IEEE Proceedings*, September 1977.)

2.3. Signaling

Signaling is the means by which switching nodes are informed of what actions to take.[11] Since signaling involves all aspects of telecommunications it is important that standards be agreed upon and utilized, particularly between countries and independently provided networks or terminals. The details of signaling standards are known as *protocols*. When signals pass over the same transmission channels used for the messages to which they apply, the signaling is known as *associated*. These signals may be within or outside the bandwidth used by the message, and are known as *in-band* or *out-of-band* signals, respectively.

In the case of associated signaling with digital transmission, in- and out-of-band are inappropriate terms. Signals are digitally encoded and may use all or part of a bit position (so-called *bit robbing*) in each message time slot or they may use a bit position devoted exclusively to signaling in a time slot assigned for this purpose. These are known, respectively, as *in-slot* and *out-of-slot* signaling.[12]

There are four basic categories of signals: alerting, supervisory, addressing, and control. *Alerting* is used to indicate a request for service by a switch or ringing a station. *Supervisory* signals deal with maintaining a request for service (attending), by indicating a channel seizure or busy/idle condition, or answer or disconnect indications. *Addressing* indicates the called number and these signals are frequently referred to as pulsing. The final category, *control*, includes tones, announcements, messages, and other indicia about a call including class of service and calling number.

Signaling is also categorized with respect to applications. Signaling over lines is known as *station signaling*. Signaling between nodes is known as *interoffice signaling*. Since signals must pass between the nodes of a network, switching systems generally are required to generate as well as receive signals. It is possible to arrange a network so that all signals are generated only at stations. But in this case in order to obtain increased signaling range the node repeats or retransmits the signals with a minimum of delay.

In order to distinguish the signals from the characteristics of the channels carrying them, various levels of protocols have been defined, particularly for digital signals. These start out at the highest level with the electrical characteristics of the medium, then address the organization of the signals within the medium, and at the lowest levels cover the meaning or interpretation of signals.

In telephone applications the signaling has evolved less formally. In particular, the electrical characteristics of lines and trunk channels carrying analog voice signals to and from telephones have been used to carry unique forms of digital signals. The direct current (dc) battery supply to the telephone transmitter for supervisory signaling is also used by the rotary dial calling device to generate dial pulses and supervisory open (on-hook) and closed (off-hook) loop signals. They are part of a general class of signalling known as *dc signaling*. A minimum loop current to power the telephone and the ability to detect the dial pulses restricts the range or path length that can most effectively use dc signalling. Techniques such as composite and simplex derived circuits and pulse repeaters and regenerators may be used in special cases to extend dc pulsing and supervisory ranges. In general, dc range extension also requires consideration of the range limits on the alerting or ringing signals, as well as transmission.

Direct current pulses are also generated by electromechanical selector switches. The most common form of pulses are used in a servo control of the switches with dc start (loop closure) signals going forward and dc pulses returning from the switch. This is known as *revertive pulsing*.

Many forms of dc signals have been used for supervision over metallic (nonderived) trunks. In particular reverse current flow (called reverse battery), high–low current and pulse or wink signals are used with detection of the change in condition usually taking place at the calling or originating end of the circuit. These signals are used to indicate attending conditions such as start signaling and answer supervision.

Other unique signals are associated with lines for purposes such as coin phone control, party identification, cable pressure, and loop activity monitoring and testing.

Direct current signaling is a special case of out-of-band digital signaling with very limited introduction of pulse repeaters. The more general case is the more accurate and higher-speed transmission of speech. For single channels such as those used from station terminal to a switching node or a pair gain terminal, CCITT (Committee Consultif International Telephonique et Telegraphique) standards for digital protocols are being developed (1981).[13]

For digital time multiplexed channels both in-slot and out-of-slot per channel signal bits are provided (see Fig. 11). If the in-slot bit is available full time for signaling, 8 bits are provided per channel with a frame repetition rate of 8K frames per second, then 56K bits per second are used for speech or other message transmission and 8K bits per second are available for signaling. Since signaling does not generally require 8K bits per second for in-slot signaling, the bit used for signaling is used only on each sixth frame giving an effective speech bit rate of 62.667K bits per second (and an effective signaling rate of 1.33K bits per second). For out-of-slot signaling the full 64K bits are available for speech or other message transmission.

Digital signaling on digital transmission facilities has a range equal to that of the voice path, such as 200 miles for repeatered cable and thousands

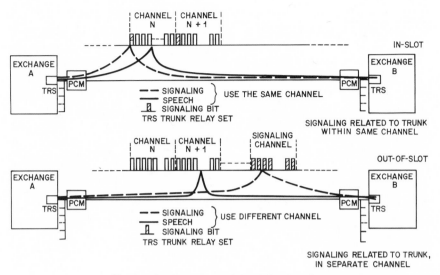

Fig. 11.   In-slot and out-of-slot digital signaling.

of miles for radio and satellite paths. Digital voice transmission at 64K bits per second is relatively wasteful of bandwidth. Therefore on longer circuits analog has been the preferred method of transmission.

Analog transmission over long distances is also repeatered. Therefore signaling over long analog channels generally is within the speech band and employs audible tone signals. For pulsing two tones per digit are generally used. This permits the use of self-checking codes and reduces the chance of simulation by voice signals. Alternating current pulsing from stations is known as *dual-tone multifrequency* (DTMF) and uses one of each of two groups of four frequencies. For ac pulsing over trunks two out of six frequencies are used. In some parts of the world digits are sent in both directions. The digits in the return direction "compel" the sending of succeeding digits and may convey information on the ability of the terminating office to complete the required connection. Compelled signaling is slower than one-way transmission of digits where the only check is the inherent redundancy in the code.[14]

For supervision, single frequencies are used, generally a different one in each direction. The presence of a frequency generally indicates an on-hook or idle condition.

Sharp bandpass filters are used to prevent the voice signals carried over the same channels from simulating supervisory signals. This can be difficult and delays are introduced to ensure that the signals persist for a minimum length of time. The presence of these filters affects the analog transmission, particularly analog data signals, much in the same manner as

in-slot signals affect digital transmission. This is one reason the trend today
is to remove signaling from the message channel, at least between switching
nodes.

2.4. Signal Networking

While signaling technology has evolved compatibility between different techniques has been the principal consideration in its development. As a
result, development of the number of useful signals has been somewhat
restricted. In earlier days of telephony a separate channel was used for
verbal signaling. These channels were used by all subscribers to reach the
central office operator and by operators to reach other offices.

These techniques using data, rather than voice transmission, are now
known as common channel signaling. The data channels are two-way and
devoted solely to signaling. The capacity of one channel far exceeds the
signaling needs of a single trunk even with a considerable increase in the
signals required by each call. Therefore many trunks may use the same
signaling channel. The use of centralized call information processing makes
common channel signaling feasible.

Common channel signaling not only speeds the call setup time, but
also enables sending more information about the call in both directions.
The common signaling channel may be associated with a single trunk group
or groups in the same route. Generally this is uneconomical except for very
large trunk groups or where a technique like out-of-slot signaling uses a
channel of a specific transmission facility.[15]

Common channel signaling is now being applied more generally on a
disassociated basis. This means that the signaling between switching nodes
does not parallel nor necessarily use the same transmission facilities or
routes as the signals that carry the calls and messages.

The signaling data messages resemble packets each with its own
address header. Messages are transmitted by separate channels in each
direction. With disassociated common signaling channels, signaling messages intended for a trunk group terminating in different centers are received
by a packet switch and routed directly or indirectly to the proper switching
center. The packet switching can be implemented using the call information
processor (CIP) (see Chapter 3, Section 2) at a trunk switching center, or by
a separate packet switch. In either case it is known as *signal transfer point*
(STP).

Networks of signal data links to and from switching centers and
packet switching nodes form a separate signaling network. Generally a
signal transfer point serves many switching centers. To ensure the reliability
of this form of signaling, where one data link carries messages for thousands
of trunks, it is expected that STPs will be duplicated. Independently routed

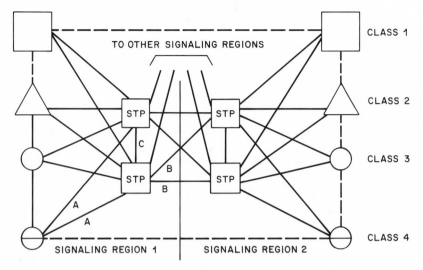

Fig. 12.   Common channel signaling network with signal transfer points.

data links connect each switching center to at least two STPs. As shown in Fig. 12, for the nationwide Bell System network in the United States signal transfer points are usually fully interconnected thereby reducing to two the maximum number of STPs through which a given signal message must pass. For international calling the STPs are in different countries. Separate STPs are required for traffic within or between contiguous local areas.

While signaling messages generally pass through STPs to and from the successive switching offices through which a call passes, it is possible to use a signaling network for sending signals from the originating office to the terminating office and back if necessary without the information being used for establishing connections. These messages may, for example, pass forward the calling number to the terminating station. Or messages may be sent back to an originating office if the called line is busy or out of service, thereby avoiding the need to establish a connection to the terminating office to receive a busy tone. Signaling which is not used for the equivalent of over-the-trunk pulsing and supervision is known as direct signaling.

Call handling data storage in the form of a data base may be added at one or more pairs of STPs. Using direct signaling this type of signaling network can and will be used to implement network-wide services and features that cannot be implemented within a switching node alone. An example of a service of this type is known as expanded 800 service. Here the data base is used to store all 800 numbers together with one or more regular network addresses (directory numbers) to be used to complete calls at different locations depending upon the point of origination, the time of day, and the day of the week.[16]

Other services may involve the user changing the information in the data base so that calls may be redirected by reference to the data base before starting to establish a connection. This type of operation is known as *direct service dialing capability* (DSDC).[17] As shown in Fig. 13 the location of the data base is known as a *network control point* (NCP). Initial access to the NCP via the signaling network takes place at an *action point* where the called number is examined. Detecting a call for which an inquiry to a NCP is required takes place at the ACP. In the example given in Fig. 13 the action point is shown at an operator system (TSPS) location, but it could be at the first toll office or at the originating office location. At the action point, direct signaling messages are formatted to indicate that the call should be first referred to an STP that includes an NCP.

Signaling networks have generally been used only where the call information processing is centralized and uses high-speed electronic technology. The data transmission between processors may be analog or digital. As in data communications, the latter is generally favored for signaling networks since the processor produces digital information.

Common channel signaling (CCS) is a generic term. A separate (common) signaling channel uses digital signals for a number of message circuits. International standards have been set for CCS. There is one standard for analog transmission and one for digital transmission known, respectively, as CCITT No. 6 and No. 7 systems.[18] In the United States a variation of the No. 6 system known as *common channel interoffice signal 6* (CCIS 6) has been placed into service. The country has been divided into

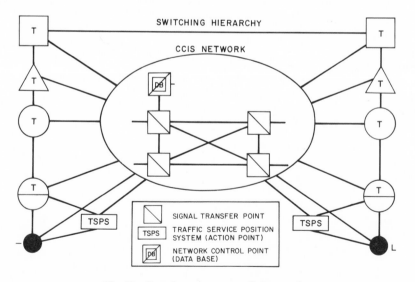

Fig. 13. Stored program controlled network.

	IN-BAND SIGNALING	OUT-BAND SIGNALING	COMMON-CHANNEL SIGNALING	ANALOG TWO-FREQUENCY SIGNALING	ANALOG MULTIFREQUENCY SIGNALING	DIGITAL	SUITABLE FOR OPERATION OVER SATELLITES	SUITABLE FOR OPERATION WITH TASI CIRCUITS	RECOMMENDED FOR OPERATION BETWEEN SPC EXCHANGES
CCITT SIGNALING SYSTEM NO. 3 (OBSOLETE)	X						NO	NO	NO
CCITT SIGNALING SYSTEM NO. 4	X			X			NO	NO	NO
CCITT SIGNALING SYSTEM NO. 5	X			X	X		YES	YES	NO*
CCITT SIGNALING SYSTEM NO. 6			X			X	YES	YES	YES
CCITT SIGNALING SYSTEM NO. 7			X			X	YES	YES	YES
CCITT SIGNALING SYSTEM R1 ANALOG VERSION	X				X		YES	NO	NO*
CCITT SIGNALING SYSTEM R1 DIGITAL VERSION					X	X	YES	NO	NO*
CCITT SIGNALING SYSTEM R2 ANALOG VERSION	X	X			X		NO	NO	NO*
CCITT SIGNALING SYSTEM R2 DIGITAL VERSION					X	X	NO	NO	NO*

* MAY BE USED ON LINKS CONNECTING SPC AND ELECTROMECHANICAL EXCHANGES.

Fig. 14. CCITT signaling systems.

ten signaling regions each containing duplicated STPs in different cities serving all offices within a geographical area.[19] A CCIS 7 is under development.[20] A transition from CCIS 6 to CCIS 7 in the United States is expected to occur when economics and service demands permit.

For over-the-trunk tone signaling, other international standards have been set and are used in different parts of the world. Figure 14 shows the identification of these systems that employ different combinations.[21] Also shown is the suitability of each arrangement to operate over TASI, satellites, and between the stored program-controlled (SPC) form of electronic call information processing (see Chapter 3 of this volume).

3. Circuit-Switching Systems

3.1. Switching System Design

The design of a switching system is dependent upon both *external environmental* factors and *internal design* alternatives. These requirements mostly cover a wide variety of applications to justify the development and production preparation costs.

The external environmental factors include such items as the numbering plan, dialing plan, network plan, routing plan, transmission plan, traffic, connecting offices, signaling, and service requirements and expectations.

The numbering plan identifies the addresses or directory numbers of each line or main station. Universal numbers or addresses identify stations no matter from where in the network they are called. Closed numbering plans provide for universal dialing, that is the same number of digits or other indicia are dialed from any station to reach a particular station. A dialing plan usually applies to open numbering plans where different digits are dialed to reach a particular station depending upon from where the call is placed. In the United States the numbering plan has been quasiclosed in that there are only a few well-known variations. The area code is deleted when calling in the area of the called station. Prefixes of 0, 1, 8 and 9 are dialed to distinguish calls that require an operator, toll service, a private network or to leave a PBX.

Various network plans were discussed in Section 2.2. The routing plans apply to how and when the transmission paths established in the network are used. This is particularly needed with multiple alternate routing to avoid rerouting a call to a node through which it has passed and to select among several route choices from a node.

It is very important to know and understand the characteristics of the traffic expected to be generated within and into the environment of a switching system. Once traffic-carrying objectives are set for each class of call and service, system requirements are developed so that the offered and carried traffic may be measured, and the maximum size of equipment modules postulated. This includes such items as the memory modules for software (see Chapter 4 of this volume), hardware for interfacing transmission facilities, e.g., trunk circuits, and interpreting addresses for implementing the routing plan. Other items that might be measured include cumulative holding times or the number of calls routed or overflowed to or from a particular destination to account for traffic between the different companies carrying segments of the same calls. Another concept of the environment is the provision for observing, analyzing, and controlling traffic flow. Generally these features are called *network management*. They may be automatically invoked or manually implemented by remote control after sending an indication of the condition that obtains in an office or elsewhere in the network. Figure 15 shows how effective load management can be for a particular office or for the entire network. Automatic arrangements are particularly useful in dealing with abnormally heavy offered loads or loads focused to particular terminating areas or numbers.

Some of the variations in office class-dependent functions have been described in Section 2.2. The signaling methods by which a system communicates with other switching offices and with lines are described in Section 2.3. These methods are particularly necessary since the systems deployed at other nodes and terminals may be of a different design or technology.

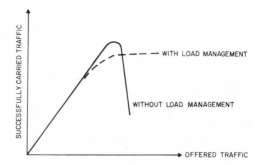

Fig. 15.   Effectiveness of local management.

The transmission plan is developed to allocate such items as gain, return loss, delay, and phase characteristics between the switching nodes and the transmission facilities of the network. The objective of such plans is to ensure uniformity of voice transmission taking into account the wide variety of combinations of switching and transmission facilities that can be used in any particular call. Such plans must account for the mix of analog and digital facilities[22] as described in Chapter 10 of this volume.

The primary purpose of a switching system is to deliver service. The variety of service needs continually increases. There appears in the offing a veritable explosion of new services, and most of these impact on the switching system design. Services are the offerings to customers that they use and for which they generally pay. Coin or certain types of public services are for cash. Most other services are billed. The basic service, or the readiness to make and receive calls or messages, might carry a fixed minimum charge. Other charges depend upon the system resources required per call attempt or message.

Part of network planning is forecasting service requirements. It is difficult to predict in what quantity and in what operating procedure a new service will develop. Engineering and marketing judgments must be made and preferably trials conducted with potential customers. Calling rates and usage of established services are more predictable but may vary with economic and rate changes.

Part of service is its perceived availability and switched services affect a multiplicity of users. Redundancy and generally automatic service restoration in most cases of trouble are requirements if service expectations are to be met. Provision must be made with switching equipment to rapidly, and preferably automatically, detect, report, locate, and isolate troubles as well as to test and connect to standby equipment to ensure service continuity. Redundancy is also useful to ensure continuing service even while making service changes that are inevitable in a growth environment.

Requirements may be specified as generic, for all switches of a given network or administration.[23] These general requirements are supplemented to take into account variations and additions created by specific switching system designs. To formalize system requirements with respect to service operations a *system description language* (SDL) has been standardized by the CCITT. It is used by many administrations to specify service uniformity among different switching systems.[24]

The internal design of a switching entity is dependent upon not only its environment but certain other factors that are not as visible or self-evident to the user. Most prominent among the design considerations is the system capacity. One would like to believe that with modern technology design objectives can always be met. However, design decisions are always required that are challenging. For example, is the system to serve as both an end office and intermediate (tandem) office? What part of the expected market should the system serve most economically? What are the expected repair times during which adequate redundancy should be provided to meet some stated objective such as out of service time from all causes not to exceed 2 hours in 40 years? What is the maximum size to which the memory capacity of the system can grow? In what size units is partial system capacity, for example, for line and trunk terminations, to be provided?

The requirements for all capabilities of a system are known as *features*. Features include the provisions made for making all service requirements. In addition there are requirements for maintenance, operation, and administration of the service. Lists of features for typical modern telephone switching systems are quite extensive, often exceeding several hundred. There were more than 700 features in the Bell System's No. 1 ESS in 1981.[25] Generally new system designs, to be useful and marketable, should contain a large subset of the features in currently deployed systems as well as some that may be unique to the new design.

Figure 16 shows the basic call-processing structure of most systems. It compares the hardware termination interfaces with the requirements for call processing. A category of features expected as part of call processing include the application of dial, ringing, reorder, receiver off-hook, and call progress tones, and congestion and number change announcements. Calls that reach unassigned and unequipped numbers are also given distinguishing tones or announcements.

Another important set of call-processing features is those that ensure proper supervision of each call. Requests for service where no address is received or calls only partially addressed must be detected and action taken to avoid their tying up call-processing facilities. These conditions, commonly knows as *permanent signals* and *partial dial*, respectively, are only two of many call abandon possibilities that must be anticipated in the system design.

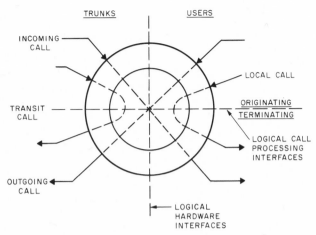

Fig. 16.   Partitioning and definitions in circuit-switching node.

3.2.   Switching System Functions

Functions are the means for providing the features. The functions are structured in the hardware and software architecture. There are three basic switching functions in circuit-switching systems. These are call signaling processing (CSP), call information processing (CIP), and call connecting or switching center network (SCN). More generally they are, as shown in Fig. 17, the interconnections, controlling, and signalling functions. Hardware is required to perform some or all of each of these functions but trades may alter the balance between hardware and software in various system designs.

These three basic functions are required for all circuit-switching entities. The interconnecting function is omitted if only store and forward switching is performed.

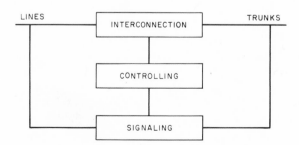

Fig. 17.   Circuit-switching functions. (From *IEEE Proceedings*, September 1977.)

3.3   Switching Networks

The principal interconnection function of a circuit switch is implemented by *switching center networks* (SCN).[26,27] Referring first to Fig. 18, the quantities of the basic system elements and the inputs (or outputs) of each function vary in typical systems over the wide range of five orders of magnitude, from a single control to as many as 100,000 lines or trunks. Since the functions must generally be fully interconnected, a set of switching networks other than SCN is needed. The internal networks are known as connectives and are shown in Fig. 19. They are named generically as access networks with adjectives indicating to what they connect. There are four types of access networks—signal access networks (SAN), control access networks (CAN), intracontrol access networks (ICAN), and network control access networks (NCAN).[28]

The *SANs* connect lines, trunks, and service circuits to call signal processing (receivers and transmitters). Generally these have been given the names *scanners* and *distributors* in electronic switching systems.

The *CANs* are used to connect call signal processing to call information processors or controllers. These are usually some form of bus system.

Typically the *ICANs* associate central controls with the memories or other processors. The NCANs are also bus systems to connect the call-processing control to the control for the SCNs. These relationships are shown in Fig. 20. In modern electronic circuit-switching systems the SCN is also used as the SAN and/or CAN. Access networks are required for all types of switching systems. Only the SCN is peculiar to circuit switches.

Terminations or ports for lines, trunks, and service circuits appear on the periphery of SCNs. Most networks, including SCNs, are topologically

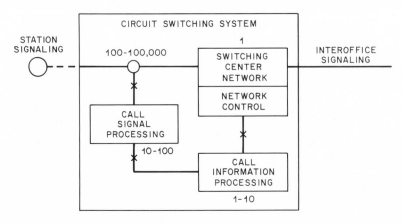

Fig. 18.   Circuit-switching function terminology.

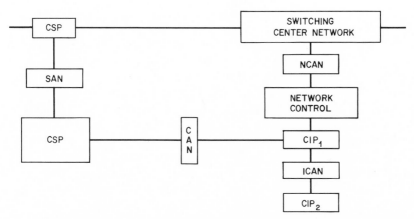

Fig. 19. Circuit-switching functions with access connectives. CSP, call signal processing; CIP, call information processing. Switching networks and their controls: SCN, switching center network; access networks: SAN, signal access networks; CAN, control access networks; NCAN, network control access networks; ICAN, intracontrol access networks. (From *IEEE Proceedings*, September 1977.)

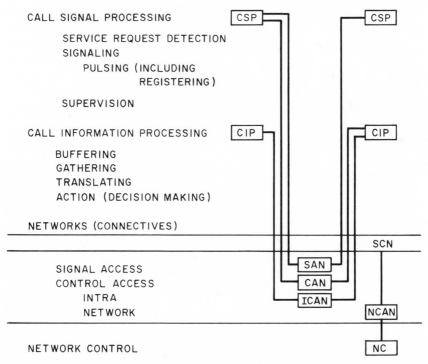

Fig. 20. Circuit-switching functional relationships. (From *IEEE Proceedings*, September 1977.)

one- or two-sided. This means that the periphery has terminals on one or two edges.

Some SCNs accept traffic in only one direction. These are known as unidirectional networks. Since most lines both originate and terminate traffic, two unidirectional SCNs must be connected together on one side to provide two-way service. Many two-sided and all one-sided networks are bidirectional, meaning that connection requests may originate from any port. Most SCNs are composed of several stages that may provide for the network functions of concentration, distributing, and expansion. Connections between stages are known as *links*. Links between networks within a switching entity are known as *junctors*. Generally the access connectives are unidirectional networks since the call signaling and processing naturally flow in this way. Almost all access connectives are two-sided.

The maximum number of simultaneous internal connections that a network can support relates to the internal topology and the number of terminals or ports it supports and how they might be subdivided into groups. Two-sided networks with the same number of terminals on each side are known as *distribution networks*. If it can carry simultaneous calls originated in any sequence equal to the number of terminals on each side, it is known as a strictly nonblocking network. If the simultaneous connection capacity is less than the number of terminals then the network is blocking. However, if it can support connections equal to the terminals on the side with the least number of terminals, it may be possible by rearranging them during calls to obtain nonblocking. Single-sided networks may also be blocking and nonblocking.

When the number of terminals on one side is greater than the other and the network is unidirectional then it is known as a *concentrator* if the inputs exceed the outputs. For the reverse situation it is an *expandor*. Bidirectional unequal networks are usually also called concentrators. Some access network expandors or concentrators have only one inlet or outlet. For this reason some connectives are not easy to discern since they are trivial.

In all networks discussed above it is assumed that each input can reach all outputs. This is known as full availability. For larger networks it is sometimes economical to provide partial access to the individual trunks of a particular group. Partial access is known as a grading when it applies to a section or stage of a network.

The economics and capacity of a network is dependent upon the technology and the way it is employed. Space division networks are those where the connection is established for the entire duration of the message or call. Where messages are long relative to the address and control time and cannot be delayed, as in telephone service, the network may use electromechanical devices with metallic contacts. All earlier switching systems were of this type. Electronic devices were first used in the access networks and are now replacing metallic contacts in SCNs.

The simplest two-sided network topology is a rectangle (concentrator) or square (distribution) with inputs in one dimension and outputs in the other. At the intersection of each row with each column a crosspoint, either a set of metallic contacts or electronic devices, establishes a path for the message. For analog signal transmission, linear response is required of the crosspoint device and wiring over the transmitted bandwidth. Space division networks have the advantage of accommodating wide bandwidths of tens of megahertz.

The costs of networks include their control (see Chapter 3 of this volume) and relate to the number of crosspoints and the number of links.[29] Minimizing crosspoints is only one factor in reducing switching network costs. To obtain large networks, successive stages of a plurality of rectangles are interconnected by links. Nonblocking may still be achieved if the number of links expands to equal $2n - r$, where n is the total number of inputs and r is the number of rectangles into which the n inputs is divided. Usually $r = \sqrt{n}$ as shown in Fig. 21. This technique to achieve nonblocking is attributable to its inventor Clos.[30] For very large networks multiple Clos three-stage networks may be accessed or the middle stages may themselves be expanded to Clos networks. Multistage nonblocking single-sided networks may also be devised.

By reducing the links and center stage matrices, blocking may be introduced. Figure 22 shows, for different values of n and r, the blocking resulting from a reduction in center stage switches by k. The number of inputs need not be a perfect square.

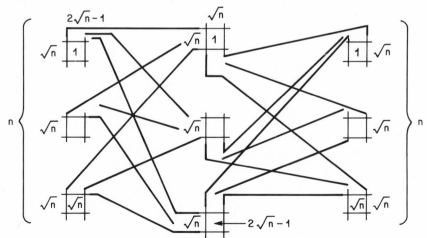

Fig. 21. Nonblocking three-stage two-sided networks. (From *IEEE Computer Magazine*, June 1979.)

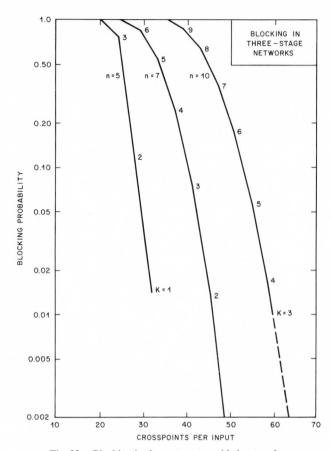

Fig. 22.   Blocking in three-stage two-sided networks.

In order to function in a space division network, crosspoints must be held operated. Holding requires memory of mechanical position as in a gross motion electromechanical switch. Some contacts are held magnetically. Electronic crosspoints can have two inherent electric states, a high or almost infinite impedance and a low linear transmission impedance. Some of these devices are *pnpn* semiconductor diodes that are held by dc and can carry only low-level ac signals. More recently, a class of high-energy gated diodes has been devised.[31] These can be used to pass high-level dc signals to operate station transmitter, ringer, and coin control devices. Some networks used semiconductor crosspoints that are held in the operated state by separate flip-flop memories.

The use of arrays of crosspoints defines a class of networks that employ multiples, that is each input, output, and link connects to a multiplicity of crosspoints. Nonmultiple space division networks are possible. An example is a simple switchboard with inputs and outputs terminating in individual jacks and connections being made by plug ended cords. Light beam systems can have the same characteristics with the possibility of a much greater capacity. The space through which cords and light beams pass has also been called a common medium since it is used by all connections.

Other switching networks that employ common media use the frequency or time domains. With frequency division switching each connection is assigned a different carrier frequency on the common medium. Variable frequency modulators associated with each input and output (demodulators) are assigned one of a plurality of frequencies that, as shown in Fig. 23, are applied through a *network control access network* (NCAN) that maintains (holding) the connection for its duration. The space division NCANs make this type of frequency division network uneconomical when compared with a space division network. Different frequencies and usually separated media and NCANs are used to obtain bidirectional (four-wire) transmission. In effect the frequencies are equivalent to links in Fig. 4.

Electromechanical space division networks may be used for either two- or four-wire transmission depending upon the number of contacts provided at each crosspoint. For analog signals, message direction need not be separated and two wires may be used. One arrangement known as "high–low" (impedance) uses two-wire crosspoint networks to look like four-wire networks.[32] This is particularly useful when digital signals, which are inherently four-wire, are passed through space division networks originally designed for two-wire analog signals.[33] It is also important for interfacing four-wire analog transmission facilities.

Electronic crosspoints may also be used in two- or four-wire arrangements. Common media switching, viz., time and frequency division, requires

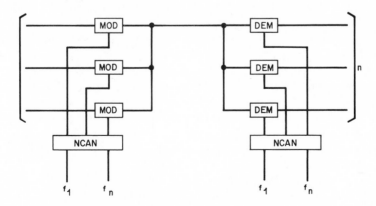

Fig. 23. Frequency division circuit switching. (From *IEEE Computer Magazine*, June 1979.)

transmission separation. Usually a duplicated network for the reciprocal connections is provided and takes advantage of using the same control.

Since time division networks employ active devices that simultaneously serve many calls it is necessary to consider path redundancy in their design to ensure service continuity. Duplication or spare independent network paths are usually provided in switching center networks (SCN) and other connectives.

The time dimension is the one that makes attractive new forms of switching. Again a medium is used in common by many calls requiring circuit switching. Circuit-switching networks can carry analog or digital signals. For time division networks the signals must be samples at a rate at least equal to twice the bandwidth of the transmitted signal. Each sample is assigned to a time period or time slot on the common medium. Analog samples of varying amplitude or width may be carried in each time slot. The analog samples may, by means described in Chapter 7 of this volume, be converted to digital signals. Generally the digital bits representing each sample are placed on the common medium during a time slot. A frame of time slots represents the sampling rate. Digitized samples representing analog signals may be sent through a space division network the same as analog signals. Usually when one refers to digital switching one is implying the use of time division switching. Figure 24 shows the relationship between continuous and sampled speech and space and time division switching. A radius may be drawn to represent practically any combination of transmission and switching techniques.

All telecommunications start from individual sources. This means they are inherently divided in space. To take messages from space-divided lines to time-divided transmission requires multiplexing (and demultiplexing), that is converting from space to time division (and vice versa). The number of inputs (outputs) may equal the number of time slots and operates as a distribution stage if the assignment of inputs (outputs) to time slots is not fixed. A first time division switching stage may concentrate, that is, the number of multiplexed inputs is greater than the number of available time slots. This is known as *space division to time division multiplexing* (SD/M). In packet switching this is known as statistical multiplexing. (Data packets may be transmitted at a random rate rather than at a fixed rate as required in transmitting speech samples.)

Multiplexing is also used to concentrate digital time division signals by mixing slower-speed inputs to form a higher-speed output. This is known as *time division to time division multiplexing* (TD/M).

A plurality of synchronized time division inputs can be switched simultaneously in each time slot to any permutation of a plurality of synchronized outputs. This is known as a *time multiplex switching* (TMS). Switching stages appear as square arrays of high-speed crosspoints. They are loosely referred to as space or *s* stages of a time division switching

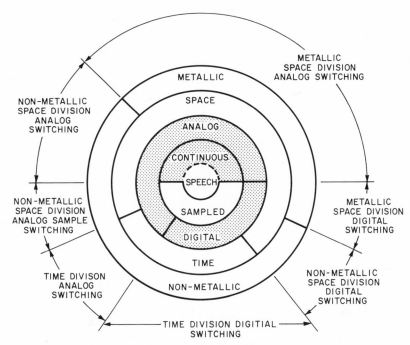

Fig. 24. Circuit-switching–transmission relationships. (From *IEEE Transactions*, July 1979.)

network. If there are several TMS stages, they operate in synchronism and each stage usually is designated by a separate *s*. These stages are usually unidirectional. (Single stages have been made bidirectional.)

Finally, for switching to take place it is necessary to be able to move samples from a time slot in one multiplexed input to a different output time slot in a multiplexed output. This requires the use of memory or delay of the samples. This operation has become known as *time slot interchanging* (TSI); the stages are known as *t* stages.

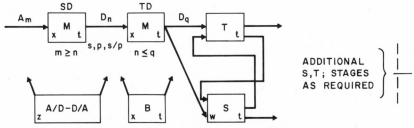

Fig. 25. Generalized time division network functional relationships. SD, space division multiplex; TD, time division multiplex; A_m, analog (*m* channels); B, buffer storage; D_n, digital (*n* channels); M, multiplex; A/D, analog-to-digital conversion; s, serial; p, parallel; s/p, serial and parallel; S, time multiplex switch stage; T, time slot interchange stage; t, time slots; w, stages; x, quantity per stage; z, inputs served. (From *IEEE Transactions*, July 1979.)

Time division networks utilize the SD/M, TD/M, TMS, and TSI stages in various arrangements shown generally in Fig. 25. Each stage requires a circulating memory that is generally part of the network, similar to contact memory in a space division network, to keep track of the connection associations for each time slot. More detail on digital time division networks is given in Chapter 5 of this volume. Note that the principles of the elements described above may in one form or another provide for the switching of sampled analog or digitally encoded signals.

4. Introduction to Digital Switching

4.1. Digital What?

Digital switching is merely the switching of digital signals.[34,35] It is important to recognize this simple definition since many have attempted to broaden the definition to include other aspects of technology in general and switching in particular.

Digital techniques are essential in all of switching, electromechanical or electronic. The controls of all types of switching systems require memory and logic. These have long been implemented by digital techniques whether using relays and electromechanical switches or more sophisticated stored program controls (see Chapter 3 of this volume). The mere fact that integrated circuit technology has come along at the same time as new switching system designs does not make them any more digital. This applies as well to any other new switching techniques such as stored program control or remote switching.

Likewise, the need to switch digital signals being transmitted by newer station devices, such as CRT terminals and computers, does not make digital switching a new technique. Switching systems for telex and other types of digital data signals have long been used in the industry and might be considered to be the forerunners of modern digital switching systems.

Finally, some writers have implied that to have digital switching one must employ time division techniques in the SCN. This is also not true in view of earlier data-switching systems and the current use of systems with space division SCNs for introducing switched digital capability into the existing United States public network.[36] A similar approach has also been introduced in East Germany.[37]

4.2. Need for Digital Switching

With the increasing use of time division multiplex transmission that includes the conversion of analog to digital signals there is a growing need to provide switching of these digitized and multiplexed inputs to nodes directly without first converting the signals to analog solely for the purpose of switching. This is illustrated in Fig. 26.

Telephony started with converting sound pressure variations to an electrical current analog of these variations. Over the years integrated networks of transmission and space division switching systems have developed for conveying these analog signals until now there is a worldwide public network. As the time division digital transmission systems proliferated the situation shown on Fig. 26b obtained where it was necessary on many connections to convert from digital to analog and back to pass through space division switches. For this reason many speak loosely of "analog switches," which is a misnomer since these space division switches are usually capable of switching digital signals.

It was quite natural that the first switching systems developed to avoid two conversions (to and from analog) were for intermediate or tandem office application where a large number of digital facilities terminated. The E10,[38] No. 4 ESS,[39] and IMA 2[40] systems were all first used in situations of this type. They employ time division (TD) digital switching. A

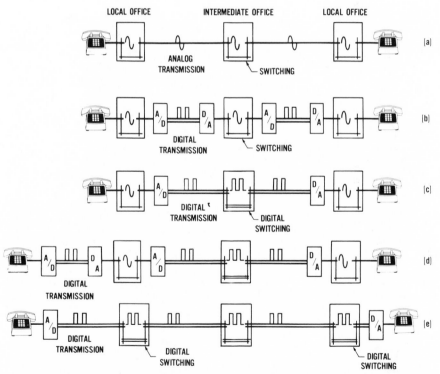

Fig. 26. Integrated switching and transmission. (a) Integrated analog switching and transmission; (b) growth of digital trunk transmission; (c) digital intermediate office and trunk transmission; (d) digital pair gain; (e) digital local office with analog-to-digital conversion at the central office (right) or at or near the station (left) integrated digital switching and transmission. (From *IEEE Transactions*, July 1979.)

different interface is required where analog facilities are terminated. These interfaces are generally the same as or similar to the reverse of a time division digital multiplex transmission terminal used to convert analog to digital.[41] In each network application there is a different transition situation. However, where new switches are required for growth or replacement there is likely to be more opportunity for using digital switches.

For local offices, most terminations (approximately 80%) are lines. Lines have, in the past and continue now, to generate analog signals, and will do so for some time to come. Where digital signals are sent from data terminals, modems are used to convert digital data signals to analog signals. The use of time division digital switching for local offices (and PBXs) is motivated primarily by the expectation of the future lower cost of analog-to-digital line interface integrated circuits.

It is interesting to note that manufacturers are able to enter the switching field, develop digital systems that include stored program controls, and skip the development of a generation of new space division technology. For the purchaser of this equipment there is the prospect of being able to obtain the synergy of digital switching and transmission as growth permits more lines to be served by digital subscriber carrier systems to save new cable pairs. This application is known as *pair gain*. Even with modest deployment of subscriber carrier, with 10%–20% of the lines served by digital pair gain systems, the synergy goes a long way to proving-in the new switching technology.[42]

It is expected that in the not too distant future digital rather than analog signaling will be used to carry voice and other digital signals over individual lines. Standards are being developed for using a single pair of wires for digital transmission in both directions[43] (see Chapter 8 of this volume). Typical standards being proposed provide for two-way 64 kilobits for speech plus one or more channels of 8 kilobits for data. Once these standards are agreed upon, the design and deployment of new telephone sets and terminals with built-in analog-to-digital conversion will proceed. However, in some countries the ratio of telephone sets to telephone line terminations is greater than one. It is expected that only where there is a need for the simultaneous transmission of voice and data service will such terminals find early application. New interfaces between digital switching systems and digital carrier systems will be required for operation with these sets.

4.3. Basic Building Blocks

For time division digital switching systems the essential elements are those associated with the switching center network (SCN). In Section 3.3 the basic elements were described as: time slot interchange (TSI), sometimes called time T switching; time multiplex switching, sometimes called space S switching; and space (SD/M) and time (TD/M) multiplexing. The SCN of a digital switch uses a chosen combination of these elements as well as memory buffers (B) for synchronization of the multiplex sources that the system serves. The choices among these combinations are discussed in detail in Chapter 5 of this volume.

Another major element of any digital switch is the clock that determines the rate at which synchronous digital pulses will pass through the switching elements.

For local applications the most important element is the line interface. This interface usually contains seven functions that spell the acronym BORSCHT. The functions these letters represent are shown in Fig. 27 and their design characteristics are discussed in Chapters 7 and 9 of this volume. Compared with space division analog systems these interfaces are complex and costly. The Codec function, including coding and decoding, has already been most successfully reduced in size and cost by the use of integrated circuits. Most system designs are predicated on the assumption that the remaining functions, generally referred to as subscriber line interface circuits (SLIC), will be made amenable to the same reductions by the application of large-scale integrated circuits.[44] The SLIC includes some common circuitry that interfaces with the control portion of the system, and the time division network. It is expected that within the next few years the SLIC cost will become low enough that local time division digital SPC systems with per line SLIC will be competitive with space division SPC systems. In the meantime some systems are employing space division concentrators ahead of the BORSCHT to reduce the average per line cost.[45]

It is important to recognize that the cost of the switching system alone is not the only factor in determining whether it is economical to employ time division digital switching. As more digital transmission facilities are deployed the synergy between them and a particular digital switch may be

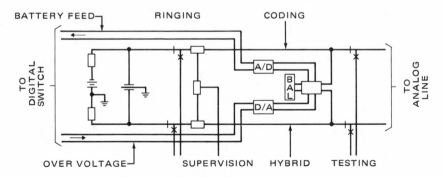

Fig. 27.   Analog-line–digital-switch interface functions. (From *IEEE Transactions*, July 1979.)

economically attractive. These situations are discussed in more detail in Chapter 10 of this volume.

The control of switching systems is discussed in Chapter 3. Distributed control appears to be the choice for most digital switching systems.[46] Many switching systems find it advantageous to also employ a central control,[47] while some rely on only distributed control with intermodule signaling.[48] Equipment units interfacing with a plurality of lines and/or trunks together with a distributed control have been referred to as switching "modules." Some systems are designed so that the modules may become remote switching units.[49]

5. Summary

This chapter has served as an introduction to the subject of digital switching. While the basic functions of a switching node in a network may be simply stated and easily understood, the design of switching entities is deceptively complex once all of the included features and services have been defined.

The basic functions that are built into the architecture of any switching system are also simple. Signaling standards have been described that ensure compatibility between old and new systems in the network. New signaling network techniques that disassociate the signaling from the message channel have been described.

Design and technology alternatives for the switching network functions have been described. Circuit switching is distinguished from other forms of switching by the inclusion of the switching center network.

The principles of space, time, and frequency division as applied to switching networks have been given. The topological factors for the growth and capacity of networks have been given. Networks have been shown to be the general connectives or access networks among other switching system functions.

Finally, the subject of digital switching has been discussed in general terms relating to its evolution and possible future trends. The building blocks and broad system architectures have been described.

Questions

1. Is the U.S. Public Telephone Network hierarchical in terms of function, or are specific switching offices used for different levels of the hierarchy?
2. What are the attributes of noncentral switching? Can noncentral switching use a star network? Does a local area network employ a noncentral switch?
3. Distinguish by definition among circuit, virtual circuit, and packet switching?

4. How many trunks are required to carry a load of 50% with a loss of one call in one hundred?

5. Is time division a circuit switching technique?

6. Name three external environmental and three internal factors that influence switching system designs.

7. Distinguish between in-band, out-of-band, and associated and nonassociated common channel signaling.

8. What are the basic building blocks of digital switching networks other than time-slot-interchange (T) and space (S) stages?

9. Can a digital time division network be built using only time stages (T)?

10. Distinguish space stages in space and time division switching systems.

11. Can space division switching systems be designed to switch digital signals? Multiplexed digital signals?

12. What are the BORSCHT functions, and explain why each is required in interfacing analog lines and trunks with digital switching.

References

1. K. B. Miller, *Telephone Theory and Practice,* vol. II, McGraw Hill, New York, 1933.

2. S. Brolin, Yo-S. Cho, W. P. Michaud, and D. H. Williamson, "Inside the New Digital Subscriber Loop System," *Bell Lab. Rec.,* pp. 110–116, April 1980.

3. U. K. Stagg, "No. 10A Remote Switching System (RSS) Overview," *IEEE Int. Commun.,* Pl. 1/1–5, 1980.

4. H. W. Kettler, G. P. O'Reilly, and R. L. Pokress, and K. A. Shulman, "The Application of Remote Switching Bell System Rural Modernization," *ISS 1981 Conf. Pub.,* vol. 4, Paper 41c2.

5. R. Landry, "Centrex—A New Concept of PBX Services," *Bell Tel. Mag.,* p. 10, Autumn 1961.

6. E. F. O'Neill, "TASI," *Bell Lab. Rec.,* pp. 82–87, March 1959.

7. T. Skeimoto and J. G. Puente, "A Satellite Time Division Multiple Access Experiment," *IEEE Trans Commun. Technol.,* No. 4, pp. 581–586, August 1968.

8. J. H. Weber, "Some Traffic Characteristics of Communications Network With Automatic Alternate Routing," *Bell Syst. Tech. J.,* p. 969, March 1962.

9. *Notes on the Network,* AT&T Pub., Basking Ridge, N.J., 1980.

10. L. A. Baxter and C. R. Baugh, "A Comparison of Architectural Alternatives for Local Voice/Data," *IEEE Comm. Mag.,* pp. 44–51, Jan. 1982.

11. C. Breen and C. A. Dahlbom, "Signaling Systems For Control of Telephone Switching," *Bell Syst. Tech. J.,* vol. 39, pp. 1381–1444, 1960.

12. CCITT *Yellow Book,* vol. VI, Recommendation Q. 315, Q. 421, *International Telecom. Union, Geneva, Switzerland,* November 1980.

13. R. G. Cornell and D. J. Stelte, "A Signaling Protocol for Digital Subscriber Lines," pp. 45.5/1–5 of *Natl. Telecommun. Conf.,* 1980.

14. J. G. Pearce, *Telecommunication Switching,* Plenum Press, New York, 1981.

15. J. S. Ryan, "CCITT Signalling System No. 6: A Story of International Cooperation," *Telecommun. J.,* vol. 41(2), pp. 77–82, February 1974.

16. J. J. Lawsen and D. Sheinbein, "Realizing The Potential of the SPC Network," *Bell Lab. Rec.,* vol. 57(3), pp. 85–89, March 1979.

17. W. O. Fleckenstein, "Switching Technology and New Network Services," *ISS '81,* Keynote Session, pp. 56–64.

18. F. Hlawa and A. Stoll, "Signaling for the Future (Explanation of Common Channel Signaling Based on CCITT System No. 7)", *Telephony*, vol. 200, pp. 85, 86, 90, 91, 96, 98, February 9, 1981.'

19. P. R. Miller and R. E. Wallace, "Common Channel Interoffice Signaling (CCIS): Signaling Network," *Bell Syst. Techn. J.*, vol. 57(2), pp. 263–282, February 1978.

20. W. J. Huckins, "Planning for the Implementation of CCITT No. 7 in the CCIS Network," *Intelexpo '81*, p. 132.

21. D. G. Fink and D. Christiansen, *Electronics Engineers' Handbook, 2nd Ed.*, McGraw-Hill Book Co., New York, 1982.

22. J. E. Abate, L. H. Brandenburg, J. C. Lawson, and others, "The Switched Digital Network Plan (No. 4 ESS)," *Bell Syst. Tech. J.*, vol. 56(7), pp. 1297–1320, September 1977; *Telephony*, vol. 193(17), pp. 25, 28, 29, 32, 33, October 24, 1977.

23. "Local Switching System General Requirements," AT&T Co., Publication No. 48501, December 1980.

24. A. Rockstrom and R. Saracco, "SDL—CCITT Specification and Description Language," *IEEE Natl. Commun. Conf., 1981*, pp. 6.3.1–6.3.5.

25. A. E. Joel, Jr. and G. Spiro, "Bell System Features and Services," *International Switching Symposium, Paris, 1979*, pp. 1247–1255.

26. A. E. Joel, Jr., "Circuit Switching: Unique Architecture and Applications," *Computer (IEEE)*, vol. 12(6), 10 June 1979.

27. M. J. Marcus, "The Theory of Connecting Networks and Their Complexity: A Review," *PROC IEEE*, vol. 65(9), pp. 1263–1270, September 1977.

28. A. E. Joel, Jr., "Classification and Unification of Switching System Functions," *Int. Switching Symp. 1972*, pp. 446–453.

29. A. Feiner and J. G. Kappel, "A Method of Deriving Efficient Switching Network Configurations," *Natl. Electronic Conf. Proc.—1970*, p. 818.

30. C. Clos, "A Study of Non-Blocking Switching Networks," *Bell Syst. Tech. J.*, vol. 32, pp. 406–424, March 1953.

31. P. W. Shackle, A. R. Hartman, T. J. Riley, and others, "A 500 V Monolithic Bidirectional 2 × 2 Crosspoint Array (Telephone Loop Switch)," pp. 170–171 of *IEEE Int. Solid-State Circuits Conf., 1980*.

32. G. Haugk, "New Peripheral System For No. 1 and No. 1A ESS," *Int. Switching Symp., 1976*.

33. S. W. Johnson and B. Litofsky, "End-to-End 56 Kb/s Switched Digital Connections in the Stored Program Controlled Network," *ISS '81 Conf. Pub.*, vol. 2, Paper 23c†

34. A. E. Joel, Jr., "Digital Switching—How It Has Developed," *IEEE Trans. Commun.*, vol. 27(7), pp. 948–1959, July 1979.

35. A. E. Joel, Jr., "Towards a Definition of Digital Switching," *Telephony*, vol. 197, p. 30, 22 October 1979.

36. G. J. Handler, "Planning Switched Data Transport Capabilities in the Bell System," *IEEE Natl. Telecommun. Conf., 1981*, pp. 2.3.1–2.3.4.

37. H. Sturz, "Electronic Telephone Switching System—ENSAD," *World Telecommun. Forum 3rd, 1979*, Part 2, pp. 1.2.8.1–1.2.8.9.

38. J. P. Coudreuse, P. Grall and C. Raphalen, "E-10 System: TDM Tandem Exchanges," *Commutation Electron. (Spec. Issue)*, pp. 43–56, June 1975; *Commutation Electron., No. 43*, pp. 71–85, October 1973 (in French).

39. H. E. Vaughan, A. E. Ritchie, and A. E. Spencer, "No. 4 ESS—A Full Fledged Toll Switching Node," *Int. Switching Symp. 1976*.

40. J. R. Baichtal and J. C. McDonald, "New Integrated Digital Switching System (IMA2)," *Natl. Telecommun. Conf. Rec., 1976*.

41. A. Como, "A Digital SPC Switching System for Transit Exchanges (AXE)," *IEEE Reg. 8 Conv., 1977*, pp. 2.5.4.1–2.5.4.6.

42. G. E. Harrington, D. H. Morgen, and J. W. Olson, "Survey of Pair Gain System Applications," *ISSLS '80*, pp. 196–200.

43. *Ibid.*, pp. 1–13.

44. L. Brown and B. G. Bynum, "One Chip Closes in on SLIC Functions," *Electron. Des.*, vol. 28(20), pp. 85, 27 September 1980.

45. N. Shimasaki, A. Kitamura, A. Saeki, and T. Yamaguchi, "NEAX-61 Digital Telephone Switching System," p. 748 of *Intelcom '80, Conf. Proc.*, Brasil, May 9–12 1980.

46. A. E. Joel, Jr., "Electronic Switching: Digital Central Office Systems of the World," *IEEE Press, 1982*, pp. 36–39.

47. S. E. Puccini and R. W. Wolff, "Architecture of the GTD-5 EAX Digital Family," *GTE Autom. Electr. World-Wide Commun. J.*, vol. 18(4), pp. 110–116, July 1980; p. 18.2/1-8 of *ICC '80. 1980 Int. Conf. on Commun., Seattle, Washington*, 8–12 June 1980, IEEE.

48. S. Dal Monte and J. Israel, "Proteo System—UT 10/3: A Combined Local and Toll Exchange," *ISS '81 Conf. Pub.*, vol. 3, Paper 32a2.

49. F. T. Andrews Jr. and W. B. Smith, "No. 5 ESS—Overview," *ISS '81 Conf. Pub.*, vol. 3, Paper 31a1.

Random Nature of Service Demands

Sushil G. Munshi

1. Introduction

In the course of conducting our normal daily business, we encounter situations where our demands are not immediately satisfied, for example, at taxi stands, banks, post offices. Some of these situations are tolerable, others are frustrating but beyond our control. The degree of importance of the service sought influences the choice between abandoning the service demand or increasing our threshold of tolerance and waiting until the demand is satisfied. In this chapter we will describe the nature of one such service demand, telephone calls, and characterize this demand in mathematical terms. The chapter is intended to provide an introduction to congestion problems and how they influence the design and engineering of digital switching systems. No attempt is made to derive the theory or offer solutions for specific congestion problems. The interested reader should consult the references listed at the end of the chapter for further study.

2. Nature of Demand

In this section, we describe what constitutes a demand and the basic elements of a demand. Then, for each element, its characteristics are discussed and defined in mathematical terms.

Sushil G. Munshi ● Technology Planning Department, United Telecommunications Inc., P.O. Box 11315, Kansas City, Missouri 64112

2.1   Elements of Demand

The basic elements comprising a demand are the *request for service* and the *duration of service*. Consider check-out counters at a supermarket. Customers in the store are potential candidates for generating requests for service. They all reach the check-out counter unless they abandon shopping altogether. Each customer has a different number of items in a cart; the service duration, in general, is approximately in proportion to the number of items in the cart. We all have, at one time or another, selected a queue (line) after a quick glance at each line, mentally analyzing the number of customers in each line and the items in their carts to minimize our waiting time. And, on occasion, our intuition has failed us when someone in our queue with expected short service time due to fewer items requires longer time for service due to, for example, check verification, refund coupons, etc. It is obvious that an individual's waiting time is dependent upon not only the number of customers ahead in the queue, but also upon their individual service times. This combination of number of customers, service requests, and the service times constitutes the *demand* or *load* on the server, the check-out clerk.

In telecommunications the load or the status of the system is not visible to the individual requesting service. That is, the individual customer is unaware of the number of customers waiting or their service times. However, overload is noticeable when a request for service cannot be satisfied immediately. This is observed by a delay in dial tone reception, or by reception of a fast busy signal or announcement indicating all paths are busy.

In telephone terminology the components of load are *calling rate* and *duration of calls*. The product of these two parameters over a fixed time unit is the traffic load. When the time unit is the same for both parameters (calling rate in calls/seconds and holding time in seconds or calling rate in calls/hour and holding time in hours) the product gives the traffic load intensity in *erlangs*. When the unit for holding time is 100 sec and the calling rate is expressed as calls/hour the product gives the traffic load in CCS (hundreds of call-seconds per hour). Since there are 3600 sec in one hour, i.e., 36 units of 100 sec each, it is easy to see that one erlang equals 36 CCS.

The number of calls per unit time is the rate at which calls arrive and the process associated with the arrivals of calls is called the *arrival process*. The reciprocal of the service time gives the rate at which calls leave the system (complete service) and the associated process is called the *departure process*. The traffic load in erlangs can be expressed as the ratio of the mean arrival rate to the mean departure rate:

$$\rho = \lambda/\mu = \lambda h \tag{1}$$

where λ is the mean arrival rate, μ is the mean departure rate, $h = 1/\mu$ is the mean service time, and ρ is the traffic load.

Some important systems of this type are studied by the theorists under the general classification of birth and death processes.

2.2. Origination of Calls

Many factors influence the call origination process, customer behavior being the strongest factor. The state of the system may also influence the call origination process. Heavy system overloads will stimulate repeated attempts. Special events and promotions cause major increases in call originations in selected areas. Catastrophic events, e.g., earthquakes and floods, create extreme overloads in limited areas. In this section we will illustrate the random nature of traffic demand. The behavior of the call origination process under special circumstances is not included.

Customers originate calls, in general, in a random fashion when the population universe is viewed as a whole. A customer originates a call independent of other customers and the state of the system.

However, many studies[1-3] have shown that the call origination process follows a pattern which can be described in probabilistic terms. The characteristics, in most cases, are such that a rational explanation can be provided.

Within a given hour, the call origination rate exhibits random fluctuations as shown in Figure 1.[4] Under normal conditions different hours exhibit similar fluctuation patterns. However, there are variations among hours of the day. During certain hours of the day the calling rate is higher than the average hourly calling rate. These hours define the daily busy periods for a central office. The morning busy period is mainly caused by

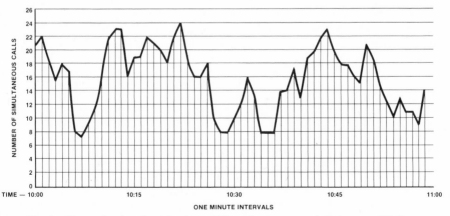

Fig. 1.   Fluctuation in call originations within an hour on a particular group of 30 lines.

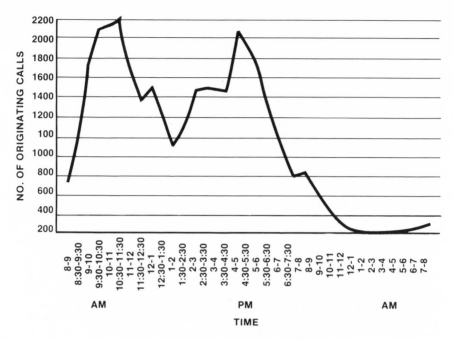

Fig. 2.   Hourly fluctuations in call originations.

business traffic. As shown in Fig. 2,[4] the calling rate increases due to business traffic about an hour after the start of the day and may increase in the late afternoon with combined business and residential traffic (after school). The reduction in calling rates around lunch period is easily recognizable.

Evening busy periods also occur in many offices. One factor causing this is the reduction in the cost of toll calls during evening hours. The cost incentive has significantly increased the residential call origination rate and there are instances where the load during the evening busy period is higher than the daytime busy period.

In many offices, there are significant variations in calling rates among different days of a week as illustrated in Fig. 3.[4]

Once again the influence of business traffic is evident; Mondays and Fridays, in general, have the highest calling rate. These variations are also observed among various weeks and months as shown in Fig. 4.[4]

The increase in call origination rates for Mothers' Day, Christmas Day, and New Year's Eve can be seen. Figures 5, 6, and 7[1] illustrate a typical call origination pattern for the morning of December 31 and the hours surrounding New Year's Day. Notice the normal pattern during the day, a rapid build-up of traffic just around midnight and a slowing down

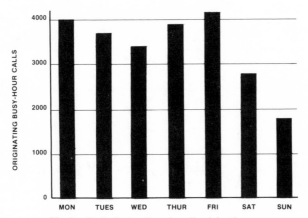

Fig. 3.   Daily fluctuations in call originations.

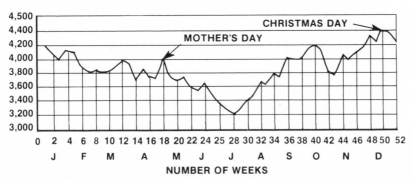

Fig. 4.   Weekly fluctuations in call originations.

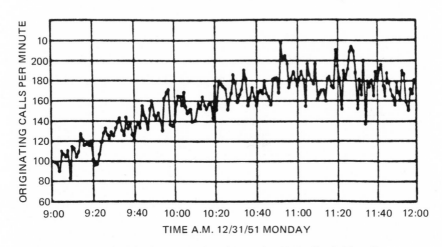

Fig. 5.   Call originations—morning of December 31, Sterling 9–Ulster 7.

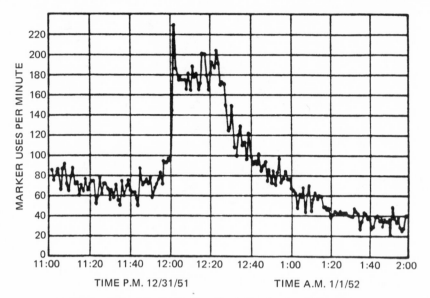

Fig. 6.   Call originations—New Year's Eve, Sterling 9–Ulster 7.

soon after midnight. The behavior on these special days is predictable even though not deterministic.

The preceding discussion describes the variations in call origination rate for fresh calls, i.e., calls that are offered to the first stage of switching. The characteristic of the call arrival process as observed at the various stages of a switching system is altered and the random nature of the process

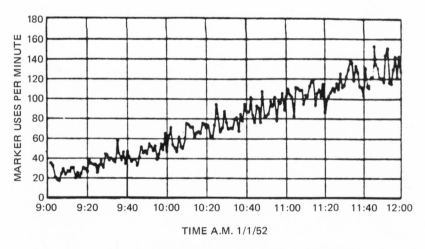

Fig. 7.   Call originations—New Year's Day, Sterling 9–Ulster 7.

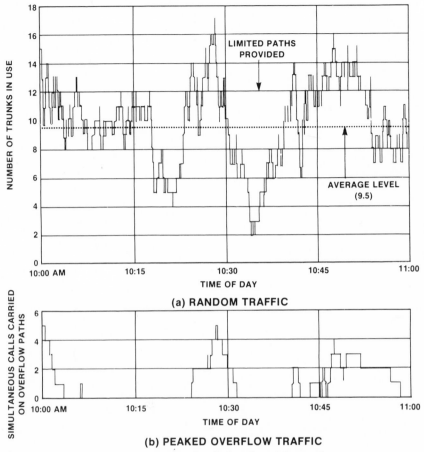

Fig. 8. Production of peakedness in overflow traffic.

is somewhat lost. One such example is the call arrival process as seen by the overflow trunk group. An overflow trunk group is an alternate choice group and the traffic is routed to this group when it cannot be carried over the first choice group. As shown in Fig. 8,[5] the traffic seen by the overflow group is significantly different from that which is seen by the first choice group. Traffic theory provides special treatment[5,6] to model this traffic, known as peaked traffic.

Another example is the case when the number of customers, sources which can originate calls, is relatively small. In this case, as sources become busy by originating a call, the chance that new calls will be originated diminishes as compared to the case where the number of customers is very large (infinite) and the mean call origination rate is virtually constant. Other situations where the calling rate may not behave as depicted is when there is a significant proportion of repeated[7,8] attempts under overload. The repetition frequency as well as the probability distribution for repeated attempts are needed, as a minimum, to study the traffic problem. In this introductory treatment we exclude such phenomena.

2.3. Service Time

The demand on a server is determined by the number of service requests and the time required to satisfy a request. The *service time*, or the *holding time* as it is commonly called, of a telephone call contains many elements. On a successful call, the customer goes off-hook and on receipt of dial tone enters the necessary digits. The call is then forwarded to the called party and the phone is rung. The called party answers, after a few ringing cycles, and two parties engage in conversation. At the end of the conversation both parties hang up and the connection is dropped.

Three major elements of holding time are evident from the above description: dialing time, ringing time, and conversation time. Note that call processing time and associated delays are not considered here. In addition to the three major elements, other elements contribute to holding time, particularly for calls which do not result in conversation. Figure 9[1] illustrates the major elements of holding time. These holding time elements affect different devices in the switching system with respect to traffic load.

False starts are customer call initiation attempts which are abandoned after a short interval with no dialing after the receipt of a dial tone. The holding times of such attempts are short and, hence, they do not burden the conversation carrying path significantly. However, they add significantly to the load on the common control equipment.

A permanent signal condition occurs when the customer's line signals

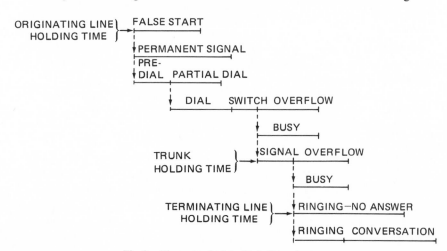

Fig. 9.   Elements of teletraffic holding times.

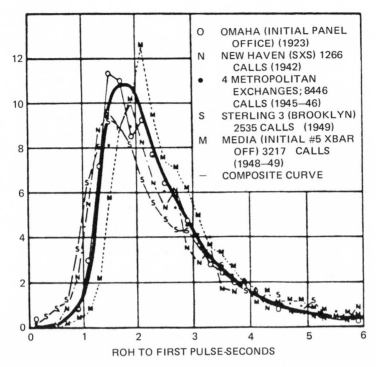

Fig. 10.   Subscribers dialing performance—receiver off-hook to first digit dialing, with good tone service.

off-hook for a long time with no dialing or any intention of call initiation. If the condition is caused by oversight, then prompt application of alerting tone signals the customer to go on-hook and this reduces the effect of a permanent signal. However, if the condition is caused by a trouble condition or intentionally by the customer, then the permanent signal condition creates an abnormally large holding time and may produce a noticeable effect on switching systems.

Predialing time or the time from removal of the telephone receiver to the first digit is critical for the digit receiving equipment in the central office. The receiver must be ready to receive the customer's dialed digits. Otherwise, the digits may be mutilated or completely lost and the call will be unsuccessful. Figure 10[1] shows typical predialing behavior.

Once the customer starts dialing, the call attempt might be abandoned prior to dialing all the necessary digits. This partial dial phenomenon could occur at any time during the dialing process. Frequently, the reason for a partial dial is that the customer recognizes a dialing error and a repeated attempt follows. On occasion the call is abandoned and is not retried in sufficient time. In this case another attempt is classified as a fresh

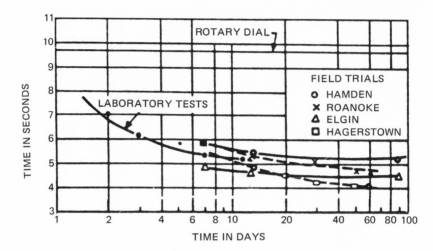

Fig. 11.   Dialing time for pushbutton and rotary dial telephones.

call rather than a retrial. These partial dial events impose a load on the common control equipment.

A customer's dialing time depends upon the number of digits to be dialed and whether the telephone is pushbutton or rotary dial. For rotary dial, the average dialing time is 10 sec. With experience, customers key in 7-digit numbers in about half the time required with rotary dial. Figure 11[1] shows the results of dialing time measurements after pushbutton telephones are installed. Dialing irregularities, such as misdialed numbers, are somewhat higher in new installations of push button telephones as compared to rotary telephones.

Once the call reaches the called party, busy tone is applied if the line is busy or a ringing tone is applied if the line is idle. The customer's behavior varies regarding the length of time before the call attempt is terminated due to a busy line or no answer. It has been found[9] that the average time to answer after the first ring is about 6 sec for business customers. On the average, the calling party hangs up after 20–30 sec if there is no answer and after 5–6 sec if the line is busy. This is explainable since the busy signal is a definite and immediate indication that the party is not available; whereas, if the telephone rings it is possible that the party is available but not in the immediate vicinity to answer.

It is expected that the time interval between successive attempts would be shorter (higher retrial frequency) when the customer receives a busy signal than if the customer encounters ringing but no answer condition.

Table 1 and Fig. 12[9] list the statistics of customer behavior under various situations for long-distance call attempts. Figure 13[9] shows the percentage disposition of long-distance calls.

Table 1. DDD Call Setup and Abandonment Time Statistics

Call setup or abandonment interval	Mean (sec)	Std. dev. (sec)	Cumulative distribution percentage points (sec)		
			10%	50%	90%
Off-hook to start dialing	1.7 ± 0.1	2.0	1	2	4
Start of dialing to end of dialing	12.1 ± 0.3	5.1	6	12	18
End of dialing to ring before answer or disconnect	10.9 ± 0.5	5.0	5	11	17
End of dialing to answer without a ring signal	11.1 ± 0.9	5.3	5	10	17
Start of ringing to answer	8.5 + 0.3	7.2	3	6	15
Start of ringing to disconnect without an answer	38.1 ± 2.5	20.7	18	33	59
Answer to disconnect for wrong numbers	18.7	8.9	—	—	—
End of dialing to busy (60 IPM) signal	10.5 ± 0.9	5.2	5	10	17
Start of busy to disconnect	4.6 ± 0.3	3.7	2	3	8
End of dialing to no circuit/reorder (120 IPM) signal	7.4 ± 2.0	7.4	0	6	15
Start of no circuit/reorder to disconnect	3.6 ± 0.4	2.3	2	3	6
End of dialing to no-such-number (NSN) tone	1.2	1.4	—	—	—
Start of NSN tone to disconnect	2.6	1.7	—	—	—
End of dialing to ring prior to NSN announcement	5.3	4.1	—	—	—
Start of ringing to NSN announcement	7.1	4.9	—	—	—
End of dialing to NSN announcement without a ring signal	7.3 ± 1.6	5.4	1	6	11
Start of NSN announcement to disconnect	7.6 ± 1.8	10.4	2	5	13
End of dialing to ring prior to intercept for number charge or disconnect (INT)	10.9 ± 1.1	4.6	6	10	19
Start of ringing to INT	8.8 ± 1.8	6.3	3	9	15
End of dialing to INT without a ring signal	13.9	4.4	—	—	—
Start of INT to disconnect	24.7 ± 14.2	24.6	4	15	81
End of dialing to customer abandonment without a system response	15.5 ± 2.8	17.8	1	12	35

Conversation time is the largest element of the various components of holding time. It exhibits variations somewhat similar to the call arrival process. The holding time averages are known to vary with the type of customers and the charging method. Business calls, on the average, have a shorter conversation time compared to residential calls. The conversation time also varies in different geographical locations. The effect of the charging method on conversation time is observed in the evening low rate period. Variations in conversation times are also observed during different days of the week and in different hours of the day. Figures 14 and 15[1] illustrate such variations. Within a given hour, the conversation times

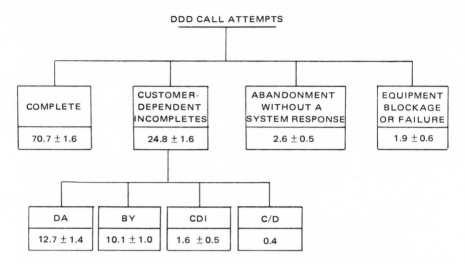

Fig. 12. Average DDD call attempts and abandonment times. DA, called station did not answer; BY, called station busy; CDI, customer dialing irregularly; C/D, called number changed or disconnected.

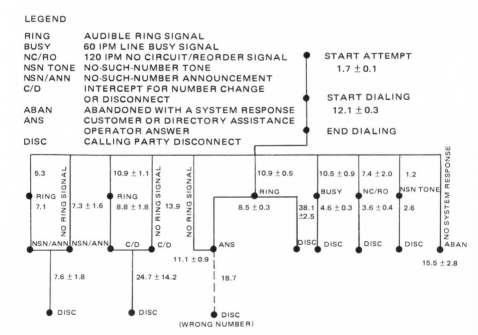

Fig. 13. DDD call attempts dispositions.

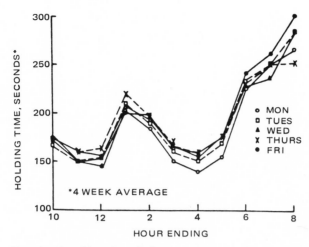

Fig. 14. Day of week and intraday toll alternate route network holding time effects.

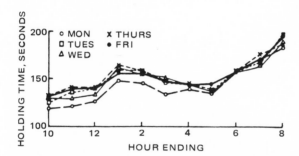

Fig. 15. Day of week and intraday local alternate route network holding time effects.

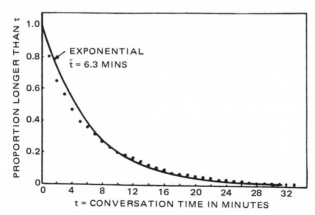

Fig. 16. Distribution of conversation times; 512 calls customer dialed, United States to United Kingdom, 1970.

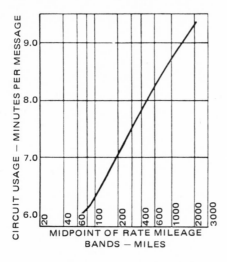

Fig. 17.　Holding time variations with distance.

follow the curve as shown in Fig. 16.[1] In the United States the conversation time shows a tendency to increase with distance as shown in Fig. 17.[1]

The characteristics of customer demand based on measurements have been described in this section. These measurements lay the foundation for the mathematical models presented in the next section.

3.　Important Probability Distribution Functions

In this section we will characterize the arrival process and the departure process (holding time) in mathematical terms. The treatment presented is by no means exhaustive; there are situations where special treatment and additional mathematical details are necessary. The intent here is to present some of the most commonly used probability distribution functions as a means to familiarize the reader with the mathematics of telecommunication traffic theory and to direct interested readers to references in the field of queuing theory.

In the previous section, it was observed that both call initiations and associated service times show a wide range of fluctuations. Even though these fluctuations appear to be endless in variety and are functions of many parameters, long-term observations[10,11] have shown that these variations can be characterized in mathematical terms with probabilistic interpretations.

3.1.　Binomial Distribution

The binomial distribution characterizes the most elementary experiment. If p is the probability of a success and $q = 1 - p$ is the probability of a failure and if the experiment is performed n times, the probability of exactly k successes is given by

$$p(k \text{ successes}) = \binom{n}{k} p^k (1 - q)^{n-k} \tag{2}$$

where

$$\binom{n}{k} = \frac{n!}{k!(n-k!)} \tag{3}$$

It is assumed that outcomes of each of these experiments are mutually independent.

This distribution is obviously applicable to coin tossing problems. In telephony, it is frequently used to describe the probability of a given number of busy or idle lines in a customer group or a given number of busy or idle links in a multistage switching system, although the required independent assumption is somewhat questionable.

3.2. Negative Exponential Distribution

One of the most important distributions in teletraffic theory is the negative exponential distribution. The distribution function, $F(x)$, is defined as

$$F(x) = \Pr\{T \leq x\} \tag{4}$$

$$= 1 - e^{-\mu x}, \quad x \geq 0$$

$$= 0, \quad x < 0 \tag{5}$$

where T is a continuous random variable, for example service time. The mean or expected value of T is μ^{-1} and variance of T is μ^{-2}. The negative exponential distribution is the only continuous distribution with the important "lack of memory" Markov property, i.e., for every $t > 0$ and $x > 0$

$$\Pr\{T > t + x \mid T > t\} = \Pr\{T > x\} \tag{6}$$

It has been well known that the service times of telephone calls, particularly conversation times, can be characterized by the negative exponential distribution. This fact, together with the Markov property of the distribution, have greatly simplified the mathematical treatment of congestion or queuing theory problems. Figure 16[1] illustrates a typical distribution of conversation time. Even though the various individual elements of service time do not follow the negative exponential distribution, it provides a good approximation for the total service time when all elements are viewed collectively.

3.3. Poisson Distribution

Another very important and widely used distribution not only in teletraffic theory but also in other fields is the Poisson distribution. The exponential distribution was discussed mainly with respect to its use for describing service times. It can just as well be used to describe the arrival process by considering the duration of elapsed time between call arrivals. If it is assumed that the distances between successive call arrivals are independently, identically, and exponentially distributed with mean λ^{-1} then the probability that j calls arrive in a time interval of length t is given by

$$\Pr\{j \text{ calls in interval } t\} = \frac{(\lambda t)^j}{j!} e^{-\lambda t} \tag{7}$$

The Poisson distribution is generally used to define the call arrival process at a central office. When call initiations occur from a large group of customers with a constant mean arrival rate, and independence of call initiations is a reasonable assumption, the Poisson distribution characterizes the call arrival process. However, there are situations where the arrival process cannot be characterized by the Poisson distribution, for example, overflow traffic, traffic from finite sources, etc.

In many cases the Poisson distribution and the negative exponential distribution can adequately describe the arrival process and service time

Table 2. Basic Congestion Formulas

Erlang B	Probability of blocking—probability of S servers busy: $$B(s, a) = \frac{a^s/s!}{\sum_{j=0}^{s} a^{j}/j!}$$	Poisson input with mean rate λ; mean service time $1/\mu$; traffic load $a = \lambda/\mu$; number of servers $= s$; blocked calls cleared
Erlang C	Probability of delay $= \Pr[W > 0] = C(s, a)$; $$C(s, a) = \frac{a^s/(s-1)! \times 1/(s-a)}{\sum_{j=0}^{s-1} a^j/j! + a^s/(s-1)!(s-a)}$$ Probability of delay greater than t: $$\Pr[W > t] = C(s, a)e^{-(1-a)s\mu t}$$ Average delay: $$EW = \frac{C(s, a)}{(1 - a)s\mu}$$	Poisson input with mean rate λ; negative exponential service time distribution with mean $1/\mu$; blocked calls delayed order of arrival service; blocked—customers wait until served
Poisson formula	Probability of blocking—probability that all S servers are busy $$P(s, a) = \sum_{j=s}^{\infty} \frac{a^j}{j!} e^{-a}$$	Poisson input with mean rate λ; negative exponential service time distribution with mean $1/\mu$; traffic load $a = \lambda/\mu$; blocked calls held

distribution. This has been of great value in solving many queuing theory problems which could have otherwise been untractable.

The mathematical expressions for the most common formulas can be found in any book on congestion theory;[12,13] Table 2 lists the three basic formulas. Of course, in practice, there are situations where the assumed conditions under which the above formulas are derived may not exist, and it is then necessary to derive the suitable formula based on mathematical analyses. It is useful to note a recursive form for the Erlang B formula which simplifies numerical evaluations:

$$E_n(A) = \frac{AE_{n-1}(A)}{n + AE_{n-1}(A)} \tag{8}$$

where $E_n(A)$ is the probability of blocking, A is the traffic offered in erlangs, n is the number of servers, and $E_0(A) = 1$.

Some useful characteristics can be observed by examining the Erlang B formula. For a given blocking or $E_n(A)$ the traffic carried increases as the number of trunks increases. That is, larger trunk groups are more efficient than smaller trunk groups. Also, for a given number of trunks, blocking increases as traffic load increases. It should be noted that the larger trunk groups, even though more efficient, are more vulnerable to overload, i.e., under overload the blocking probability increases rapidly for larger trunk groups. Figures 18 and 19 show several load service curves as a function of trunk group size.

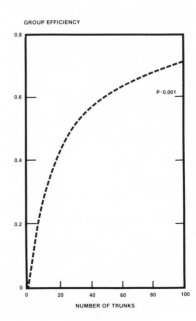

Fig. 18. Trunk group efficiency.

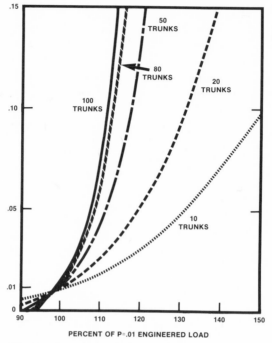

Fig. 19.   Overload performance of various trunk groups.

4.   Digital Switching Systems

Digital systems are being introduced in the telephone network. They offer a number of advantages over the current analog systems; increased capacity, reduced cost, reduced floor space, low maintenance, improved transmission quality, etc. They provide the network planners with more alternatives and flexibility. As a result an area planning concept, a broader perspective than exchange by exchange planning, is required. We discuss some traffic considerations in qualitative terms; hopefully this will provide some appreciation for the traffic-related problems.

4.1.   Class-5 Configuration

Figure 20 shows a generalized schematic of a class-5 digital system which represents a model suitable for the majority of digital systems on the market. As far as the block diagram is concerned, there is practically no difference between an analog class-5 and a digital class-5 system. Both contain a line stage (single or multistage); a switching matrix where inter- and intraoffice trunks are connected; various types of controllers (wired logic microprocessors); and service circuits (originating registers, software records). The difference is primarily in the technology used in the hardware as well as software or firmware areas. Briefly, the configuration can be described as follows.

Customer lines are connected to a line module (LM) which serves as a concentrator. Trunk circuits appear on a trunk module (TM) generally without concentration but with a proper interface device. The switching matrix is the distribution stage providing paths for connection between any two ports connected to it. There may be various microprocessors (telecommunication controllers) to handle functions associated with a call. The current trend is towards distributed control using microprocessors with a central processor acting as the brain of the processing complex. Special service circuits may be required during some phases of call setup which can be distributed according to the system philosophy.

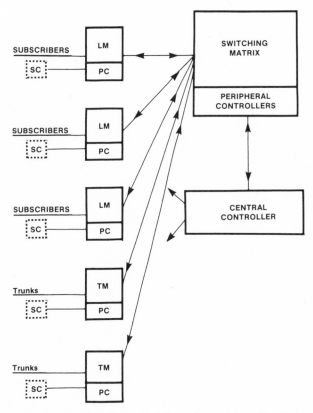

Fig. 20. Schematic diagram of a class-5 digital switching system. LM, line module: concentrator; TM, trunk module; SC, service circuit; PC, peripheral controller.

The fundamental considerations are essentially identical in analog as well as digital switching systems except digital systems may provide more flexibility in applications. One could say that the responsibility for "traffic engineering" is shifted, to a certain extent, from the operating company traffic engineer to the engineer designing the system. For example, the traffic engineer has been responsible for determining the number of dial tone markers or originating registers in the electromechanical systems; but in a digital switching system the design engineer is responsible for ascertaining that the line module controller has adequate real time capacity to meet the demands and that enough storage memory is provided to register the necessary digits for call processing. Next, we consider these aspects in connection with the generalized configuration shown in Fig. 20.

4.2. Traffic Considerations

4.2.1. Line Stage

Traffic on subscriber lines is usually low, on the order of 0.1 erlang or so during the busy hour. For efficient use of equipment it is concentrated before forwarding it to the high-capacity switching matrix. The concentration stage thus introduces blocking which depends upon the concentration ratio and the total traffic from the group of customers. The link between the line module and the switching matrix is a digital multiplex such as the standard 24- or 32-channel multiplier. The traffic capacity is determined by the number of channels and the criteria for grade of service; i.e., probability of blocking and probability of dial tone delay exceeding a preset limit. Note that the originated as well as terminated traffic occupies a channel. Probability of blocking can be estimated by using the straightforward Erlang B formula or applying the formula for finite sources (called Engset formula) depending upon the concentration ratio.

The estimate of the dial tone delay distribution is complicated due to the need for a connection to a receiving device. For example, when a connection to a DTMF receiver is required, in most cases, two channels are needed, one for the originating customer and one for the DTMF receiver, as shown in Fig. 21. Call processing delay as well as channel congestion must be evaluated.

Note that these channels are used to carry conversation traffic (long holding time) as well as digit reception traffic (short holding time) with

Fig. 21. Service circuit connection.

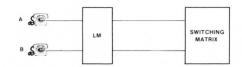

Fig. 22.   Intramodule call connection.

different arrival rates, since not all attempts result in conversation. In certain systems the channel to the service circuits is dedicated. Also, the conversation traffic is on a blocked calls cleared (BCC) basis while the digit reception or dial tone is on a blocked calls delayed (BCD) basis. The delay for a dial tone could be because the channel for the caller is not available, the channel leading to the receiver or the receiver itself is not available or the processors are busy. This presents an interesting problem in queuing theory. Arthur and Stuck[13] and others have considered one such model which could be expanded to cover other models.

Calls which are confined to the same line module (when calling and called party both are served by the same line module) require two channels, one for each customer, from the given group of channels assigned to the line module, Fig. 22. It is obvious that a significant amount of this type of traffic would greatly impact the capacity of line modules. In some systems special links called intralinks are provided to accommodate a portion of such traffic. Proper account should be taken of channel usage, intralink usage, and traffic overflow when all intralinks are busy.

4.2.2. Switching Matrix

The switching matrices can be of many types as described in Chapter 5 of this volume. Technological advances have made the design of economical, high-capacity, nearly nonblocking matrices possible. From the user's point of view, there are practically no traffic considerations in this area. High capacity and extremely low blocking eliminate the need for inlet load balancing. The designer is concerned with modularity, expansion, number of stages required, path searching routines, and other design considerations. A detailed description of blocking in a TST switching matrix is given in Chapter 9 of this volume.

Some systems utilize a four-stage matrix where two mirror images of two-stage matrices are interconnected via links generally referred to as junctors. The traffic capacity in such systems is limited by the number of junctors provided between the switching groups. Figure 23 depicts the schematic of such a configuration. The links between the incoming and outgoing groups are redistributed as the network grows. Under uniform load distribution among various groups, the number of links is calculated for the resultant traffic between a pair of incoming and outgoing groups. (It is seen that reassignment of incoming and outgoing termination may be required

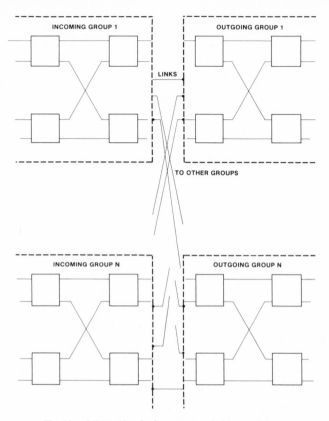

Fig. 23.   Schematic of a four-stage switching matrix.

to maintain the uniform load distribution.) That is, if traffic from an incoming group is A and there are N groups, then traffic between a pair is assumed to be A/N. If the load is not uniformly distributed then each pair must be treated individually.

4.2.3. Processors

Traffic considerations for controllers or processors are not unique to the digital environment; they are the same as those in any stored program control system. The basic consideration is the call-processing capacity. Busy hour call attempt capacity could vary with traffic mix since the type of call defines the functions to be performed, which, in turn, determines the processing time required. Real time available for call processing depends upon the traffic-independent load, overhead, and the margin reserved for overload conditions as described in Chapter 3 of this volume. The system should satisfy all grade-of-service criteria under normal or engineered load and should specify the performance under various overload conditions. Digital systems usually employ distributed control. The distributed control philosophy reduces the load on the system processor by performing routine non-time-critical functions and add a little overhead due to the need for communication among various controllers. The software architecture and task partitioning in distributed control may increase the number of internal queues, interaction between processors, and contention situations, all of which should be carefully analyzed.

Each line module might be controlled by a pair of microprocessors in a load-sharing mode. Each microprocessor may be associated with one multiplex. When one of the multiplexes or one of the controllers associated with a line module fails, the entire load must then be carried by the working controller. This could result in an overload of the controllers even though the total load from the line module may not exceed the designed load. The performance under these conditions should be evaluated. Similar considerations apply to other peripheral processors.

4.2.4. Remote Units

The introduction of digital switching systems has encouraged the development of a satellite unit, usually referred to as a remote unit, and has promoted host–remote configurations. A new set of traffic considerations emerges under this approach.

Remote units usually serve a small community remotely located from the host office when, for economic reasons, a complete digital switch cannot be justified. The approach enables the system to offer the small community services equivalent to those available to the customers served by the host office. It has been found[15] that for a small group of customers the traditional time-consistent busy-hour method of engineering is not applicable. The fluctuations are greater than those seen by a system which serves a large group of customers with a mixture of calling behaviors. In such cases the method called extreme value engineering (EVE)[16,17] may be applicable. EVE originated as an application for remote line concentrators and then for small step-by-step offices.

The application of remote switching units should be examined from the service availability (reliability) point of view. The availability of service to the customers connected to a remote switching unit depends upon the availability of the link(s), i.e., the Tl lines, to the hub office. Different methods exist to improve the system availability, each providing a varying degree of service capability.

Reliability of links to the hub office can be significantly increased by providing an adequate number of backup lines and span switching. Diversified routing is another means of improving the system availability.

Emergency switching or intralink switching is also used to provide protection from total service denial. In one philosophy, a number of remote units (collocated) communicate with each other via emergency switching modules in case of failure of the primary links to the hub. This method permits local calling among the customers served by the cluster of remote units; however, no nonlocal call can be handled. This method places all the associated remote units in emergency mode when all lines from one or more remote units fail.

In some systems intralinks are distributed among various collocated remotes. The distribution is selected by the user. The call handling capability under emergency strongly depends upon the intra-link distribution.

Note that all methods of improving system availability cost money. The decision to select a particular method, e.g., diversified routing or emergency switching, requires a service trade-off study using economic considerations.

4.2.5. Service Circuits

In a telecommunication system, means to receive information for a call setup must be provided. These can be accomplished via either software registers or hardware devices. In general, stored program control (SPC) systems provide software registers to receive information transmitted via dial pulse signaling; e.g., digits dialed via rotary dial or DP signaling over an incoming trunk. At present, reception of DTMF and MF signaling requires hardware devices which are referred to as service circuits in this chapter. The system may employ other types of service circuits, e.g., conference circuits.

These devices affect the delay experienced by the service request, either as a dial tone delay or as a receiver attachment delay seen by an incoming trunk. Estimates of traffic should include traffic load due to incomplete calls as well as completed calls; a call encountering line busy or all trunks busy places the same demand on the receiving device as a completed call. Therefore, attempts rather than completed calls should be used for calculating traffic load. Complete service time for a request should be accounted for properly and requires a clear understanding of the call-processing philosophy employed.

The hardware devices such as DTMF and MF receivers are connected in the system in different ways. They can be connected to the network the same way as digital trunks; i.e., there is a dedicated channel for every service circuit, and, therefore, an idle service circuit implies an idle channel associated with it. When this approach is taken for service circuits, the reliability aspects should be carefully examined. For example, when 24 service circuits are linked to the network via one 24-channel multiplex, it is important to consider the consequences when that multiplex fails. In some cases, service circuits are distributed over all line modules, thus providing protection against single multiplex failure. However, when these devices are distributed among line modules, the requests for connection to a service circuit must compete with other traffic to secure a channel. This adds an extra element which could cause blocking. Of course, channels could be dedicated to distributed service circuits at the expense of a reduction in the traffic capacity for line modules.

When remote units with emergency switching for local calls are considered for application, it is necessary to provide adequate service circuits at remote locations. In some systems the service circuits are treated as a pool regardless of the location; i.e., at a remote office or at the host office. Special consideration must be given to the distribution of these circuits so that an adequate number of service circuits are available to customers at the host office, even though the total number of service circuits in the system may be reduced due to failure of the link at the remote office.

Detailed analysis in special cases may be required to ascertain the quality of service. For example, circuits designed to provide conference capabilities may require a group of channels per call, thus effectively increasing the load on channels or reducing the number of channels available to other traffic. In such complex situations, simulation studies are very useful in evaluating the performance of the system.

5. Traffic Engineering

Traffic engineering of a digital system is, fundamentally, no different from its analog counterpart. This is to say that for each traffic-sensitive element of the system appropriate parameters such as load, attempts, holding times, and service criteria, should be defined and applicable congestion formulas should be used. It is beyond the scope of this chapter to address traffic engineering of a switching exchange. In the following we will briefly describe some new or atypical methods of interest.

Extreme-value-engineering[16,17] concepts have their origin in traffic engineering and administration of remote line concentrators. They are also applied to small step-by-step offices. Basically, the EVE concept recommends the use of peak load monitoring and the use of peak load distribution with a peak load service criterion for engineering small offices instead of the traditional time-consistent busy-hour (TCBH) approach. It was observed that only about one-fifth of the time does the peak load occur in the TCBH. The grade of service—i.e., dial tone delays or blocking—deteriorates rather rapidly under peak load in a digital system. The study in the references cited above suggests a normal distribution raised to the sixth power for the extreme value distribution function. For this service criterion a monthly frequency of occurrence is preferred and the criterion for line finders is, for example, that the probability of delay greater than 3 sec should not exceed 8% more often than once a month. The application of EVE to small step-by-step offices has resulted in improved service during the peak load period and maintains at least as good an overall service as other methods. The reader is advised to consult the references cited if the application of EVE is considered, as an example, for remote units.

The modular trunk engineering[18] approach addresses the cost benefits of the method for digital networks. The introduction of new digital terminals for the No. 1/1A ESS (the digital carrier trunk, DCT) and for No. 4 (ESS (the digital interface frame, DIF) requires that the trunk groups that terminate on either of these switches must be provided on separate T-carrier systems. The traditional method of engineering high-usage groups based on ECCS (economical CCS) assumes a linear cost function. The approach described in the reference cited suggests that the size of the high-usage group should be constrained to be multiples of a fixed size (module). The study results recommend a module of 12 trunks for one-way groups and a module of 24 trunks for two-way groups with a round-up threshold of half a module. An optional threshold could differ from one-half module depending on the particular network, since the network cost is not very sensitive to the threshold value. This approach reduces the network administrative costs and the number of high-usage groups but increases the network terminations in the study model. It may be necessary to carefully examine the cost penalties for an accelerated switch exhaust against the savings identified with modern engineering.

It was stated earlier that the digital switching systems offer flexibilities in network configurations (remote, host). When various network alternatives are considered, their impact on the traffic engineering of the area network should be carefully analyzed. For example, when a small local office is replaced by a remote unit, the flow of traffic is considerably different. The local traffic in the nonremote configuration was handled by the local office. Under a remote unit configuration all traffic may flow to the host thus increasing the number of call attempts on the host controller, requiring additional links to host (versus links for trunk traffic only) and increasing the termination requirements for the host. A similar situation arises when the collocation of a digital system with the existing analog system is considered to accommodate growth and eventually retire the analog system. Many other situations may occur while planning for digital networks and a careful analyses of traffic flow and its impact on the network deserve special attention.

6. Conclusions

In this chapter, we have described the random nature of service demand: calling rate, service time, and their characteristics. Key probability distribution functions and congestion formulas were discussed in Section 2.2. Digital systems with emphasis on traffic sensitive elements were then qualitatively discussed. As stated in the beginning, the objective of the chapter is to provide an introduction to and appreciation for the traffic engineering related issues and not to present a treatise on congestion theory. The field of congestion theory is very rich in literature. The interested reader is advised to consult the references for further reading. The list is rather short but directs the reader to further readings. The *Bell System Technical Journal*, the *Proceedings of the International Teletraffic Congress* (ITC), and the journal *Operations Research* are excellent sources for keeping informed of developments in this field.

Questions

1. Describe the similarities between the arrival of telephone calls at a switching system and the arrival of customers at the check-out stand at a supermarket. How many servers can be available in both cases?
2. It has been observed that the calling rate in a public switching system often increases when new trunks are added to eliminate congestion. What do you feel are the reasons behind this phenomenon?
3. During a busy period of 10:00 A.M. to 12 Noon, 1600 calls arrive at a certain telephone exchange. The average service time for a call is three minutes. What is the traffic load in (a) Erlangs, (b) CCS?
4. Describe the characteristics of the basic elements comprising the traffic demand, viz, service time and call arrival rate.
5. For the situation described in question 3, what is the blocking probability if the demand is served by a group of 50 trunks? How many trunks would be required for a blocking probability of 0.01? With 50 trunks, what is the probability of delay?
6. Describe the hourly, daily, weekly, and seasonal variation in telephone traffic.
7. Probability theory can be used to establish a mathematical model for the traffic offered and processed by a switching system. Describe the key assumptions necessary to make the theory valid.
8. Give some examples of situations where Poisson distribution and negative exponential distribution are not applicable.
9. List the traffic sensitive devices in a typical digital switching system.
10. What steps should be taken in a stored programmed control system to prevent a "crash" when there are a large number of simultaneous seizures as is the case, for example, in public reaction to a sonic boom?
11. A certain processor requires 120 ms to service a complete call. What is the processor's busy-hour call-attempt rating? Make assumptions relative to partial dials, ineffective attempts, reserve for traffic peaks, and allowance for dial administration and traffic reporting.

References

1. W. S. Hayward, Jr. and R. I. Wilkinson, "Human Factors in Telephone Systems and Their Influence on Traffic Theory, Especially with Regard to Future Facilities," *Sixth International Teletraffic Congress* (ITC), Paper 431, 1970.
2. P. K. Roy Choudhury, M. N. Shukla, and T. R. Wadhwa, "Effect of Subscriber Behaviour and Traffic Administration on the Design of SPC Exchanges," *Ninth ITC*. Paper 148, 1979.
3. A. Myskja and O. O. Walmann, "A Statistical Study of Telephone Traffic Data with Emphasis on Subscriber Behaviour," *Seventh ITC*, Paper 132, 1973.
4. R. R. Mina, *Introduction to Teletraffic Engineering*, Telephony Publishing Corporation, Chicago, 1974.
5. R. I. Wilkinson, "Theories for Toll Traffic Engineering in the U.S.A.," *Bell Syst. Tech. J.*, vol. 35, pp. 421–514, 1956.
6. A. Kuczura, "Loss Systems with Mixed Renewal and Poisson Inputs," *Seventh ITC*, Paper 412, 1973.
7. K. S. Liu, "Direct Distance Call Completion and Customer Retrial Behaviour," *Ninth ITC*, Paper 144, 1979.
8. P. LeGall, "Sur L'Influence des Repititions d'Appels dans l'Ecoulement du Traffic Telephonique," *Sixth ITC*, Paper 432, 1970.
9. F. Duffy and R. A. Mercer, "A Study of Network Performance and Customer Behaviour During Direct Distance Dialing Call Attempts in the U.S.A.," *Bell Syst. Tech. J.*, vol. 57, No. 1, 1978.
10. K. Rahko, "A Study of the Traffic Process Based on Measurements," *Sixth ITC*, Paper 537, 1970.
11. D. Bear, "Some Theories of Telephone Traffic Distribution: A Critical Survey," *Seventh ITC*, Paper 531, 1973.
12. R. Syski, *Congestion Theory in Telephone Systems*, Oliver and Boyd, London, 1960.
13. R. B. Cooper, *Introduction to Queuing Theory*, The Macmillan Company, New York and London, 1972.
14. E. Arthurs and B. W. Stuck, A Theoretical Performance Analysis of Markovian Nodes, *IEEE Trans. Commun.*, vol. COM-26, No. 11, 1978.
15. R. V. Laue and R. K. Even, "Traffic Consideration for Line Concentrators," *National Telecommunication Conference*, 1977.
16. D. H. Barnes, "Extreme Value Engineering of Small Switching Offices," *Eighth ITC*, Paper 242, 1976.
17. K. A. Friedman, "Extreme Value Analysis Techniques," *Ninth ITC*, Paper 313, 1979.
18. W. B. Elsner, "Dimensioning Trunk Groups for Digital Networks," *Ninth ITC*, Paper 421, 1979.

3

Switching System Controls

A. E. Joel, Jr.

1. Introduction

No area of switching system architecture is more difficult to understand than the various aspects of control. There are many functions and trades that may be made in both the technology and architecture in implementing the control portion of a switching system.

"Control" is the term generally used to include many functions that cannot be described as unique to switching such as the use of memory and software. Similarly the terms "processor" and "central processing unit", are associated with control and may have or imply different characteristics when used in a switching system.

Control is used also to cover several specific system functions already mentioned in Section 3.2 in Chapter 1. These are network control (NC) and call information processing (CIP), and their related connectives or access networks as described in Section 3.3 of Chapter 1. Control includes both hardware and software. *Processor* is a broad term and generally includes the control logic, memory, input/output, and administrative equipment.

Also included in this chapter is the consideration of redundancy to ensure service continuity. This involves both controls and networks.

With the trends towards distributed switching there is also a contrary trend towards the greater centralization of some functions that have traditionally been part of call information processing. The centralized systems serving one or more offices are known generally as operations support

---

A. E. Joel, Jr. ● Bell Telephone Laboratories, Holmdel, New Jersey

systems (OSS). In some system environments they play an active role in the CIP function and are therefore considered as part of the control.

Normally the architecture of a switching system does not include separate functions for its maintenance, operation, and administration (MOA). Maintenance, operation, and administration features are embedded in the architecture of the switching system functions. With the exception of test sets, MOA is part of the control function including the operations support systems.

No discussion of control would be complete without illuminating the software dimension that in modern systems is a major consideration in stored program controls (see Section 3.5 and Chapter 4 of this volume).

2. Switching Center Network Controls

Controls for networks generally involve receipt of a network address to which it is desired to establish a connection, a search for a desired path through one or more stages of the network, and the establishment, and at a later time, the release of the selected connection. It may include the interpretation of the input and output addresses and memory of the links and terminations that are busy. In time division networks it includes the periodic use of the memory of established connections.

The network control functions may be divided and found to reside in separate system blocks. For example a network map may be located with call processing data in a common store. Since the switching center network (SCN) is the most important circuit switching function, some system architectures assume that the network control responds directly to call signal reception.

2.1. Progressive versus Common Control

A progressive network control is one with direct association of the call signal processing (CSP), SCN, and NC. The earliest electromechanical switching systems, such as step-by-step, panel, and rotary,[1] used progressive control. Step-by-step generally uses progressive control directly from the station calling device. Other progressive systems permit the call signal processing from the station to be indirect progressive control of the SCN and is used in the panel and rotary systems. Both direct and indirect progressive control permits some call information processing (CIP) (see Section 3) to be introduced. These combinations are shown in Figs 1 and 2.

Progressive network controls advance calls stage by stage through the SCN and from office to office. Since the NC is used only to establish the connection in one stage for one call it is relatively inefficient. Common NC

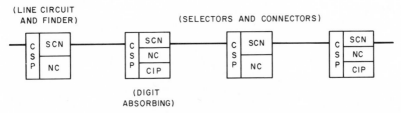

Fig. 1. Direct control.

may be provided for each stage or even a plurality of stages.[2] The common NC is accessed through combined or separate signal access networks (SANs) and network control access networks (NCANs) (see Chapter 1, Section 3.3).

Finally there are the more intelligent and advanced common or centralized controls. This type of control has another attribute. It is able to "look ahead", that is, it may select an output of a multistage network and then select and establish an idle path through all of the stages.[3] This type of control can establish only one call at a time through those portions of each stage selected for a particular call. Much of the selection process may be performed in a portion of the CIP, and then transmitted to the NC that actually establishes the connections.

In circuit switching, memory is required for all switching network elements. This memory keeps track of their busy/idle state. For electromechanical switching the memory may be associated with the operated/nonoperated position of the device. In time division networks, control memory as shown in Fig. 3 is used to periodically access the TSI memory or TMS crosspoints (Chapter 1, Section 3.3).[4]

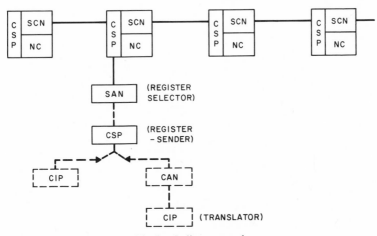

Fig. 2. Indirect control.

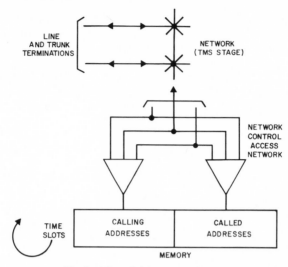

Fig. 3.   Time division network control.

In space division networks the memory may be integrated to varying degrees with the crosspoint elements as shown in Fig. 4. The ultimate is to utilize, as in the time division case, separate bulk memory, sometimes referred to as a network map.[5] The map shows the busy/idle state of links rather than crosspoints. In some systems the map is included in the memory used for other system functions.

Supervision of network connections also includes their release. Networks may be electrically held so that upon release the links will once again

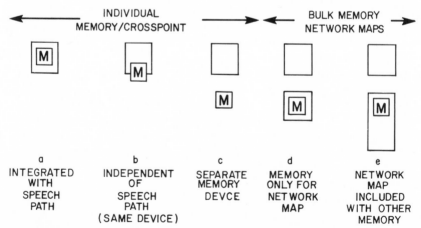

Fig. 4.   Memory association with networks: (a) Integrated with speech path; (b) independent of speech path (same device); (c) separate memory device; (d) memory only for network map; (e) network map included with other memory.

test idle. Networks with magnetically or mechanically held switches, and time division networks, must include a specific release function. This includes restoring link images to idle in network maps. One technique used to actually restore previously operated but now idle crosspoints is to release them as part of and only when their operation conflicts with the establishment of a new path. This is known as destructive marking.[6]

2.2. Network Control Access

Except in progressive and some distributed control (see Section 3.3) systems, where it may be thought of as being conbined with the SNC, a separate network control access network (NCAN) is required to access network elements and memory.[7] Thus we have a recursive function with networks requiring networks to control their operation.

Both time and space division are used for NCANs and this is not necessarily related to the type of SCN employed. For time division as shown in Fig. 3 a trivial form of time division NCAN is required to actuate the sample-carrying SCN network TMS stage. A similar access function is provided for the TSI and network map memories. This function is more commonly associated with a function known as addressing.

For NCANs associated with the common control of electrochemical crosspoints, the NCAN may be bidirectional. It may carry busy/idle information to the network control, and it is also used to carry the signals that actuate the crosspoints.[8]

NCAN may access several or all stages of an SCN through which a call is to pass. NCAN may be used to associate one NC with several different SCNs, for example one for wide band and one for voice application.[9] Within an office the network control may be divided, and an NCAN may be required to interrelate these NC functions, particularly for redundant (see Section 3.6) or multiprocessing (see Section 3) controls. NCANs may be combined with signal access networks (SANs) as in certain progressive systems with common network controls[10] or where the SAN is used to address a termination on an SCN[11] used for call originations, or combined with SCNs as in some distributed control systems (see Section 3.3).[12] Figure 5 summarizes the possible progressive and common network control arrangements with single and plural controls operating on a single or plurality of network stages or an entire network.

3. Call Information Processing

Call information processing (CIP) differs from general purpose computer processing in that it must function in almost real time. In most cases delays greater than a second or two are considered excessive. Teletraffic (see

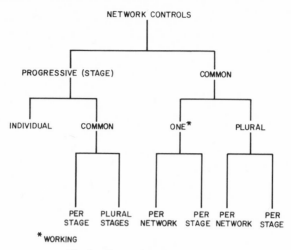

Fig. 5.   Types of network controls.

Chapter 2 of this volume) as applied to circuit switches deals generally with blocking or loss of calls. In the control portion of systems we are generally dealing with contention and delay. Each attempt must be served.

For switching center networks call holding time distributions are assumed exponential or binomial. For controls, the holding time for a call event or occupancy is usually a constant. To avoid excessive delay in serving expected offered load, more than one control unit or server may be required. Figure 6 shows the average delay, measured as a multiple number of holding times, for a given average occupancy. As the number of servers, n (available to all requesters), increases, the average wait decreases for the same average occupancy.

The internal functions that implement CIP are memory and logic. These are further divided by the uses generally made of them. Memory is used to record call data. Memory is also used to store semipermanent information such as the identification, class of service, and addresses of network terminations, known generally as translations, and information about the size and grouping of control functions and network terminations (known as parameters).

Logic circuitry is used in performing operations on data, decision making, checking, information coding and interpretation (decoding), and the controlling of trivial intracontrol access networks such as internal buses. The most important use of these functions is in feature and service implementation which is the primary purpose of CIP.

A critical issue in CIP design and engineering is the matter of capacity. Many variables are involved such as the technology (including software), the dividing of the functions the CIP is to perform, and the way redundancy is employed. Some CIPs can serve only 6000 calls per hour while others may serve 750,000 calls per hour. The difference is due generally to the type of technology and the degree of subdivision by which the CIP is implemented. To a lesser degree hardware and software trades may affect capacity.

The control must deal with each offered message. Many false starts occur so that typically in a local office the attempts may be more than double the acutal messages served. Capacity is generally referred to as busy-hour call attempts (BHCA). The required capacity is engineered to be less than the peak BHCA the system architecture might permit (for example, less than 3600 1-sec attempts). Typically to allow for unexpected

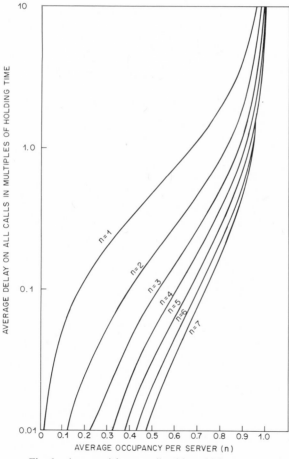

Fig. 6.   Average delay on calls with multiple servers.

overload or change in expected percentage of different types of calls (call mix) (coin, PBX, intraoffice, etc.) the engineered BHCA capacity is usually chosen as no more than 90% of the peak BHCA capability.

3.1. Traffic versus Functional Division

High-speed electronic technology has generally permitted, in most systems, one or at most a few processors to provide all or most of the CIP functions required by the offered traffic.[13]

The term *central processing* means that a major portion of the CIP features are implemented in one functional block accessible for all call attempts (see Fig. 7). However, the control function block may be divided to serve specific call functions and/or to serve a portion of the traffic. These two techniques are known as functional and traffic CIP division.

One form of traffic division is where the system input terminations are arbitrarily grouped and each group is served by a different CIP. This is known as distributed control (see Section 3.3). Generally in centralized traffic division, calls detected by the CSP are distributed more or less equally via a control access network (CAN) to an idle processor of a group of identical processors (see Fig. 8).[14] Sometimes a subset of both techniques, known as load sharing, permits each processor to be accessible to serve all inputs, but under normal circumstances (no processor out of service) it serves only a predetermined group of inputs (see Fig. 9).[15]

Traffic division is any division of a CIP control when all or most of the same functions are performed by each resulting portion. Conversely, with functional division, portions of what would be a centralized control are separated so that additional call attempt capacity results when all of the required control functions are not placed together.[16]

The ultimate in traffic division is separate offices. When one office outgrows its line, trunk, network, and/or control, a separate entity may be

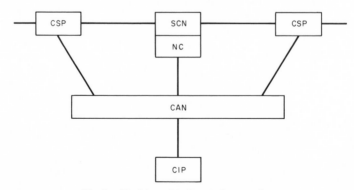

Fig. 7.   Nonhierarchical central processing.

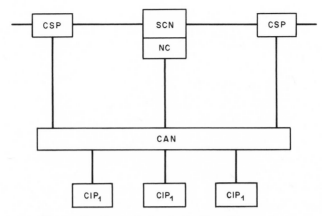

Fig. 8. Nonhierarchical central traffic multiprocessing.

established. However, this may be costly, particularly since trunking from other wire centers requires separate trunk groups to each entity or for all traffic to be tandemed (screened) through one, usually the larger, of the two or more entities. Line numbering (central office and station codes) is also a consideration since the office code is used to identify the destination of calls for call charging purposes.

One technique that has been considered by designers to reduce the penalties associated with this problem is known as sectoring or cooperative call processing (see Fig. 10).[17] With this technique the entities employ separate common channel signaling links and larger trunk groups among them to pass information and calls between the entities. In effect each unit acts to screen calls for all units and tandems the traffic as required.

Functional division occurs when the call processing functions are divided and carried out by different processors or groups of processors. For

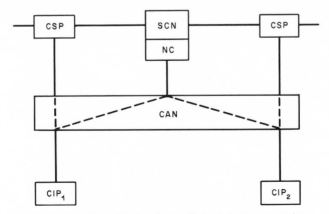

Fig. 9. Nonhierarchical central traffic load sharing processing.

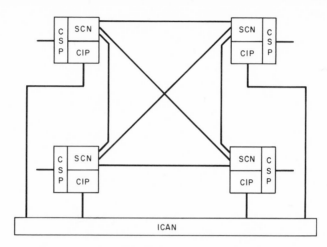

Fig. 10.   Nonhierarchical sector distributed multiprocessing.

example the receipt and interpretation of information from CSP may take place in one group of CIPs, and the output termination(s) to be used on a call is selected by another (see Fig. 11).[18] Figure 12 shows an arrangement where the CSP 1, CAN 1, and CIP_{0x} are for one type of traffic, viz. originating, and the CSP_2, CAN_2, and CIP_{1x} might be for terminating traffic.[19] Where call-processing functions are performed in sequence by different processors operating in tandem, the process is known as *pipeline*.

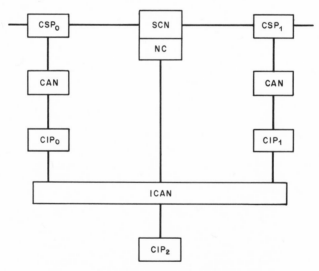

Fig. 11.   Hierarchical functional multiprocessing.

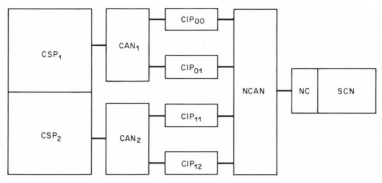

Fig. 12. Nonhierarchical functional multiprocessing.

Systems may make use of both traffic and functional division techniques simultaneously. Where there is more than one active central processor the technique is known as *multiprocessing.*

3.2. Controller Access

There are two basic types of connectives used for access to and between CIP controls. Control access networks (CAN) are used to connect other system functions to a central CIP or to division of a CIP.

Intracontrol access networks (ICAN) are used to interconnect divisions of CIP.[20] ICANs may also be used for exclusive interconnection between CIP and NC.

A so-called peripheral bus between CSP and SAN scanners is a typical CAN.[21] Connectivity between a control and a plurality of stores is provided by an ICAN.

As with other connectives the CAN and ICAN may be part of other connectives, particularly the SCN.[22] Certain arrangements of connectives for functional division have been given recognition based upon general system architecture.

The use of ICAN implies both multiprocessing and functional control. Even where traffic division is a predominant feature, functional division may also be present, for example to access a common memory for a network map or translation or even infrequently used programs as shown in Fig. 13.[23] This figure also shows that the central processors ($CIP_{10, 11, 2x}$) need not all be alike. Each has equal ability to process calls and is provided with memory (CIP_2) for call data recording. But only CIPs of type 1X ($CIP_{10, 11}$) provide access to CIP memory type 4, e.g., disk or drum files. When a type-2 processor needs type-4 memory, it applies for it by means of the common memory CIP_3. CIP_3 is used for such functions as low-frequency call processing programs and common data areas such as the

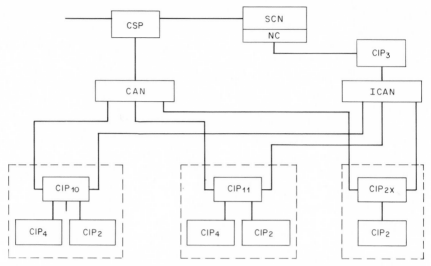

Fig. 13.   Hierarchical traffic multiprocessing—common memory.

network map. Each memory CIP_2 provides sufficient capacity for basic call processing, but the CIP_3 and CIP_4 memories may be much larger.

Figure 14 shows the typical content of memory in the processors and the use of memory common to all processors. Using common memory (or processor—sometimes called an auxiliary processor) introduces possible contention and delay. The relative volume of common memory to processor memory (or functions) determines the average delay.

Where functional division is employed to enable greater traffic handling capability, a hierarchy of controls usually occurs as shown in Fig. 11. A

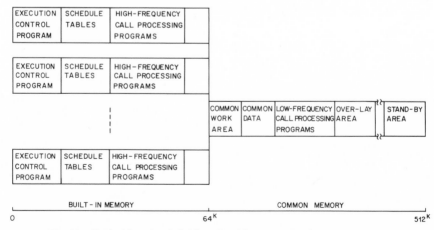

Fig. 14.   Typical functional division of multiprocessors and common memory.

distributed or load-sharing traffic divided CIP most closely associated with CSP receives and filters or preprocesses the input call information. When it determines that sufficient call information has been received it calls upon another control element, perhaps centrally located, to complete less time-consuming and routine CIP functions. When confined to the CSP and interpretation CIP functions, this part of the control is generally known as a signal processor.

A separate ICAN (Fig. 15)[24] or the SCN (Fig. 16)[25] may be used for hierarchical control connectivity. In the latter case, the intercontrol signals use the same paths as the messages. To use the same paths as the messages requires the functional control signals to simulate the message format, usually of the serial type. This is a type of distributed switching (see Section 1.1) which has been widely known as *distributed control*. The use of SCN for intercontrol access is also known as *indirect ICAN*.

3.3   Distributed Control

Distributed control is a particular combination of traffic and functional control divisions. It may use direct or indirect ICAN. Since it is usually associated with distributed switching (see Chapter 1, Section 1.1), indirect ICAN is being used increasingly in modern system design.

The first CIP to serve calls is divided trafficwise, each division serving a portion of the total lines and/or trunks to be served by the entity. The central control of other portions of the system control serving less routine or more complex CIP functions may be accessed through the SCN (indirect) (Fig. 17)[26] or ICAN (direct) (Fig. 18).[27] Where these remaining

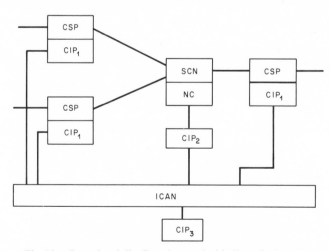

Fig. 15.   Central and distributed control with direct (bus) access.

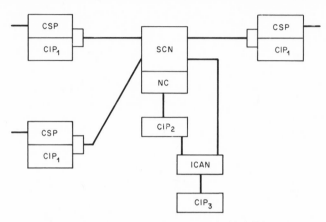

Fig. 16.   Central and distributed control with SAN access.

functions are further subdivided so that all functions reside in a distributed control unit, or module (including network control), the control is said to be fully distributed.[28] Indirect access is usually employed to facilitate the use of the same modules in distributed switching.

For a distributed control the cost per control is generally lower than the getting started cost for a central control since the capacity requirements are less. However, many memory and other functions increase more rapidly as more modules are added to the system. Figure 19 compares the relative costs between distributed and central control. A single central control can

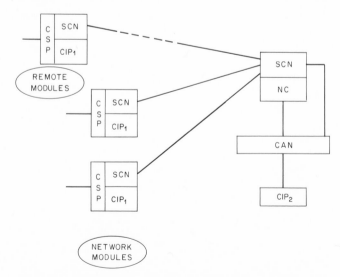

Fig. 17.   Central and distributed switching and control with SAN access.

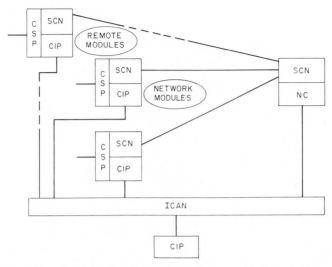

Fig. 18. Central and distributed switching and control with direct (bus) access.

provide the same functions more economically than distributed controls beyond a certain size.

Distributed control for circuit switching also requires consideration of the network control access. Emerging fully distributed control systems employ progressive control of the switching center networks (see Fig. 20).[29] For common network control, an ICAN between some if not all CIPs and the NC(s) is required.[30] For this arrangement the CIP associated with route selection and perhaps including a network map is usually designated as a central control. Also network control for a portion of the SCN collocated with distributed CIP may be included with the distributed control.[31] NC information may originate in the central CIP to provide for a coordinated SCN path through the distributed as well as the centrally located SCN.

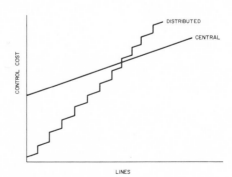

Fig. 19. Control cost relationships.

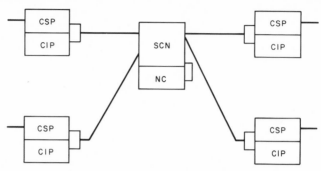

Fig. 20.   Fully distributed control.

Another CIP function associated with distributed control is control signal formating. This is always required for control access but is more formal when the messages must pass through the same network (SCN) as the service (voice, data, etc.) messages.[32]

Figure 21 summarizes the various types of system control and control access arrangements described in the last three sections.

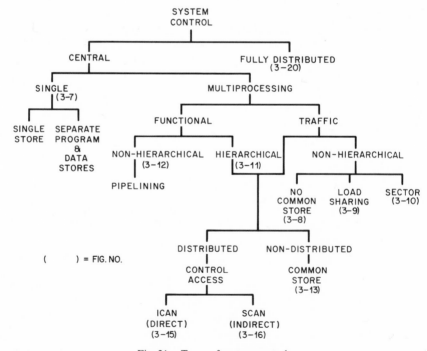

Fig. 21.   Types of system controls.

3.4. Scheduling

Electromechanical central control systems are generally driven asynchronously; that is, they respond to traffic as it originates. In such systems the control functions are also performed in a fixed or deterministic order.

The CIP in many electronic systems includes the driver or motivator for the synchronous operation of the system. This not only includes a clock for setting the relative rate(s) at which the various functions are performed, but also a set of logic known as the scheduling functions. Scheduling is employed to allocate real (available) time to the CIP resources, and also to functions such as SANs in their quest for service requests. It is used in multiprocessing to spread the offered load equitably among the controls.

Scheduling is used by functionally divided controls, particularly those in an hierarchical array. The various divisions of a control may have autonomous scheduling or be coordinated by a master scheduler.

While each function of a control generally has a logical location in the sequence of control actions, the relative real time importance of certain system actions may require the suspension or delay of some system actions. Such actions are known as interrupts. They may occur due to the detected presence of call or maintenance actions requiring higher priority or because of a real time constraint such as the speed of signaling, e.g., detecting dial pulses. Figure 22 illustrates a typical schedule.[33] In effect this is time division as applied to the control portion of the system. Interrupts are also invoked between independent processes, such as those with autonomous scheduling.

Figure 23 shows the basic relations of real time utilization.[34] The routine repetitive operations are referred to as overhead. The overhead is divided into a fixed or basic overhead that is required to order the sequence

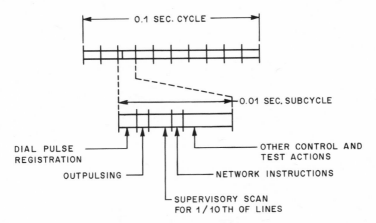

Fig. 22. Time division control.

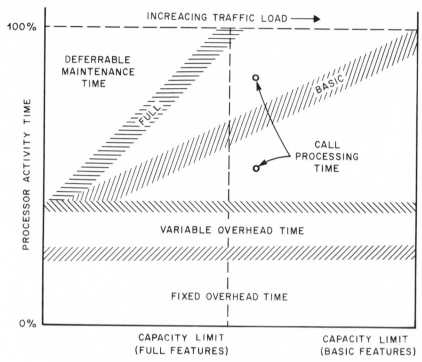

Fig. 23.   Use of real time by central processor.

of system events that take place even in the absence of traffic. Some over-head items are added as the office size (lines, trunks, etc.) increases.

In addition to overhead there are traffic-dependent items. As more features are added to the basic call processing functions more real time is utilized, thereby reducing the traffic that may be served. Routine mainten-ance features are scheduled during light traffic periods.

With multiprocessing the system control capacity is not increased in proportion to the number of active processors.[35] Figure 24 shows that to double the capacity requires about three processors. It also shows for a typical system with only common memory (CIP_3) such as shown in Figure 13, very little is gained in the way of capacity. These curves form a limit with systems using both common and individual memory realizing capac-ities in between these curves.

3.5. Stored Program Control and the Software Dimension

Prior to the advent of electronics all system controls were implemen-ted using relay logic circuits and memory, in the form of cross-connected or threaded wire placements.[36] In effect these determine the sequence and decision elements of the call-processing functions. These were the "wired"

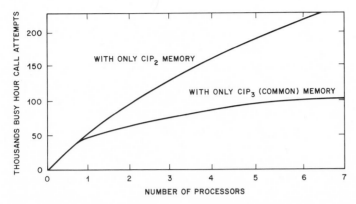

Fig. 24. Central multiprocessor capacity with and without common memory. (From *Proceedings of the Third Int. Conf. on Software Eng. for Telecom. Switching Systems*, Helsinki, June 1978, pp. 27–29.)

logic program of the system. The logic was designed specifically for each system and required modification as each feature or service was added or modified.

The concept of applying computer programming to switching systems has radically changed control design. The use of programs to control switching systems is generally known as *stored program control* (SPC) as contrasted to wired program control referred to above. Stored program control contrasts with most general purpose computer data processing in requirements for real time execution and high availability (reliability and service continuity).

There are many varieties of stored program controls—almost a continuous spectrum from wired logic to what has been called fully stored program control (FSPC).[37] Each design chooses a different proportion or mix of logic hardware and the software stored in one or more memories. The basic differences in the hardware may be characterized as general purpose or special purpose. General purpose SPC hardware logic and associated ICAN connectives are characteristic with full SPC. These controls execute instructions that are written in a language that is independent of call processing or other switching system functions. (Programs for fault detection and location are also independent of the call processing logic and other features in FSPC systems.) As the degree of independence lessens the controls become more specific to particular system organizations and features.

One popular type of control, loosely called action translator, utilizes a macro instruction set in the control circuitry specific to system operations, such as "establish network connection between X and Y" or "scan line Z." The instructions appear in a translationlike table that defines the different sequences of system operations and decision points.[38] Corresponding decision logic is also provided in the hardware.

Programs are stored in a bulk memory. This memory may be the same one used for storing call or office data or a separate one. The instruction words are read out at a rate determined by the system clock and the speed of the memory. The speed at which the memory can provide successive instructions and the rapidity with which it can respond with an instruction are both major factors in setting the processing capacity of an SPC control.

Memory is also used to store data bases or tables, known in earlier switching systems as translations. Data bases include such items as equipment to directory number, directory to equipment number, trunk equipment number and route translations, as well as office parameters. System designs include engineering limitations. In specific offices only a portion of the maximum possible equipment is installed. In SPC systems parameters on office data define these limitations in both the hardware and software.

Distinguishing between hardware, software, and different forms of SPC becomes difficult when some of the modern forms of memory are used. Because of service reliability requirements programs are loaded into nonvolatile read-only memories (ROM) or volatile memories with rapid automatic reload ("pump up") from nonvolatile back up (such as a disk, tape, or drum).

Electrically programmable read only memories (EPROM) provide the advantages of nonvolatile memories with remote loading. Programs can also be delivered to an office site recorded in a ROM. Prerecorded ROMs are known as *firmware*. They can be used to provide specific system features in software. This is just one of many growing tradeoffs between software and hardware that are possible with modern technology. Firmware can also be used to provide different instruction set interpretations so that programs can be run on different processors. Processors with changeable firmware can also be used to effectively execute programs written in different "languages" for different applications.

When programs, data bases, and parameters are maintained in ROMs provision must be made for temporarily changing this information before new ROMs are set to the office, or before ROMs are rewritten off-line in the central office. Temporary memory and programs are used for this process known as "recent change."

The software dimension of an SPC system is extensive and involves many development and administrative considerations before a program becomes resident and working in a control. Briefly these steps are the following:

(1)   Before any program or wired logic may be considered for development the system services and features must be specified. These are known

as system requirements and include the engineering parameters such as given in Chapter 1, Section 3.1.

(2) As mentioned above basic design choices are between hardware, firmware, and software. The latter two elements are part of the software dimension.

(3) The structure of memory allocations for call and other data must be determined including the partitioning of all memory words.

(4) For call processing the sequence of operations is formally documented in flow charts. A system description language (SDL) has been standardized for this purpose.[39]

(5) The instruction or order code set for the control is designed taking into account the efficient movement and execution of instructions.[40] This includes the fetching of call data. The same or different storage communities may be used for call data and/or programs. Different types of instructions will result. The way general purposes hardware registers are used influences the instruction designs. Also, control hierarchies may call for distinctive instructions to provide efficient, noninterfacing of intercontrol communications.

(6) The size of instruction and memory words is a function of the anticipated total memory address requirements and the fields that are included in the instruction set. The instruction set of a real time processor is generally unlike that used in most general purpose computers. Generally switching systems have little need for high-speed arithmetic operations that are fundamental in computers.

(7) The language used in writing the program or sequence of instructions that appear in a switching system can range from the assembled sequence of instructions to a high-level language (HLL). A high-level language specifies the system call processing program requirements in a form that may be translated by a general purpose computer into the sequences of instructions that may be utilized by the control. Generally the use of high-level languages and repetitive sequences of instructions known as macro instructions or subroutines are less efficient in the use of real time and memory. High-level language also require more memory. The principal advantage of the use of high-level languages is its portability, so that much of the call-processing development effort may be used with other systems, and for administrations employing many different SPC systems. CCITT has standardized a high-level language known as CHILL.[41]

(8) Once the language and flow charts have been decided upon, the actual programming and production of system instruction set (coding) may begin. High-level languages are translated into (machine) code by a general purpose computer executing an assembly program. Sections of the program are compiled before assembly into machine code. The act of programming is generally understood as the most important factor in the software dimension.

(9)   After a section or all of the program has been written and compiled to the extent practicable, an advantage of SPC is that the program can be partially tested independent of the control hardware. This step is known as simulation and generally uses a general purpose computer to test the logic of the sequence of the programs and decision points.[42]

(10)   One of the most difficult design judgments in SPC systems is the call attempt capacity of a particular program under various load conditions (basic or mixes with more elaborate features) (see Section 3.4). This difficulty arises out of attempts to determine the number of instructions that must be executed per call before the program is written. This is even more difficult when a high-level language is used. Again, using a general purpose computer interfacing with the actual system hardware, usually a laboratory model, it is possible to examine the system control performance under various load and call mix conditions. This is known as load testing, and key time indicators may be used to interpret system control performance and capacity.

(11)   Also part of the software is the data required to define specific installation parameters. These are generally referred to as data bases. Typical data bases are those that provide translations such as directory to line equipment number and trunk group address information. Other parameters that are required define the size of the SCN and various equipment groups including storage and control modules.

(12)   Not only does the program use this information, but provision must also be made for entering these data into the office before and after cut-over while the system is processing calls. This is known as office data administration (ODA). Another aspect of software for ODA is the routine insertion of translation changes into the data base or in a separate "recent change" section of the data base. Insertion is readily possible when EPROMs are used for the translation memory, but with ROMs separate recent change call processing and memory update procedures may be required.

(13)   Once programs, data bases, and office data are prepared, provision must be made to assemble them and to insert them into the office memories. Again the assembly is usually performed using a general purpose computer that not only assigns actual addresses to the program sections, including maintenance programs, but also converts the programs where necessary, into actual processor readable instructions. These actions are repeated each time a change or new version of the program is written. A procedure must be provided to enable these changes to be made in the office while it processes calls with the program and/or translations to be replaced.

(14)   While specific reference has not been made to the programs required for maintenance, operation, and administration (MOA), they are a

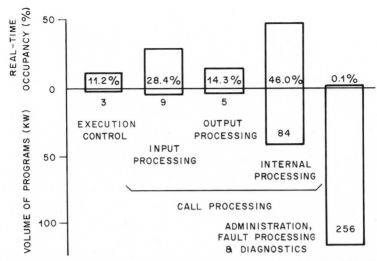

Fig. 25. Quantity and usage of system software. (From *Proceedings of the Third Int. Conf. on Software Eng. for Telecom. Switching Systems*, Helsinki, June 1978, pp. 27–29.)

most important factor in the software dimension of SPC systems. In most SPC systems more than half of the programs are devoted to MOA (see Fig. 25).[43] However, as shown in the figure, the MOA programs consume very little real time. Unlike most of the call-processing programs these programs are dependent upon the details of the hardware design. Hardware may be added for test purposes. Also the programs for fault locating are dependent upon the specific equipment and logic circuit configurations. Programs are also provided for initialization of an office when it is not running through its scheduled events and for aiding in the cutover process when an SPC system replaces another system.

The characteristics of software are described in more detail in Chapter 4 of this volume.

While simple in concept, SPC is the most sophisticated type of control introduced to date. The hardware, firmware, and software must be integrated into a working and administratable entity. SPC is possibly because modern computer and data processing techniques have been adapted to the specific real time, availability, and continuity of service requirements of switching system controls.

Most of the advantages attributable to the application of electronics to switching have been made possible by the adoption of SPC. Typically the control represents about 30% of the office cost, but a much higher portion of the development cost due to the software effort involved. Therefore, to recover the cost of new programs with added features, the software is increasingly being sold or leased as separate items, raising the cost of control to as much as 50%.

The advantages of SPC are (1) the flexibility of programming new features; (2) the ability to adapt to new technology; (3) high capacity; (4) space savings; (5) lower operating and maintenance expenses due to both more reliable components and the programmable MOA features: and (6) increases in revenues made possible by including available new services.

3.6. Redundancy

It is necessary to include in the system architecture extra equipment defensive hardware, and program strategies to ensure continuity of service in the face of failed components and wiring, faulty software, and human operating errors. While all areas of switching systems require reliability considerations, the control portions of systems demonstrate most of the principles employed to ensure high service availability and are therefore presented in this chapter.

Figure 26 summarizes the factors involved in the hardware, software, and procedures requiring attention in the design and operation of switching systems. The principal emphasis here is on the system structure. However, not until a system is placed into stable operation in several offices is it possible to take a most important step, viz., evaluation.

To make a dependable system possible the anticipated component failure rate is taken into account in adding redundancy to the system architecture.[44] The most obvious and useful architectural modification is the use of multiple system subunits. These units are chosen so that the objective system capacity, usually call attempts for controls, will be maintained even if one of the identical units becomes defective. Most provisions for continuity of service are based upon sufficient redundancy during the time a single

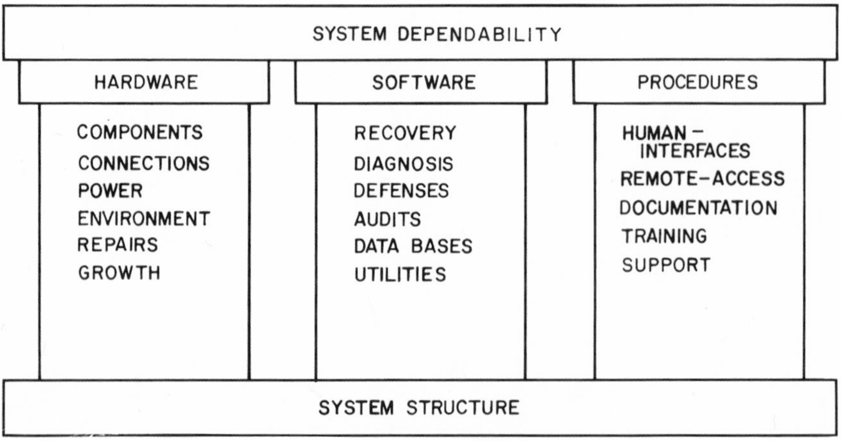

SYSTEM DEPENDABILITY		
HARDWARE	SOFTWARE	PROCEDURES
COMPONENTS CONNECTIONS POWER ENVIRONMENT REPAIRS GROWTH	RECOVERY DIAGNOSIS DEFENSES AUDITS DATA BASES UTILITIES	HUMAN − INTERFACES REMOTE−ACCESS DOCUMENTATION TRAINING SUPPORT
SYSTEM STRUCTURE		

Fig. 26.   Design for reliability.

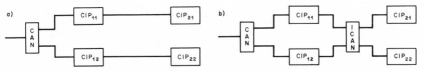

Fig. 27. Use of connectives (ICAN) to improve reliability. (a) Separate controls (CIP_{1x}) with memory (CIP_{2x}). (b) Independent controls and memories.

trouble exists, with the expectation of rapid repair. This is generally defined as a single trouble in the system subunit of a particular type. By augmenting connections in the system architecture, strategies may be automatically invoked to provide service when other types of subunits are also in trouble. These strategies generally involve the manner in which the connectivity for the redundancy is introduced.

Figure 27 shows how the introduction of connectives between control subunits can provide greater tolerance to hardware troubles.[45] Assume that CIP_{11} and CIP_{12} are duplicated central controls and CIP_{21} and CIP_{22} are associated memories. Should either the control *or* memory of either pair (Fig. 27a) experience trouble, then the system depends upon the other pair. By introducing the ICAN (Fig. 27b) to permit full interconnectability of controls and memories, the system may continue to function should either memory *and* either control fail. The reliability of the ICAN must also be considered.

When complete duplication of subunits is provided then several operating modes for their use may be chosen. These are shown in Fig. 28 where the basic modes are one or both running, i.e., processing information. While this chart shows duplex modes it does not evaluate them from the standpoint of other service continuity factors. For example, with the synchronous mode matching takes place between controls on each clock cycle or sub-

MODE	TYPE		CONTROL 1	CONTROL 2
	SYNCHRONOUS		CONTROLLING	MATCHING
BOTH RUNNING	TRAFFIC	LOAD SHARING	A CALLS	B CALLS
		ALTERNATING	EVEN CALLS MATCHING	MATCHING ODD CALLS
	FUNCTION DIVISION		I/O	SCHEDULING
	FUNCTION DIVISION		CALL PROCESSING	ADMINISTRATION
ONE RUNNING	HOT STANDBY		ACTIVE	UPDATE MEMORY
	WARM STANDBY		ACTIVE	POWERED
	COLD STANDBY		ACTIVE	AVAILABLE

Fig. 28. Modes of application of duplicated controls.

cycle. With this mode of operation it is possible to detect troubles immediately.[36] With various traffic and functional divisions it is assumed that full system capacity can be carried by a single operating control.

Space division networks have adequate or inherent redundancy. Network maps are generally associated with system control and provided in duplicate. Time division networks have active elements that require redundancy considerations in much the same manner as described above for controls. Providing working spare line and trunk interface circuits can facilitate service continuity as well as in the testing and replacement of defective units.

Memories and other system components such as networks are usually provided in modules. To build a large memory capacity requires many modules, i.e., a memory subsystem. Redundancy can be provided either by duplicating the entire subsystem or by providing spare module(s). When less than a duplicated subsystem is provided then service restoration may be hindered. In the case of memory a substituted call data module is unlikely to contain the call information that has been most due to module failure. Generally modular redundancy is referred to as $n + m$ redundancy where n and m are the required number of operating and spare modules, respectively.

Redundancy goes deeper than the subunits themselves. It must also be possible to automatically isolate power distribution and the communication paths into and out of connectives so that there exists no common electrical paths that could prevent the use of redundant units. Serious consideration should also be given to avoid physical associations that if damaged by fire, etc., might also prevent restoration of service with the remaining viable subunits. This is not generally a requirement but an important physical design consideration. With integrated circuits, the physical design may greatly simplify the trouble locating programming procedure, since many more components are on a single printed wiring board.

Trouble detection is implemented in the hardware, firmware, and software.[47] The hardware checks include error checking (parity and error-correction), matching (in the synchronous mode), out of range address detection, and clock and other time checks (one such check is called "all-seems-well"). Also included in hardware checks are specific circuits that place calls and check that the resulting processing takes place within a prescribed time and reach a predetermined address.

Typical duplex processor arrangements are shown in Figs 29 and 30 for the Bell System's 1A and 3A processors, respectively. They differ primarily in the degree of coupling and the number of functions accessed by the central controls. The two 1A central controls run hot and match on each clock pulse.[48] They access all store communities (c = call, p = program, f = file, d = disk) with address and answer buses (part of

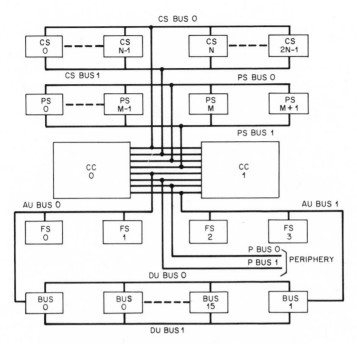

Fig. 29. Typical control configuration—1A processor.

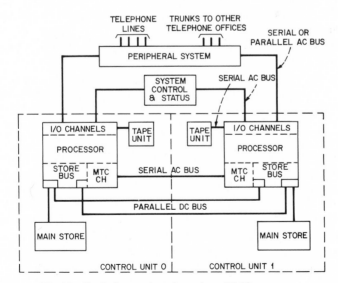

Fig. 30. Typical control configuration—3B 20 processor.

ICAN) and a separate duplicated bus to the periphery, including input–output equipment. All buses carry data words in parallel.

The 3A processors are self-checking.[49] Serial and parallel buses access the periphery. One store community is used by each control for all of its memory needs. Memory update information is passed on a parallel basis between controls. A serial (MTC) channel between units is used by one control to diagnose the other. Each unit has a tape unit to load program and office data.

Software and firmware checks are both offensive and defensive in nature. Many software difficulties are programming errors that were not detected during the design check out. Frequently they manifest themselves when a particular mix or quantity of regular traffic is being processed as occurs only when a system is in service or under a load with appropriate call mixes.

Hardware troubles may be intermittent and thereby cause errors in executing programs. For example a wrong bit inserted after a parity check is made might cause wrong data to be processed. Also continuity of service can be greatly assisted by considering when and where error detecting circuits are used together with synchronous or hot standby redundancy. Error correcting, for example, can be valuable to overcome intermittent troubles, particularly in memories.

The elements of service continuity in modern SPC systems are (1) trouble detection (as soon as possible to prevent call-processing errors); (2) trouble isolation; (3) trouble recovery (switching to return to call-processing capability including updating of information in memory such as entries lost during the trouble detection and isolation phases); (4) trouble locating (generally automatic with the aid of programs specifically designed for this purpose and executed by the operating control); (5) repair (as rapidly as possible to mitigate the possibility of more than one simultaneous trouble); (6) check testing of the repair; and (7) restoring the redundant unit to running or standby mode.

4. Operations Support

With wired logic, and initially with SPC, the portions of switching systems devoted to MOA features were incorporated into the system with most of the burden falling on the system control when central control was introduced. However, the reliability of SPC systems has made the centralization of the man–machine interface important to ensure continuous availability of skilled and well-honed maintenance capability. The success of this approach by the Bell System in the United States resulted in extending the centralization concept to many other MOA features. These centralized

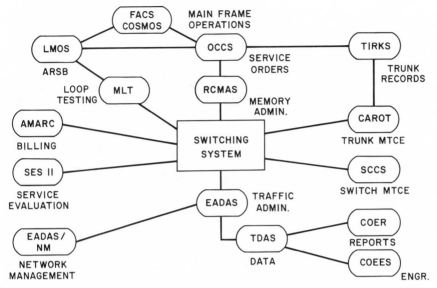

Fig. 31.   Typical operation support functions for switching systems.

facilities usually employ general purpose computers that serve from 5 to 50 offices and have been called operations support systems (OSSs).[50] Other administrations have not only centralized many MOA features, but even call processing for services that are required on a very small percentage of calls.[51]

While these features have been removed from the control of the switch, the switch still must gather and transmit the basic information for use by the OSSs. Figure 31 shows a few of the recently deployed OSSs for local United States Bell System switches, identified by acronyms.[35] It is expected that this trend towards centralization of the MOA features will continue. Considering also the growth of distributed switching, this centralization becomes twice removed from the location of many of the smaller end offices.

5. Summary

This chapter has described many variations in the organization of switching system controls. Control redundancy is essential to the public use of switching systems. Many factors must be considered in providing redundancy.

The way technology is employed also results in different approaches to system control. The subject of software, basic to most modern systems, is introduced.

The coupling between controls and the remainder of the system, particularly the switching center networks, is described as are the various types of access connectives used between portions of the control and with the periphery.

Adequate capacity is provided by traffic or functional division. One approach is a class of distributed control architectures. Trades between logic and memory and between hardware and software are also discussed.

Questions

1. Distinguish switching networks, switching center, and signal access networks. Which is not required in store and forward switching systems?
2. Give two reasons why more than one control information processor (CIP) may be employed in a switching system.
3. Distinguish distributed switching and distributed control.
4. Distinguish hierarchical from nonhierarchical control access.
5. Name the characteristics that distinguish wired logic, action translators, and stored program controls. How is memory used with each?
6. How is memory associated with switching network functions? What particular technique is required for time division networks?
7. What functions constitute the largest portion of programs for SPC systems used in public networks?
8. Name two techniques for detecting hardware faults in control information processors.
9. How might software faults be detected in SPC systems?
10. How have operations support systems influenced switching system design?
11. Does the use of SPC relate to digital switching?
12. Why does the application of multiple call information processors not increase call carrying capacity linearly?

References

1. K. B. Miller, *Telephone Theory and Practice*, vol. III, Automatic Switching, McGraw-Hill, New York, 1933.
2. R. Taylor and C. E. Beale, "Common Control System," *Post Off. Electr. Eng. J.*, vol. 24(2), pp. 125–131, July 1931.
3. O. Myers, "Markers for the Crossbar Toll System," *Bell Lab. Rec.*, vol. 22, pp. 499–504, August 1944.
4. H. E. Vaughan, "Introduction to No. 4 ESS," *Int. Switching Symp.*, Boston, Massachusetts, 1972, pp. 19–25.
5. D. H. Carbaugh, G. G. Drew, H. Ghiron, and E. S. Hoover, "No. 1 Call Processing," *Bell Syst. Tech. J.*, vol 43(5), pt. 2, pp. 2483–2531, September 1964.
6. D. Danielson, K. S. Dunlap, and H. R. Hoffman, "Switching Network Frames and Circuits", *Bell Syst. Tech. J.*, vol. 43(5), part 2, pp. 2221–2254, September 1964.
7. J. B. Connell, L. W. Hussey, and R. W. Ketchledge, "No. 1 ESS Bus System," *Bell Syst. Tech. J.*, vol. 43(5), pt. 1, pp. 2021–2054, September 1964.

8. O. Myers, "Markers for the Crossbar Toll System," *Bell Lab. Rec.*, vol. 22, pp. 499–504, August 1944.

9. P. N. Burgess and J. E. Stickel, "The Picturephone System: Central Office Switching," *Bell Syst. Tech. J.*, vol. 50, pp. 533–566, February 1971.

10. W. Hatton and J. Friuthof, "The 7-D Rotary Automatic Telephone System," *Electr. Commun.*, vol. 14, pp. 311–347, April 1935.

11. F. J. Scudder and J. N. Reynolds, "Crossbar Dial Telephone System," *Bell Syst. Tech. J.*, vol. 18, pp. 76–118, January 1939.

12. H. S. McDonald, "A Note on the Structure of Common Controls for TDM Local Switching Systems," *Int. Switching Symp.*, Kyoto, Japan, October 1976, p. 422-1.

13. A. E. Joel, Jr., "Experimental Switching System Using New Electronic Techniques," *Bell Syst. Tech. J.*, vol. 37, pp. 1091–1124, 1958.

14. G. S. Bishop, "Connectors for No. 5 Crossbar System," *Bell Lab. Rec.*, vol. 28, pp. 56–61, 1950.

15. J. D. Beierle, "10-C Toll Telephone Switching System Central Processor," *IEEE-ICC, 1970, Conf. Rec.*, vol. 2, pp. 27–19.

16. J. W. Dehn and R. E. Hersey, "Recent New Features for No. 5 Crossbar Switching System," *Trans. Am. Inst. Electr. Eng.*, vol. 75, pt. 1, pp. 457–466, 1956.

17. R. K. Holm, "No. 3 EAX System Description," *GTE Autom. Electr. Tech. J.*, vol. 15(8), pp. 334–341, July 1977.

18. A. H. Doblmaier and S. M. Neville, "No. 1 ESS Signal Processor," *Bell Lab. Rec.*, vol. 47, pp. 120–124, April 1969.

19. F. F. Shipley, "Crossbar Toll Switching System," *Bell Lab. Rec.*, vol. 22, pp. 355–359, April 1944.

20. R. M. Morris, "Crossbar Tandem TSP," *Bell Lab. Rec.*, vol. 42(5), pp. 146–157, May 1964.

21. L. Freimanis, A. M. Guerico, and H. F. May, "No. 1 ESS Scanner, Signal Distributor and Central Pulse Distributor," *Bell Syst. Tech. J.*, vol. 43, part 2, pp. 2255–2282, September 1964.

22. H. G. Alles, "The Intelligent Communications Switching Network," *IEEE Trans. Commun.*, vol. 27(7), pp. 1080–1087, July 1979.

23. Y. Tokita, T. Suzuki, A. Shoda, and K. Hiyama, "ESS Software Architecture for Multi-Processor System (HDX-10)," *Conf. Software Eng. Telecommun. Switch.*, 1978, pp. 132–136.

24. J. Muerling, "The AXE Switching System—New Standards for Telephone Exchanges," *Int. Telecommun. Expo.*, 1977 VI, pp. 384–390.

25. J. H. Davis, J. Janik, R. D. Royer, and B. J. Yokelson, "No. 5 ESS System Architecture," *Int. Switching Symp.*, Montreal, September 1981, vol. 3, p. 31A2.

26. C. G. Svala, "DSS-1, A Digital Local Switching System with Remote Line Switches," *IEEE Natl. Telecommun. Conf.*, 1977, pp. 39:5/1–7.

27. T. H. McKinney and W. H. Stewart, "Digital Central Office Hardware Architecture (DCO)," *IEEE Natl. Telecommun. Conf.*, 1977, pp. 15:4/1–4.

28. P. C. Richards, "ITT 1240 Digital Exchange. Cost Effective Digital Switching for up to 100,000 Lines," *Electr. Commun.*, vol. 54(3), pp. 205–214, 1979.

29. R. Galimberti, G. Perucca, and P. Semprini, "Proteo System: An Overview," *Int. Switching Symp.*, 1981—Conf. Pub., vol. 3, p. 32A1.

30. J. Muerling, "The AXE Switching System—New Standards for Telephone Exchanges," *Int. Telecommun. Expo.*, 1977 VI, pp. 384–390.

31. R. Galimberti, G. Perucca, and P. Semprini, "Proteo System: An Overview," *Int. Switching Symp.*, 1981, Conf. Pub., vol. 3, p. 32A1.

32. J. H. Davis, J. Janik, R. D. Royer, and B. J. Yokelson, "No. 5 ESS System Architecture," *Int. Switching Symp.*, 1981, vol. 3, p. 31A2.

33. A. E. Joel, Jr., "Experimental Switching System Using New Electronic Techniques," *Bell Syst. Tech. J.,* vol 37, pp. 1091–1124, 1958.
34. J. E. Brand and J. C. Warner, "Processor Call Carrying Capacity Estimation for Stored Program Control Switching Systems," *Proc. IEEE,* vol. 65(9), pp. 1342–1349, September 1977.
35. Y. Tokita, T. Suzuki, A. Shoda, and K. Hiyama, "ESS Software Architecture for Multi-Processor System (HDX-10)," *Conf. Software Eng. Telecommun. Switch.,* 1978, pp. 132–136.
36. A. E. Joel, Jr., "Communication Switching Systems As Real-Time Computer," *Eastern Joint Computer Conf., 1957, Proc. IRE,* pp. 197–203, 1958.
37. A. E. Joel, Jr., "Realization of The Advantages of SPC," *Int. Switching Symp. Rec.,* Munich, September 1974, p. 143.
38. J. H. Augustus, J. P. Dufton, and R. W. Duthie, "C-1 EAX Software and Real-Time Considerations in a Small Stored Program Switching Machine," *Int. Switching Symp.,* Boston, June 1972, pp. 577–584.
39. C. Carrelli and D. H. Roche, "CCITT Languages for SPC Switching Systems: Development, Status and Prospects," *Natl. Telecommun. Conf.,* 1981, pp. G6.1.1–6.1.5.
40. J. A. Harr, F. F. Taylor, and W. Ulrich, "Organization of the No. 1 ESS Central Processor," *Bell Syst. Tech. J.,* vol. 43(5), part 1, pp. 1845–1922, September 1964.
41. R. H. Bourgonjon, "The CCITT High Level Programming Language," *Conf. Software Engineering Telecomm. Switching,* 1978, pp. 36–39.
42. W. A. Budlong, "Simulating Electronic Switching with a Computer," *Bell Lab. Rec.,* vol. 38, pp. 328–333, 1960.
43. Y. Tokita, T. Suzuki, A. Shoda, and K. Hiyama, "ESS Software Architecture for Multi-Processor System (HDX-10)," *Conf. Software Eng. Telecommun. Switch.,* 1978, pp. 132–136.
44. G. F. Clement, W. C. Jones, and R. J. Watters, "No. 1 ESS Processors: How Dependable Have They Been?" *Bell Lab. Rec.,* vol. 52, pp. 21–25, January 1974.
45. J. B. Connell, L. W. Hussey, and R. W. Ketchledge, "No. 1 ESS Bus System," *Bell Syst. Tech. J.,* vol. 43(5), pt. 1, pp. 2021–2054, September 1964.
46. G. R. Durney, H. W. Kettler, E. M. Prell, G. Riddell, and W. B. Rohn, "TSPS No. 1: Stored Program Control No. 1A," *Bell Syst. Techn. J.,* vol. 49, pp. 2445–2507, December 1970.
47. R. W. Downing, J. S. Nowak, and L. S. Tuomenoksa, "Maintenance Plan on No. 1 Electronic Switching System," *Bell Syst. Tech. J.,* vol. 43, part 1, pp. 1961–2020, September 1964.
48. R. E. Staehler, "1A Processor Organization and Objectives," *Bell Syst. Tech. J.,* vol. 56(2), pp. 119–134, February 1977.
49. T. F. Storey, "Design of a Microprocessor Control for a Processor in an Electronic Switching System (ESS 2B, ESS No. 3)," *Bell Syst. Tech. J.,* vol. 55(2), pp. 183–232, February 1976.
50. E. E. Sumner, "Operations Systems for the Local Telecommunications Network," *Int. Zurich Seminar Digital Commun.,* 1978, p. F6.
51. H. E. Binder, "Automation of Operating and Maintenance Centers for EWS Using the Service Computer," *IEEE Region 8 Conv. (EUROCON),* 1977, pp. 460–466.

4

Switching System Software

D. H. Carbaugh and N. L. Marselos

1. Introduction

The intent of this chapter is to familiarize the reader with the basic design concepts and architecture of software for stored program control in central offices. It describes the criteria the designer must consider in developing central office software, and then details the structure and operation of a basic design to provide plain-old-telephone service, a few custom calling features, and central office maintenance.

The chapter also presents an "ideal" model for future stored program switching machines. This model leads to a software design which encompasses multiprocessing as a basic machine architecture. This "ideal" design provides increased modularity, enhanced flexibility, and reduced maintenance of the central office software.

2. Historical Introduction of Switching System Software

The Von Neuman computer brought new insights into improving switching systems. By using a computerlike device called a switching processor, a new type of switching system could be developed that could be controlled via a stored program in the processor. This made possible central control over the system. It also provided economical advantages since many changes could be effected by modifying the stored program rather

D. H. Carbaugh and N. L. Marselos ● Western Electric, 2600 Warrenville Road, Lisle, Illinois 60532

than the more costly hardware. Owing to the inherent speed of electronics and the capability of memory, the stored program switching processor made it possible for switching systems to offer a wide range of new services.

2.1 Early Developments of Stored Program Control for Telecommunications

The Bell System in the United States began investigating the concept of stored program control for switching in the early 1940s. These early investigations led to a trial office put into service in Morris, Illinois in 1960.

The Morris switch used a computer with a unique memory called the flying spot store. It worked by using a photographic plate as memory for the program logic. Memory access was accomplished through an optical mechanism. To change the memory one was required to scratch out or cover over "bits" in the photographic plate. This proved to be an arduous and error-prone task for inserting "quick" program fixes.

The Morris switch had an "endmarked" switching center network that consisted of gas tubes for crosspoint connections. Network connections were made by applying a difference in voltage potential across the network end points. The gas tubes which were the path of least resistance would conduct establishing a voice connection.

The Morris switch provided some key insights into electronic switching that formed the basis for future stored program control switchers. From the Morris trial, it was obvious that a bit-serial computer, one that looked at one bit at a time, was too slow. It was also learned that a gas tube network would not support the heavy voltages needed for ringing conventional telephones and coin control functions for pay telephones.

The results of the Morris, Illinois trial were used in a series of steps that led to the development of the full-scale commercial electronic central office. The first in a series of electronic switching systems was the No. 101 Private Business Exchange (PBX), which was followed by the Class-5 Electronic Switching System, the No. 1 ESS.[1]

The first No. 1 ESS went into service in Succasunna, New Jersey on May 30, 1965. This switching system used a processor which was word addressable, an instruction set which contained many unique instructions required for switching functions, and a ferreed crosspoint network. Besides providing plain-old-telephone services, (POTS), it had three additional custom calling features: (1) three-way calling, (2) speed calling, and (3) call forwarding. The software in the Succasunna switch consisted of approximately 100,000 memory words of 44 bits each. The call-processing software required 40% of this space and the remaining 60% was used to do system maintenance, diagnostics, and fault recovery.

2.2 Early Software Design to Accommodate Commercial Electronic Telecommunications

The advent of stored program control resulted in the centralization of all the logic in the central office. The wired (relay) logic that had resided in the individual trunk, service, and control circuits in mechanical systems, like the Bell System's No. 5 Crossbar, were put into software. It was reasoned that software was cheaper than hardware and unlimited in what it could do. Thus, in the early electronic switching systems, the circuits were reduced to their simplest physical components and put under complete control of the software.

The Bell System implemented the concept of a generic program in its electronic system switches. The idea was to have one identical common control program in every office. This program would process calls, identify and diagnose faults, and perform administrative functions like taking traffic counts. This generic program would always be resident in the system's memory and only required maintenance and new feature development support for the one program to be used for all offices.

Although the generic program would be the same in each central office, the physical environment and directory numbers of each office could be quite different. In order to define the environment for the generic program, an office data base would be used. The office data base would also contain the hardware configurations of frames and circuits as well as the network and line configurations.

This concept proved to be a wide choice for the first 10 years of stored program control systems. However, as many business features, for example *CENTREX*, were added to the program, the memory requirements placed a significant penalty on the one generic concept. As a result, the concept of one generic for all offices has been modified to provide the central offices with feature set options. This is accomplished by deleting unwanted feature code from a master generic program at load time. The result is a program load tape for the central office with a generic program tailored specifically for a set of features. This saves the telephone company money because the tailored feature set generic is smaller and requires less memory than the fully generic. In addition, it still requires maintenance and new feature development for only one "super" program that has all the features in it.

3. Central Office Design Criteria

One of the first considerations in designing effective switching software is to design for customer satisfaction. Unfortunately, switching software has two customers, each with different criteria to satisfy: the communications company (usually a telephone company) and the end user (customer). These considerations are driven primarily by cost factors of both the hardware and the software for the switching system.

The telephone company is obviously the primary customer for the manufacturer since they purchase the switching machines. But the telephone company's customers must be satisfied if they are going to use the features provided by the system and thus increase the telephone company's revenues. The question of how each can be satisfied can only be answered by understanding what each one wants.

3.1. Telephone Company Criteria

One of the telephone company's main considerations is life cycle cost. They are looking for a switch with a low first cost, reasonable growth costs, and low maintenance cost as well as opportunities to increase their revenues through the offering or of new features to their customers. This assumes, of course, that the switching system meets the capacity and feature requirements of the telephone company.

3.1.1 Cost

The tradeoff between first cost and growth costs is an important consideration in designing the switch, as Fig. 1 shows. First cost, the initial cost of the switch, may appear large in economic studies. However, a switch with a high first cost might provide for incremental growth at comparably small costs as the capacity of the switch is increased. At some point in the switch's growth, another large cost increment might be required due, for instance, to the need to add another processor. The point at which an increase in capacity requires another major investment is a result of the switch's design. This design tradeoff must take into consideration the telephone company's interests in keeping first costs down and in minimizing growth costs. Although a small first cost may make the switch more inviting to purchase, the ultimate measure of the switch's cost for the capacity of

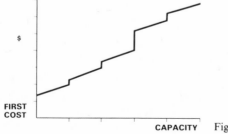

CAPACITY   Fig. 1.   Product cost.

service it provides is the combination of the first cost and the slope of the step function shown on Fig. 1.

3.1.2. Reliability and Performance

After first cost and growth cost, the telephone company is concerned about the cost of maintenance. This covers the areas of reliability and ease of servicing. For the system to be reliable, it must stay active. This means the software and hardware must have a high degree of fault tolerance and recovery capabilities designed into it.

The ease of servicing the switching system would include the day-to-day administration interfaces and growth. On a daily basis, the interfaces between the switch and its human operation support must be simple and straightforward. This requires well-written manuals for the operators and clear, unambiguous messages from the switch to its human monitors. It also requires simple procedures for bringing the switch from a fault condition back into service.

In terms of growth, the telephone company wants simple procedures. The switching software should be designed so as to make growth as simple as adding items to a list. So, as new hardware is added to the switch, the changes in software are reasonably transparent to the telephone company.

3.2. Customer Criteria

The telephone company's customer must be satisfied with service provided by the switch. The customer's criterion is slightly different from that of the telephone company. The customer wants features, and features that operate the same way from one switch to another; whether they are in New York or Chicago, the customer wants a feature to work the same. Unfortunately, the customer often has to be reeducated on how to use a feature on each new switch, and the variability from country to country is worse.

The customer is also concerned with reliability and performance. The customer essentially wants the switching system dedicated to his requirements. Reliability to the customer means having calls go through on the first attempt. For performance, the customer expects immediate dial tone, and uninhibited access to features. However, completely satisfying the customer's needs could require an unrealistic investment in hardware and software. And so, the system must be designed so that the customers feel the system is satisfying their needs. This essentially places a real-time, time-shared requirement on the switching system. It must share its facilities between the 100s or 1000s of terminals that might be using the switching system where each terminal seems to have total control of the system's resources while in reality a process of constant swapping takes place.

3.3. System Cost Considerations

The switching system software designer must take into consideration another set of criteria that have direct impact on the system's cost. The system cost is strongly influenced by the software implementation. In this context, implementation means the actual written program code and its packaging into executable modules. The criteria that must be considered relate to the physical environment of the switch:

- Processor speed,
- Memory usage,
- Code design.

Each of these plays an important part in establishing the criteria for implementing the switching software.

3.3.1. Processor Speed

The instruction cycle time for a switching system controller, as for any computer, is an indication of how much work that system can do. Early commercial switching systems had cycle times of about 5 μsec. Today's switches operate ten times faster. This means that the current system can do what the old ones did in one-tenth the time, or do ten times as much work in the same time.

The number of customer calls that can be processed in a time interval is a function of the number of cycles available to the call-processing program units. However, determining the call-processing capacity of the switch is not a simple matter. Consider the case shown in Fig. 2. Here the number of machine cycles available per hour for call processing is plotted as a straight line against the number of calls per busy hour (this representation has been simplified by omitting the constant overhead load which absorbs a fixed number of cycles). Assume also that only 95% of the total machine

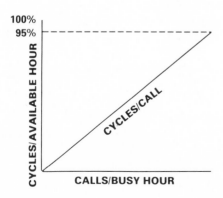

Fig. 2.   Representation of call processing capacity.

cycles are available to the call processing software during peak hours. Then, in this model, it is easy to determine the number of calls given the number of cycles used per call, which is the slope of the line.

Unfortunately, this model is not realistic because it depends on all calls being similar in the number of cycles they use. In a real system, a call taken to the talking state might require 5000 cycles. If, however, that call originates from a coin phone, it might require 20,000 cycles; the added cycles are needed for coin control functions. Thus, different types of calls differ in the number of cycles they use.

The varying requirements of cycles by different types of calls require sophisticated analysis to determine the switch's capacity. One method to solve this problem is by simulation. The simulator can be a program in which the number of cycles for each type of call is known. Then, by giving the simulation program various traffic mixes, it will identify the capacity requirements for that configuration.

3.3.2. Memory Usage

Partitioning between fixed and variable memory in the switch is a balance between considerations of cost and processing tradeoffs. To keep first costs down it is desirable to keep memory to a minimum. This is done by designing a software architecture that uses a fixed and variable memory structure.

The fixed memory is the minimum memory necessary to process one call. This would contain the generic program and portions of the office data base, i.e., routing information. Whether the switch handles one or one-hundred thousand calls, it needs the fixed memory. The cost of the fixed memory is part of the switch's first cost.

The variable memory is dependent on the engineered capacity of the system and the subscriber's calling characteristics, e.g., holding times, attempts per hour, feature usage, etc. Each call uses some of the variable memory. Customer information and equipment information is stored in the variable memory. As the office grows, the variable memory needs to be increased. So the increase in the variable memory is part of the growth costs.

The designer of the switching software has to consider the tradeoff between fixed and variable memory. To have low first costs the fixed memory can be kept at a minimum at the expense of design flexibility and/or real time. This memory optimizing is generally achieved by designing and implementing programs which use a high degree of program loops and tight data packing. This unfortunately results in a program and data structure that cannot easily be changed to accommodate future extensions, like new features.

3.3.3. Program Design

When a program is compressed to use less memory, the tradeoff is usually at the expense of real time or program complexity. Consider an example of scanning 32 rows of scan points. The commands needed are SCAN ROW x, where x is alternatively each of the rows, and OUTPUT RESULT. Figure 3 shows two alternative approaches to this problem. Alternative 1 uses a counter to specify the scan row and a looping structure. It has six instructions. Alternative 2 is a straight line implementation of the problem: SCAN ROW 1 OUTPUT RESULT, SCAN ROW 2 OUTPUT RESULT, etc. There are 64 instructions in alternative 2.

The two alternative program implementations in Fig. 3 show the tradeoff of memory versus real time. Alternative 1 saves memory, but it uses up 161 machine cycles to perform the scanning: after the first instruction, the next five are repeated 32 times ($1 + 5 \times 32 = 161$). Alternative 2, however, requires more memory but only 64 machine cycles. The tradeoff here is to conserve memory at the expense of real time and keep first costs down, as in alternative 1, or conserve real time at the expense of memory, as in alternative 2. The designers have to face this problem and realize the tradeoff and its economic implications for both present and future situations. The quality of these types of decisions is what distinguishes good designers from poor ones.

A way to design for optimization is to provide specialized call-processing instructions through hardware design in the processor. For example, assume that to do network path hunts for a large switching center network it is necessary to rotate the middle 8 bits of a 23-bit word while not affecting the other bits in the word. An algorithm to accomplish this on a general purpose computer would be quite expensive in terms of machine cycles. But switching machines are not general purpose computers. They are tailored to perform these operations with special instructions. Thus, the 8-bit rotation which might normally take 10 cycles in a general purpose

ALTERNATIVE 1	ALTERNATIVE 2
SET CTR TO 32	SCAN ROW 1
AA : SCAN ROW (CTR)	OUTPUT RESULT
OUTPUT RESULT	SCAN ROW 2
DECREMENT CTR	OUTPUT RESULT
TEST CTR	.
BRANCH [IF CTR] $\neq$ 0 TO AA	.
	SCAN ROW 32
	OUTPUT RESULT
NO. INSTRUCTIONS = 6	64
NO. CYCLES = 161	64

Fig. 3.   Program implementation of scanning example.

computer could be reduced to 2 cycles. This is an important saving if the operation were performed 30 times per call.

The tradeoff between processor speed and memory usage is an issue that switching system software designers must consider carefully. The issues are economics and process capacity. The objective is to keep first costs low and yet find an effective balance between the processor's memory, fixed memory, and its real-time capability. This can be done by determining the processor's capacity through simulation. Specialized instructions can be developed to save real time by minimizing the number of machine cycles needed for often used operations.

4. Basic Electronic Switching Software

A commonly used design architecture for switching software consists of two major components. The first is a program that contains all the logical instructions necessary to perform the switching system's functions. The program is often called a "generic" because it is designed to allow its switching system to operate in any central office. It does this by obtaining the specific characteristics of the office from a data base.

The office data base is the second major component of the current design. It is unique to each central office. It stores the specific information on the office's equipment and customers that the generic program needs for processing calls.

4.1. Generic Program

The generic program provides a variety of functions for the central office. Foremost among these is processing calls. This includes providing intraoffice and interoffice calls, and all the custom calling features offered by the office to its customers. In addition to call processing, the generic program provides system maintenance and administration functions: system maintenance provides for diagnostic and recovery procedures; administration assists the telephone company in updating and monitoring the switching machine.

The generic program is not a single program but an aggregate of many program modules. Each of these performs a specific functional task. Their operation is coordinated by an executive control program that calls them into execution at the appropriate time. For these programs to communicate with each other, buffers and temporary memory storage areas are needed. This can be best explained by looking at a functional model of call processing.

4.1.1. Functional Model of Call Processing

The basic requirement for the generic program is to provide a message path between two customers on request. For an intraoffice call this is a six-step process:

1. Detecting a request for service.
2. Interpreting dialed digits.
3. Alerting the called customer.
4. Establishing a talking connection.
5. Disconnecting the call.
6. Charging.

These are the six basic functions of the call-processing programs.[2] Other services such as interoffice call processing and custom calling features (like conference calling, call waiting, etc.) are really extensions to these six basic functions.

The component programs of the generic that perform call processing begin with detecting a request for service. This is done by scan programs that look at each trunk for a call from other offices (call termination) and each line for a request for service (call origination). The scan programs must look at each line or trunk approximately every 100 msec.

When the scan program detects a request for origination, a customer in the office going off-hook, it stores the terminal number for that customer in the service request buffer as shown in Fig. 4. This buffer is used to bridge the higher speeds of the scan programs with the slower running executive control program. On a regular visitation basis, the executive control program inspects the service request buffer. If it finds a request for origination, it passes the terminal number to the origination program.

The origination program prepares the switching machine to receive digits from the originating terminal. This includes identifying the terminal's characteristics (e.g., will the digits be received by dial pulses or dual tone multifrequencies), then finding an idle digit receiver, and finally finding a network path to connect the digit receiver to the terminal. The terminal's characteristics are obtained from the office data base using the terminal number as an index. However, it is then necessary to store this information in a piece of transient memory (called a call record) that can be used for the duration of the call.

The call record is a scratch pad which keeps the state of an active call or an active terminal for the switching system software. Call records are a pooled resource. Once an event is initiated, like a terminal going off hook, the next free call record is assigned to it. When the event has terminated, such as at disconnect of the call, the call record goes back into the pool for further use.

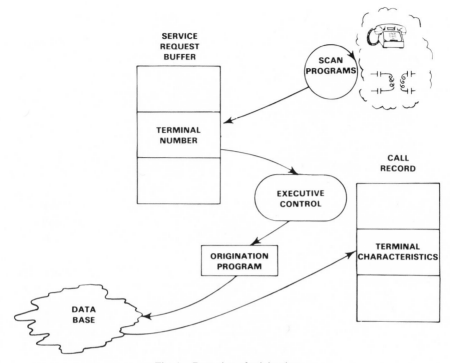

Fig. 4.   Detection of origination.

The call record will generally contain three basic segments of information about a call as shown in Fig. 5. The first is a control block that contains the state of progress of the call, timing areas (such as for timing out digits or for timing out disconnects), scanning (when it is desirable to adjust the scanning rate such as to speed it up to receive digits), and a communication area that allows other call records and temporary memory to be linked together throughout the course of a call.

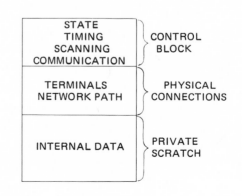

Fig. 5.   Call record.

The second segment of the control block stores information on the physical connections in the switching system used by the call. This is the hardware and path information for the call during processing. The third, and final, segment of the call record is a private scratch pad for the generic programs. It is here that internal data are stored by the generic programs. It is also here that detailed digits and billing information are stored.

Once the origination program has recorded the terminal characteristics in the call record, it must prepare the way to receive digits from the terminal. First, it must find an idle hardware digit receiver and then it must reference the switching center network map to find a path through the switching center's network for connecting the receiver to the terminal as illustrated in Fig. 6.

The network map is simply a data table in which the busy or idle condition of network paths are recorded. When a path is selected, its status is changed from idle to busy in the network map. When the path is no longer needed, it is returned to the idle state.

The origination program will store data associated with the receiver in temporary memory that is then linked to the call record. The temporary memory is used to keep the overall size of the call record at a minimum. Each block of temporary memory serves a specific function. Several blocks of temporary memory may be linked together during the processing of a call. The linkage between temporary memory and the call record is bidirec-

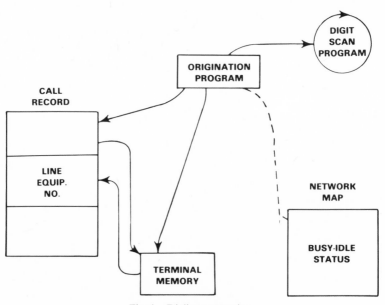

Fig. 6.   Dialing connection.

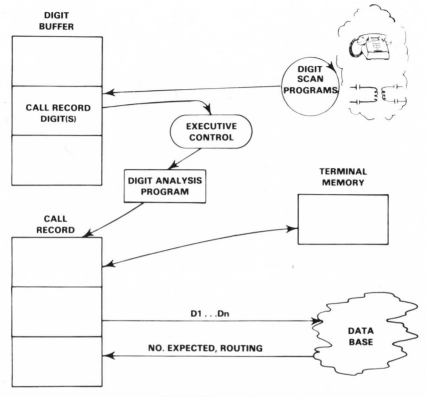

Fig. 7.   Digit reception.

tional; each points to the other. When a temporary memory block is no longer needed, it will be disconnected from the communication linkage of the active call record.

When the origination program has the terminal connected to a digit receiver, it has completed its function. The digit scan program now begins to scan the receiver for dialed digits. The scanning for digits must be fast, typically at a 10-msec scanning rate. The rapid scanning requires a digit buffer for collecting the dialed digits, Fig. 7. This buffer is associated with the call record during dialing.

As the digits are collected, the executive control program activates the digit analysis program to analyze for valid dialing. The valid terminating directory number is used to access the data base to obtain the expected termination for the dialed directory number and to obtain routing information for the call, Fig. 8. The terminating line (LEN_T) must be checked to determine that it can receive the call (e.g., not busy). Then network paths for talking must be found between the originating and terminating line, and

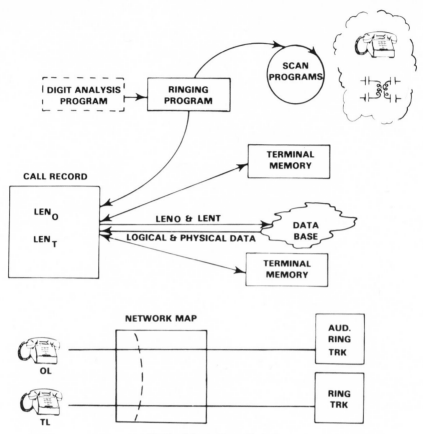

Fig. 8.   Line-to-line call alert.

between the ringing circuit and the terminating line. It is important to assure a talking path before ringing since it does not make sense to ring a party for which a talking path cannot be established.

The logical and physical data on the LEN_O and LEN_T connections are obtained from the data base and stored in the call record. The network map is prepared for ringing by the ringing program and audible ring is given to the originating line (OL) and ringing to the terminating line (TL). Once this is done, the scan program is activated to look for an answer from the terminating line or a disconnect from the originating line.

When the scan programs detect answer, they store that terminal number in an answer buffer, Fig. 9. The executive control program deactivates the ringing program and activates other program modules to establish the talking path between the OL and TL. At this point, the call is in a stable state and much of the temporary memory can be freed. The scan

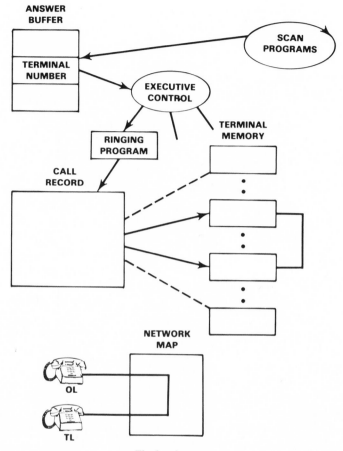

Fig. 9.   Answer.

programs will continue to check for disconnect, and at that time the disconnect and billing programs will be activated, after which the OL and TL
will be returned to their original idle states and the call record will be freed.

4.1.2.   System Maintenance

The principal function of the generic program is call processing, but in
most cases only 20% of the generic code is traversed under successful,
normal call processing. A far larger segment of generic program is devoted
to the system maintenance functions:

- Fault recognition,
- Fault recovery,

- Overload controls,
- Audits,
- System recovery.

Together they maintain the correct operation of the switching machine.

The fault recognition and fault recovery functions of the generic program work together. When a fault such as a hardware failure or a software bug is encountered, the fault recognition program must identify the nature of the problem. The fault recovery program then remedies the situation if possible. For example, if a hardware unit fails, the software must find a bad hardware unit, remove it from service, and quickly switch to a good unit.

The overload controls monitor the load on the switching machine. It gives a picture of the state of the whole machine which is used by the call-processing programs to maintain sanity as the switch reaches its real-time or traffic engineered capacity.

Audits have two purposes. One is to recover lost memory, such as temporary memory blocks or call records that have been lost from the active or idle lists. The second audit purpose is to assist in call program recovery when it finds itself in an unexpected situation. In essence, the audits provide centralized "garbage" handling and collection for the switching system software.

System recovery is used to bring the system back when it encounters a major, system-affecting problem. This can go in levels of action or phases, the worst phase, or highest level, being a total reload of the program from permanent storage. The system recovery should always begin with the lowest-level phase first. These might do some simple house-keeping like reinitializing an area where constant data used by the software are stored. If that does not bring the switching machine back to sanity, then the next higher phase should be activated. This process of cleaning-up or purging should continue escalating upward with the switching machine's sanity checked after each phase. No higher phase should be executed than necessary. Under automatic control, a reload should be limited to removing only transient calls, calls that are not already in the talking state. Thus, vital stable calls, like monitoring a cardiac patient's condition, are maintained.

The system recovery phases and their respective escalation processes may be triggered by the relative activity in fault recovery, overload, and audits. These three systems can be used to indicate the severity of system degradation. System recovery will successively apply more severe remedial activity until the system is restored to a healthy process.

4.1.3. Administrative Functions

The generic program also provides support for the telephone company to administer the switching machine. This includes keeping traffic counts for the telephone company traffic engineer, providing a change capability to overwrite the office data base with current information, and a change verification mechanism to inspect the switching system's memory and data base interactively.

4.2. Office Data Base

The second most important component of switching system software after the generic program is the office data base. The generic program depends on the office data base to uniquely define the central office for it. This makes it possible to use the same generic software in any installation.

4.2.1. Office Data Base Contents

To provide the central office information required by the generic program, the office data base consists of two types of data:

- Customer,
- Equipment.

The customer data provides customer related information. This includes the following:

- The lines that terminate local customers,
- Directory number to terminal correspondences,
- The trunks that are available to distant offices,
- Features available to each customer,
- How calls will be routed,
- How calls will be billed.

Although not an exhaustive list, the above define some of the key information the office data base must contain about the customer.

The equipment data within the office data base provides the generic program with the hardware configuration of the central office. This includes the number of frames and the number of circuits within the frames, and how each can be addressed by the software. It contains information on the processor configuration defining the size of memory, and it includes the switching center network configuration. From this information, the generic program can determine the physical environment of the central office.

4.2.2. Office Data Base Architecture

The uniqueness of each central office will be reflected in both the size and content of the office data base. Yet to the generic program, the structure of the data base must minimize the impact of this uniqueness. The office data base can accomplish this by being structured into a hierarchical link list. Each node of the list is a table that can contain data and pointers to lower-level tables in the hierarchy as shown in Fig. 10. At the top of the hierarchy is a Master Head Table which resides in a fixed location in memory. The rest of the tables, which can be linked down for several levels, are accessed through the Master Head Table and are thus relocatable in memory.

The generic program accesses data from the office data base by hunting down the link list until the data are found. The search begins at a fixed location in the Master Head Table designated for the address of a specific Head Table. Once the head Table is found, the generic program indexes down the hierarchical structure to the specific subtranslator containing the desired information as shown in Fig. 11. The hardware location and type of ringing for a terminating party are retrieved from the Director Number Translations by using the called number as indexed into two levels of tables.

4.3. Current Design of Switching Software

Switching software designs today are based on the concept of maximizing efficiency. The idea is to put through the most calls, in the fastest time, using the fewest possible resources. The measuring stick for this objective is the switching system's cost versus capacity as described in the previous section on Central Office Design Criteria.

The early designs for switching system software were for plain old telephone service (POTS) with only a few features. Current designs incor-

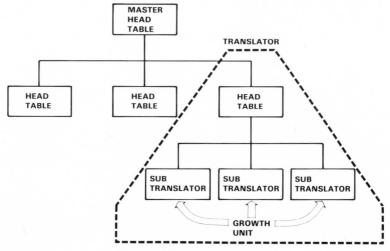

Fig. 10.   Office data base structure.

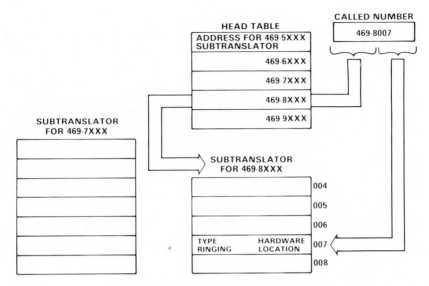

Fig. 11. Directory number translator.

porate many features, but basically they are modeled after the early designs. This section describes the general architecture and operation of current designs, and the problems inherent in them.

4.3.1. Architectural Structure

The conceptual architecture for switching software can be defined as a lattice structure as shown in Fig. 12. The switching system is input driven and perceives its stimuli by input programs. These programs operate at the real time rates required to receive the inputs; for example, digit reception checks every 10 msec for more digits. In a similar way, output programs send responses from the switching system. Input hoppers and output buffers are used to bridge the external interfaces with the faster speed of the processor. Switching software is constructed of a set of reentrant program modules. Each module performs a specific task, such as origination or digit analysis. The module is designed to contain only the program's logic. It uses data storage that is managed externally to the module and which is provided to it each time it executes. In this way, the module can be reentered after it relinquishes control, and have its data restored in such a way as to make the interruption transparent. This makes it possible for one program to have many sets of data associated with it at one time. The reentry of the program modules is made possible by the allocation of transient memory as described in Section 4.1.1.

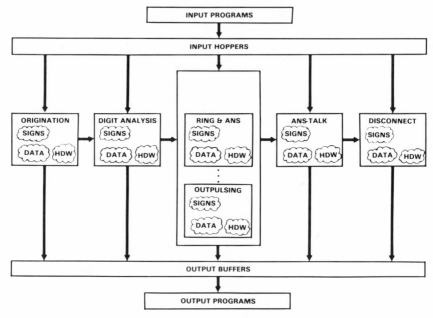

Fig. 12.   Conceptual representation of switching software architecture.

Each switching software program module has direct control over its interfaces with the switching system. The module interprets its own input signals, signs, and controls the hardware associated with its task. The modules also directly change the common transient memory, the call record, and write data directly in the output buffers for the output programs. Thus, the program modules and physical resources form a tightly coupled network.

4.3.2.   Program Scheduling

Scheduling of switching software program modules is done through priority levels and interrupts. The call processing and normal maintenance switching software comprise the base-level programs as shown in the right side in Fig. 13. Each program is permanently assigned to a preference class A through E; although five classes are shown here, many switching systems use fewer.

The preference class is a priority level with A levels higher than B, and B higher than C, etc. Programs with higher-priority levels run before or more frequently than those with lower ones. So programs that collect digits or detect answers are assigned a higher preference level because these activities must be checked more frequently. And programs with less initial de-

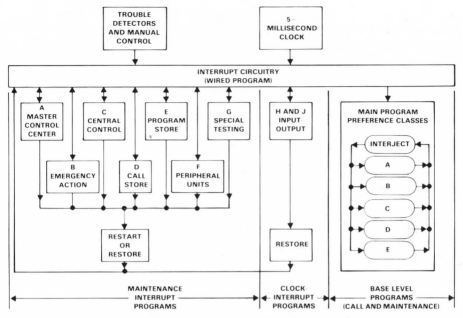

Fig. 13.   Program scheduling plan.

mands, such as connecting up to an outpulsing trunk circuit, are assigned a lower preference class.

Interrupts play an important part in the switching system. An interrupt will temporarily take control from the current running task, perform its operation, and restore control without the task realizing anything has happened. In severe cases, the interrupt may have to issue a restart to clear the problem. This will usually lose tasks that were in progress at the time the interrupt occurred.

Interrupts themselves must be assigned levels of priority because it is possible for an interrupt to occur while the handling of a previous interrupt is in progress. The priority scheme for interrupts in Fig. 13 shows priority levels A through G for maintenance interruption programs, and priority levels H and J for clock interrupts. The level of highest priority is A down through the lowest priority J. A lower-priority interrupt cannot cause an interrupt while a higher priority one is in progress. The highest-priority interrupt, A, is normally a manual override interrupt. The next priority interrupt is Emergency Action. This is an automatic attempt to analyze and correct situations when the machine begins to lose sanity. Interrupts C through G are to correct various hardware problems.

Tasks that require close timing tolerances are controlled by the clock interrupts. The 5-msec hardware clock is used to drive these tasks designated by priority levels H and J. They are used for tasks such as input processing, line scanning, and for output processing, like transferring billing information to tape.

4.3.3. Limitation in Prior Software Designs

The current designs of switching software are partitioned into temporal operations in which the program's origination, digit analysis, answer, etc. conform to the chronological events in the calling process. However, in order to make this design viable, it was necessary to have each program intimately knowledgeable about its environment. Thus, the origination program has to know about all the kinds of signaling it will receive: the timing for on-hook and for off-hook, distinguishing flash from disconnect. Also, the programs have to know details about the hardware they must interface and control.

The result of having each switching software program module control its immediate environment as per Fig. 12 is to have it do a great deal. Under ordinary circumstances, this would require large programs. However, the constraints of low memory usage and high efficiency require a considerable amount of optimization of the program code. In this way, the programs are reduced to small efficient modules. This works well for basic call processing, but not for vertical services of customer features.

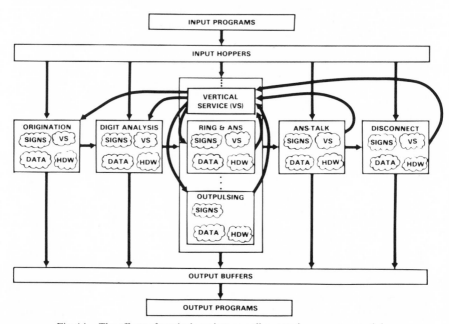

Fig. 14.   The effects of vertical services on call-processing program modules.

Vertical services such as call waiting, conference calling, etc. have an effect over many of the call-processing program modules as illustrated in Fig. 14. Each module has to have an intimate knowledge of the vertical service woven into it, which in turn more tightly couples the modules together. A change to a vertical service might require a change in several program modules. The result was a complex network of dependencies between program modules.

Switching software systems that are built around these design concepts are efficient in real time and memory, but are costly to enhance and test. The tightly coupled nature of these designs can result in unexpected side-effect errors when changes are made to the switching software. To ensure that the integrity of the system is maintained, a change to the software requires significant testing.

The difficulty of adding vertical services to this type of switching software makes enhancing it costly. However, the number and sophistication of vertical services will significantly increase in the future. It may well be that these software switching designs will not provide the flexibility to meet future demands. It is obvious that a new model for switching software is necessary.

5. New Model for Switching System Software

Switching systems are rapidly changing in this era of expanding telecommunications. There is increasing use of data transmission, there are needs to enrich switching systems with features, and data switching is becoming more popular. And, as the need for faster yet reasonably priced processors grows, distributed processing is increasing in use.

The switching systems software designer is faced with this changing environment and is aware of the problems that have resulted from prior switching software designs. There is a need for a new model for switching systems software that addresses these issues. This section describes such a model.

5.1. Architectural Objectives

A new model for switching system software has to be based on an architecture that avoids the problems of prior designs. The efficiency built into these designs results in its lack of flexibility. For a new model to meet the ever-changing demands being placed on switching systems, it has to be built around the concept of flexibility. This flexibility has to allow it to accommodate the many sophisticated customer features switching systems will be offering in the future, facilitate the rapid introduction of these features, and give the telephone company the ability to add their own features. And it must do all of this while still meeting the basic customer criterion of reasonable cost.

The objectives of an "ideal" architecture for switching system software are demanding. It must result in software that can be partitioned to run in separate processors of a distributed processing environment or be used on a single processor. It must isolate hardware and data structure dependencies from feature programs. It must be modular with well-defined interfaces to simplify testing and adding features. And it must minimize the cross-feature dependencies.

Although this may seem like an ambitious goal for a new software model to accomplish, the framework for these basic objectives is already being addressed in an approach to software called "software engineering." This discipline has been demonstrated in general applications software to produce high-quality software while improving the productivity of the software developers. It can be equally effective for switching systems software. These techniques might initially be considered too costly in real-time and memory usage. This argument is similar to that used by assembly language programmers when faced with the possible use of high-level languages. However, by applying well-known optimization techniques after the design is complete, it is possible to recover these valuable resources.

5.1.1. Software Engineering Concepts

Software engineering has been introduced as a way to improve both the productivity of the software developers and the quality of software products. There is substantial evidence to indicate that it has been successful in both areas.[3,4] As shown in Fig. 15, software engineering compared with prior development practices has realized a decrease in effort of 50% for development and 75% for maintenance. Software engineering achieves these results by addressing the major components of the software development process:

1. Software structure,
2. Development methodology,
3. Development tools.

Each of these areas have a supportive effect on the other.

5.1.1.a. Software Structure. The software system's designer is most concerned with the concepts of software structure. Software engineering has shown that a functional partitioned system's design is the most flexible one. A function is a specific well-defined activity. A software design is segmented into component functions and subfunctions which require minimal interface between each other. Thus, a switching software design might have a line

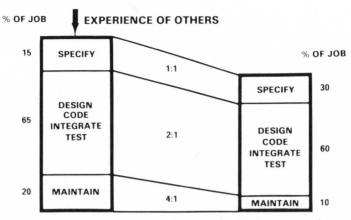

Fig. 15.   Software engineering benefits over prior development practices.

identification function which tests for off-hook and returns a yes or no answer. The interface between this subfunction and its parent function would be the exchange of the line identification for the test reply.

When a system has been defined functionally, it can be easily partitioned into program modules. These modules are executable segments of the program. They should be defined to approximate the functions of the system's design. Experience has shown that small program modules, less than 100 statements, are more easily written, tested, and changed.

Another software engineering concept that is an important part of software structure is data abstraction. The more the structure of the data is known by the program module, the more impact a change of that data will have on the module. To minimize this effect it is important to hide the structure of the data from the program modules. This can be done through an intermediary such as a data base manager subsystem. When a datum is needed by the program module, it is received from the data base manager in the format it needs the datum without knowledge of how it is actually stored in the system's data base.

5.1.1.b. Development Methodology. Software engineering has shown that the quality of the software can be enhanced by the way it is developed. One useful technique is top-down development. It is the process of developing and testing a hierarchically structured software system design by beginning at the top module of the hierarchy and proceeding down the legs of the branches. Each node of the hierarchy is a program module that must be tested before the nodes beneath it are. In a functional design, this implies that the parent functions are tested before their subordinant subfunctions. The results of this development technique have shown a significant improvement in quality of the software accompanied by a decrease in the time needed to develop it.

The structure and composition of the software team is another part of the development methodology that has been influenced by the software engineering concept. Modern software development teams can be made more effective if they are structured around the concepts of the Chief Programmer team developed by IBM.[5] This is a team of specialists, with one person, the chief programmer, responsible for the overall design and technical coordination of the software development. Each person in the team can be a specialist in their own areas of software. They are brought together to use their expertise in the areas for which they are best suited.

The coordination of a team can be significantly improved by using structured walk-throughs. These are reviews conducted by the team members on each other's work. The reviews have a precise format and are conducted for all stages of development process. Their purpose is to improve the quality of the final product and increase the team's supportive commitment to that goal.

5.1.1.c. Development Tools. Improved tools to develop software are another contribution made by software engineering. One of these is the use of a high-level language instead of assembler language. Studies have shown that a high-level language can have a threefold increase in programming productivity over an assembler language.[6] The reason that switching system software developers have favored assembly language has been a need for memory and real-time savings. However, an evaluation of switching software shows that only a small percentage of the code actually needs to be that efficient and, thus, should be written in assembly language. For the largest percentage of generic code, a high-level language can be used and the memory size penalty is less severe with low-cost semiconductor memory. This will allow the developer to concentrate on solving the problems of the switching logic without being inhibited by the limitations of the programming language. Once this high-level language code is written, it can be processed by an automatic code optimizer to achieve a reasonable level of efficiency. Such languages as CHILL, of the Consultative Committee on international Telephone and Telegraphs, and C, from the United States Bell System, represent the trend to higher-level languages for telecommunications software.

The use of support libraries and program librarians are also tools that aid the development process. A support library is a repository for the development documentation. Both design and program code are stored in the library. It is administered by a program librarian whose function is to handle many of the clerical activities required by software development teams. This gives the developers more time to work on their software. The program librarian is the sole owner of the program documentation stored in the support library. In this capacity, the librarian can ensure the integrity of the support libraries so program code under development does not accidently get mixed in with already issued product code before it is properly tested.

The support library provides a safe place where control over the program development products can be administered. It also makes it simpler to perform regression testing to ensure that changes to the program are localized to what they were intended to do so that these changes do not create side effects in the program or other parts of the system.

5.1.2. Consideration for Distributed Processing

Future switching machines will move away from the single processor to distributed processing. This is motivated by a need for faster yet still economical switching machines. In the past, it has been possible to increase the speed by building bigger, faster processors. But the speed of a single processor will ultimately be limited by physical laws and the software designers' insatiable consumption of available processing resources.

One answer to this ultimate limit is to replace the serial processing of a single processor with the simultaneous processing of a distributed system. In such a system, several processors are linked together. Actions of the system are happening simultaneously rather than in serial. The effective speed of such a system could far exceed that of a single processor.

The switching system software designer must design future software to be flexible enough to operate in either a single or distributed processor environment. The question is how to do this. As complex as this seems, the answer is quite simple. The designer should design for the distributed processor environment. If programs work in a distributed environment, they can easily be put into a single processor.

The approach to take in designing software for a distributed processing environment is to functionally separate the software processes. The more separation between these processes, the more distributed an environment in which the system can operate. However, this is only possible if the communication between processes is minimal. If the design has processes too tightly connected by shared communications, a distributed system would degrade in capability to that of a single processor.

5.2. An Ideal Software Architecture Model

An ideal model for the architecture of a software system would incorporate the design objectives of distributed processing and the concepts of software engineering. The model should be defined with separate functional subsystems. These could be called processors because they could be physically distinct processors of a distributed system, or they could reside together in a single processor. The model would have minimal interfaces between processors to reduce interprocessor dependancy and communication. And finally, the model must have a data base manager to provide a level of data abstraction to isolate the software from the physical data structures.

5.2.1. Structural Overview

There are many possible ways to structure an ideal software architecture model. The structure in Fig. 16 is one. It consists of five processors:

- Sign interpreter,
- Feature processor,
- Task processor,
- Peripheral interface,
- Data base manager.

Each processor performs a specific function. They communicate with each other via message buffers, and access data from a central data source. The processors do not store any permanent data within them.

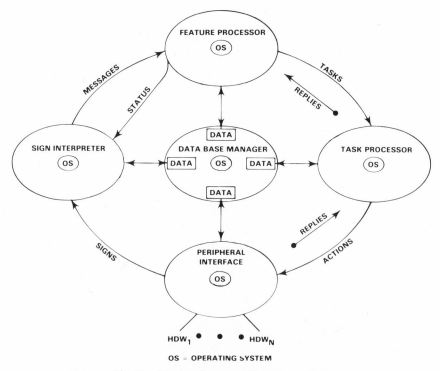

Fig. 16. "Ideal" software architecture overview.

The processors are supported by an operating system. Each processor in Fig. 16 is in a separate hardware machine of a distributed environment and, consequently, each machine has its own operating system.

The processors are an interconnected network. Each processor operates independently to perform its specific functions but is driven by stimulus from the others. Action is initiated by the direct result of inputs coming from external hardware signals, $HDW_1, \ldots, HDW_N$, to the switching system.

5.2.1.a.   Peripheral Interface. The peripheral interface (PI) is the only processor that communicates directly with the hardware of the switching system. Its purpose is to provide a level of abstraction for the rest of the switching system's software that masks the physical operations of the hardware. Thus, the PI must know the specific characteristics of the hardware for the family of switching machines it supports.

The PI has a relatively simple view of the switching system. It performs the hardware manipulations as it is directed by the task processor (TP). The TP sends actions to the PI as a series of logical tasks. The PI translates these logical tasks into physical actions and then signals their successful or unsuccessful completion as replies back to the TP. For example, the TP would specify an action to the PI for connecting a ringing circuit to a line by sending a series of tasks that symbolically identifies the line, ringing circuit, and a path to connect them together. The PI translates these symbolic identifiers into their specific hardware counterparts using the data base. It then proceeds to perform the connections as designated, allowing the required timing delays and applying proper voltages required by the specific hardware. When all tasks for the action have been completed, their overall success or failure is recorded in replies to the TP.

The PI also performs the software scanning functions of the switching system. It scans each terminal as an independent entity since it has no knowledge of connections between terminals. It knows the type of scanning it must perform for each terminal from the data base. As it receives electrical signals from the hardware, it translates these into logical messages or signs that are meaningful to the sign interpreter (SI) processor. The physical activities of the terminal become signs like off-hook and answer. The electrical impulses or tones from digits dialed on the subscribers telephone terminal are translated back to digits before being passed to the SI.

5.2.1.b.   Sign Interpreter. The sign interpreter (SI) processor translates sequences of input signals received from the peripheral interface into logical messages. The SI interprets the signs from the PI on the basis of a single terminal; it has no view of calls or connections between terminals. The PI sends signs to the SI which translates these signs into their logical interpretation of the state of the call. For example, the PI would pass the on-hook sign to the SI which in turn would perform the timing necessary to determine if this were a flash request or a disconnect. It would then send the appropriate message identifying the specific change (either flash or disconnect) to the feature processor (FP).

The messages sent by the SI are interpreted by the FP which then sends a new status for that terminal to the SI. The SI has only the view of a terminal. It is thus necessary for the FP to inform the SI what logical actions it should expect next from the terminal. This it does by sending simple status messages to the SI.

   5.2.1.c.   Feature Processor. The feature processor (FP) performs logical feature control. It sees the entire call at a high level of abstraction, and controls the calls progress at that level through a series of logical tasks passed to the task processor (TP). The FP receives stimulus from the messages sent by the SI. These identify the actions if the terminal which the FP interprets in view of the call. For example, the SI sends a message that a terminal has flashed, the FP determines by the state of the call that this is a request for connecting to a call waiting party. It then specifies the tasks for the TP to put the current talking party on-hold and connect the call waiting terminal and the flashing terminal for talking.

The level of abstraction used by the FP to process calls makes it machine independent. The FP does not need to know the details of how a change in state is determined or how to realign the network. It is shielded from these details by the other processors. This frees the FP to contend with the complexities of feature processing.

The FP retains the current high-level logical condition of each of the terminals in the data base. When the terminals are connected directly, such as via a talking path, or indirectly, such as a terminal on-hold, the FP identifies the relationship between terminals in the data base. When the SI sends a message of a state change, the FP inspects the data base for the current status and proceeds accordingly.

   5.2.1.d.   Task Processor. The logical tasks requested by the feature processor are translated by the task processor (TP) into a series of actions to be performed by the peripheral interface (PI) processor. The TP provides a bridge between the high level of abstraction of the FP and the detailed processing of the PI. To do this, the TP must know certain protocols of the switching system since it will directly drive the hardware through the actions sent to the PI.

The tasks sent to the TP from the FP are functional requests, for example, bring dial tone up for terminal X. The TP translates this functional request into procedural actions for the PI to perform. These actions are still abstract tasks since the TP does not know the details of activating the hardware resource—this is left to the PI—but they are specific enough to control the resource and must reflect the temporal nature of the outside environment and system requirements. The communications between the

FP, TP, and PI are two way. The FP issues a task for the TP which in turn issues actions for the PI. The PI replies to the TP as to the successful completion of the actions, and the TP in turn replies to the FP. This communication link gives the subsystems feedback on their requests. An absence of a reply indicates a problem which can either cause a resending of the original task request or a request to cancel and reset the hardware.

5.2.1.e. Data Base Manager. The data base manager (DBM) provides access to the data base for the other processors. The DBM is itself a processor. It handles all the details of storing and retrieving data from the data base. Thus, the other processors do not require detailed knowledge of the data structures in the data base. They simply make a request to access or store a datum to the DBM, and let it handle the details.

The DBM can provide the communications organization (e.g., the telephone company) a direct mechanism for updating the data base through an independent hardware interface to the DBM. Feature and service changes to the data base can be made through the DBM. The DBM can also be used to monitor the data activities of the other processors. This can give the communications organization an instantaneous or long-term view of the switching system's data activities. It simplifies the switching system's design for the update and monitoring data usage by localizing them in the DBM.

5.2.2. Operating System

The operating system (OS) provides continuity and control for the switching system. It coordinates the activities of the processor and the exchange of communications between processors. The operating system can also be used to monitor the traffic and measure the capacity level of the switching machine.

The operating system makes it possible for the switching software to be ignorant of its host environment. As depicted in Fig. 17, the operating system buffers the application subsystems of the switching software from the details of the bare processor. The same switching software can therefore be used in a single processor or distributed processor environment. It does not need to be modified for the physical environment because the operating system provides the buffer.

Another objective of the operating system is to make it possible for the communications company to put its own programs into the switching system. This is becoming a more desirable feature for them. There is, however, a problem in allowing communications company programs to be closely tied to the call-processing programs. If the company programming is inefficient, it can severely degrade the call processing capacity of the switching machine.

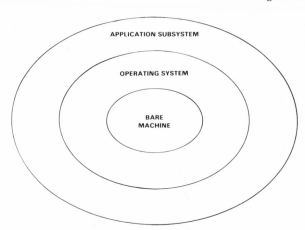

Fig. 17.   Operation system subsystem.

The operating system can be used both to link the company programs into the switching software and to monitor it. If the company programs are degrading service, a sufficiently intelligent operating system can be designed to automatically decouple them from the system.

5.2.3.   Benefits of the Model

The new model for switching system software provides an architecture that meets the objectives of an "ideal" model:

- Partitions the software into separate processors,
- Isolates hardware and data structure dependencies from feature programs,
- Is modular with well-defined interfaces to simply testing and feature packaging,
- Minimizes cross feature dependencies.

One of the major benefits of the new model architecture is that it reduces the complexity of the switching software modules. Prior switching system software was designed so all originating features knew about all terminating features. Thus, the software module complexity is the product of the number of originating and terminating features as shown in Fig. 18. In the new model, however, a uniform language is used to reduce this complexity to a simple summation of the number of originating and terminating features. In the prior design, if a module for an originating feature wanted to release a trunk, it had to know what type of trunk it was and the specific details on how to release that specific trunk. In the new model, the uniform language allows the originating features to release a trunk without knowing what kind of trunk it has since this is handled by a terminating features module. By separating the logic of originating and terminating features and

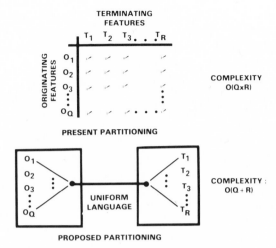

Fig. 18. Module complexity reduction.

using a uniform language, the module complexity can be significantly reduced.

This model also makes it possible to develop switching software that is applicable over a family of switching machines or processor types. The mechanism for this lies in the levels of abstraction between processors. At the least abstract end is the peripheral interface processor which directly interfaces with the hardware. The PI is dedicated to a specific switching machine. However, from the PI through the sign interpreter and task processor to the feature processor, call processing becomes more abstract. The FP does not look at calls as line-to-line or line-to-trunk, but rather local-to-local and local-to-distant. This abstraction makes it possible to use the same FP in any of a family of switching machines, and reduces the cost of many developments for feature software.

Another strength of the new model's architecture is its adaptability to either a single processor or distributed processor environment. Switching systems are moving toward distributed processing. It is only in this kind of environment where the speed and capacity of the switching system can be significantly enhanced to meet the demands that will be placed on switching systems in the future.

6. Conclusions

This chapter has presented central office switching system software: its origins, an example of a typical existing architecture and its operation, and a description of the criteria that must be considered by its software designer. The chapter has also described the benefits software engineering can have on enhancing both the quality of switching software and the productivity of those who develop it. Finally, this chapter has presented a model architecture for a distributed processing switching system. The purpose of this model is to illustrate the types of problems and possible solutions the switching system's software designer may encounter in the future.

The introduction of the stored program switching processor brought about the centralization of control in switching systems. Decentralized activities that were previously controlled by hardware could be performed by software which resulted in economic advantages to the communications companies and provided more sophisticated features to the customers they served. The trend toward switching systems using distributed processing will reverse this process of centralization of control. Software will play a major role in this and future developments in the evolution of switching system technology.

Questions

1. What advantages does stored program control provide to switching systems?
2. What is a generic program?
3. What is the relationship between the generic program and the office data base? How do they interact to process calls?
4. What are some of the primary considerations in designing switching software? (a) What are the telephone company's main considerations? (b) What are the subscriber's main considerations?
5. What role does processor speed, memory usage, and program design play in the implementation of switching software?
6. What are the functions of maintenance software in a switching system?
7. How are priority levels and interrupts used in call processing?
8. What are some of the limitations of earlier switching system software designs?
9. What are some of the key objectives of future designs for switching system software?
10. What are some of the beneficial aspects of software engineering concepts in developing switching software?
11. What are some of the objectives of an ideal switching system software architecture?

References

1. W. Keister, R. W. Ketchledge, and H. E. Vaughan, "No. 1 ESS: System Organization and Objectives," *Bell Syst. Tech. J.,* vol. 43, pp. 1831–1844, September 1964.
2. D. H. Carbaugh, G. G. Drew, H. Ghiron, and Mrs. E. S. Hoover, "No. 1 ESS Call Processing," *Bell Syst. Tech. J.,* vol. 43, pp. 2483–2531, September 1964.

3. N. L. Marselos and R. J. Grellner, "A Structured Approach to Software Development," *West. Electr. Eng.,* vol XX(4), pp. 42–50, October 1976.

4. F. T. Baker, "System Quality through Structured Programming," *Fall Joint Computer Conf.,* pp. 339–343, December 1972.

5. F. T. Baker, "Chief Programmer Team Management of Production Programming," *IBM Syst. J.,* vol. 11(1), pp. 56–73, 1972.

6. E. A. Nelson, "Management Handbook for the Estimation of Computer Programming Costs," *System Development Corp. report No. TM-3225,* pp. 66–67.

5

Time-Division Networks

Matthew F. Slana

1. Introduction

Previous chapters have dealt with general topics related to switching, such as circuit switching networks, traffic theory, and control, which are independent of whether the switch is analog or digital. As the topics were discussed, the areas where these technologies were unique to digital switching were highlighted.

This chapter introduces the concept of time-division networks, and illustrates how this concept forms the basis for digital switching, first by discussing time-divided analog networks, and then advancing to time-divided digital networks. The time-divided network becomes the switching center network of a switching system as described in Chapter 1 of this volume. The discussion here centers around the techniques and components associated with those networks generally characterized as circuit switches. Later chapters will discuss the differences between circuit switching and packet switching, the analog and digital interface to digital networks, and digital switching architectures.

2. Sampling and Modulation

The basis for all time-division switching resides in a method where the signal to be switched is conditioned and sent through the time-division network. The conditioning process which performs this function includes

Matthew F. Slana • Bell Laboratories, Room 1100, Warrenville Road, Naperville, Illinois 60566.

sampling and modulation. Sampling is a process which repetitively investigates the amplitude of the incoming signal at fixed instants of time. Modulation forms a representation of the amplitude of the signal at each of these investigation times. Properly conditioned signals are sent to the time-division network. Samples are taken at a fixed rate, and the system is synchronized to this rate.

The process by which these "samples" are obtained is based on the *sampling theorem.*[1] The sampling theorem, originally developed by C. Shannon, requires that the signal to be sampled be band-limited (i.e., has a specified maximum frequency component) and contain a finite energy spectrum in the band. Under these conditions, the sampling theorem can be stated as follows:

> If a band-limited signal of finite energy is sampled at a frequency twice as high as the maximum frequency component in the signal, all the informational content of the signal is available in the samples and may be completely recovered from the knowledge of the samples.

The sampling rate of $2f$ samples per second, for a maximum signal frequency of f Hz, is often called the *Nyquist rate*, or Shannon sampling rate.

The sampling theorem provides the basis for conversion between discrete analog signals and sampled (analog or digital) signals, which is the foundation for digital transmission and switching systems.

In practical applications, a sampling rate slightly higher than the Nyquist rate is normally used, to allow for band-limiting with practical filters.

The sampling theorem thus allows transmittal of the complete information content of a band-limited signal by using samples taken at a uniform rate at or above the Nyquist rate. Since these samples may be converted through the process of modulation into analog or digital pulses and these pulses can be transmitted using only a small portion of the available time on a transmission channel, the remainder of the channel can be used for other independent signals on a time-shared basis thus providing the process of time-division multiplexing.

A practical example of this occurs in the telephone network, where the voice frequency spectrum is limited by filters to a maximum upper frequency of 3400 Hz. Typical pulse amplitude modulation (PAM) or pulse code modulation (PCM) systems sample the filtered analog signal at an 8-kHz rate (i.e., once every 125 μsec). A PAM system will then transmit or switch these amplitude samples directly, using a pulse of constant width whose height is proportional to the analog information. A PCM system will normally encode the sample into an 8-bit *code word* which represents a discrete amplitude value approximating the signal sample and then transmits or switches the eight bits. The eight bits are sampled at an 8-kHz rate and thus create a 64-kbit/sec digital channel. PCM is described in more detail in Chapter 7.

3. The Time-Division Switching Concept

Conceptually, a time-division network can be represented in the form shown in Fig. 1. The customer (subscriber) lines are represented on the left side by three lines, A, B, and C. The lines terminate on a *line function module* (LFM) which, for customer loops in the telephony network, provides the *BORSHT* (*b*attery, *o*vervoltage, *r*inging, *s*ignaling, *h*ybrid, and *t*esting) functions, as described in Chapter 7.

In those cases where the incoming line is not a customer loop, the line function module will provide other appropriate functions. An example would be the Bell System's digital No. 4 ESS, where analog trunks are connected to the office and the line function module provides appropriate trunk termination functions including analog-to-digital conversion. In all cases, the line function module "conditions" the incoming signal to the form appropriate for the time-divided network.

The signals are then switched through *time-division gates* onto a *time-division bus*. The control of the appropriate connections is maintained via a *time-division gate memory*, which contains the information as to which lines are to be connected and when. A highly stable and accurate clock (not shown) reads words from the memory at a fixed rate (e.g., once every

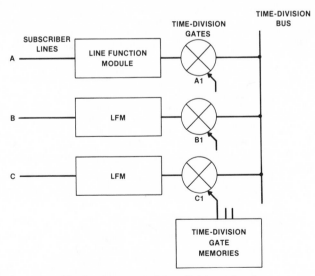

Fig. 1.   A conceptual time-division network.

125 μsec per connection). Memory words provide the information to "close" the appropriate time-division gates, allowing the sampled information to pass from one LFM to the other. If it is desired to have subscriber A connect to subscriber C, a word in the memory must contain the information required to close the gates connected between subscriber A and the bus and between subscriber C and the bus, at the appropriate time.

This word would be "read" from the memory once every 125 μsec (the "frame" time), and the gates would be closed for the amount of time required to transmit the information (the "time slot"). The ratio of the frame time to the time slot time gives a measure of the maximum number of conversations which the time-division bus is capable of simultaneously carrying. For example, if 5 μsec is required to transmit the samples between LFMs, the time-division bus with a 125-μsec frame time is capable of handling 25 simultaneous conversations. Since the sampling interval is fixed at 125 μsec, the only variable which can be modified to yield more capacity for the bus is the time-slot period. The time-slot period is limited by a combination of gate speed, memory speed, and the transmission properties of the bus.

However, another method is available to increase the network conversation capacity. If a number of time-division buses are supplied and the time-division gates are modified to provide access to all buses, the conversation capacity of the system can be increased as a function of the number of buses provided to a maximum determined by the time-division gate complexity. This provides a "spatial" addition to the time-division network, as shown in Fig. 2. The time-division memory, often called the *time-slot*

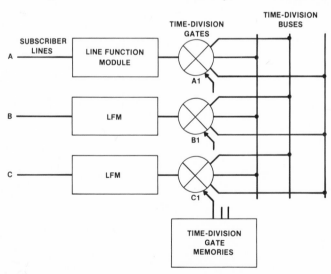

Fig. 2. A conceptual time-division network showing additional time-division buses.

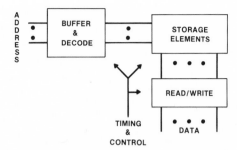

Fig. 3.   Functional components of a time-division memory.

memory, is a critical component in the network. As shown in Fig. 3, the time-slot memory is normally a random access memory consisting of storage elements, data read/write circuitry, and address buffer and decode circuitry. The storage elements contain the connect information that exists for calls in progress at a particular instant of time. Each word must be read once each frame in order to provide the connect information for a particular call. The connect information in the storage elements is changed only when a conversation is established or removed. In other words, if a call lasts for 3 min, connect information for the call will remain in memory for 3 min, and will be accessed once every 125 μsec to set up the path. A new call or termination of an existing call will cause the control to write a new word in a location.

Now, how does this memory control the switch? It is easiest to visualize this by looking at a system with six customer lines plus a single time-division bus as shown in Fig. 4. A time-division memory is shown

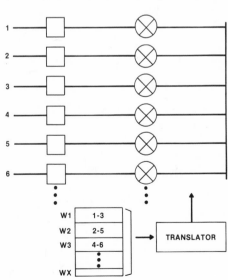

Fig. 4.   Example of the control process for a time-division switch.

connected to a translator which translates the path data from the memory and enables the appropriate time-division gates at the correct times. This memory will be read for each time slot. In order to analyze the operation, three particular words ($W1$, $W2$, $W3$) will be studied. In the first time slot, word $W1$ is read. Word $W1$ contains data to connect customers 1 and 3 together. The translator takes that word and enables the time-division gates which are associated with lines 1 and 3 and allows the information from line 1 to pass to line 3, and from line 3 to pass back to line 1. At this point, these gates are shown conceptually as two-way gates. In some systems, in particular digital switching systems, two conversation paths are required, consisting of a forward and a reverse path, each handling transmission in only one direction.

Thus in time slot 1, which might be 1 μsec wide, the two gates are enabled, and information is passed back and forth between customers 1 and 3. In the next time slot, 1 μsec later, word $W2$ is read indicating that customers 2 and 5 are to be connected together. Customer 2 and customer 5 are connected by virtue of the fact that their gates are enabled, and the information is transmitted between the two customers. Notice that this time-division bus contains information from a number of different conversations. However, the conversations are all time separated, with no two conversations existing on this bus at exactly the same instant of time. This is one of the basic concepts of time-division switching. This bus can be a digital bus or an analog bus; both types of network are described in the following sections.

Continuing with the previous call progress, customers 4 and 6 could be connected together in time slot 3. In the remaining time slots of the frame, other customer connections could also be established. Since the control allows connection of any customer to any other customer, control information may be changed or rearranged without affecting conversations and a very high usage of the bus can occur which allows for very efficient network utilization.

Different types of time division networks exist. These include lossless analog, lossy analog, and digital. The first two will be briefly described in the following sections, then digital time division networks will be covered.

4.   Lossless Analog Time-Division Switching

As mentioned in the previous section, a variety of time-division systems are feasible. The first of the systems to be described in this chapter provides "lossless analog" time-division switching. "Lossless analog" time-division switching transmits the analog samples of the signals from one customer to another with essentially no loss and without the use of gain elements. This type of system is used in the Bell System's 101 ESS Switch Units[2] to provide the switching center network for a family of private branch exchange (PBX) switching systems. The principle by which the signals are interchanged is referred to as *resonant transfer*.[3]

In order to describe the concept of resonant transfer and how it provides a lossless analog time-division switching capability, consider a call between two customers A and B. The line function module contains a low-pass filter which band-limits the signal to 3.4 kHz as discussed. The bus side of the low-pass filters can be represented as a fairly large capacitor. The voltage across this capacitor represents the amplitude of the voice signal as a function of time. Two customers are connected by a resonant equivalent circuit as shown in Fig. 5. Capacitor voltages are $V_{CA}(t)$ for customer A, and $V_{CB}(t)$ for customer B. The connection between the two capacitors is represented by a lossless bidirectional analog gate, capable of transmitting signals in either direction equally well, a controlled inductance, and the time-division bus. The resonant transfer process begins by closing the switches associated with customer A and customer B simultaneously, allowing the charge which is on capacitor A to transfer to capacitor B and the charge from capacitor B to transfer to capacitor A. Since the capacitor charge is directly proportional to the voltage ($Q = CV$), and the voltage represents the voice signal, the charge is also directly proportional to the amplitude of the voice signal of each customer. If all the charge is transferred from one capacitor to the other a lossless transfer of information has taken place.

An analysis of the charge transfer will indicate what is occurring and the criteria which limit the expansion of the system. Begin by considering what happens to the voltages on capacitor A and capacitor B when the switches close. If capacitor A has a voltage $V_{CA}(t)$ and capacitor B has a voltage $V_{CB}(t)$ at the time that these two switches are closed, an essentially constant amplitude oscillation will occur, as shown in Fig. 6, since the circuit is a simple LC circuit. This oscillation would continue indefinitely in

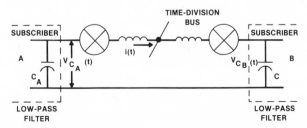

Fig. 5. Schematic of subscriber-to-subscriber circuitry involved in a lossless analog time-division connection.

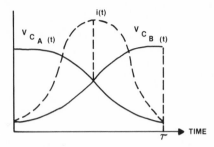

Fig. 6. Voltage waveforms at capacitors A and B and current through the connection of Fig. 5.

a lossless circuit. Now if the gates are opened at the precise instant of time, τ, at which all the charge has transferred from customer A to customer B, then we have succeeded in transferring all the information from customer A to customer B, and, by superposition, whatever information was on customer B's line, transfers back into customer A's line. Since charge can be neither created nor destroyed, all the charge originally on the capacitors must remain in the LC circuit (assuming that τ is short compared to the rate at which the voice signal on the capacitors can change).

This is the principle of resonant transfer. The resonance property of the circuit is used to provide a complete transfer of information from one side to the other. This requires precise control of the network capacitance and inductance, as well as timing.

An equivalent circuit analysis for the current flow through the gates, as also shown in Fig. 6, shows $\sin^2 \omega t$ shape. When the switches are first closed no current can instantaneously flow because of the inductances present in the circuit. As the current builds up, it reaches a maximum and then decreases with a $\frac{1}{2}\tau$ peak at the maximum slope point of the voltage. In order to maximize the number of circuits in a time-division system, the designer must provide as many time slots as possible within the 125-μsec sampling intervals. If more time slots can be provided, more customers can be connected together.

If 32 time slots are to be provided, each time slot will occupy 3.9 μsec. This is the maximum time which can be used for the transfer of information. Doubling the time slots reduces transfer time by a factor of 2. For a resonant transfer lossless analog time-division system, the maximum number of channels which can be implemented with any reliability is between 24 and 32 time slots. This requires a gate sampling period in the range of 4 to 5 μsec. A number of factors contribute to limit capacity. One of the major limitations is the turn-on and turn-off time of the time-division gate. The shorter the time slot, the faster the gate must switch. Since the area under the current waveform represents the charge transferred, the peak current will increase as the gating period decreases. This requires that the semiconductor devices used for the sampling gate operate faster, and at the same time requires that they handle higher current levels. These requirements lead to conflicting device requirements, since the faster operating speed is generally obtained by reducing device size, while higher current-carrying capacity is obtained by increasing the device size.

Another major limitation in the number of possible time slots lies in the control of the LC time constant of the circuit, and its relationship to the gate interval, τ. If all components are not identical or if τ is slightly off, then either some charge will not be transferred, or some charge will "reflect back" to the originator. This will appear as a loss of amplitude to the recipient. In addition, the "real world" time-division bus will have some capacitance associated with it. If all components and timing are not chosen correctly, a small residual charge may appear on the bus capacitance. This charge, related to the amplitude of the signal for that time slot, will remain for the next time slot and will be transferred into the capacitors of the next conversation path. This process will cause crosstalk. Stray bus capacitances must be reduced to minimize crosstalk. One method used to reduce crosstalk is to connect another time-division gate between the time-division bus and ground, while providing a guard interval between each transmission time slot to short the bus to ground, discharging the stray charge on the bus. Another method sometimes employed is to provide a split bus system, doubling the number of buses and increasing the time slot interval to provide a system with two interconnections in one time slot. This technique is used in the 2A switch unit of the Bell System's 101 ESS.[2]

In the 2A switch unit, 30 talking time slots and five data time slots are provided in the frame for switch half zero, and 30 talking time slots plus four data time slots in the frame for switch half one. With the duration of each time slot set at 2.464 μsec, the sampling rates are 11.9 and 11.6 kHz, respectively, which lead to a periodic motion of the time slots in one frame relative to the other. Crosstalk between switch halves thus appears as unintelligible noise. With tone sources, digit receiving trunks, and test lines excluded, this system has a total busy hour traffic capacity, at 70% time slot occupancy, of 151,000 call seconds, and can be arranged to handle any combination of lines and trunks totaling 420.

In most systems designed to date, an upper limit of 24 to 32 time slots per bus appears to represent a practical limit for this switching technique.

5. Lossy Analog Time-Division Switching

If loss is allowed to occur in a controlled manner, the device limitations mentioned previously can be reduced. Then the number of time slots can be increased without requiring increased current-carrying capacity. The losses must be compensated for by gain, but, with appropriate amplifiers, the system is now only required to switch an analog time-division representation of the signal without switching the full energy content of the signal. This method is commonly referred to as *lossy analog time division*.

The limitation of this technique arises from the active gain requirement since amplifiers are unidirectional devices. Some bidirectional active devices such as negative impedance converters do exist, but their gain is generally difficult to control. Certainly the gain control problem is compounded in something like a time-division system requiring fast response.

A representative block diagram of a lossy analog system is shown in Fig. 7. As shown, the signal comes from customer A's low-pass filter through an analog hybrid which splits the bidirectional signal into incoming and outgoing unidirectional signals. The incoming signal next passes through a buffer with a controlled amount of loss, and through a sampling gate. Two buses, send and receive, are connected by an isolation amplifier which buffers the signal on the send bus and passes the signal to the receive bus. At this point the customer B time-division gate switches the analog sample to a sample and hold (S&H) circuit. The S&H circuit accepts this analog sample, and holds this voltage until the next input sample arrives. Thus the input signal energy is restored. The signal then passes through the analog hybrid in the outgoing direction to customer B's low-pass filter. In a similar manner, signal energy from customer B is passed through the switch to customer A, providing for a bidirectional transfer of information. However, the system in Fig. 7 now requires two time slots in the send and receive buses to handle the bidirectional signals resulting from unidirectional gain elements. Therefore, a significant portion of the potential increase in capacity may be lost.

This describes the principle of lossy analog time-division switching. Figure 8 shows typical waveforms at various nodes of this system. At node a, the analog input signal is shown as it might exist in a conversation. At node b, the signal is shown sampled into fairly wide samples. In an actual case, the samples, on the scale shown, would appear as impulses, separated by wide spaces. A number of samples from other conversations would be

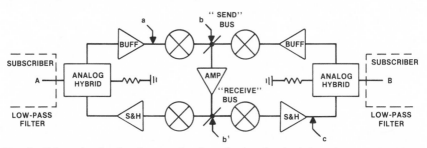

Fig. 7. Schematic of subscriber-to-subscriber circuitry involved in a lossy analog time-division connection.

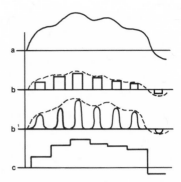

Fig. 8.   Voltage waveform in circuit of Fig. 7.

interleaved. The samples must, of course, be 125 μsec apart if 8-kHz sampling is maintained.

The samples then pass through the amplifier from node b to node b' ("send" bus to "receive" bus). Since the amplifier has a finite frequency characteristic, or slew rate, the "sharp" pulses at b are slightly degraded to a more Gaussian form at b', although the linear characteristics at the peak are maintained. These pulses are then sent to the S&H, which amplifies and "stretches" them into a continuous discrete signal. The pulses then pass through the hybrid to the low-pass filter, where the discrete signal is smoothed into an accurate representation of the input signal.

These techniques, although in slightly different form, have been used in commercial switching systems for Private Branch Exchanges. In particular, the Bell System's DIMENSION® PBX uses a variant of this technique which requires only one slot per conversation.

6.   Digital Encoding and Multiplexing

In the systems discussed to this point, the signals being switched were analog modulated samples of the inputs. However, the particular requirements for switching analog signals lead to difficulties in the design and capability of these systems. If analog performance requirements within the switch fabric could be alleviated or diverted to other system modules, then appreciable advances in technology could be applied. In particular, if the analog signals are converted to digital and standard digital techniques are used to switch the signals, then all the advances currently being applied to digital devices, including large-scale integration, may be utilized in digital switching networks.

The first portion of the problem then involves the task of converting the analog signals into a digital form. As mentioned previously, the analog signals must be sampled and the analog samples then converted into digitally coded samples. A wide variety of possible coding methods are available to implement this digital coding. Pulse-code modulation (PCM), using the Nyquist sampling criterion, is an important form as discussed in Chapter 9. Other methods, such as delta modulation, are also possible. The PCM technique is described in detail in Chapter 7. It is sufficient to recognize that an 8-bit PCM "code" is created for each analog sample, and the code words are sent at the sampling rate. This is basically the same principle used in PCM channel banks which take analog input signals and convert them into a 24-channel PCM format as in the Bell System T1 system.[4]

The analog–digital conversion process is performed at the input to any digital system. This input could be at any point, from the line or trunk interface to the network, to a remote unit, pair gain system, or the telephone itself. The signals might be in digital format directly as might occur when a terminal talks to a computer, or for computer-to-computer communication. These bits are then switched like PCM in 8-bit bytes.

If the cost is low enough, the PCM conversion can be performed on a per-line basis (one coder–decoder for each line). Many current systems use a coder shared over a number of lines by time-sharing one coder over 12 or 24 lines, or by concentrating the analog terminations ahead of a group of coders. The resulting digital signal is multiplexed along with other signals and used by the switching system to connect input and output terminations.

A typical channel bank frame format is shown in Fig. 9. This is the standard format used by the Bell System in their T1 carrier systems and Digital Data System.[5] In some systems, the least-significant bit is used every sixth frame for channel-associated signaling (*A–B* signaling). The switching network will, however, switch this as a full 8-bit byte. The 193-bit frame is repeated every 125 μsec, and is divided into 24 8-bit channels in a byte format, plus one additional bit designated as the *F*-bit, which is used

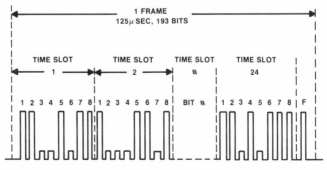

Fig. 9.   Typical PCM frame format.

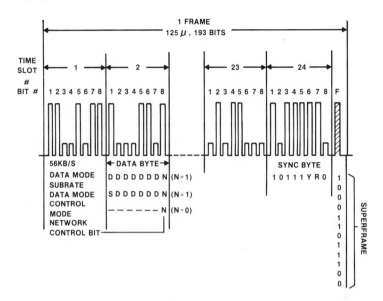

Fig. 10.   Frame format for a T1DM data multiplexer.

for framing identification (see Chapter 8 in this volume). Each 8-bit byte, repeated every 125 μsec, represents a 64-kbit/sec channel and each bit carries 8 kbit/sec of information. If a T1WB4 data-voice multiplexer[5] is used, the 24 channels may carry data or digitized voice. If a T1 data multiplexer (T1DM)[5] is used for a second-stage multiplexer, all the channels except the 24th are data channels.

The 24th channel for the T1DM is used to provide increased protection against loss of synchronization. To accomplish this, six bits of the 24th channel are used in conjunction with the framing bit for synchronization detection. This is shown in Fig. 10, where the fixed pattern of the six bits, plus the repeating pattern of the framing bit over a 12 frame "super-frame," are shown. The bits marked as Y and R are used internally within the T1DM for housekeeping purposes.

In addition, as mentioned previously, the 64-kbit/sec channels may be used for data channels as shown. Two formats exist for the data channel,[5] as shown in Fig. 10. If the channels are used as 56-kbit/sec channels, 7 of the 8 bits (7/8 × 64 kbit/sec = 56 kbit/sec) would carry the data, with the eighth bit always a 1 to signify the data mode (if voice was being carried by this channel, the eighth bit would average half zeros and half ones). If the channel is used for a multiplexed data channel, six of the channel bits are used to carry the data, thus providing a 48-kbit/sec channel capable of carrying five 9.6-kbit/sec multiplexed channels, ten 4.8-kbit/sec multiplexed channels, or twenty 2.4 kbit/sec channels. The additional bit *s* of the eight (6-data bits, one data mode bit) is used as a subrate control bit, with a fixed pattern which allows the terminal equipment to determine which of the 5, 10, or 20 subrate channels the current 48-kbit/sec channel byte contains. This knowledge is required if a subrate switch is being designed.

For the time-divided networks being considered, it is sufficient to recognize that the digital switch will switch bytes of information in a specified format as required. In most cases digital switches operate with PCM encoded voice, as described in Fig. 9.

7. Time-Division Switching

Having laid the groundwork, we can now describe the two major techniques involved in implementing time-division switching. These techniques are time-slot interchanging, and time-shared space division switching. Although a network can conceptually be built using either of these techniques alone, application of both techniques is used to implement practical networks. These techniques will be individually described and then a network combining the two techniques will be presented.

7.1. Time-Slot Interchanging

Incoming data occur during time slots in a frame format. To establish a communications channel, information in time slots must be switched from their incoming appearance on the network to the outgoing time slot which represents the termination of the call. Each channel on a switch has a specified time slot in a particular data stream, and the task for the switching network is to move a time slot from one data stream to a time slot in another data stream. The process of interchanging time slots from one stream to another is referred to as *time-slot interchanging*.

The diagram of Fig. 11 describes the process of time-slot interchanging. The incoming time slots are placed in a scratch pad or buffer memory for temporary storage. As shown, the incoming time slots are consecutively numbered from 1 through X in the frame representing the incoming stream. These time slots are stored in the buffer memory's locations 1 through X. Data from time slot 1 will always reside in word 1, time slot 2 in word 2, etc. Of course, the data will be overwritten with new data once per frame. The time-slot interchange function provides for the moving of data from any time slot in the incoming stream, say time slot 7, to any chosen time slot in the output stream, say time slot 2. This allows the information coming from the subscriber represented by incoming time slot 7 to go to the subscriber represented by outgoing time slot 2. As shown in the example,

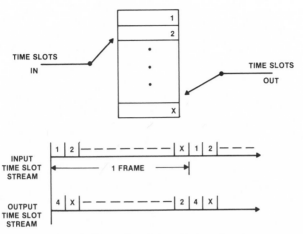

Fig. 11.   Schematic illustration of time-slot interchanging process.

the first time slot of the outgoing stream contains the information from incoming time slot 4, the second from time slot X, etc. The purpose of the buffer should now be readily apparent—the information must be stored for a period of time which may range from one time slot to as many as $X - 1$ times slots, depending on the particular relationship between input and output which exists at any time.

For a two-way conversation to occur, another channel through the network is required to complete a two-way path. Let us assume that two streams of data are coming in, and the network is to switch a customer who appears in time slot 2 on the incoming line to a customer who appears in time slot 9 on the outgoing line. In that case, the information must be moved from time slot 2 of the incoming line to time slot 9 of the outgoing line, and the same function must also occur for transmission in the opposite direction, i.e., time slot 9 to time slot 2.

In this example, the memory is categorized for control purposes as "sequential-write–random-read" or functionally can be thought of as "output time-slot interchanging," as shown in Fig. 12.

Output time-slot interchanging is accomplished by providing a memory which is controlled by a time slot counter such that the input time slot sequences of 1, 2, 3, 4, 5, to X, are put into the appropriate words of memory. The controller places the data byte of time slot 1 into word 1 of the memory, time slot 2 into word 2, and so on. This is a direct sequential write into the memory. The output time-slot contents are controlled from another memory, the time-slot memory. The time-slot memory contains the control information that causes interchanging of the X time slots. Control information is loaded from the call-processing software. In the figure, control is provided by the time-slot memory, a translator for the output data, a

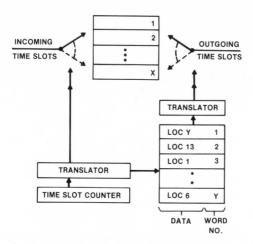

Fig. 12.   Output control of the time-slot interchanging process.

time-slot counter which is synchronized with incoming and outgoing data streams, and a translator for the time-slot counter. The counter counts 1 when the incoming and outgoing time slots are 1, etc. The counter translator translates this count of 1 into the address for word 1 of both the buffer memory and the time-slot memory. Thus, the translator causes the data in the first incoming time slot to be written into word 1, the second time slot into 2, third time slot into 3, and so on. The time-slot count also translates into the time-slot memory so that in time slot 1, the translator reads out the data stored in word 1, in time slot 2 the data stored in word 2, and so forth. However, the data from the time-slot memory address the cells of memory which contain the data to be placed in the outgoing time slot. As shown in the example, the data in word y of the buffer memory would be placed in outgoing time slot 1, word 13 in time slot 2, word 1 in time slot 3, etc., thus effecting the time-slot interchange.

Control may also be reversed, leading to a "random-write–sequential-read" algorithm, or "input time-slot interchanging," as shown in Fig. 13.

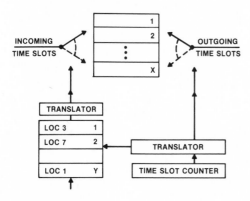

Fig. 13.   Input control of the time-slot interchanging process.

The control information shown in the time-slot memory will allow the same time-slot interchanging to take place as the algorithm previously discussed in Fig. 12. In this case, incoming time slot 1 would be placed in word 3 of the buffer memory, and read out in time slot 3, thus allowing subscriber 1's data to be switched to subscriber 3 in both systems.

An even more sophisticated control system might allow a "random-read–random-write" algorithm to be implemented if separate time-slot memories are provided. This allows the input time slots to be written randomly in the buffer memory, while the output time slots are randomly read from the buffer memory. The added hardware complexity provides little additional in the way of flexibility.

7.2. Time-Shared Space-Division Switching

The interchanging of time slots between incoming and outgoing time-slot streams as described previously provides a full switching function for all time slots. If a network is to handle M customers with a single time-slot interchange stage, an M-word memory, operating at the appropriate speed, would be required.

For small switches this implementation could serve the system. For instance, a 128 time-slot system would require a memory capable of being written and read once every 976 nsec. A 128 time-slot system, sampled at an 8-kHz rate requires 976 nsec per time slot (125 μsec/128). However, as larger systems are proposed, the memory and access speeds required go beyond the component technology available. For instance, a 16,384 time-slot system would require the capability of reading *and* writing the memory on a semirandom basis every 76.3 nsec (125 μsec/16,384).

In order to increase the usefulness of the system, a method of increasing the capacity using standard components is required. One method of achieving this objective is to connect groups of time-slot interchangers together by a set of logic gates which allow the switching of time slots in the time-slot streams in a pattern determined by the required network connectivity. This technique can be referred to as time-shared space-division switching, using a space array. The array is similar to a relay contact arrangement except that the rearrangement of the array every time slot requires high-speed logic gates. The array consists of a number of input horizontals and a number of output verticals, with a logic gate at every crosspoint as shown in Fig. 14. In a given time slot the appropriate connection is made to enable the chosen logic gate and information passes from the input horizontal to the output vertical. For instance, one time slot on a serial input stream containing K different PCM words can be switched onto the chosen vertical by enabling the appropriate gate. The other $m - 1$ horizontals can have the same time slot in each of their streams switched into

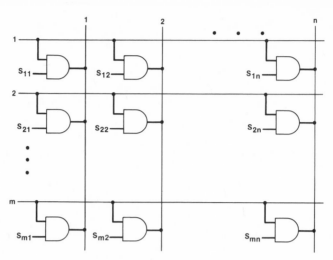

Fig. 14.   Time-division network space array.

other verticals by enabling other gates. In the next time slot, a completely different path configuration could occur, again allowing time slots from the horizontals to be switched to chosen verticals.

Note that the occurrences of time slots are identical on horizontal and vertical. Thus no switching of time slots occurs in the array. A control memory will contain information to enable gates at the desired time slot. As shown, a system could have m inputs and n outputs, where m or n might be equal or unequal depending on whether the system is designed to produce a concentration, distribution, or expansion function. Thus, the space network might be a multistage array. If it is desired to send a signal from input 1 to output 2, the gate at the intersection would be activated by putting an enable signal on S_{12} during the desired time slot. The information bits would then pass through the logic gate onto the vertical. In the same time slot an enable signal on S_{m1} would allow the signal on the mth horizontal to transmit to vertical 1. Thus, as many simultaneous connections as the smallest of m or n could be carried through this array simultaneously during one time slot. If a time-slot interchanger is placed on each input line, and the interchanger system handles 128 time slots, a space array of ten inputs and ten outputs can then serve 1280 different time slots.

Control of the space array, shown in Fig. 15, occurs in basically the same way as control of the time-slot interchanger. The system controller (processor) provides two types of connect information to the control memory: gate data and control address. The address applied to the memory is the count of the time-slot counter. The contents at that address is a word of memory which enables the desired gates. The read register holds the gate

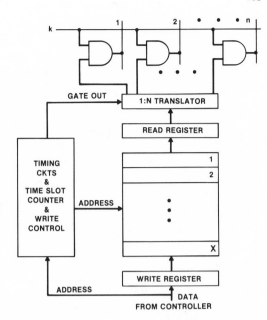

Fig. 15. Space-array control
architecture.

control information during a time slot and a translator enables the gate to be switched.

To change the path during a given time slot, the controller provides information relating to a new or terminating call. The controller places gate data into a write register and provides the time slot address information to the write control to signify where the data are to be stored. This new information will be retained unchanged for the duration of the call, or until removed or changed by the controller.

In a philosophical sense, a time-shared space-division array can be viewed as a set of parallel layers, as shown in Fig. 16. The array, shown as a 4×4 matrix, appears X times in parallel at the input and output, where X represents the number of time slots in a given horizontal. If each time slot is represented as a layer, then the connectivity represented in the first time slot could be shown as a configuration of closed gates represented by the dots in the topmost layer, or Array 1. The figure shows four connections during the first time slot. A totally different interconnection pattern between the four inputs and four outputs could take place in the second time slot, and so on through the Xth time slot, as represented by the bottom layer, Array X. In the next frame, the pattern repeats for each layer in the same sequence. The power of time-division switching begins to appear in this example, since X of these 4×4 arrays would be required to provide the same connectivity in a space-division array of relays or crossbar switches.

The time-shared space-division arrays can be configured to handle

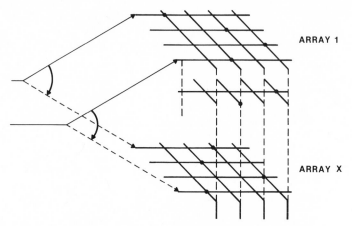

Fig. 16.   Equivalency of digital space arrays to analog space arrays.

serial or parallel transmission. Each method has its advantages and disadvantages, as discussed below.

In the case of serial transmission, shown in Fig. 17, the incoming data are represented by the bit patterns shown for two time slots on a typical line, k. Control signals are applied to the gates connecting the input line to output lines 1 through n. Figure 17 shows the input line connected to output line 1 in the first time slot (S_{k1} enabled in TS1), and to output line n in the second time slot (S_{kn} enabled in TS2). The bits in TS1 are then switched to output line 1 in TS1, and output line n in TS2, as shown. Notice that the gates must be enabled for the full time-slot period and that the timing of the enable must be precise. Notice further that the gates must be capable of passing the high-speed bit rate of the serial stream.

If the array were constructed instead to handle parallel transmission, then 8-bit lines would now appear where one line appeared before, on both input and output. Eight gates would also be required for each single gate required before, as shown in Fig. 18. A single control lead per "crosspoint" is sufficient to enable the gates. As indicated, the input signals now appear as parallel words rather than serial. The two time slots of data shown entering the array on the left represent the same data patterns of the previous serial example, with the most significant bit of each sample appearing

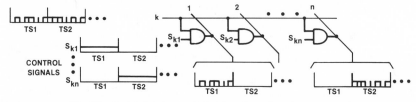

Fig. 17.   Serial data transmission in a time-shared space array.

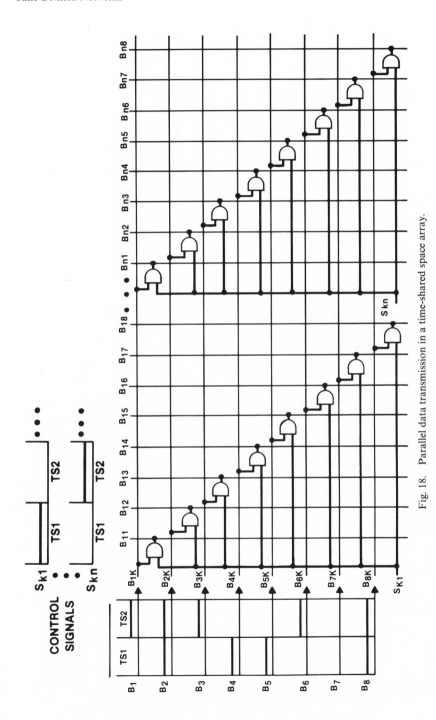

Fig. 18. Parallel data transmission in a time-shared space array.

on line S1. The same enable signal would cause the eight bits in TS1 on input leads B_{1k} through B_{8k} to appear on output leads B_{11} through B_{18}, and the eight bits in TS2 on the input leads to appear on output leads B_{n1} through B_{n8}.

Some significant differences between serial and parallel operation can be studied. The parallel network requires eight lines for every line of a serial network and eight gates for every gate of the serial network. This substantially increases the wiring complexity and, even if the gates are cheap compared to wiring, parallel operation leads to higher cost. The advantage of the parallel system is a speed improvement of up to 8 times. A tradeoff thus occurs between the complexity of wiring and the number of gates versus the speed or transmission requirements. If the design requires an extremely high-capacity network, the choice could be made to develop a parallel network, especially if it is not a very large one. If a very large parallel network is desired at nominal speeds, the system may become limited by the wire buildup on circuit boards and equipment frames.

Various tradeoffs between serial and parallel operation can be made. In a serial network, gates have to be faster for the same performance, but increased wiring of the parallel system might not give an 8:1 speed improvement. One of the advantages of a serial transmission and switching system lies in the effect of failures. In a parallel system, if one gate fails, the system loses one bit of the information word, and parity error detection is required, which adds an extra bit to be switched. If one gate is lost in a serial system, the full time-slot sample is lost. The latter case may be more easily detectable, and may provide better fault isolation by rerouting calls.

7.3. Network Functions

As in analog space-division networks, the functions of concentration, distribution, and expansion can be constructed in time-division networks from the components discussed in the previous two sections. The general network functions are shown in Fig. 19. Concentration is defined as a net-

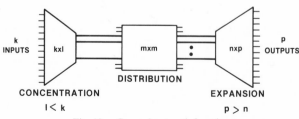

Fig. 19.   General network functions.

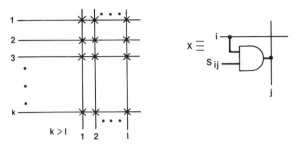

Fig. 20. Schematic of a space-array concentration module.

work function with k inputs and l outputs where l is less than k. A distribution function has the same number of inputs (m) and outputs (m), while an expansion function will have n inputs and p outputs, where p is greater than n. The figure pictures a network containing one or more concentrators on the input, distribution in the center of the network, and one or more expansion functions on the output. This is a common form although networks can also be constructed with expansion on the input, distribution in the middle, and concentration on the output. This latter architecture generally yields a lower blocking probability network at increased cost for a given number of terminations. The individual network functions will be implemented in both time-slot interchange and time-shared space-division forms in the following discussion.

Considering the concentration module first, the network function must be capable of making a connection between a number of input lines or time slots, k, to a number of output lines or time slots, l, where k is greater than l ($k > l$). Only the lesser of the two, l in this case, can be accommodated at any time through the network. Blockage will occur if the l plus first connection is attempted.

A space-division concentrator is shown in Fig. 20. There are k input lines (each handling a number of time slots T) and l output lines (each also handling a number of slots T). The array is capable of handling T time slots and a complete reconfiguration of the network occurs at each of the T time slots, as discussed previously in Section 7.2.

A time-division concentrator performing the same concentration function is shown in simplified form in Fig. 21, which shows a time-slot interchanger of the form discussed in Section 7.1. In this case, a data stream containing k incoming time slots is sequentially stored in the buffer memory. The output channel, however, contains only l time slots, where l is less than k. Thus a concentration function is realized. Call data to be placed in the outgoing time slots are contained in the I-word time-slot memory, as illustrated. For the example shown, data from incoming time slot i are placed in output time slot 1, j in 2, etc. Write control on the input with

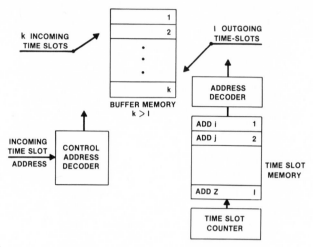

Fig. 21. Schematic of a time-slot interchanger concentrator module.

sequential read control of the output (random-in–sequential-out) could also be used as discussed previously.

The distribution module provides switching for a number of input lines or time slots to an equal number of output lines or time slots. Full access from any input line or time slot to any output line or time slot is provided.

A space distribution function, shown in Fig. 22, contains m input lines and m output lines which are connected by an $m \times m$ array of logic gates. Reconfiguration of the network occurs for each time slot. Thus, a total of mT connections can be made through the space module shown.

A time distribution function is shown in Fig. 23. In this case, there are m incoming time slots and m outgoing time slots. In the figure, a complete time-slot interchanger is shown in the sense that the incoming time slots can be put in any location in the buffer memory under control of an input time-slot memory. The output can also be randomly read by virtue of the

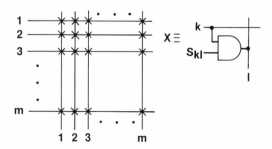

Fig. 22. Schematic of a space-array distribution module.

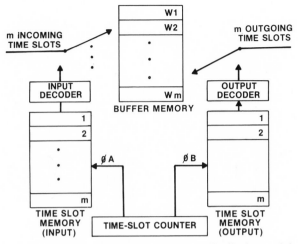

Fig. 23.   Schematic of a time-slot interchange distribution module.

equipped output time-slot memory. The added complexity provided by the double time-slot memories provides little, if any, performance advantage for the added cost, however.

The expansion module in a network is required to expand from a set of n input lines or time slots to a set of p output lines or time slots, where p is greater than n $(p > n)$. A space expansion function, shown in Fig. 24, and a time expansion function, shown in Fig. 25, can be easily visualized when related to the previous discussions of the concentration function. In the space expansion module, n inputs, each containing T time slots, are switched to p outputs, each containing T time slots, and the network is reconfigured each time slot. A maximum of nT connections can be accommodated. The time-division expansion module consists of a buffer memory of p words, with n incoming time slots placed in n of the p words $(p > k)$, and p outgoing time slots being read out.

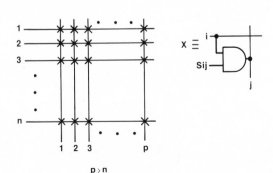

Fig. 24.   Schematic of a space-
array expansion module.

$p > n$

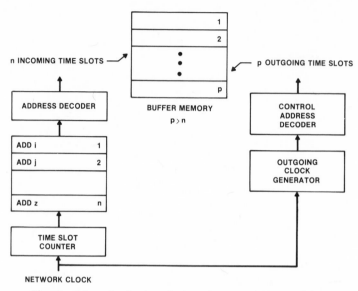

Fig. 25.   Schematic of a time-slot interchange expansion module.

Now that network functions have been described, the details of various network architectures can be analyzed. As discussed in this and previous sections, the networks may be constructed out of time-slot interchangers or time-shared space-division arrays, and can contain concentration, distribution, or expansion stages.

7.4.   Network Architectures

In constructing networks, the architecture may contain time-slot interchanging or time-shared space switching, or a combination of both. As a method of characterizing a network, a time-slot interchange stage will be classified as a T-stage, and a time-shared space stage as an S-stage.[6] Thus, networks can be the following:

    a. T only,
    b. S only,
    c. $T–S$,
    d. $S–T$,
    e. $T–S–T$,
    f. $S–T–S$,
    g. More complex combinations of S and T.

An analysis of each of these, with their characteristics and limitations, will be presented in the following paragraphs. In all cases, it will be assumed that a constant number of time slots, T, are to be switched.

7.4.1. T Only

In a time-only network, the only switching stage which exists is time switching. As shown in Fig. 26, a *T*-only network contains only a single stage time-slot interchanger. As indicated, this network would contain *T* incoming time slots and *T* outgoing time slots, and could switch *T* customers. The incoming time slots could be written sequentially and the outgoing time slots read randomly, or the incoming time slots could be written randomly and the outgoing time slots read sequentially, or both random writing and reading could be done for flexibility. However, due to the limitations of a system capable of switching only *T* customers, and the memory access time requirements, such a system would be limited to a rather small capacity application (although the system would be nonblocking).

7.4.2. S Only

A single-stage space system could be constructed, as shown in Fig. 27. The *S*-only stage cannot give full availability. The space-only network cannot complete a connection from time slot *j* in one of the incoming channels to another time slot *k* in one of the outgoing time slots. This seriously restricts the ability to connect all subscribers together. In a general array (i.e., $m \times n$), the total possible connectivity which can occur under ideal conditions is mT or nT, whichever is smaller. The space-only network is sufficiently restrictive that most practical networks are constructed as *T* only or as combinations of time and space stages.

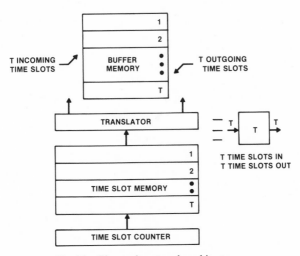

Fig. 26.   Time-only network architecture.

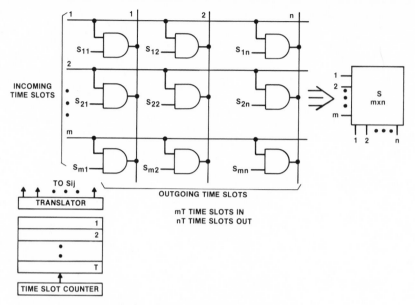

INCOMING TIME SLOTS

TO Sij

TRANSLATOR

TIME SLOT COUNTER

OUTGOING TIME SLOTS

mT TIME SLOTS IN
nT TIME SLOTS OUT

Fig. 27.   Space-only network architecture.

7.4.3.   T–S

Two simple combinations of time and space stages are possible. The first of these, shown in Fig. 28, consists of a time stage on each of the m incoming lines, followed by an $m \times n$ space stage. The time stage, functioning as a time-slot interchanger, places the incoming time slots into the proper time slot for connectivity through the space stage to the proper output. As an example, suppose a customer whose input appears in time slot 7 of input multiplex 2 desires to be connected to a customer in time slot 9 of multiplex 6. The nature of a digital switch, since it is unilateral, requires that each customer have an appearance at both input and output ends of the network. Thus, customer A will appear in time slot 7 of input multiplex 2 *and* S-stage output multiplex 2, while customer B appears in time slot 9 of input multiplex 6 *and* S-stage output multiplex 6. The switching network is

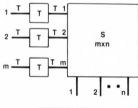

mT TIME SLOTS IN
n T TIME SLOTS OUT

Fig. 28.   A time–space network architecture.

thus required to place time slot 7 of input multiplex 2 into time slot 9 of output multiplex 6, and time slot 9 of input multiplex 6 into time slot 7 of output multiplex 2, in order to effect a 2-way conversation. The time stages perform the time-slot interchange functions, and the space stage performs the multiplex switching functions. For this case, $m = n$.

Thus, the time-slot interchanger on input multiplex 2 places information at time slot 7 of its input stream into time slot 9 of its output stream, where it then passes into the space stage on horizontal line 2, then to be switched into vertical line 6, where it passes out as time slot 9 of output multiplex 6. Half of the connection is thereby provided. In a like manner, the second half of the connection is made by transferring information from time slot 9 of input multiplex 6, through the time-slot interchanger which places the data into time slot 7 on horizontal level 6 of the space stage, which switches the data to vertical line 2, where it proceeds on time slot 7 of output multiplex 2. This network structure can reasonably function as a moderate size network, since a 128 time-slot system feeding a 16×16 switch would provide the capability of handling 2048 time slots, or one-way connections. This network structure will block calls if, for instance, two time slots on input k are to be switched to two customers on outputs n and $n - 1$ who exist at the identical time slot p.

Larger networks require either more time slots or a larger array, or both. More time slots require faster devices, and decrease timing margins. Larger arrays require adding more crosspoints which increase, in the single stage as shown, as the square of the number of inputs or outputs.

7.4.4. S–T

The second combination of space and time stages consists of a space stage, followed by a time stage, as shown in Fig. 29. This network provides the space switching of the input channels first, followed by the time switch-

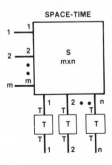

Fig. 29.   A space–time network architecture.

m T   TIME SLOTS IN
n T   TIME SLOTS OUT

ing of the channels to place them into the proper outgoing time slots. Switching proceeds in an analogous manner to the T–S combination described previously.

7.4.5. T–S–T

A somewhat more complex, but more flexible, arrangement comes about when additional time or space stages are added. The most common arrangements are those which either place space stages on either side of a time stage (S–T–S) or time stages on either side of a space stage (T–S–T).

The first case considered is the time–space–time arrangement, shown in Fig. 30. In the arrangement shown the time-slot interchanger will interchange information between external channels and internal (space array) channels. The space stage provides connectivity between time stages at the input and output.

This arrangement provides improved capability for handling calls without blocking. The network control does not associate a time slot on the input or output channel with a particular space-stage time slot. Any intermediate network time slot may be chosen for space interconnectivity. For example, connection of input time slot 3 to output time slot 17 can be made via network time slot 9. In the T–S or S–T cases, discussed in Sections 7.4.3 and 7.4.4, the time-slot interchange had a fixed translation when the connection was specified. If either prescribed time slot was already being used for a path through the network, the call became blocked.

In the T–S–T case, an incoming channel time slot may be connected to an outgoing channel time slot by any possible space array time slot. There are more possible paths between a prescribed input and output which makes the T–S–T network a much more powerful network.

In order to illustrate blocking in a digital network, assume a call is to be made from time slot 3 on a given input to time slot 17 on a given output. First consider the case where no input time switch exists (i.e., an S–T network only). An interchange must be made between time slot 3 and time slot 17 assuming the space stage is capable of providing a path from the input horizontal to the output vertical. If both time slot 3 on the input and time slot 17 on the output are free, the connection can be made, with only a single path possible. If a call is already in existence on time slot 3 (from another input level) on the vertical to the time stage, the call is blocked, even if time slot 17 on the output channel is available.

Now, add an input time stage to the S–T network. The input time-slot interchanger could use any of the available time slots between time-slot interchangers on the input and output sides. If 128 time slots are postulated for the incoming, outgoing, and space stage multiplexes, the incoming call

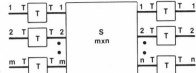

Fig. 30.   A time–space–time network architecture.

on time slot 3 has access to all 128 space stage time slots, minus any time slots used by calls which occupy the desired horizontal or vertical at the time the call is being set up. The path-hunting process then becomes a task of finding an available time slot at each end of the space array. In many cases, the network will provide more than one possible time slot from any input to any output. As in most networks, deloading will decrease the probability of blocking. Blocking in a T–S–T network is discussed in more detail in Chapter 9 of this volume.

7.4.6. S–T–S

A similar process may be accomplished with a time-shared space stage following the time-shot interchange stage of the S–T network, thereby implementing a space–time–space (S–T–S) network, as shown in Fig. 31. The S–T–S network conssts of a space matrix at the input, an array of time-slot interchangers in the middle, and a space matrix in the output. In this case, the choice of input and output time slots is fixed by the desired connection. The ability to access any time-slot interchanger by means of network connections in the two space arrays provides flexibility in the connectivity pattern.

In the S–T–S case, an incoming time slot, say 7, which must be connected to an output time slot, say 16, requires a time-slot interchanger which is available to interchange time slots 7 and 16. This can be accomplished in any of the n time-slot interchangers in the time stage.

Both T–S–T and S–T–S networks can be designed with identical call-carrying capacities and blocking probabilities. It can be shown that a direct one-to-one mapping exists between time-division and space-division networks.

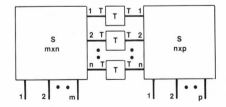

Fig. 31.   A space–time–space network architecture.

7.4.7. More Complex Arrangements

In an analogous manner, the network designer can create more complex network arrangements by adding additional stages as required to meet design requirements. More complex networks can be designed to provide increased capacity, more flexibility, or less blockage.

8. No. 4 ESS

In order to illustrate how the concepts discussed in this chapter have been incorporated into a commercial digital switching system, the architecture and system design philosophy which was applied to the development of the United States Bell System's No. 4 ESS[7] network will be described.

The No. 4 ESS system is a large digital time-division switching system intended to provide for toll switching needs in the Bell System. The network is designed to allow economic growth to a maximum of 107,520 terminations. The system interfaces only with trunks, so the switching center network is required to handle traffic with high trunk occupancy and remain almost nonblocking.

A skeletonized view of the No. 4 ESS network is shown in Fig. 32. The network is architecturally constructed as a time–space–time network.

A set of input buffers provides the input to the network. Those buffers are used to synchronize the input signals to the network. In previous sections, synchronization of all inputs in time and frequency was assumed. In the No. 4 ESS System, frequency synchronization is required and time synchronization of incoming signals is performed in buffers as discussed in Chapter 10. The network requires that all time slots "1" appear at the network at the same instant of time. Time slots "1" of the incoming transmission facilities most likely will appear at the input to the buffers at different times. All frames are 125 μsec long, as determined by the standard 8-kHz sampling rate. Signals are clocked into the input buffers on the left-hand side of the figure from a clock derived from the signal, which is external to the switching center network. This clock is controlled by the

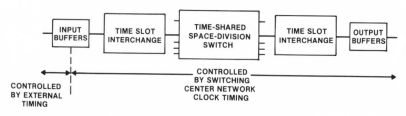

Fig. 32.   Architecture of the No. 4 ESS network.

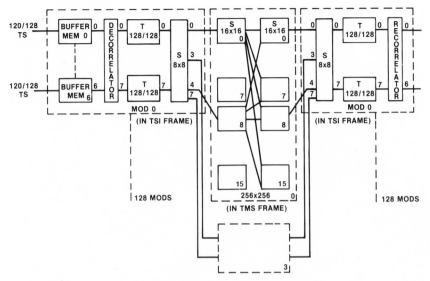

Fig. 33. Schematic of the No. 4 ESS network.

sending office or by the clock in the transmission facilities. If analog trunks terminate on the No. 4 ESS, the encoding function occurs within the office in an analog-to-digital converter frame. This frame may be placed up to 1000 feet away from the switching network frames, leading to differences in round trip delays of 0 to 3000 nsec. Control of the encoding frame frequency is easily implemented, but control of the phase or delay is difficult. Thus the input buffer also provides delay synchronization. Since the input data to the buffer are controlled by external timing, and the output timing is controlled by the time-division network, the buffer functions as an asynchronous delay line for that multiplex. The time-slot interchanger thereby sees time slot 1 simultaneously from all inputs.

Time-slot data from the input buffers proceed into the time–space–time switch consisting of a time-slot interchanger, a four-stage time-shared space-division switch, and another time-slot interchanger, and then into output buffers. The time–space–time switch is controlled by the switching center's network clock timing, and data leaving the output buffers are in synchronism with the switch. All outgoing channels are in synchronism, both in frequency and in phase.

The No. 4 ESS System is constructed with a 128 time-slot architecture. The detailed architecture of the No. 4 ESS, shown in Fig. 33, will now be discussed. The switching center network is composed of two types of frames, time-slot interchange (TSI) frames, and time-multiplexed switch (TMS) frames. This provides a growable network with a somewhat constant cost per termination over the complete range of possible trunks. The TMS frame is a two-stage space division array which is arranged as a distribution stage. It is a two-stage array of 16 × 16 grids, wired to provide 256 inputs by 256 outputs.

The No. 4 ESS System operates on a 128 time slot basis with a basic clock frequency of 16.384 MHz producing clock pulses with a 61-nsec period. Sixteen clock pulses occur per 976 nsec time slot, and 128 time slots with a 976-nsec duration fill the 125-μsec frame (8 kHz sampling). Selection of 128 time slots and 16 clock pulses per time slot is due to the circuit efficiencies allowed in designing digital systems using powers of 2. Interfacing digital switches with transmission systems based on 12 and 24 trunk modules creates unique timing synthesis problems.

The TMS frame thus consists of 256 inputs, each carrying 128 time slots. Multiplying these numbers, the capacity of a TMS frame thus becomes 32,768 time slots. The network is designed to grow to four TMS frames in the maximum size network. Four 256 × 256 grids provide a total of 131,072 time slots across the network. The TMS frame provides the two center stages of the four-stage time-shared space-division portion of the network.

The TSI frames contain the remaining portions of the network. These frames are structured into an originating portion, shown on the left side of the figure, and a terminating portion, shown on the right side. The frames contain two to four modules each with originating and terminating capabilities. The TSI frame provides a growable unit of the system, with 128 modules contained in a full system.

Incoming channels arrive on the originating portion of the modules and outgoing channels leave from the terminating portion of the modules. The incoming time slots are placed in a buffer memory operating as an asynchronous delay line as previously described. The incoming stream contains its own clock information and provides the address for each incoming time slot in the channel. The time-slot positions derived from the incoming data are used to address buffer memory words during the first portion of a No. 4 ESS time slot, so that incoming data can be stored (i.e., data in time slot 16 are loaded into buffer address 16). Many separate multiplexes are simultaneously terminated on the No. 4 ESS. At the same time one time slot from one multiplex is loaded into one buffer, another time slot from another multiplex is applied to another buffer. Time slots in different incoming multiplexes are most likely at different phases, and each data word from each multiplex must be loaded into its corresponding buffer at its appropriate time. Thus, differences in phase from the many inputs can be accommodated. This assumes that the input multiplex frequency is identical to the No. 4 ESS system clock frequency.

The interface between the No. 4 ESS and transmission systems based on 12 or 24 trunk groups uses only 120 (10 × 12 or 5 × 24) time slots of the incoming 128 time-slot stream. The remaining eight time slots are used for diagnostic and maintenance purposes.

This provides some deloading of the network since only 120 of the 128 time slots active contain calls. The buffer memories pass information to a decorrelator, which has seven inputs and eight outputs, and provides a distribution and an expansion function which reduces switching center network blocking. The decorrelator also reduces the impact of high-occupancy trunk groups by spreading the traffic from seven 128 time-slot streams equally over eight 128 time-slot streams. The net effect of the decorrelator is to provide only 105 active time slots in the 128 time-slot stream ($\frac{7}{8} \times 120$). This function is analogous to a combined distribution and expansion function. The major difference between the decorrelator and a normal distribution/expansion function is that decorrelation occurs with a fixed wiring pattern.

The operation of the decorrelator is controlled by the network time-slot counter (not shown in Fig. 33) which also controls the buffer memories and the time-slot memories denoted as T. These memories are all 128-word random access memories, corresponding to the 128 time slots in the streams. The memories are synchronized and operation occurs as follows. The time-slot counter in time slot 0 reads word 0 out of each of the buffer memories 0 through 6. These words move across the decorrelator and the counter addresses word 0 in each of the time-slot memories, 0 through 6, into which the words are written. The last T memory ($T7$) does not receive data, since no eighth input exists. In the next time slot, the time-slot counter contains a count of 1. The decorrelator receives the new count and shifts the outputs with respect to the inputs by one time slot, connecting input 0 to output 1, 1 to 2, etc., including 6 to 7. At the same time, each word 1 is read out of buffer memories 0 through 6, transmitted across the decorrelator to time-slot memories 1 through 7, and placed in the word 1 address of each of these memories. In time slot 2, the outputs of the decorrelator are indexed by 2 with respect to inputs (0 to 2, 1 to 3, etc., including 6 to 0), word 2 is read out of the buffer memories, transmitted across the decorrelator, and written into the appropriate time-slot memories in the word 2 address.

Each of the time-slot memories thus sees 1/8 of the traffic from each of the buffer memories. If one of the input multiplexers has 100% occupancy on each channel, data would be distributed over the eight time-slot memories equally with only 1/8 the occupancy in each one. Since blocking can exist in the No. 4 ESS switching center network, this reduces the possibility of blockage due to multiplexers with abnormally high occupancy.

The time-slot interchanger (T) is a 128-word memory in which information during the incoming time slots is sequentially written (word 0 in time slot 0, word 1 in time slot 1, etc.). The T memory is read in a sequence determined by call processing data placed in the time-slot control memory.

The desired address is accessed during each time slot and the address contents (call information) is transmitted in that time slot over the four-stage time-shared space-division portion of the network. As mentioned before, a maximum of 105 of the time slots can be active.

The first and fourth stages of the space-division network are 8 × 8 single-stage space switches which are connected to eight time-slot interchanger memories. These space-division stages are contained in the TSI frame. The 8 × 8 space switch connects to the TMS frames containing the 256 × 256 arrays to the initial and final T stage. With four TMS frames, the 8 × 8 space stage has two connections to each TMS frame.

The four TMS frames are connected to the 8 × 8 space stages at either side and create a network which appears as a 1024 × 1024 array. With 128 time slots available, connectivity is possible for 131,072 total time slots. Only 107,520 are used (1024 × 105), due to the deloading mentioned previously. This provides a very high-capacity network with essentially non-blocking properties.

The terminating portion of the TSI frame contains the final 8 × 8 space array, plus an additional time stage, as shown in the figure. The overall network therefore has a T–S–S–S–S–T configuration. An 8 × 7 re-correlator follows the final T stage and performs the inverse mapping of the decorrelator function. Call information, after passing through the recorrelator, is transmitted on the output channels.

Each frame has its own local controller which is accessed from a large special purpose central control processor which performs all call-processing and path-finding functions. The central controller sends messages to the switching network frame controller which cause the connections to be enabled.

In order to provide high system availability to service the subscribers and to provide a reliable, maintainable system, the switching center network is completely duplicated. In addition, parity generators and checkers and matchers between the duplicated halves of the network are placed at appropriate points in the network to provide a method of determining where faults exist. All memories, both buffer and time slot, contain parity checkers.

The contents of every time-slot memory contain parity over address and data, which is checked on every read cycle. Each buffer memory checks parity on the bit stream passing through the system. In addition, data between the two redundant halves of the system are matched in the decorrelator and the recorrelator. Since time is required to test for a match, the recorrelator and decorrelator are designed in bit parallel format, which provides the additional time needed to match between the two halves of the network. Data leaving the decorrelator are converted back to serial.

Two additional bits are added to the 8-bit PCM signal passing across the network. A "leading one" is placed to precede the data, and a parity bit over the data placed following the data. A 10-bit word is thus transmitted across the network. With 16 clock pulses in a time slot, six extra bit times are available to enable and disable the gates in the network before and after the pulse stream proceeds through. If any paths fail, the system control can switch to the redundant standby half, which maintains the identical path configuration. Diagnostics can be run on the half with the fault.

9. Conclusions

Digital switching makes use of the most advanced semiconductor components. Hence, new technological developments play a significant role in the development of the three major elements required for a digital switch—control, memory, and network fabric. Semiconductor technology is undergoing rapid change with substantial effect on the design of these elements. For example, the control portion of the system is proceeding more and more towards a distributed architecture. Microprocessors are providing more flexible and intelligent peripheral controllers. Some form of central control will probably be retained but it will become more like a system manager. More of the diagnostic and maintenance functions may also be distributed on a per frame basis. Some overall maintenance and control functions will still be done by a central processor.

Memories are becoming less expensive and faster. One problem which exists for time-division networks lies in the configuration of semiconductor memory components. The trends in chip architectures are toward larger word structures, such as 256K words by 1 bit, which are not useful for 128 or 256 time-slot systems. These systems need 256×8 or 256×10 memory structures. Technology trends toward faster memories will lead to more time slots per channel.

Similar trends help the network fabric. Faster logic gates will allow more time slots in the system. This will lead to smaller systems and lower propagation delays, which again leads to faster systems. Systems will be fabricated in smaller and smaller spaces which will continue to handle the same number of lines or trunks. The advent of high-speed, economical fiber optic links will alleviate the problems associated with communication between frames, and may also lead to new architectures, such as distributed or remote network components.

Questions

1. You are attempting to design a high-quality, resonant transfer, PAM switch for a space station. The telephones are capable of handling 12 KHZ bandwidth. You have, as time-division gates, a low-current, very fast semiconductor device, with zero transition times from on to off, and vice versa. You have determined

that ζ, the "on" period, must be 10 μsec, due to the current carrying capability of gates. (a) What is the maximum number of simultaneous calls which the switch can handle? (b) What is the maximum number of simultaneous calls which the switch can handle if you are forced to "ground" the bus between time slots?

2. You are designing an analog time division, multiplexer switch for wideband signals. The PAM samples are taken from 600-KHZ low-rate video signals. You would like to multiplex twelve such signals on a high-bandwidth resonant transfer analog transmission signal. With ideal gates (zero transition times), what is the sampling period T, and what is the maximum time slot ζ?

3. An 8-KHZ PAM switch is to be built. Describe the effects of gate transition times (gate speed) on the number of time slots which could be handled. If a memory read requires 2 μsec, what effect would this have on the carrying capacity of a 25-time-slot switch?

4. Discuss the advantages and disadvantages of placing the amplifier, which restores the gain in a lossy analog time-division system, between the "send" and "receive" busses as shown in Fig. 7 versus placing the amplifier in series with the sample-and-hold (S&H) circuit. Why is it advisable not to place the amplifier ahead of the "send" bus?

5. In order to reduce the bandwidth required for transmission, a number of coding schemes other than PCM have been formulated. One such scheme is a differential-PCM (DPCM), which encodes only the difference in amplitude between PCM samples. Assume such a system is to be used, which requires a 3-bit DPCM sample to be switched every 125 μsec for each channel. Assuming a 128-channel (128-time-slot) system, what is the period of a time slot? What is the period per bit? How does this affect the memory sizes and access times?

6. A low-voice-grade field switch is to be built. In order to allow the individual phones to be independent and cost effective, an adaptive delta modulation encoding scheme, involving transmission of a single bit sample every 62.5 μsec (a 16-KHZ sampling rate), is to be used. Design a single-stage time-division switch which can interconnect 32 such phones. Describe all gate and memory speeds and timing constraints. What are the network time slot periods?

7. A time–space switch is to be designed for switching 64-kbit/s PCM channels, for an international switch. The channels, encoded in 8-bit samples, are contained in a 32-time-slot transmission system. The switching system is designed to switch sixteen such transmission systems (512 channels). Design the switch, and provide the requirements for all memories and clock rates.

8. A switch is needed to switch 1536 PCM channels, derived from 4-KHZ telephone channels, and packaged in a standard 24-channel transmission system. Four such transmission systems are multiplexed together, providing 96 channels on a link to the network. Design a $T-S-T$ switch to handle this capacity, using a single stage of space switching. Describe all memory and timing parameters.

9. A gateway switch is to be designed, to connect continental T1 PCM systems (24 channels) and international PCM systems (32 channels). Assume the same PCM coding scheme and sampling rate (8 KHZ) are used by both types of systems. Design a $T-S-T$ system capable of switching between 768 channels of continental traffic and 768 channels of international traffic. Use concentrators or channel banks as appropriate. Provide the requirements for all modules used by the network.

10. A small PBX switch is to be designed, using a time stage only. A total of 232 telephones, plus a 24-channel T1 transmission system providing access out of

the system, are to have full access out of the system, and are to have full access to each other. Describe the appropriate architecture, and define the requirements of the time stage.

11. It is possible to have not only serial and parallel operation within a network, but also a mixed serial–parallel operation. As an example, consider a network which adds a parity bit to a standard 8-bit PCM sample and then switches these through a 3-wire parallel network, with three serial bits on each wire of the three parallel wires. Describe the potential advantages of this example. What are the disadvantages?

12. As described in this chapter, many possible network arrangements can be devised which meet the needs of a given system. Two of the important economic parameters are the numbers of bits of memory (buffer and time-slot) and of gates of space array needed per conversation. Analyze the number of memory bits and space array gates required for a T–S–T and an S–T–S network handling the same number of 8-bit PCM channels in a 24-time-slot, 1024-input by 1024-output network. If memory bits cost 1% of gate costs, which is cheaper? If memory bits cost 10% of gate costs, does the result remain the same?

References

1. S. Haykin, *Communication Systems*, John Wiley and Sons, New York, 1978. Pages 430–435 contain a derivation of the sampling theorem.

2. T. E. Browne, D. J. Wadsworth, and R. K. York, "New Time Division Switch Units for No. 101 ESS," *Bell Syst. Tech. J.,* vol. 48, 443–476, 1969.

3. K. W. Cattermole, "Efficiency and Reciprocity in Pulse-Amplitude Modulation: Part 1, Principles," *Proc. IEE, England,* vol. 105, pp. 449–462, 1958.

4. M. R. Aaron, "PCM Transmission in the Exchange Plant," *Bell Syst. Tech. J.,* vol. 41, pp. 99–141, 1962.

5. P. Benowitz, S. J. Butterfield, M. P. Chichetti, Jr., and T. G. Cross, "Digital Multiplexer," *Bell Syst. Tech. J.,* vol. 54, pp. 893–918, 1975.

6. A. W. Kobylar, "Method for Isolating a Set of Near Optimum PCM Digital Network Configurations," *Int. Conf. Commun.* (August, 1974), Paper 3YE. Also see a companion paper by S. G. Pitroda, Paper 3YD, in the same conference.

7. J. H. Huttenhoff, J. Janik, Jr., G. D. Johnson, W. R. Schleicher, M. F. Slana, and F. H. Tendick, Jr., "Peripheral System," *Bell Syst. Tech. J.,* vol. 56, pp. 1029–1956, 1977.

6

Circuit versus Packet Switching

Myron J. Ross

1. Introduction

In addition to voice, other types of communications network services are becoming increasingly more important. These are narrowband data traffic types and include interactive data, facsimile, slow scan image, and bulk data. Typically, these services are delivered by separate networks using various kinds of switching technology, e.g., packet, circuit, or message switching. If we could handle all voice and data in a single network, with a unified switching and transmission approach, then it might be possible to reduce costs, since separate resources for each network, such as switching and transmission facilities, would not be required. This is the foundation for the Integrated Services Digital Network discussed in Chapter 10 of this volume.

In this chapter, we will examine integrated digital voice and data via circuit and packet switching. We will place particular emphasis on the unified treatment of voice and data traffic. The relative advantages of circuit and packet switching will be studied as they apply to various types of data. In Section 2 we describe future developments in the field of communications networks and establish the need for integrated voice and data. We discuss voice and data characteristics in Section 3; circuit, message, and packet switching in Section 4; and in Section 5, compare the various alternatives

Myron J. Ross • GTE Products Corporation, Sylvania Systems Group, 77A Street, Needham Heights, Massachusetts 02194

for integrating voice and data in a common system. An example of a system design approach directed toward implementing an integrated voice/data network is covered in Section 6. Finally, in Section 7, we describe the transition to an integrated network with the equipment required and the services offered.

In Chapter 1 of this volume, we saw that circuit switching depends on the preallocation of transmission bandwidth in order to effect a continuous path for information transfer. Signaling and routing are used to establish the path connection on an end-to-end basis so that information will flow through the network in an uninterrupted manner. Thus, in the telephone, telex, and TWX systems, a fixed bandwidth is preallocated for the duration of the call, while for radio, the spectrum is preallocated, either permanently or for a single transaction.[1]

Packet switching is an example of the dynamic allocation of bandwidth, on a link-by-link basis rather than allocation of bandwidth over the whole source to destination path.[1-3] Message systems operate in this fashion. Under this technique, data do not flow uninterrupted through the network but instead are transferred through a series of "transactions." Each transaction includes a transfer of the message along with signaling, control, and address information in order to determine how the transaction will be handled at each intervening node along the way. The procedure for handling these transactions is referred to as the data transfer protocol of the network.

In packet-switching networks, information is exchanged in the form of blocks of limited size called *packets*, as illustrated in Fig. 1. Long messages are handled by dividing the message into multiple packets for transmission

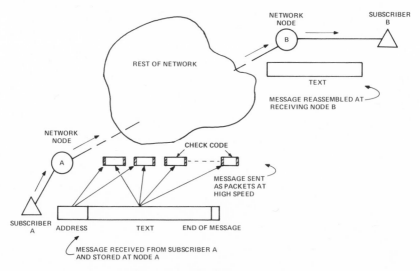

Fig. 1.   Principle of packet switching.

through the network, and subsequent reassembly again at the destination. All packets are similar, each having a header derived from the original message address, a portion of message text, and an error check code. Transit times for packets through the network are purposely kept small, typically involving delays on the order of 10 to 100 msec. This implies an overall message delay which can reach seconds. The packets can be thought of as envelopes into which data are placed in much the same way that mail is delivered via the postal system (although much faster). Transmission through the network should not interfere with the data inside the envelopes.

Many of the advantages of packet switching derive from the ability to time-share expensive long-haul transmission facilities over many users and to adaptively route individual packets of a long message. The network bit rate is made much higher than that required for a single user. Through the use of rapid line scanning and high-speed switching, the network is able to share its resources effectively among many users. Buffer storage is used to provide a smooth flow of traffic and to reconcile user and network mismatches in speed. The ability to reallocate resources also provides the network with a means of overcoming temporary congestion or link/switch failures.

Packet switching was first proposed by Baran in 1964 as a means of survivable voice and data communications for military systems that contained no critical central components.[1] In 1967 the ARPANET was planned as a pilot project to link time-shared computer systems in the United States together into a widespread packet-switching network. At about the same time, a multinode packet-switching network was being conceived and studied by the British. Today, the ARPANET consists of over 60 packet-switching nodes, with minicomputers used as the packet switch and interfacing device at each node, and interconnected by high-speed leased lines. The ARPANET proved that dynamic allocation techniques such as packet switching could be organized to provide an efficient and responsive interactive data communications facility for the sharing of computer resources. Other early applications of packet switching included the following networks: Societé Internationale de Telecommunications Aeronautiques (SITA), Tymnet, Cyclades/Cigale, Reseau à Commutation par Paquets (RCP), European Informatics Network (EIN), Telenet, Transpac, and Datapac. Today, the rapid growth in interactive computer applications, in both commercial and military operations, indicates that the major areas of growth in data communication networks will be in packet-switching technology.

2. Present and Future Communications Networks

The transmission and switching structure of current voice communication systems is based primarily on 3.4-kHz bandwidth analog channels. Examples of this are the national Direct Distance Dialing network and

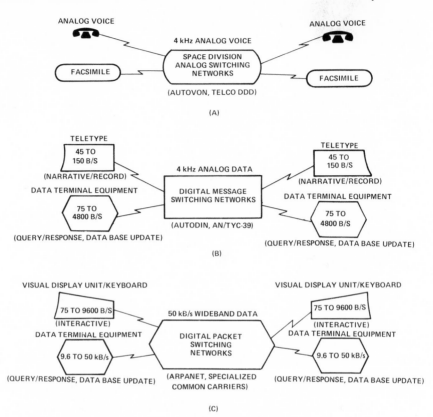

Fig. 2. Current customer communication systems.

special networks such as the United States AUTOVON network shown in Fig. 2a. The 3.4-kHz bandwidth provides adequate analog voice transmission and is a good compromise between high-fidelity speech and efficient use of the available transmission spectrum. Until recently, facsimile has been treated as if it were voice. The majority of facsimile machines installed to date use analog transmission for transmitting information.

Conventional data networks for narrative/record message transmission are separate from voice networks and are also based on 3.4-kHz bandwidths. Examples are the United States AUTODIN I store-and-forward network[4] and the network composed of AN/TYC-39 store-and-forward switches, shown in Fig. 2b. Narrative/record traffic in these cases tends to require 45–150 bit/sec teletype communications and/or 75-4800 bit/sec terminal/computer communications.

Currently, secure voice and packet-switching networks are implemented only in separate networks or via dedicated circuits. The same is true for high-speed facsimile and video. Packet-switching networks are used for interactive data traffic while store-and-forward networks are used for narrative/record traffic. Examples of packet-switching networks are shown in Fig. 2c.

Future communication systems, Fig. 3, must adapt to evolutionary developments in both data and voice systems. Networks will have to interact with a multiplicity of voice digitization techniques at transmission rates ranging from 2400 bit/sec to 64 kbit/sec. These techniques are expected to be incompatible with each other, such as voice encoded in PCM and Vocoders. New services, such as low-speed video and facsimile, must also be handled. Future data communications must be able to handle interactive, query/response, data base update, and bulk data traffic interchangeably and efficiently.

Communication networks in use today utilize combinations of landline, line-of-site radio, and satellite radio trunks for links between switching nodes, shown in Fig. 4. Communication links feature a wide variety of trunk data rates. Typically, these trunks are used for multiplexed voice and/or data (the latter are generally converted by modems to 3.4-kHz analog bandwidths).

Future communication networks, also shown in Fig. 4, will make use of all the current types of links as well as new communication links based on techniques such as TDMA satellite and various types of microwave and optical links. There may be new transmission rates to consider. Future systems must be adaptable enough to efficiently utilize interswitch trunk groups with a variety of characteristics over a wide range of transmission rates. In addition, they must be capable of maintaining link and network

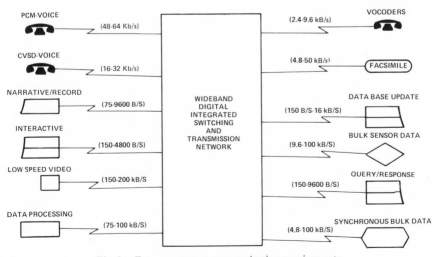

Fig. 3.   Future customer communication requirements.

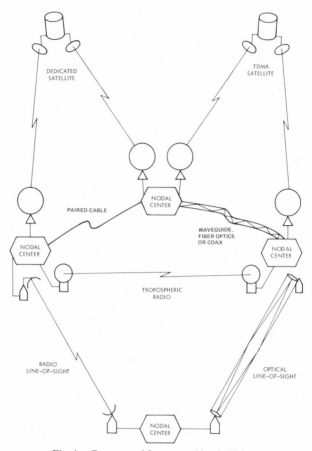

Fig. 4. Current and future trunking facilities.

synchronization necessary for large-scale networks while simultaneously utilizing transmission capacity efficiently.

Many of the current networks shown in Fig. 2 are of intercontinental or global proportions. It is likely that future communications systems will assume similar global proportions. The present networks employ separate transmission facilities for voice and data; in many instances they utilize parallel path connections. Since a significant portion of the cost of a net-work lies in its transmission segment, integrating the different transmission types can lead in the future to economically practical systems where switch-ing equipment, as well as transmission capacity, can be shared, thereby reducing expenses for the entire network. Another advantage to integrating the differing traffic types is the ability to provide interconnection between the broadest community of subscriber terminals possible. A consequence of this could be the provision of graphics or high-speed facsimile service.

Therefore, the need for a unified network is justified on the basis of cost and a maximum interconnectivity of diverse terminal types at various voice and data transmission rates.

3. Voice and Data Traffic Characteristics

Three main types of traffic are handled by an integrated network: voice, interactive data, and bulk data. Each has special service requirements. Voice traffic requires low delay and high throughput, but can have relaxed error rate constraints. If an occasional bit error occurs, the effect on the transmitted voice quality is usually not objectionable. Interactive data traffic, like that between a terminal and computer, requires low delay. It also requires a low bit error rate because a single error can distort the transmitted information completely. However, it does not have a particularly high throughput requirement.

Bulk data traffic requires high throughput because of the large amount of information that must be handled. Also, it requires a low bit error rate for the same reasons as for interactive data. However, low delay is not as critical a requirement as for the voice or the interactive data traffic. For different mixtures of the three traffic types, the performance parameters of the network should be selected accordingly.

Table 1 shows the performance characteristics of the different types of traffic served by an integrated voice/data system. Class I traffic is characterized by long messages requiring continuous real-time delivery, such as voice, facsimile, or video. This type of call is accepted or blocked; if accepted, it is maintained for the duration of the call. Class I traffic is generally associated with circuit-switching techniques. Error protection is not required for voice calls, since occasional errors in the voice waveform are almost imperceptible to a listener. However, forward error correction may be implemented in the case of facsimile to control bit errors.

Class II traffic ranges from short, discrete data messages requiring near real-time delivery, such as interactive data, to long messages of the store-and-forward type, requiring neither continuity nor immediate delivery. This type of traffic may experience some delay. Long messages, typified by bulk data traffic, experience more delay than short messages and may even be queued prior to transfer. The short, discrete Class II traffic is efficiently handled by packet-switching techniques, while bulk data traffic can be handled by either circuit or packet switching.

Table 1. Characteristics of Different Types of Network Traffic

	Class 1	Class II	
Type of traffic	Digitized voice, video, facsimile, sensor bulk data	Narrative/record, interactive, query/response, data base update	Nonsensor bulk data
Call duration	Several minutes	Seconds to minutes	Minutes to hours
Error control	Generally none (possibly forward error correction for video and facsimile)	Automatic repeat request, forward error correction/automatic repeat request	May or may not be required
Cross network delay	Less than 200 msec	Less than 1 sec	Minutes to hours
Message length	10^5–10^7 bits	600–6000 bits	10^6–10^8 bits
Transmission rates	2.4–200 kbit/sec	45 BPS to 100 kbit/sec	4.8–100 kbit/sec
Availability	Blocking	No blocking, but may be delayed	No blocking, but may be throttled

4. Circuit, Message, and Packet Switching

4.1. Circuit-Switched Networks

The choice of switching method used to construct the communications network serving the various traffic classes is a major design decision. There are three main switching technologies: circuit switching, message switching, and packet switching. Each of these switching techniques has advantages with respect to voice or data transmission. Therefore, it is important to understand their capabilities and limitations in order to be able to apply the techniques to meet a particular communication requirement.

Figure 5 illustrates a circuit-switched network providing service by setting up a dedicated physical path between communicating customers. The public telephone and telex (switched teleprinter) systems are examples of this. A person or terminal places a call by entering into the switching system the directory number of the person or terminal to be called. The switch then sets up a connection between subscribers, consisting of a sequence of point-to-point circuits, joined together by switches at the junctions between them. The connection is set up by a signaling message which passes all the way through the network. A return signal tells the source that voice or data transmission can begin. The connection exists between the two communicating parties until they decide to "hang up," or terminate the connection. They use the circuit exclusively. Although some multiplexing may take place in a portion of the transmission system, the parties will not notice it.

Circuit switching has several advantages. It allows customers to interact until they are satisfied that the information transmitted is correct. It is appropriate if the users need to communicate at a fairly constant rate for a long period of time. It is interactive, i.e., customers or machines can converse with one another as rapidly as they please. If a question is asked, the other person answers right away.

Disadvantages are that the connection between customers must be

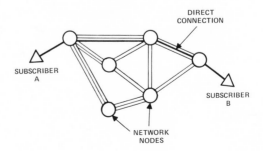

Fig. 5.   Circuit-switched network.

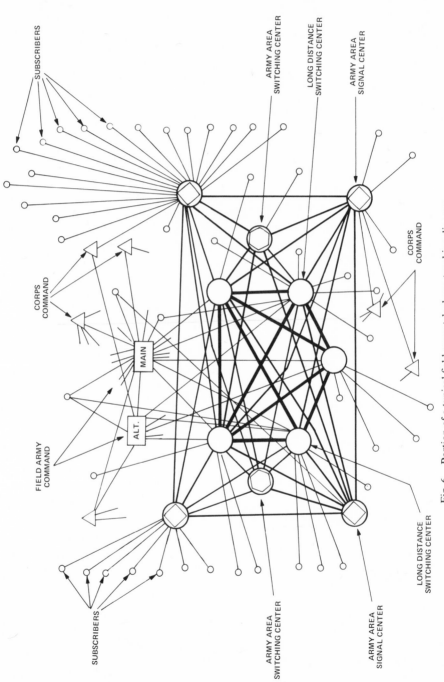

Fig. 6.   Portion of a typical field army telephone trunking diagram.

made before they can communicate, and the connection (consisting of links and switches) must be available for the full duration of the conversation (or transaction). Also, circuit switching is inefficient for bursty traffic which has a high peak-to-average information transfer rate.

There are various categories of circuit-switched network topologies. Most countries use a hierarchical network for their public telephone system. Calls progress up the hierarchy until a path downward is possible. The advantages of this network structure include efficient use of trunk groups and the ability to route traffic in a reasonably efficient manner (e.g., avoiding loop-arounds) with simple and inexpensive nodal control schemes.

Figure 6 is an example of another type of circuit-switched network: a portion of a tactical military telephone communications network used by the United States 7th Army in Europe on maneuvers several years ago. It features a highly interconnected distributed backbone network, and an access area command network arranged in a hierarchical fashion, feeding into the backbone network. A mesh backbone network is more flexible (provides more alternate routes) and, very important from the military standpoint, is more survivable than the hierarchical approach. In addition to the public telephone system there are other circuit-switched networks, and these networks can be quite complex, as illustrated in Fig. 6.

4.2. Message-Switched Networks

Another communication technique is message switching, or store-and-forward switching, where customers exchange information by sending each other discrete messages, Fig. 7. A message which the user wishes to have

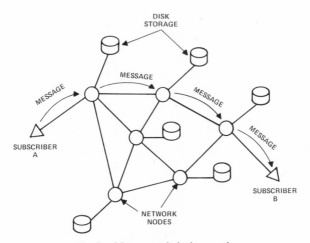

Fig. 7.   Message-switched network.

transported as a whole is moved from node to node. The message works its way through the network, from link to link, queuing at specific nodal points. Small computers are used for entry into the network, for buffering, and for routing messages to subsequent nodes towards the destination.

Initially, a narrative/record message is sent to a switching center, where it is stored. When facilities become available to send it on to another switching center closer to the destination, the message is forwarded over these facilities to be stored at the next point. Each node in the path stores the message on disk. When the selected channel is busy, queuing delays result at the node. This storing and forwarding process continues until the message reaches its destination. Examples of message-switching networks include the AUTODIN I military network[4] and the SITA Airline reservation network.[5]

Message switching is designed for the one-way delivery of messages. It is not suitable for real-time conversational interactions between people or computers. However, it has certain advantages over circuit-switching. It can operate more efficiently with a higher trunk utilization. Messages occupy the channel just long enough to transmit the information. The channel can then be made available for some other use. Not so with circuit switching, where there are intervals of "dead-time" when data is not being transferred between parties on a switched circuit. The channel cannot be used to carry data associated with a different circuit-switched call or transaction.

Message switching is more flexible in adapting to traffic peaks, since it can store messages during the peaks and send them on their way later when a path becomes free. Therefore, systems do not have to be designed for peak loads, and thus cost less. Since a higher percentage of attempted calls are completed, more revenue is collected for a given capital investment.

Another message-switching advantage is that simultaneous availability of the calling and called party is not necessary. In addition, speed and code conversion can be performed, in order to allow terminals with different operating characteristics to converse with one another.

The SITA network, Fig. 8, is a message-switching network providing worldwide communications to over 160 international air carriers. In 1969, SITA began updating its design by replacing the major nodes of its message-switching network with "high-level network" nodes interconnected with voice grade lines, and organized to act like a packet-switching network. The backbone network consists of nine computer centers, interconnected by 4800-bit/sec voice grade transmission circuits. Two types of traffic are carried: conversational (inquiry/response) traffic and telegraphic traffic. Conversational traffic comprises inquiry messages and responses flowing between agent terminals located in airline offices, and their associated reservation computers located geographically distant. Telegraphic traffic consists of messages destined for and generated by airline teleprinters and com-

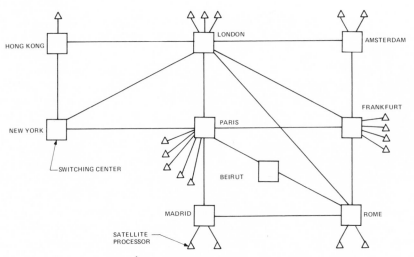

Fig. 8. The SITA high-level network, 1975.

puters, as well as local telex networks. Telegraphic traffic also flows over a complex low-speed network, interconnected with the high-level network.

Agent sets are connected to satellite processors and reservation computers to the high-level centers. Sets are polled cyclically by the processor, asking them to transmit any waiting inquiry messages. If no messages are waiting, the next terminal is interrogated.

4.3. Packet-Switched Networks

Data traffic, although it covers a wide range of characteristics depending on its source, is broadly characterized by having fairly short messages, less than 2000 bits in length, often exchanged at quite high speeds. For example, for a message of 1000 bits and a transmission speed of 48 kbits/sec, the transmission time is 21 msec. Because the message transmission times are so short, circuit switching is really inappropriate, because the time to set up and clear circuits is much longer than the message transfer time. The message-switching principle, particularly the technique known as packet switching, is more appropriate for data traffic than circuit switching.

Packet switching is similar to message switching except that the complete message is not sent at one time. As shown in Fig. 9, messages are divided into segments, called packets, for transmission through the network. Each packet must have additional bits added for address and administrative purposes. Packets are treated individually, each forwarded along the best available path at any given instant. Each packet is error-checked along the way, each time another wideband link is traversed. At the destination,

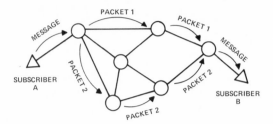

Fig. 9.   Packet-switched network.

another switch reassembles packets into complete messages, which are then presented to the subscriber.

An advantage of packet switching is that, similar to message switching, the transmission channel is occupied for the duration of transmission of the packet only. The channel is then available for use by packets being transferred between different data terminals. Also, many packets of the same message may be in transmission simultaneously. Thus packet switching fully utilizes the relatively expensive transmission facilities.

The main difference between message-switching and packet-switching systems is the speed of the network. With conventional message-switching systems, the emphasis is on low errors, rather than speed, in the information transfer between customers. It is not intended that customers should interact rapidly with each other through a message-switching network. In packet-switched systems, customers are expected to interact with each other by exchanging packets, in much the same way that they would interact by exchanging information through a circuit-switched connection. Information is exchanged in the form of short packets, and the time of transit of these messages is kept low. Thus a packet-switching network can be expected to deliver its packet in a fraction of a second, while a message-switching system delivers its message in a fraction of an hour.

Packet switching therefore combines the major advantages of both circuit and message switching, i.e., speed and transmission efficiency. This makes it appropriate for handling the interchange of information between computer systems.

Two basic modes of packet switching operation have evolved. In the virtual circuit mode, each packet travels the same path through the network after being set up by a pathfinder packet. Packets arrive in the order in which they are sent. In the datagram mode, packets travel along any available path to the destination and are delivered in the sequence they arrive at the receiving terminal. No attempt is made to deliver packets in the sequence they entered the network. Electronic funds transfer or network mail systems, which require the exchange of short unrelated segments of information, are ideal for datagram usage. Multipacket messages are best handled by virtual circuit operation.

An information transfer protocol defines the functions which must be performed to achieve reliable operation in a packet network. The current view of the International Standards Organization (ISO) uses the concept of layering to divide all actions of a protocol into seven layers:

(a) The topmost layer is the Applications layer, which provides the user-to-user protocol and the system management functions.

(b) The Presentation layer provides required format transformations of data being transferred between processes.

(c) The Session layer provides the "sessions," or high-level cooperative relationships, to support the dialog between processes.

(d) The Transport layer provides reliable end-to-end transport of messages across one or more networks.

(e) The Network layer provides logical channels for transferring information between two end points in a single communication network.

(f) The Data Link layer allows logical sequences of messages to be exchanged reliably across a single physical data link.

(g) The Physical layer provides the actual means of signaling and bit transmission across a physical medium.

Figure 10a identifies these layers. Layers (1) through (4) are commonly associated with transport services, while layers (5) through (7) constitute the higher-order protocols.

The rate at which packets flow from one node to the next is regulated by a data link line control procedure such as HDLC (high-level data link control). The basic format of an HDLC packet is shown in Fig. 10b. It is bounded by two 8-bit flags and contains an address field, control field, information field, and frame check sequence for error control. The control field is used to set up and take down virtual circuit connections, provide

(a) SEVEN LAYER ARCHITECTURE MODEL

FLAG	ADDRESS	CONTROL	INFORMATION	FRAME CHECK SEQUENCE	FLAG
01111110	8 BITS	8 BITS	VARIABLE SIZE FIELD	16 BITS	01111110

(b) HDLC PACKET FORMAT STRUCTURE

Fig. 10.   Packet-switching network protocol.

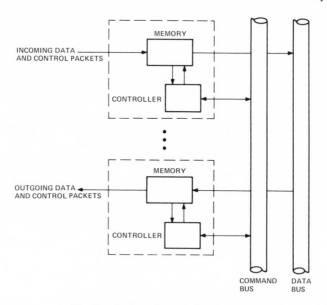

Fig. 11.   Basic packet switch architecture.

acknowledgments and sequence information, and restrict the flow of packets for control purposes. Error control consists of detection using a 16-bit
polynomial check, along with a request for retransmission (Automatic
Repeat Request) of packets in which errors have been detected.

The basic principle of a packet switch is shown in Fig. 11.[7] Incoming
data and control packets are delivered to a buffer, where they are checked
for errors. Following this they are held ready for transfer to the data bus or
interpreted by the controller to produce a control action. An incoming
packet may be transferred to the data bus in series or in parallel. For
implementation over satellites, the bus effectively becomes a serial satellite
channel in which there is a significant delay. The data packet is transferred
from the bus to an outgoing buffer by a controller which recognizes the
address as one it serves on the basis of the routing information to which it
has access.

A common feature of satellite, packet radio, and wideband cable systems is the transmission of packets from packet sources by means of a
common communications channel. All three systems suffer from the possibility of a clash in transmission, when two or more transmitting terminals
overlap. The resolution of contention for use of the transmission medium is
therefore very important.[6,7]

Transfer of data packets to the transmission medium may occur randomly. In this case if a collision occurs with a packet inserted by another
terminal, the packet is repeated after a random delay. In the satellite case

this mode of operation is known as ALOHA. As an alternative to random transfer, each terminal may be restricted to transmitting at the beginning of any timeslot (slotted ALOHA), or required to sense that a packet is not present in the communications medium before transferring its next data packet (carrier sense, multiple access—CSMA). There are several variations of CSMA. One method—listening not only before transmitting but also while transmitting a packet, so that a collision is detected more quickly—is called carrier sense multiple access with collision detection (CSMA-CD), and is the method used in the Ethernet local area network.[8] In general, CSMA techniques provide superior performance (e.g., throughput, delay) over ALOHA techniques.

Other alternatives exist. A terminal receiving priority packets may inhibit all others during transfer of its packets (virtual circuit) or specific time slots may be assigned to each port (time division multiple access). Messages passed between controllers are used to set up these operating modes.

Table 2 identifies some services which use packet data communications. Many of these services are being provided today. Others are planned to be implemented in the near future.

Telenet, Fig. 12, is an example of a fully operational public packet-switching network, which employs distributed network architecture, redundant equipment, and dynamic alternate routing. Telenet operates as a multilevel hierarchical network consisting of a high-speed backbone network and local distribution networks. The backbone is used for long-haul transmission of data at speeds of 56 kbit/sec. This results in a network transit time of less than 200 msec. Each node interconnects to at least three other nodes and operates independently of the rest of the network. This ensures continuation of service even if one or two backbone lines fail. Each node forms the hub of a local distribution network, linking intelligent concentrators in outlying cities via one or more access lines at speeds up to 9.6 kbit/sec.

AT&T has announced their Advanced Communications Service (ACS), which will provide a complex interface through which a wide variety of otherwise incompatible terminal systems can talk to one another, Fig. 13.

Table 2. Applications of Packet Switching

Time sharing	Travel reservations
Remote job entry	Electronic mail
Data-base access and information services	Supply and demand matching services
Financial transactions	Facsimile transmission
Order entry, inventory control and goods handling	Utility metering and security Instructional systems

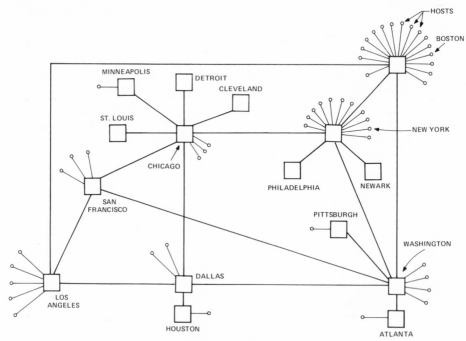

Fig. 12.   Telenet.

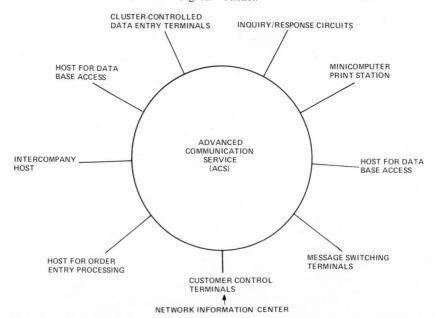

Fig. 13.   Advanced communications service (ACS). [NOTE IN PROOF: Recently changed to Advanced Information Systems (AIS).]

This packet-switching network provides the capability of interconnecting different types of terminals and computers in a user's data communication network.

Historically, users have tended to develop data communications systems to solve one business problem at a time, thereby creating a multiplicity of single application networks. These networks underutilize user personnel, equipment, and transmission facilities. ACS will integrate these diverse networks so that any one terminal will have communication access to multiple applications and data bases. ACS will do this by providing the code conversion, protocol translation, and speed matching needed for equipment compatibility.

4.4. Comparison of Circuit, Message, and Packet Switching

The choice of which switching technique to use is dependent on the particular application, performance requirements, cost, etc. Figure 14, adapted here from a paper by Miyahara, Hasegawa, and Teshigawara,[9] shows the message delay and throughput of circuit, message, and packet switching, for a fixed line utilization of $\rho = 0.5$, as a function of the average message length. For message and packet switching, a network queuing model incorporating the queuing delay at individual nodes, retransmission of packets or messages in error, and reassembly of packets at the destination node, is used to yield an average message transmission delay. The delay analysis of circuit switching is used to develop a comparable circuit-switched delay which is a combination of message transmission delay and line setup time. This setup time is measured from the time a request to transmit a message occurs to the time an idle channel is reserved in order to transmit that message.

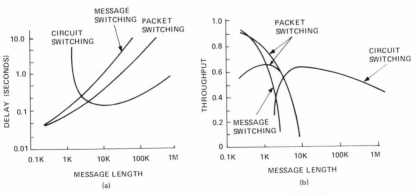

Fig. 14.   Delay and throughput versus message length.

Under a fixed line utilization, as the message size decreases, the number of messages increases. Thus, there is more delay experienced under circuit switching in trying to reserve a channel in order to transmit the message. In fact, line setup time tends to saturate at short message lengths, which accounts for the sharp increase in the delay curve representing circuit switching in Fig. 14a as the message length decreases. Although the time to transmit a message decreases at short message lengths, this is more than offset by the saturation effect of line setup time.

At long message lengths, the message transmission time increases. This effect is predominant over line setup time and results in an overall increase in delay for circuit switching as the message length increases. For message and packet switching, long messages mean a longer time spent waiting in queue, causing an increase in overall message transmission delay. This effect is greater for message switching than it is for packet switching where the long messages can be broken up into small packets so that long queuing delays can be avoided.

In Fig. 14a, we note that there are regions in which each type of switching technology is effective. Packet switching has lower average delay than message switching over the whole range of average message lengths. Circuit switching delay is less than that of packet switching above message lengths of approximately 5000 bits.

In Fig. 14b, throughput for message and packet switching is defined as the volume of traffic which the source node of an n-node, sequential network model can process during a unit time for a message transmission delay of 200 msec. The throughput for circuit switching, however, must take into account the saturation effect of line setup time at short message lengths. At a certain value of line utilization, line setup time increases sharply. This value is different, depending on the average message length specified. Traffic throughput is defined as the line utilization at which the rate of change of this increase is approximately the greatest. This quantity, which is dimensionless, is arbitrarily taken to be 0.9 times the saturation point of line utilization for the different message lengths.

Note that the top curve for packet switching corresponds to a maximum packet size of 1000 bits while the bottom curve corresponds to a variable packet size, chosen to give the maximum packetizing efficiency for buffer utilization. Packet switching is always better than message switching in the former case while, in the latter case, message switching has a higher throughput until a message length of about 1000 bits.

These results illustrate that for time-sharing systems, where average message length is on the order of 1000 bits, packet switching can be very effective. However, for remote job entry or file transfer traffic, where messages are several thousand bits long or more, and should be sent at the same time, circuit switching is more useful.

Figure 15 further illustrates the properties of the three switching technologies from the point of view of user delay.[10,11] In circuit switching there is a delay in setting up the path through the network which increases as the load on the network increases. However, once the path is established, information exchange takes place at transmission rate R, dependent only on the physical properties of the circuits, and customer equipments, which make up the path connection. Call setup consists of a connection delay at the switch followed by transmission of a setup signal. This cycle is repeated until the terminating switch is reached, at which point a return signal is generated and sent back to the originating switch. The data are then sent from originating to terminating switch with relatively little delay. Thus, with circuit switching, the start of an interaction will be delayed as the load

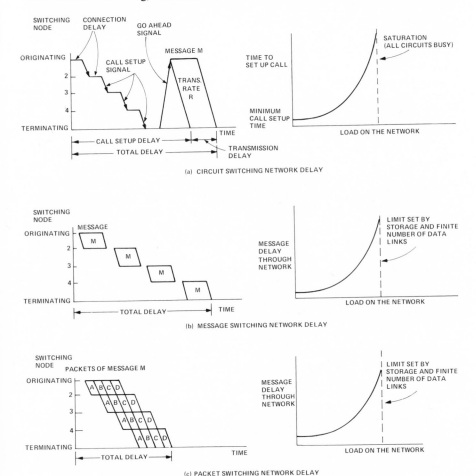

Fig. 15. Network delays for various switching technologies.

on the network increases, but once begun it will proceed at a speed unaffected by loading on the network.

In message switching there is a small setup delay, after which the entire message is transmitted from the originating switch to the next switch along the network path. Following the receipt of the message, the sequence is repeated, until the terminating switch is reached. The time necessary to transfer a message through the network consists of the time to travel between switches at the transmission rates of the respective links, and a message handling time at each switch, including the time taken to read the message into and out of storage. An increase in load causes queues to develop at switches while messages wait to be processed, or for links to become free. This increases the time required for messages to pass through the network.

An increase in load can result in congestion. To the user, this may not be apparent for a while, because the network continues to accept messages, storing them for later delivery. However, messages may not be able to be forwarded for some time. Eventually, the system breaks down and no messages are forwarded unless the congestion is relieved.

In packet switching, messages are broken up into smaller packets prior to transmission. Following the receipt of the first packet at a node, it can be relayed to the next node while the second packet is being received. Similar to message switching, the time of transit of a message through a packet-switched network is a function of network load. However, the transit time for individual packets is purposely kept low, as a result of using high-speed lines and not having to read the message into and out of off-line storage at each switch. Thus, in general, messages experience lower delay in a packet-switching network than in a message-switching network.

5. Approaches to the Integration of Voice and Data

At this point we have examined circuit-, message-, and packet-switching networks. We have seen that packet switching is a deluxe form of message switching: a packet-switching network can carry message-switched traffic (narrative/record) as well as packet-switched traffic (interactive) and yield good performance (low delay). Therefore, with regard to the integration of voice and data, we are left with the following possibilities:

(a) Circuit switching of data as well as voice.
(b) Packet switching of voice as well as data.
(c) Hybrid (circuit/packet) switching—an arrangement where voice could be circuit-switched while interactive data would be packet-switched. Bulk data would be either circuit-, or packet-switched, depending on the application.

In this section, we examine these alternative switching technologies for the integration of voice and data.

5.1. Circuit Switching

There are three variations of circuit switching: traditional circuit switching, fast circuit switching, and circuit switching using time assignment speech interpolation (TASI) techniques.[12,13]

In traditional circuit switching, a complete end-to-end circuit is established for each pair of voice or data users and is dedicated for the full duration of use. The circuit is disconnected when either party terminates the call. This is like our present telephone system and has the advantage that once the circuit is established, the transfer of information takes place independent of the load on the network. However, there are some problems associated with this method. For example, call establishment times after dialing are on the order of one second or more. This can mean a significant delay for data users with bursty interactive data if the call is reestablished for each burst. If the circuit is established only once per conversation, inefficient use of the circuit occurs since the dedicated channel is not used at all during user "think-time." In addition, link-by-link error control typically is not applied to circuit-switched data transmission. Instead, user-to-user error control is applied on an end-to-end basis after the circuit-switched connection has been established. With a large amount of noise present on the links, this will result in a considerable number of end-to-end retransmissions, and could reduce the network throughput.

Figure 16a illustrates the format for the AT&T D3 frame structure in

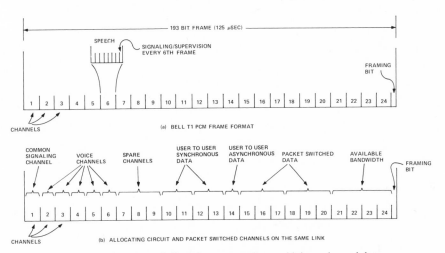

Fig. 16. TDM channel allocation strategy for combining voice and data.

which provision is made for 64 kbit/sec channels which are multiplexed for transmission at a T1 rate of 1.544 Mbit/sec. Individual channels contain 8 bits which repeat at a basic frame duration of 125 μsec. Every 6th frame, the 8th bit of a channel is used for signaling, in order to set up, send signaling, return answer supervision, and take down individual calls. The last bit in each frame, the 193rd bit, is used for establishing and maintaining frame synchronization.

One way to handle voice and data in the same system is to time-share the network to provide data transfer during idle periods. For example, voice facilities could be used at night for batch data transmission. Another technique is to dedicate certain predetermined channels to be used for data transmission. Alternatively, contiguous channels could be grouped together to form separate voice and data regions. During idle periods, the traffic assigned to one region would make use of capacity nominally assigned to the other region.

Figure 16b shows an interleaved approach in which channels (individually and in groups) are assigned to voice or data customers on demand. Channels are reserved prior to transmission and cannot be used for any other purpose unless disconnected. This technique is suitable for user-to-user synchronous data, such as voice, facsimile, or long data files, which require continuous transmission, since fragments of these calls can fit nicely into preassigned time slots. The same techniques can be used to carry user-to-user asynchronous traffic, e.g., packet-switched interactive data between a terminal and computer. Here the traffic is bursty, i.e., it occurs in time according to a nonregular pattern. Allocating entire channel widths to these types of calls for the full duration of the connection can be very wasteful of bandwidth, particularly in the case of asynchronous, low-speed customers.

Another form of circuit switching is "fast" circuit switching. Fast circuit switching causes a circuit to be established more quickly than conventional circuit switching for every message which is to be sent. The circuit is then rapidly disconnected after transmission. As switching technology progresses, it is predicted that switching systems will be developed that will enable the setup of a call circuit in 140 msec or less. Long-haul common channel signaling could speed up end-to-end connections. This would be sufficient to satisfy all requirements for voice and data traffic within the circuit-switching structure. Typically, voice and bulk data applications would use the traditional circuit-switching method, while interactive data would be fast-circuit-switched. For interactive data traffic, a circuit would be established for every message, held for the duration of the transaction, and then disconnected. The strict delay requirements for interactive data applications would thus be satisfied. Only a small amount of transmission capacity would be wasted during circuit setup and disconnection because of the increased speeds involved. The recovered capacity could be used to transfer more data, thus improving network efficiency.

A factor that works against fast circuit switching is that, while the 140-msec connect time is generally agreed to, no known architecture and design to achieve this exists today. In addition, although this technique provides for the unification of voice and data, it is not as suitable to the servicing of voice and data subscribers at various channel rates as, for example, packet switching.

During a voice conversation, only one speaker at a time is using the channel. Even then, the speaker has pauses between words. For a large number of speakers and channels, it is estimated that the channel is in use an average of about 40% of the time.

A way to improve the relatively poor transmission efficiency of circuit switching is another form of circuit switching called *time assignment speech interpolation* (TASI).[14,15] TASI is a well-known technique used in submarine cables, in which the idle time during conversational voice calls is used to accommodate additional calls. During speech silence intervals, transmission ceases, and the available capacity can be used to transmit the "talkspurts" from other calls. The original speech is said to be interpolated. A control channel is used to select which talkspurts to apply to the channel. If the number of channels is large enough, most of the idle time on the transmission link can be filled, giving an enhancement in transmission capacity greater than twofold.

A disadvantage of this technique is that talkspurts cannot be managed by delay, but must be treated with a loss or blocking strategy. This will tend to decrease overall network efficiency, since talkspurts are either accepted or blocked; they cannot be stored and transmitted later when capacity becomes available.

Figure 17 shows how 46 voice conversations can "time-share" 23 PCM channels, giving a TASI advantage of 2 to 1. The circled numbers represent active speech sources. During this time-slice, talkspurt No. 1 is carried by channel 2, talkspurt No. 4 by channel 3, talkspurt No. 7 by channel 4, etc. At subsequent periods of time, voice sources become active and inactive on a dynamic basis. When, as will occasionally happen, more than 23 customers are active at once, a random selection is made of the voice sources to be included in that frame, and the remainder are TASI-clipped. This process, called "hashing," ensures that the same customer will not always be clipped when contention for voice slots occurs.

One method of control is illustrated here—a TASI map is transmitted in the signaling channel, made up of 46 bits sent during multiple frames with a 6-bit error correcting code. Each bit indicates whether there is voice activity in that frame on any of the 46 simultaneous voice connections being sustained. When voice activity exists, a minimum of 10 msec is trans-

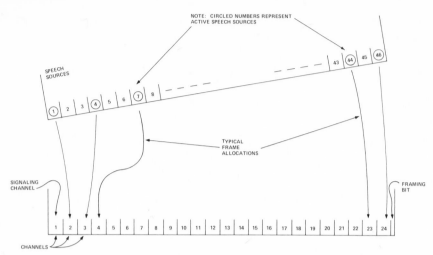

Fig. 17.   Use of TASI to carry additional voice conversations.

mitted at 64 kbit/sec PCM voice, or 640 bits. This corresponds to 10 msec/125 μsec or 80 T1 frames.

Of course, data could be sent instead of voice during a TASI interval.

5.2.   Packet Switching

Under the packet-switching concept, both voice and data can be packetized, sent through the network, and reassembled into complete messages or voice streams at the receiver. However, different packet sizes and different transport protocols may be used for speech and data depending on the application.[16] For a fixed-path transport protocol, signaling messages in the form of packets are propagated from the source switch to the destination switch to establish a path connection for the subsequent voice or data call. Software pointers set up at the tandem switching nodes along the path determine the outgoing link for every packet entering the node. During conversation or data transfer, packets transit this fixed path. Upon termination of the connections, the path is released. Of course, trunks along the path are time-shared by many packet users. During the conversation, no channel capacity is reserved along the fixed path, nor is any switch capacity dedicated to the call.

Two other concepts incorporate the voice packetizing technique. In the first approach, voice packets are routed over a fixed path, but data packets are independently routed to avoid congestion points. In the second approach, both voice and data packets are independently routed. No path is set up for the duration of the call. Each voice packet is transported across the network to its destination independently of other packets for the same connection. Individual packets can be alternately routed as appropriate. This approach is a "pure" packet network, and could result in high transmission efficiency and low network delays. However, there is a price to be paid in both approaches: increasing complexity and delay, due to the reassembly process (for both voice and data), and increasing software complexity of the routing algorithm.

Figure 18a shows a packet-voice network and a typical packet-voice information flow. Speech is digitized at the customer headset but packetized at the source switch. We will assume that signaling has been completed so that a connection has been established between customers. Conversation ensues.

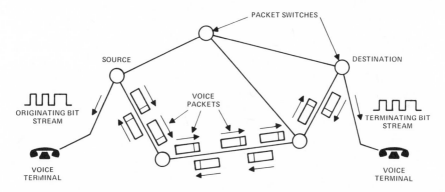

(a) PACKET-SWITCHED VOICE SYSTEM INFORMATION FLOW

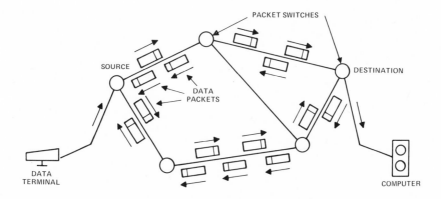

(b) PACKET-SWITCHED DATA INFORMATION FLOW

Fig. 18.   Packet-switched voice and data information flow.

At the source switch, the incoming information bit stream is divided into information packets, a header containing appropriate address and control information is appended, and the packet is placed on a channel output queue. Packets are routed along a fixed path to the destination. No link-by-link error control, i.e., error detection and retransmission, is provided. At tandem switches, packet processing is kept to a minimum (consisting of read-in, header analysis, read-out). Packets arriving at the destination node are analyzed, and the header removed. Packets arrive in the order in which they are sent, therefore reassembly is not required. The resulting information bit stream is collected and then presented to the customer.

Figure 18b shows the information flow for a typical packet-switched data transaction. At the source switch, the incoming bit stream is packetized as in Fig. 18a. However, individual packets can take one of many routes to their destination. At the destination node, reassembly of packet order may be required before presentation of the delivered bit stream to the destination terminal (in this case, the computer).

The packetizing of voice is receiving considerable interest as an approach for integrated voice and data networks.[17–23] Packetized speech lends itself well to the use of TASI techniques, and hence, provides a gain in transmission efficiency. It also lends itself well to the servicing of voice customers at various transmission rates. (For a constant sampling interval, different bit rates for encoding voice yield different packet sizes, or the packet size could be made constant by changing the sampling interval for each voice rate.) Packet voice has been demonstrated on the ARPANET, during the Packet Radio experiments at SRI, and during the Atlantic Satellite Packet experiment.

There are several system issues in the packet switching of voice which must be resolved. For example, packets may become queued up at nodes, causing delays for the packetized voice which are psychologically intolerable. The problem becomes worse when many tandem links are used.

Packets which are lost through misrouting, or discarded by the network because of late delivery, affect the continuity of the reconstituted bit stream presented to a listener, resulting in missing speech segments. This deterioration in voice quality worsens under congested load conditions.

The longer one makes the voice packet, the better the transmission efficiency, but the longer the delay—with the resulting psychological effect. Alternatively, the longer one makes the control segment of the voice packet, the more uniform the supervisory processing, but the worse the network delay and transmission efficiency.

The processing requirements for voice traffic are expected to be more demanding than those of data traffic because voice has a greater traffic load than interactive data traffic. In addition, one would like to make buffer sizes small enough to keep average delay small but large enough to hold the voice packets.

An increase in network connectivity leads to a decrease in voice delay. However, this results in increased network transmission cost. Finally, standard packet switch protocols, such as CCITT X.25, do not conveniently accommodate voice.

Thus, packet switching for data meets most requirements for a network. However, packet switching for voice is still in the research stage.

5.3.   Hybrid Switching

There are several reasons to consider a switching approach for integrating voice and data which uses the best features of circuit and packet switching. We saw that circuit switching was ill suited for satisfying all classes of data traffic. The results for packet switching of voice and data show that further work is required to evaluate the effects of delay, the approaches to packetization, and their impact on speech quality and the increase in processor loading due to packetized voice. In addition, various studies have shown that circuit switching is more cost-effective for data traffic which is characterized by long continuous messages, while packet switching is more cost-effective for traffic composed of short messages (see Fig. 14). Therefore, a case can be made that the user would benefit by providing both circuit and packet switching services in the same network. We will call this a hybrid approach to switching.[24-26]

The approach is to divide wideband digital trunk capacity into contiguous master frames in the time domain with a constant period, as shown in Fig. 19. The frame period, once selected, would be constant (e.g., 10 or 20 msec) throughout a system. Within a frame, bits will be utilized for synchronism to indicate the start of a frame, a Class I region which contains those types of traffic normally associated with circuit-switched traffic, and a Class II region which incorporates packet-switched or message-switched traffic and is handled as packet-switched data. Also within a frame, traffic of varying bandwidths can be accommodated simultaneously by allocating bits as needed, until the total capacity of the wideband trunk has been allocated.

For example, if the period of the master frame were 10 msec and the transmission rate were 1.544 Mbit/sec, then 15,440 bits would be provided

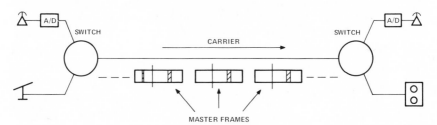

Fig. 19.   Master frame concept.

within each master frame. Frames would be transmitted at a rate of 100 frames per second. Digitized voice at 16 kbit/sec would require a 160-bit allocation per frame. Interactive data between a terminal and computer would be transmitted in the form of packets. Incorporated into the packet format will be information necessary for routing, security, identity, and precedence.

There are several variations of the basic hybrid switching generic concept. In the *slotted envelope network*, or SENET, scheme, voice is circuit-switched, interactive data are packet-switched, and bulk data are either circuit- or packet-switched.[24] TASI can be used to improve the transmission efficiency by making use of the silent intervals in the circuit-switched speech conversations. Another hybrid switching scheme is the Flexible Hybrid approach. In this scheme, voice and interactive data are packet-switched, while bulk data messages are circuit-switched.[27] There is also a scheme where the frame interval itself is allowed to vary in order to help eliminate unused capacity at the end of a master frame.[28,29]

There are several options for sharing transmission capacity in the SENET scheme. Fixed portions of the available transmission capacity can be reserved for circuit-switched traffic (e.g., voice) and packet-switched traffic (e.g., interactive data). This is called a fixed boundary arrangement. Each form of traffic coexists with the other on the same transmission link but cannot make use of capacity which has not been preassigned to it. The chief disadvantage of this approach is an inefficient use of transmission capacity, since one type of traffic cannot utilize capacity reserved for the other even though unused capacity may be available.

Some of the disadvantages of the fixed boundary arrangement are eliminated by allowing the boundary to move. This approach, while somewhat more difficult to implement, allows both types of traffic to coexist on the same link according to a flexible boundary rule in which transmission capacity is dynamically shared between the two classes. While a boundary is assigned between packet- and circuit-switched capacity, one type of traffic can utilize idle channel capacity normally assigned to the other. This leads to a system that requires less overall capacity than separate systems for equivalent performance, at the expense of organizational complexity and memory.

Miyahara and Hasegawa have proposed a hybrid switching method in which the portion of the frame containing packet-switched data is allowed to vary.[28,29] Circuit-switched user-to-user synchronous data are placed in the circuit-switched portion of the frame. Packets fit into that part of the frame following the circuit-switched portion. It would be desirable to transmit as many packets as possible, and thus minimize the idle capacity at the end of the frame. But, because of the constant frame size, the last packet in the frame may be too long, in which case the capacity would be wasted, or if the packet length is shortened, the overhead of that packet relative to its information field increases. However, if the frame interval is allowed to vary, a packet which exceeds the capacity of a frame can be transmitted over two consecutive nominal frame periods. This will result in increased transmission efficiency.

However, when a packet is being transmitted over two frame periods, the circuit-switched region of the next consecutive frame cannot begin its scheduled transmission. Under these conditions the arrival times of successive circuit-switched bit-groups will no longer be equal to the constant frame interval (e.g., 10 msec), but will vary as the frame interval is allowed to vary. Thus, the transmission delay of the circuit-switched data will no longer be constant. However, if the variance of the frame length can be upper bounded to a maximum value, which has negligible impact on voice quality and intelligibility, the transparency to delay, which is a natural consequence of circuit switching, can still be offered.

One of the disadvantages of the SENET approach discussed earlier is that the transmission efficiency suffers as a result of the inefficiency in transmitting circuit-switched voice. TASI is one method to improve the efficiency, but at the price of adding a considerable amount of complexity. An alternative approach is the previously described flexible hybrid concept, shown in Fig. 20.[27,30] Here, voice is transmitted as packet-switched data without error control via fixed path routing. Interactive and narrative/record data are transmitted as error-protected packet-switched data via independent, or adaptive routing. Bulk, facsimile, and burst data are transmitted as circuit-switched data in one direction with error control provided via packets or a small circuit-switched transmission capacity allocated in the reverse direction.

The result is an increase in transmission efficiency, since the packet switching of voice provides a TASI-like advantage. During speech silences,

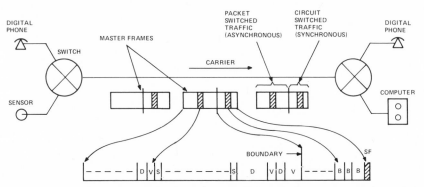

Fig. 20.   Flexible hybrid channel capacity structure. KEY: SF, start of frame marker; B, bulk data; V, packet-switched voice; D, packet-switched data; S, signaling message.

packet voice transmission ceases, hence the capacity not being used is available for other users. In addition, the bulk data class is transmitted efficiently, since long messages tend to favor circuit-switched operation and short messages favor packet-switched operation. Some difficulties in this bulk data scheme are that the simplex transmission of data requires additional control maps (in addition to the packet data) at either end of the communication link. Further, it is necessary to provide error control in the reverse direction via packets in the packet-switched data region.

5.4. Comparison of Integrated Switching Technologies

There are a number of opinions among investigators concerning which switching technology is best for integrating voice and data.[31-33] Gitman and Frank have concluded that packet-switching networks are more economical than networks using any other switching technology, under a wide range of assumptions about traffic, cost, and other parameters, see Fig. 21.[31] However, the differences between packet and hybrid are small.

McAuliffe states that because of the large number of packets necessary for voice communication, "a purely packet communications approach to an integrated system does not appear the most optimum," and that a hybrid system is preferable.[32]

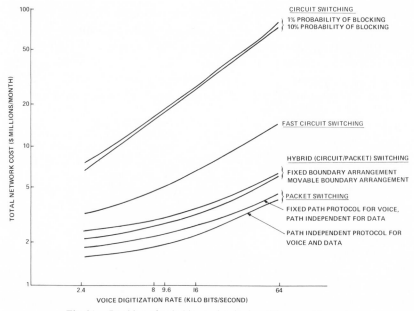

Fig. 21.   Ranking of switching technologies with respect to cost.

Rudin takes a middle course, and concludes that the ideal is "an integrated system wherein network resources could easily be allocated to either circuit switching or packet switching users."[33] He notes that, "for a spectrum of users and certainly in an environment where future applications and traffic patterns are unknown, a good case can be made for the provision of both circuit and packet switching services." His approach is a form of hybrid system, in which packet-switching services are added to a circuit-switching backbone. The boundary between packet and circuit switching is a function of message length, transmission distance, and other factors.

6. Example of an Integrated Packet- and Circuit-Switching Approach

In this section, we examine briefly the slotted envelope network (SENET) concept in order to get a better feel for the design issues involved with implementing an integrated voice/data system.[24,26] The SENET concept divides the trunk occupancy into constant-period, self-synchronizing master frames. A start-of-frame (SOF) marker provides the self-synchronizing feature for identifying each master frame. Following this marker, there are two frame regions: Class I and Class II. The Class I region contains those types of traffic normally associated with circuit-switched traffic. The Class II region contains those types of traffic normally associated with packet- or message-switched traffic. Connections in the Class I region are allocated and maintained by frame allocation maps located in switch software at each end of the link between two switches. Changes in these maps are implemented by common channel signaling messages, which are signaling messages handled as Class II packet data. Both common channel signaling messages and packet/message-switched data are consistent with the proposed American National Standard for Advanced Data Communications Control Procedures (ADCCP) format.[34]

Figure 22 illustrates a typical master frame with a constant 10-msec period, synchronized by a start-of-frame marker and sent over a T1 carrier. The Class I region is shown carrying channel connections for various voice, facsimile, video, and bulk data characterized by a variety of digitization techniques and transmission rates, all dynamically allocated to the common master frame. Each of the wedges in the Class I region represents the bits associated with a specific call. For example, the 7th call allocated in the frame is a 16-kbit/sec continuous variable slope delta modulated (CVSD) voice call handled by reserving 160 bits in each master frame for the duration of the conversation. If a call lasts 5 min, then 160 bits are reserved for 30,000 master frames.

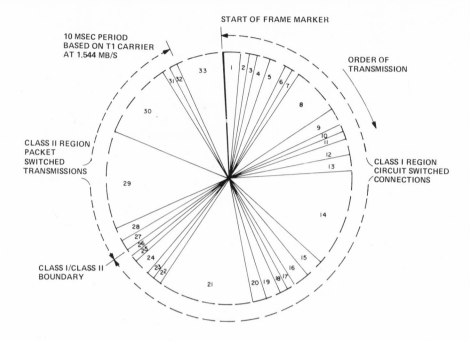

MASTER FRAME BIT ASSIGNMENTS

NO.	START	WIDTH	IDENTITY
−	1	16	FRAME MARKER
1	17	320	VOICE
2	337	160	VOICE
3	497	160	VOICE
7	1,457	160	VOICE
8	1,617	1,000	BULK DATA
9	2,617	320	VOICE
13	3,577	320	VOICE
14	3,897	2,000	VIDEO
15	5,897	320	VOICE
20	7,177	320	VOICE
21	7,497	2,000	FACSIMILE
22	9,497	160	VOICE
24	9,817	320	VOICE
25	10,137	160	VOICE
26	10,297	160	VOICE
−	10,457	−	CLASS I/II BOUND
27	10,457	224	SIGNALING
28	10,681	224	SIGNALING
29	10,905	2,000	PACKET
30	10,985	1,080	PACKET
31	14,065	168	SIGNALING
32	14,233	120	SIGNALING
33	14,345	1,095	IDLE CAPACITY

Fig. 22.   Integrated voice/data master frame structure.

The Class II region of packet-switched transmissions is shown in this specific frame carrying four common channel signaling messages and two data messages of different sizes and ordered by precedence. Precedence is a rank assigned to indicate the degree of preference or priority to be given in processing or protecting the offered message or packet. The remaining portion of the frame is shown as idle capacity. The end of each master frame is marked by the start-of-frame marker of the next subsequent frame.

Within the Class I region, call location tends to reflect primarily the age of the call. The closer a given call is to the SOF marker, the older, in general, that call is. As calls are terminated, the Class I region shrinks and the Class I/II boundary moves toward the start-of-frame marker. This shrinking of the Class I region causes the Class II region to expand, thereby allowing more data packets to be transmitted. In this way the regions react dynamically to changes in one another, resulting in a maximization of the throughput.

For the duration of a call, the minimum Class I region is fixed. However, the number of data packets within the Class II region is dynamic, depending on the available remaining capacity.

Figure 23 shows Class I channel allocations for 15 different rates of transmission of 10 different kinds of real and near-real-time communications. Included are digitization techniques such as linear predictive coding (LPC), adaptive predictive coding (APC), continuous variable slope delta modulation (CVSD), pulse code modulation (PCM), differential pulse code modulation (DPCM), vocoders, forward error-corrected (FEC) facsimile, FEC-bulk sensor data, facsimile, and low-speed video. For a 10-msec master frame period these calls would require 24 to 2000 bits per frame depending on the types of traffic present, for each of the 100 frames per second.

Additions to the Class I region are made at the end of the region. As calls terminate, all subsequent allocations would move up toward the SOF marker. Thus, the Class I region will vary dynamically, but always in a direction to provide the minimum size for Class I calls currently being serviced and therefore providing the maximum amount of master frame capacity for Class II transmissions.

The Class I region is bounded by the SOF marker and by the allocation maps maintained in switch software at both ends of each link. These allocation maps are specific as to call identity, starting points of the allocation in the master frame, and magnitude of allocation per connection, as well as precedence of the call. The Class II region is self-identifying, occurring at the first Advanced Data Communications Control Procedures flag sequence following the SOF marker. This location can be cross-checked by integrating the total map allocations for Class I with respect to the individual width per allocation. No end-of-frame marker is necessary;

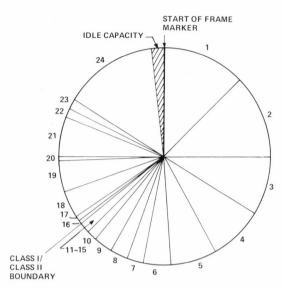

Fig. 23. Typical master frame map allocations for the SENET concept.

the start-of-frame of each successive master frame serves as the end-of-frame of the preceding master frame. Idle capacity is filled with synchronous characters (e.g., Advanced Data Communications Control Procedures flag sequences).

Figure 23 also shows four different common channel signaling messages and four packets. Allocations to the Class II region are made by first-come/first-served service with respect to precedence as long as Class II space is available. Typical data transmission (interactive, query/response, data base update, and narrative/record traffic) lengths range from 600 to 7500 bits per transfer while bulk traffic ranges in length from 1 million to 100 million bits per transfer. Common channel signaling messages are normally equated to the precedence of the Class I connection which they concern. If the common channel signaling message concerns terminating a Class I call (thereby releasing Class I capacity), the message is handled at an artifically high level of precedence. Automatic Repeat Request (ARQ), in the event of errors, would be at the same precedence level as the message or packet it concerns.

Interactive, query/response (Q/R) and data base update transactions would be set up analogous to Class I calls where there must be an assurance of a receiver for transmission before accepting data from the originator. Narrative/Record (N/R), bulk data and automatic repeat request-facsimile data would be stored-and-forwarded.

Figure 24 shows the functional block diagram of an integrated voice/data switch having a distributed system architecture employing distributed

TYPICAL MASTER FRAME BIT ALLOCATIONS

NO.	START	WIDTH	IDENTITY	ALLOCATION PURPOSE (TYPICAL)
–	1	16	FRAME MARKER	16-BIT PSEUDO RANDOM CODE
1	17	2,000	200 kB/s DATA	FEC-FACSIMILE, FEC-BULK SENSOR DATA, OR LOW SPEED VIDEO
2	2,017	1,800	180 kB/s DATA	FEC-FACSIMILE, FEC-BULK SENSOR DATA, OR LOW SPEED VIDEO
3	3,817	1,500	150 kB/s DATA	FEC-FACSIMILE, FEC-BULK SENSOR DATA, OR LOW SPEED VIDEO
4	5,317	1,200	120 kB/s DATA	FEC-FACSIMILE OR FEC-BULK SENSOR DATA
5	6,517	1,000	100 kB/s DATA	FEC-FACSIMILE OR FEC-BULK SENSOR DATA
6	7,517	640	64 kB/s VOICE	PULSE CODE MODULATION
7	8,517	500	50 kB/s VOICE	PULSE CODE MODULATION
8	8,657	480	48 kB/s VOICE	DIFFERENTIAL PULSE CODE MODULATION
9	9,137	320	32 kB/s VOICE	CONTINUOUS VARIABLE SLOPE DELTA MODULATION
10	9,457	160	16 kB/s VOICE	CONTINUOUS VARIABLE SLOPE DELTA MODULATION
11	9,617	96	9.6 kB/s VOICE	ADAPTIVE PREDICTIVE CODING
12	9,713	80	8 kB/s VOICE	ADAPTIVE PREDICTIVE CODING
13	9,793	48	4.8 kB/s DATA	FACSIMILE
14	9,841	40	4 kB/s VOICE	LINEAR PREDICTIVE CODING
15	9,881	24	2.4 kB/s VOICE	CHANNEL VOCODER
–	9,905	–	–	CLASS I/II BOUNDARY
16	9,905	112	SIGNALING	CALL ANSWERBACK, RELEASE, PREEMPT RELEASE, OPERATOR RECALL
17	10,017	104	SIGNALING	ACKNOWLEDGE, GLARE, CALLED PARTY UNAVAILABLE, INVALID NUMBER
18	10,121	752	PACKET	INTERACTIVE, QUERY, DATA BASE UPDATE
19	10,873	712	PACKET	NARRATIVE/RECORD – ONE OF MULTIPLE PACKET INTERCHANGE
20	11,585	104	SIGNALING	ALL TRUNKS BUSY, EQUIPMENT BUSY, INVALID ROUTE
21	11,689	1,080	PACKET	INTERACTIVE, RESPONSE – ONE OF MULTIPLE PACKET INTERCHANGE
22	12,769	224	SIGNALING	CALL INITIATE
23	12,993	160	SIGNALING	CALL COMPLETE, ACKNOWLEDGE, CALL INIT.
24	13,153	2,080	PACKET	BULK DATA, NON SENSOR BULK DATA, ARQ-FACSIMILE
–	15,233	207	–	IDLE CAPACITY

Fig. 23 *(continued)*

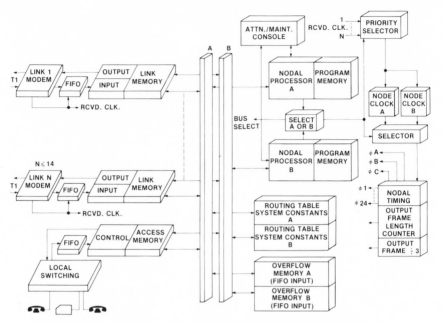

Fig. 24.   Integrated voice/data switch using the SENET concept.

data memory and distributed processors with their associated I/O hardware. The distributed control structure places link (or interconnecting switch) control functions and access area control functions (for customer access to a switch) at the link/access level, away from the nodal functions. This is efficient because it isolates the nodal processor equipment from real-time operations.

The main switch artery is the redundant tristate level common buses *A* and *B*. Redundant nodal control processors access the buses and provide a maximum service capability of 14 DS1 trunk links and approximately 600 local subscribers. One bus port will service one DS1 interface or approximately 300 local customers.

The nodal processor equipment group contains the system clocks, routing table, and nodal processor. All bus activity and system input/output are coordinated by the system clocks. The nodal processor performs supervisory control over nodal activities, e.g., updating the routing table and interfacing with the attendant console. Diagnostic routines are also run by the nodal group. Since so much of the intelligence has been allocated to the links, the need for redundancy in the nodal group (e.g., routing table) is reduced. Also, the minimization of nodal functions suggests the use of a microprocessor for nodal processing.

The link memory is distributed with a port memory module at every bus port. The incoming bit stream is read into the link memory on a frame-by-frame basis. For circuit-switched calls (Class I), the input link processor gets internal routing instructions during call setup from the routing table which tells it which bus port is to retransmit the bits associated with the particular call or transaction. The transmitting output processor (not necessarily associated with the same link) is given the memory address of the data to be switched by the input link processor via the tristate bus. During the ensuing call, the output processor directs the extraction of bits stored in memory associated with that call by providing output hardware with the memory address plus byte count of the data to be transmitted. The transmitting output processor retrieves the stored data and incorporates it into its transmitted serial bit stream, along with the data from other circuit-switched calls and transactions.

For packet-switched transactions (Class II), after incoming data are stored in link memory, the outgoing link is determined from examination of the address and routing fields of individual packets by the input processor. This information is then passed to the output processor along with the address of the stored data, for retrieval and incorporation into the transmitted output bit stream.

The arrangement is efficient in terms of memory utilization because of the nonredundant data storage and the fact that memory is dynamically allocatable by each set of input/output processors. If additional memory is required by a port processor, the nodal processor can assign up to eight port processors to temporarily use portions of the overflow memory.

Timing is based on parallel 8-bit data transfers. Three timing phases are contained in each bit time. Therefore, 8 bit times provide 24 discrete time positions (the selection of three phases per bit time was dictated by a solid-state memory having a cycle time of 215 nsec). In this scheme, two timing phases allow for direct memory access (DMA) transfer of 8-bit bytes into individual link port memories within a single processor memory cycle, while the remaining phases are assigned for such functions as output or routing table update. Note that bus contention does not exist with this arrangement. Every processor function (input, output, etc.) has its own time on the bus.

7.   New Developments and Services

Some alternative strategies for transition to an integrated network are shown in Fig. 25.[35] In the first example, the user community is divided into two classes: those requiring circuit-switched service and those requiring packet-switched service. In order to maximize the use of existing switching and transmission facilities, packet-switched service is considered

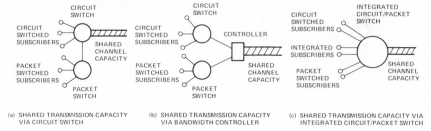

Fig. 25.   Alternative strategies for transition to an integrated network.

as simply an adjunct to circuit switching. Requests for a portion of the shared transmission bandwidth by packet-switched customers are carried out under a circuit superstructure. After channel capacity is allocated for packet-switched transactions, information transmission is carried out using packet-switching techniques. The primary advantage of this method is the ease of transition into the integrated network environment based on maximal use of existing facilities.

The second strategy breaks customers up into two classes as before with existing switching facilities used to gain access to a bandwidth controller. The controller allocates specific channel capacity for use by circuit- or packet-switch customers on a per call basis. In this way it controls sharing of the transmission capacity between both types of customers. Thus, packet-switching transactions obtain channel allocations according to their own packet-switching protocols (as opposed to circuit-switching protocols).

The third strategy includes strategy two but also accommodates an "integrated" customer, who can transmit information under either switching discipline. The switch CPU determines the switching mode to be used when an integrated customer requests transmission capacity. Potential savings can accrue due to sharing of the switch hardware/software resources; however, this could be offset by an increased functional complexity.

New developments in the field of integrated voice and data are continuing to take place.[36–39] The TRAN system dynamically assigns trunk capacity to different traffic types. Although specifically designed for data, it will eventually include voice and FAX as well. Time division multiplexing is used to assign trunk bandwidth to circuit-switched, packet-switched, or PACUIT-switched connections. The PACUIT technique makes use of a composite packet, containing data from many users, all traveling between the same source and destination. The result is an efficient use of bandwidth, particularly for asynchronous low-speed users.

Computerized private branch exchanges (CBXs) are now available which mix voice and data on a circuit-switched basis. Table 3 identifies several CBXs and some of their characteristics. In a CBX, all traffic within the switch is digitized and handled as if it were data. The CBX is a

Table 3. Computerized Private Branch Exchange (CBX) Characteristics

Manufacturer	CBX Model	Modulation technique	Data-handling capability	Comments
Intecom	IBX	Pulse code modulation	56 kbit/sec asynchronous and synchronous	Offers analog-to-digital voice conversion at the phone set (using proprietary phones)
Lexar	LBX	Adaptive delta modulation	19.2 kbit/sec asynchronous	One of the few CBXs not using PCM as the modulation technique
Datapoint	ISX	Pulse code modulation	56 kbit/sec asynchronous and synchronous	Able to interface with attached resource computer local network and thereby provide customer with hybrid, local network/CBX configuration
Northern Telecom	SL-1	Pulse code modulation	9.6 kbit/sec asynchronous	Plans to offer the digital switching of synchronous devices (terminals or processors)
Rolm	CBX	Pulse code modulation	19.2 kbit/sec asynchronous	Offers one of the least expensive per-port prices
AT&T	Dimension	Pulse amplitude modulation	4.8 kbit/sec asynchronous and synchronous	AT&T's replacement for the dimension will be the antelope, an all-digital CBX

computer-driven PBX that contains its operating instructions in programmable storage. Because of this, the user can usually define and alter a CBX's operation.

Table 4 shows some of the major advanced networks provided by the common carriers and identifies the traffic—voice, data, message, and FAX—available either now or in the near future.[40,41] Various services include circuit and packet switching, satellite access, message transfer, intercity, and international service.

Most carriers can be placed in one of three categories—voice, data, or message services. In the United States, those involved primarily with voice are AT&T, GTE, ITT, MCI, Southern Pacific, RCA Americom; with message, Western Union, Graphnet, and the International record carriers; with data/message, Tymnet, Telenet, ITT, and ACS: and with voice/data/message, SBS and American Satellite. Some carriers may carry traffic in addition to that listed: Western Union offers some voice communications although they are primarily involved with message traffic. Carriers have specialized in one or two areas because of the separate networks that exist in the voice/data/message fields. Until recently, the trend has been toward separate, rather than integrated networks.

However, the trend is toward integrated networks and the reason is the overlapping network requirements of users. SBS will provide users with voice, wideband data, video teleconferencing, electronic mail, and computer and voice resource sharing. American Satellite will offer similar services. ACS will provide packet switching for interactive data, message switching with various priority levels, and simple facilities for the preparation and

Table 4. Advanced Networks and the Services Offered

Network	Traffic	Service
Satellite Business Systems (SBS)	Voice/data/video/message	Point-to-point satellite
American Satellite Corp.	Voice/data/video/message	Point-to-point satellite
ACS (AT&T)	Data/message	Narrowband data; format/speed conversion
GTE Telenet	Data/message	Packet switching
Tymnet	Data/message	Packet switching
ITT (FAXPAK)	FAX/Data/message	Store and forward facsimile
MCI	Voice	Intercity transmission via microwave
Southern Pacific	Voice	Intercity transmission via microwave
RCA	Voice	Intercity satellite
Graphnet	Message	Intercity packet switching
Western Union	Message	Circuit switch message service

editing of messages. FAXPAK (ITT) will initially offer store-and-forward message services for FAX, followed by packet switching later on.

As the demand for integrated service grows, a more comprehensive set of services will be provided by the common carriers. Carriers must determine whether enough users will subscribe to a particular service to justify the large capital outlay. Users must decide whether integrated services will increase productivity enough to make their investment worthwhile.

8. Summary and Conclusions

In this chapter we have described the differences between circuit and packet switching. Each has a set of strengths and weaknesses, and an optimum switching approach has been suggested through the integration of the best features of both techniques. The integration of voice and data should provide lower network costs and give the capability of servicing diverse customer terminal types at various transmission rates.

After examining the characteristics of voice and data traffic, we investigated three generic switching concepts for integrating voice and data into a common network—circuit switching, packet switching, and hybrid (circuit/packet) switching. We examined several variations within each switching category and looked closely at the issues in packetized speech.

We then turned to a specific design approach to illustrate a typical integrated voice/data switch. This design is based on a hybrid switching concept and a distributed architecture in which microprocessors are assigned the tasks of servicing a variable number of trunks and subscribers. We concluded our investigation into integrated digital voice and data switching by identifying some strategies for transition to an integrated network from an existing network. Some new development work which is currently taking place was also discussed.

In conclusion, integrated voice/data systems appear to offer considerable advantages over conventional approaches in terms of cost and meeting customer requirements. However, further study, experiment, and development are required to answer many of the questions raised.

Questions

1. Table 1 identifies characteristics of different network traffic types as a function of various parameters, e.g., call duration, error control, etc. Consider the two additional parameters: transmission continuity and out-of-sequence data. Describe the characteristics of each traffic type for each of these new parameters.

2. In Section 4.3, it states that data traffic is characterized by a tendency to fairly short messages, often exchanged at high speeds. For time-sharing systems, where

messages are on the order of 1000 bits, would circuit switching be appropriate for a transmission rate of 56 kbit/s? 9.6 kbit/s? 150 bit/s? Why?

3. For file transfer systems, where messages are several thousand bits or more and should be sent at the same time, would circuit switching be appropriate for a transmission rate of 56 kbit/s? 9.6 kbit/s? 150 bit/s?

4. In circuit switching, a physical connection is provided between end users in a network. What sort of connection is provided between end users in a packet or message switching network?

5. Delayed delivery of data is possible with packet and message switching, but not with circuit-switching. Explain why not.

6. Circuit switching and packet switching both provide essentially real-time delivery of information. Message switching does not. Why?

7. Is this statement true or false? The following are characteristics of the circuit switching of data: multiaddressing, speed–code conversion, blocking under overload. Explain your answers.

8. Is blocking with overload a characteristic of message and packet switching? Speed–code conversion? Multiaddressing? Explain.

9. In the hybrid (circuit–packet) switching model, describe how connections in the Class I region are allocated and maintained.

10. Explain how synchronization of the master frames in a hybrid (circuit–packet) system could be implemented.

References

1 L. Roberts, "The Evolution of Packet Switching," *Proc. IEEE*, vol. 66, pp. 1307–1313, November, 1978.

2. G. Coviello and R. Lyons, "Conceptual Approaches to Switching in Future Military Networks," *IEEE Trans. Comm.* vol. COM-28, pp. 1491–1498, September, 1980.

3. J. Martin, *Telecommunications and the Computer*, Prentice-Hall, Englewood Cliffs, New Jersey, 1976.

4. R. Howe and R. Cournoyer, "The Integrated AUTODIN System," *Signal*, vol. 33, No. 8, 105–110, May/June, 1979.

5. M. Schwartz, *Computer Communications Network Design and Analysis*, Prentice-Hall, Englewood Cliffs, New Jersey, 1977.

6. D. Davies, D. Barber, W. Price, and C. Solomonides, *Computer Networks and Their Protocols*, John Wiley & Sons, Chichester, Great Britain, 1979.

7. E. Carne, "On Signals, Channels, Switches and Networks," GTE Laboratories, Inc., Waltham, Massachusetts, September 1981.

8. H. Cravis, "Local Networks for the 1980s," *Datamation*, vol. 27, No. 3, 98–104, March 1981.

9. H. Miyahara, T. Hasegawa, and Y. Teshigawara, "A Comparative Evaluation of Switching Methods in Computer Communication Networks," *International Communications Conference*, San Francisco, pp. 6-6–6-10, June 1975.

10. J. McQuillan and V. Cerf, "A Practical View of Computer Communications Protocols," The Institute of Electrical and Electronic Engineers, Inc., New York, 1978.

11. D. Davies and D. Barber, *Communication Networks for Computers*, Wiley, New York, 1973.

12. K. Schneider, I. Frisch, and W. Hsieh, "Integrating Voice and Data on Circuit Switched Networks," *EASCON*, Washington, D.C., pp. 720–732, 1978.

13. E. A. Harrington, "Voice/Data Integration Using Circuit Switched Networks," *IEEE Trans. Commun.*, vol. COM-28, pp. 781–793, June 1980.

14. K. Bullington and J. Fraser, "Engineering Aspects of TASI," *Bell Syst. Tech. J., vol. 38*, pp. 353–364, March 1959.

15. J. Fraser, D. Bullock, and N. Long, "Overall Characteristics of a TASI System," *Bell Syst. Tech. J., vol. XLI*, No. 4, pp. 1439–1454, July 1962.

16. O. A. Mowafi and W. J. Kelly, "Integrated Voice/Data Packet Switching Techniques for Future Military Networks," *IEEE Trans. Commun.*, vol. COM-28, pp. 1655–1662, September 1980.

17. G. J. Coviello, "Comparative Discussion of Circuit- vs Packet-Switched Voice," *National Telecommunication Conference*, Alabama, pp. 12.1.1–12.1.7, December 1978.

18. J. Forgie, "Speech Transmission in Packet-Switched Store and Forward Networks," *AFIPS National Computer Conference*, Anaheim, California, pp. 137–142, May 1975.

19. W. Naylor, "Stream Traffic Communication in Packet Switched Networks," Ph.D. thesis, UCLA, 1977.

20. Lincoln Laboratories, "Network Speech System Implication of Packetized Speech," Annual Report ESD-TR-77-178 September 20, 1976.

21. G. Coviello, E. Lake, and G. Redinbo, "System Design Implications of Packetized Voice," *International Communications Conference*, Chicago, Illinois, pp. 38.3–49 to 38.3–53, June 1976.

22. C. Weinstein, "Fractional Speech Loss and Talker Activity Model for TASI and for Packet-Switched Speech," *IEEE Trans. Commun.*, vol. COM-26, pp. 1253–1257, August 1978.

23. C. J. Weinstein and E. M. Hofstetter, "The Tradeoff between Delay and TASI Advantage in a Packetized Speech Multiplexer," *IEEE Trans. Commun.*, vol. COM-27, pp. 1716–1720, November 1979.

24. G. Coveillo and P. Vena, "Integration of Circuit/Packet Switching by a SENET (Slotted Envelope Network) Concept," *National Telecommunications Conference*, New Orleans, Louisiana, pp. 42-12 to 42-17, December 1975.

25. B. Ochiogrosso, I. Gitman, W. Hsieh, and H. Frank, "Performance Analysis of Integrated Switching Communication Systems," *National Telecommunications Conference*, Los Angeles, California, pp. 12:4-1 to 12:4-13, December 1977.

26. M. Ross, A. Tabbot, and J. Waite, "Design Approaches and Performance Criteria for Integrated Voice and Data Switching," *Proc. IEEE, vol. 65*, pp. 1283–1295, September 1977.

27. M. J. Ross and C. M. Sidlo, "Approaches to the Integration of Voice and Data Telecommunications," *National Telecommunications Conference*, Washington, D.C., pp. 46.6.1–46.6.8, November 1979.

28. H. Miyahara and T. Hasegawa, "Integrated Switching with Variable Frame and Packet," *International Conference on Communications*, Toronto, Canada, pp. 20.3.1–20.3.5, June 1978.

29. H. Miyahara and T. Hasegawa, "Performance Evaluation of Modified Multiplexing Technique with Two Types of Packets for Circuit and Packet Switched Traffic," *International Conference on Communications*, Boston, Massachusetts, 20.5.1–20.5.5, June 1979.

30. M. J. Ross, J. H. Gottschalck, and E. A. Harrington, "An Architecture for a Flexible Integrated Voice/Data Switch," *International Conference on Communications*, Seattle, Washington, pp. 21.6.1–21.6.5, June 1980.

31. I. Gitman and H. Frank, "Economic Analysis of Integrated Voice and Data Networks: A Case Study," *Proc. IEEE*, vol. 66(11), pp. 1549–1576, November 1978.

32. McAuliffe, D., "An Integrated Approach to Communications Switching," *International Conference on Communications*, Toronto, Canada, pp. 20.4.1–20.4.5, June 1978.

33. H. Rudin, "Studies on the Integration of Circuit and Packet Switching," *International Conference on Communications*, Toronto, Canada, pp. 20.2.1–20.2.7, June 1978.

34. Proposed American National Standard for Advanced Data Communications Control Procedures (ADCCP), Seventh Draft *American National Standards Institute*, December 14, 1977.

35. I. Gitman, H. Frank, B. Occhiogrosso, and H. Hsieh, "Issues in Integrated Network Design," *International Conference on Communications*, Chicago, Illinois, pp. 38.1-36 to 38.1-43, June 1977.

36. G. Davis, "The Changing Face of the Private Branch Exchange," *Data Commun.*, vol. 8, No. 8, pp. 43–49, August 1979.

37. S. Hester, "Managing the Combined Virtual Network," *Data Commun.*, vol. 8, No. 12, pp. 41–53, December 1979.

38. R. Sarch, "Drawing a Deep Breath for Next Year's Advances," *Data Commun.*, vol. 8, No. 12, pp. 71–81, December 1979.

39. E. Mier, "CBX's Have Inside Track in Office Race," *Data Commun.*, vol. 10, No. 6, pp. 48–53, June 1981.

40. S. Caswell, "Coming to Grips with Planned Carrier Services," *Data Commun.*, vol. 8, No. 11, pp. 48–54, November 1979.

41. C. Ungaro, "Federal and Local Issues Mark an Active Election Year," *Data Commun.*, vol. 8, No. 12, pp. 77–87, December 1980.

7

The Analog Termination

John C. McDonald

1. Introduction

Digital switching systems are frequently used to replace old and obsolete analog switching systems. The digital switch must have suitable analog terminations which are directly compatible with the existing analog telephone plant. In public applications, the digital switch should not exclusively require digital telephone instruments since it would be very difficult and costly to introduce a new type of telephone at the time of switching system cutover. In some cases, customers might already own their telephones and the new switching system should not preclude their use. In private applications, there is more flexibility in introducing digital telephones. But the private digital switch must have suitable analog terminations for trunks.

This chapter discusses the analog termination of a digital switch. This termination is the means by which a digital switching system delivers communication services using analog facilities. These facilities include analog customer loops connecting analog telephones to the switch, analog trunks connecting the switch to the network, and analog service circuits for devices such as multifrequency receivers. Previous chapters have described other elements of a digital switching system including time-divided networks and system control. Subsequent chapters will discuss the digital termination, digital signal processing, digital switching architectures, and networks of digital switching systems.

John C. McDonald • MBX Inc., 54 Comstock Hill Road, New Canaan, Connecticut 06840.

The analog termination is an extremely important element of a digital switching system. There are large quantities of analog terminations in a given system and these terminations establish many system parameters including cost, size, and power consumption. A large number of telephones are connected to the digital switch at the analog termination called the line circuit. The number of line circuit printed circuit boards in a local switching system far exceeds any other type in the system. Studies have shown[1] that the line circuit can represent up to 80% of the total manufacturing cost for such a system. Because of high line circuit usage, there is a potential for cost reduction through the use of very large scale integrated circuits (VLSI). The semiconductor industry has therefore become an important member of the digital switching system design team.

The analog terminations described in this chapter can be used in many types of communication systems including central office switching, PABX switching, and digital pair gain systems. While the role that the analog termination plays in the network is different for each of these system types, the analog termination technology discussed in this chapter applies to each. Section 2 defines the analog termination and describes its functional role in the digital switch. Requirements for analog terminations including the interface to telephone instruments and trunks are discussed in Section 3. Section 4 presents technology for digitizing the analog signal, which is, of course, prerequisite for digital switching. The chapter concludes with a description of the customer line circuit.

2. Line and Trunk Terminations

A digital switching system must provide a means to interface analog customer lines and analog interoffice trunks. This means is the analog termination. Analog line and trunk terminations are described in this section. A typical digital switching system is presented and the functions performed by the analog termination are described.

A typical digital switching system is shown in Fig. 1. Analog customer information sources include residence, business, and coin telephones. Data modems are also analog information sources since the modem is necessary to prepare digital information for transmission over analog circuits designed for voice. Analog information sources also include trunks to other switching systems, to operator positions, and to service circuits such as recorded announcement machines and multifrequency receivers.

Analog information is applied to the digital switch from a main distributing frame (MDF). The main distributing frame provides a convenient point for connecting the switch to the outside plant wiring and provides for mounting devices which limit the amplitude of overvoltage faults resulting

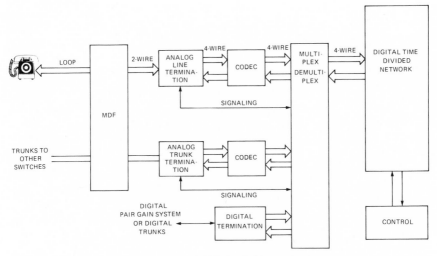

Fig. 1.   Typical digital switching system.

from lightning strikes and other high-voltage faults. This primary protection in combination with secondary protection in the analog termination prevents failure of sensitive electrical circuits in the digital switch.

The analog line termination performs many functions. First, it must supply battery feed to energize the transmitter in the telephone. This causes current to flow in the customer loop which carries signaling and conversation energy. Next, the line termination detects customer signaling such as off-hook and dial pulses. The line termination also converts the 2-wire subscriber loop signal into a 4-wire signal which is necessary for digital conversion and switching.

The process of 4-wire transmission is illustrated in Fig. 2. In a 2-wire circuit, information flows simultaneously in both directions of transmission. In a 4-wire circuit, information flows in one direction. The circuit device which performs the 2 to 4-wire conversion is called a "hybrid." (The hybrid transformer should not be confused with a hybrid microcircuit.) Analog signals originating at the telephone are applied to hybrid port *a* as shown. The hybrid provides for low transmission loss between ports *a* and *b*. Therefore, the analog signal originating at the telephone appears at hybrid port *b* and is applied to an analog-to-digital converter. The converter output is switched by a digital time divided network represented by Gates 1 and 2. Digital information at the output of Gate 2 is applied to a digital-to-analog converter which drives hybrid port *c*. The hybrid provides low transmission loss between ports *c* and *a* and the analog information is received by the far end telephone. Transmission in the opposite direction occurs by an identical process. Since analog-to-digital and digital-to-analog

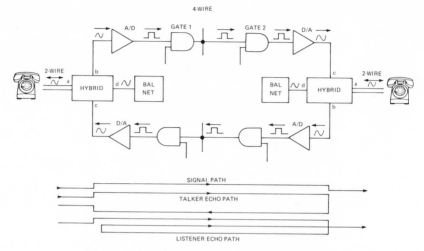

Fig. 2.   Four-wire transmission through a digital switch.

conversion and digital switching are unidirectional in transmission, it is necessary to establish a 4-wire circuit to perform the digital switching function.

Note that the 4-wire circuit forms a closed loop and therefore there is a potential for oscillation (commonly called singing). The hybrid circuit must therefore provide high transmission loss between ports *c* and *b*. The balance network attached to hybrid port *d* causes this transhybrid loss to be high as will be described in Section 5.

Referring again to Fig. 1, the analog line termination includes a hybrid and speech is digitized by the codec (coder/decoder). The outputs of many coders are multiplexed together and switched by the time-divided switching center network as described in Chapter 5 of this volume. Information from the time-divided network is demultiplexed and applied to a decoder. The decoder output is then sent to the customer loop via the hybrid.

Signaling information is similarly applied to the multiplexer and sent to the system control element as described in Chapters 3, 4, and 9 of this volume. Signaling is received from the demultiplexer to cause the line termination to perform such functions as applying ringing to the loop.

The functions of the analog trunk termination are similar to the line termination. However, trunks are often 4-wire and no hybrid is required. There are many varieties of trunks as will be discussed in Section 3. A digital trunk termination is also shown in Fig. 1. This termination provides an interface for messages which are already in a digital format. The digital termination is further discussed in Chapter 8 of this volume.

The analog termination will be discussed in more detail in the following sections. Requirements for the analog termination are first presented. Then, various techniques for digitizing speech are summarized. Finally, analog line circuits are described in detail.

3. Analog Termination Requirements

Performance requirements for analog terminations are discussed in this section. Because of the large number of installed telephones and trunks, any new switching system must be compatible with the already installed plant. It is impractical to design a digital switching system which requires a special telephone instrument in most public network applications. In private networks, it is possible that a digital switching system will be installed in a new building and there is more flexibility to introduce new technology since new telephones must be purchased and installed in any case.

This section will describe the requirements for interfacing standard telephones which might be found in a public network. A new digital switching system must be compatible with these telephones. Requirements for standard trunk interfaces are also presented. Transmission requirements including voltage levels, frequency response, and means for echo control are discussed. High voltages which a digital switching system might encounter are described. The section continues with a summary of common customer loop design procedures and their impact on the analog termination. The requirements for customer loop testing are presented and the section concludes with a summary of analog termination requirements.

3.1. Telephone Instruments

Analog terminations are tailored for a particular application. The analog termination for telephone instruments is established by the type of instrument in-place at the time of cutover. Telephone instruments have undergone a substantial evolution since Bell's invention in 1876. A significant improvement to Bell's apparatus was made by Thomas Edison, who invented the carbon transmitter in 1877. This transmitter must be energized with a direct current and is used today with very little change from Edison's original idea. However, the means for providing the energizing current has undergone substantial evolution. Initially, the transmitter energizing current was derived from a battery located with each telephone. Switching systems associated with these telephones did not provide direct current to the customer loop.

Maintenance and replacement cost for individual batteries at each telephone were high and the common battery current feed approach shown

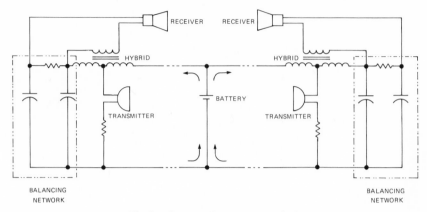

Fig. 3.   Common battery current feed.

in Fig. 3 was established. In the common battery scheme, current is applied to the loop by the switch. Today's telephone instruments are designed for common battery operation and therefore the analog termination must provide this battery feed. Figure 3 illustrates the flow of current through the customer loop to energize the carbon transmitter. The common battery arrangement supplies current from a negative voltage with respect to ground. The negative battery feed causes all customer loop voltages to be negative with respect to ground. Since the wires in a telephone cable can be exposed to moisture and leakage to ground, the negative potential prevents ions in the moisture solution from removing copper from the wires by a plating-off process. Plating-off would cause corrosion and ultimately the copper wires would open.

The functional elements of the telephone are also shown in Fig. 3. A transformer hybrid is located in the telephone to separate the 2-wire subscriber loop signal into a transmit and receive path. (The human head is 4-wire!) The hybrid minimizes the receiver signal which is caused by voice at the corresponding transmitter. A small amount of receiver signal called sidetone is desired to allow the speaker to hear himself as an indication that the telephone is working.

Telephone signaling involves off-hook sending, dialed digit sending, and station ringing. Evolution has occurred in each of these areas. The magneto telephone provides off-hook signaling by a voltage created manually with a crank. In modern telephones, the presence of loop current is sensed to detect off-hook. Dialing has evolved from manual coded ringing from a magneto telephone to the present dual tone multifrequency (DTMF) dialing.

When two parties share a single loop, means must be provided to identify the calling station to properly bill calls. Means must also be provided for selectively ringing each telephone. In some countries, the subscriber instrument has the capability to display telephone call charging.

Many types of telephones might exist in the same network including single-party telephones, multiparty telephones, and coin telephones. Coin telephones require a special analog termination to provide the voltages required for detecting the presence of coins and for coin collect or refund functions.

The Model 500 telephone[2] shown in Fig. 4 will now be described in more detail. When the telephone is on-hook, the contact "dial" is open. The ringer is activated by applying a voltage across the tip and ring. This is called bridged ringing. In normal single-party applications, the ringer will respond to a voltage of 90 V rms at 20 Hz. In some multiparty applications, the ringer is tuned and is responsive only to a single frequency. The desired telephone is rung when many are in parallel by applying the proper ringing frequency. Another means for providing selective ringing to many telephones in parallel is to connect the ringer between either the tip and ground or the ring and ground. The ringing voltage is then applied between one loop conductor and ground. This is called divided ringing. If ringers can be tuned to 5 different frequencies, divided ringing can selectively ring 1 of 10 multiparty customers.

A capacitor is shown in series with a ringer in Fig. 4. This prevents the ringer from drawing dc current and falsely indicating an off-hook. A gas tube can be substituted for the capacitor to provide another form of selective ringing known as superimposed ringing. In this case, a dc voltage must be applied to the loop in addition to the ac ringing voltage in order to cause the ringer to respond.

If the ringer is attached between the tip and ground, a dc path is formed due to the ringer resistance (2650 Ω for some telephones). This

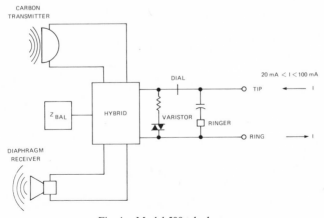

Fig. 4.   Model 500 telephone.

resistance can be used to identify one of two parties in a two-party line. One party will have a resistance between the tip and ground and the other party will not.

When the customer goes off-hook, the "dial" contact in Fig. 4 closes and current flows in the customer loop as indicated. This current is detected and interpreted as a request for service. The customer dials his number (in a dial telephone) by moving his dial off-normal, and as the dial restores to normal the current is interrupted in the loop corresponding to the number dialed.

The current flowing through the telephone varies in proportion to the dc loop resistance in series with the telephone resistance. The telephone resistance is typically 135 Ω (200 Ω worst case) and the loop resistance can vary from zero to an upper limit set by the grade of service and the sensitivity of the analog termination. The model 500 telephone provides transmission level compensation depending upon the magnitude of this dc current. The varistor (nonlinear resistor) shown in Fig. 4 provides this function. The telephone set receiver sensitivity depends on loop current as shown in Fig. 5. As loop current decreases (the telephone moves away from the switch), the loop loss increases and the telephone set loss decreases. This compensates for the higher customer loop loss.

Typical transmission levels for the model 500 telephone are shown in Fig. 6. A normal voice sound pressure level of 90 dB (sound energy, not electrical energy) is applied to the transmitter of the telephone instrument. This causes a voltage of 150 mV to appear across the tip and ring. The

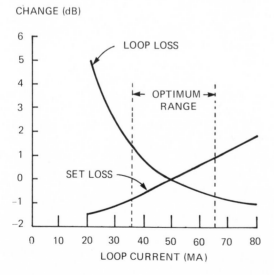

Fig. 5. Model 500 telephone sensitivity to loop current.

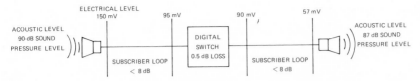

Fig. 6.   Typical speech signal levels for a local telephone call.

customer (subscriber) loop is designed to have a maximum loss of approximately 8 dB. A customer loop loss of 4 dB is shown and a voltage of
95 mV is applied to the analog termination. If the switch has a cross office
loss of 0.5 dB, the analog termination connecting the other party has an
output of 90 mV. The second customer loop is also assumed to have a 4 dB
loss and the voltage at the distant telephone is 57 mV. This causes an
acoustic level in the telephone receiver of 87 dB.

Since some individuals speak more loudly than others and network
losses vary, the range of voltages applied to the analog termination can
vary by more than 25 dB. The impact of this range of signals on the design
of the analog termination is discussed in more detail in Section 4.

Maximum power transfer from the telephone and customer loop to
the analog termination will occur when a conjugate impedance match is
provided by the analog termination. This requires a knowledge of the telephone output impedance in series with the impedance of the subscriber
loop. This impedance is plotted in Fig. 7 for loaded and nonloaded subscriber loops. Loading is a technique where inductors are periodically
placed in series with the loop to boost the high-frequency response. This
technique is discussed in Section 3.5.

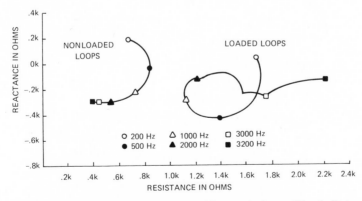

Fig. 7.   Customer loop driving point impedance with one telephone off-hook. Data courtesy
of the United Telecommunications Inc. 1975 survey of subscriber loops.

3.2. Analog Trunk Terminations

Customer loops are pairs of wire which are dedicated 100% of the time to a single customer or to a small group of party line customers. The loop connects the customer's telephone to the local switching system. Trunks are a common resource which can be accessed by any customer in the office. The switching system connects customers to trunks which allow them to reach other switching systems in the network or network resources such as operators or recorded announcement machines. The digital switching system must provide analog terminations for a wide variety of analog trunk types. This section discusses some of these types.

The analog trunk termination can be 2-wire or 4-wire with various signaling capabilities. Unlike the 2-wire customer loop, trunks are often 4-wire to minimize the number of hybrids in tandem on a long-distance connection. Since each hybrid is a source of echo, the use of 4-wire trunks and 4-wire tandem switching minimizes the number of points along a circuit where echo is introduced.

Trunks can be one-way or two-way depending upon the signaling protocol. One-way trunks are always seized at the same trunk end. Two-way trunks can be seized at either end and therefore a means must be provided to resolve simultaneous seizure at both ends (glare).

Common trunk types are shown in Table 1. A digital switching system might be required to terminate any of these trunk types which can be associated with paired cable or analog carrier systems using frequency division multiplexing on paired cable, radio, or coaxial cable. The digital switching system might also provide a special interface for a PABX.

A switching system signals by going off-hook to seize a trunk just as a customer goes off-hook to request dial tone. This trunk seizure is transmitted over the trunk to the far end where the distant switching system detects the off-hook at its trunk termination and prepares to respond. If multifrequency (MF) signaling is used, the distant office attaches a MF receiver to the trunk and signals off-hook back to the originating switch under one type of signaling protocol. The originating office can then send the dialed number. Thus, the trunk termination must provide the required message channel transmission and signaling interface.

Two types of trunk terminations for a digital switch are shown in Fig.

Table 1. Common Trunk Types

Analog transmission mode	Signaling and supervision
2-wire	E & M
2-wire	Loop
2-wire	Sleeve
4-wire	E & M

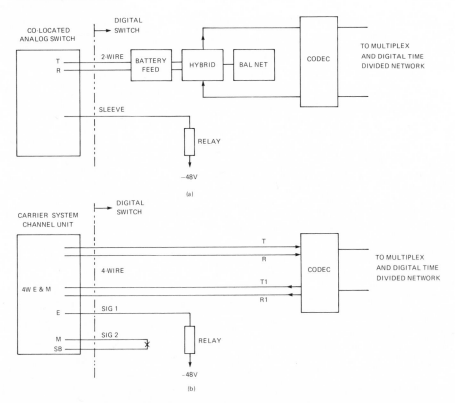

Fig. 8.   Two types of analog trunk terminations for a digital switch.

8. A digital switch interface to a colocated analog switch is shown in Fig. 8a. This analog termination is a one-way trunk which must provide battery feed through the analog switch to the customer loop. The analog switch seizes the trunk by grounding the sleeve lead. A hybrid is required to convert the 2-wire trunk into the necessary 4-wire format for the digital switch.

A 4-wire E&M analog trunk termination is shown in Fig. 8b. Referring to the carrier system channel unit illustrated, the M lead refers to the transmit or signaling from the switch to the carrier system. The switch seizes the trunk by grounding the switch termination SIG 1 lead which is connected to the M lead. This seizure controls the recieve or E lead at the distant end of the carrier system. Signals from the distant switch cause a closure of the switching termination relay shown. Neither a hybrid nor a battery feed is required for this termination. The trunk can be one-way or two-way.

In summary, there are many similarities and differences between analog line and trunk terminations. The line termination must satisfy the requirements of the telephone instrument for battery feed, signaling, over-voltage protection, ringing and 2- to 4-wire conversion. The trunk termination must satisfy similar requirements for transmission and signaling between switching entities.

3.3. Transmission Requirements

A digital switching system must provide a message channel between two terminations which allows customer information to pass with a minimum of distortion and noise accumulation. This section describes some of the important requirements for the transmission of analog information through a digital switch.

Speech must be converted into a digital form for digital switching. The digital switching process involves coding, transmission, switching, and decoding. Overall message channel quality is difficult to specify quantitatively because it involves human perception. In general, words must be intelligible and the listener should be able to recognize the speaker. The message channel might also carry voice band data and tone signaling which have different quality requirements. The requirements for speech will be discussed first.

The energy in speech is concentrated in a band of frequencies between 100 Hz and 5 kHz. This is a result of the natural characteristics of human voice and band limiting introduced by the telephone set and the customer loop. This bandwidth is wider than that required for intelligibility, and a trade-off between equipment cost and message channel quality usually forces a restriction of voice energy to between 200 and 3400 Hz. Most of the energy in speech is below 2.2 kHz. The higher frequencies aid in speaker identification. The amplitude of the speech signal varies considerably and is concentrated in talk spurts of about 1 sec in average duration with a separation of 1 or more seconds. The peak to average power ratio is highly dependent upon the individual talker but is typically 19 dB.[3] The average power can range between -16 and -25 dBm at the input to a local switching system.

Noise is introduced into the message channel at many points in the digital switch. While the signal is in analog form, it is susceptible to crosstalk between channels and impulse noise can be introduced by large voltage transitions when ringing or test relays are closed. Longitudinal noise from power mains near the subscriber loop can be converted into "metallic" or in-band noise due to an imperfect balance in the line circuit. Once longitudinal noise is converted into in-band noise, filtering cannot be used since the filter would equally attenuate signals as well as noise. Longitudinal noise amplitudes are shown in Fig. 9. Another source of noise is quantizing noise which is introduced by the digital coding and decoding process as

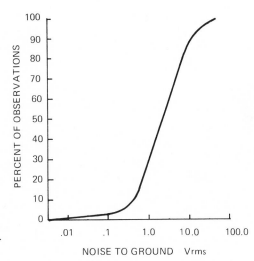

Fig. 9. Distribution of longitudinal noise voltages from a United Telecommunications Inc. survey.

described in Section 4. Once the information is in digital form, additional quantizing noise might be introduced by digital attenuation, digital conferencing, or other digital signal processing described in Chapter 8 of this volume.

Voice-band data are distorted by the same means. In addition, nonlinearities in the phase characteristics of filters and the coding and decoding process add distortion in data.

A digital switching system uses a 4-wire transmission path as shown in Fig. 2. If the hybrids are not perfectly balanced for all message channel frequencies, a portion of the signal energy will traverse the hybrid between ports c and b and two types of echo will be created: talker echo and listener echo. Talker echo comes from energy originating at the talker which is returned to the talker from the hybrid associated with the listener as shown. Listener echo comes from energy originating at the talker which is returned to the listener after traversing both hybrids.

Means to control echo in a local digital switch have been studied.[4] Subjective tests have been conducted[5] where echo is introduced into a voice channel and listeners are asked to judge the circuit as good, fair, poor, or unsatisfactory. Results of these tests are shown in Fig. 10 where subjective transmission quality is given for various amounts of loop delay and singing margin (the amount of gain inside the 4-wire loop required to marginally cause oscillation). Figure 10 shows that the singing margin required to provide a given grade of service depends on the loop delay. For example, the singing margin must be at least 5.5 dB if the loop delay is 2 msec in order to provide "good" transmission.

The singing margin shown in Fig. 10 is assumed to be constant with

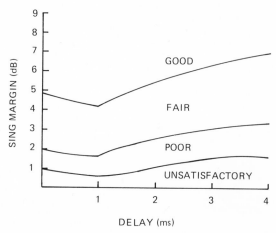

Fig. 10.   Echo grade of service versus singing margin and loop delay.

frequency. In actual practice, studies have shown[6] that the loss around the 4-wire loop varies with frequency as illustrated in Fig. 11. The singing margin is the point of minimum attenuation.

Since the loop attenuation varies with frequency, a term called weighted echo path loss (WEPL) has been defined to judge listener echo performance, where

$$\text{WEPL} = -20 \log \frac{1}{3200} \int_{200}^{3400} 10^{-L(f)/20} \, df \tag{1}$$

Here $L(f)$ is the listener echo path loss in decibels.

The WEPL objective assuming a 4-msec switch delay is shown in Fig. 12.[6] This curve shows that WEPL for all connections with a 4-msec delay should exceed 9 dB. Methods of controlling echo to meet these WEPL objectives are discussed in Section 5.2.1.

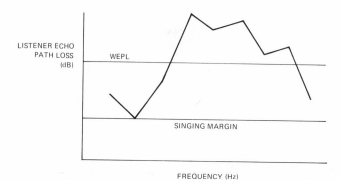

Fig. 11.   Singing margin and WEPL for a typical analog termination.

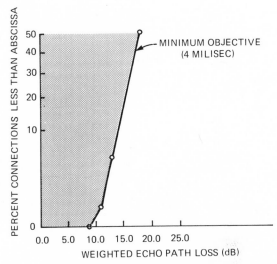

Fig. 12.   Statistical WEPL objective for a loop delay of 4 msec.

3.4.   Overvoltage Protection

Adequate protection must be provided to prevent damage to sensitive electrical circuits in the analog termination when the system is subjected to high voltages. These voltages result from lightning strikes or power line crosses and are transported to the switching system by outside plant wiring.

Protection devices must be installed to allow the switching system to withstand, without damage or excessive protector maintenance, the dielectric stresses and currents which are produced by these overvoltage sources. Currents can be produced in the tip to ring circuit or between the tip or ring and ground.

Studies have been made to determine the proper laboratory simulation for these overvoltage conditions.[7] Five types of laboratory tests have been identified to properly simulate the overvoltage conditions actually found in the field.

The first test involves a current surge which simulates the stress before the protectors at the main distributing frame breakdown. The peak current applied from the tip or ring through the analog termination to ground is 500 A with the waveform shown in Fig. 13. For this test, the rise time is 10 μsec and the one-half value decay time is 1000 μsec.

The second test involves the simulation of an ac power fault where a 10-A current is applied from either the tip or ring through the analog termination to ground. This test is limited to 11 cycles of a 60-Hz signal.

The third test involves a voltage surge at the input to ac power supplies. This test simulates an ac power source surge and involves the

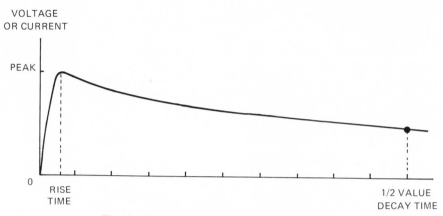

Fig. 13.   Waveform for voltage or current stress tests.

waveform of Fig. 13. The peak voltage is 2500 V, the waveform rise time is 1.2 μsec, and the one-half value decay time is 50 μsec.

The fourth test involves a voltage surge which simulates a stress from a relatively high impedance source. The waveform of Fig. 13 is applied between the tip and the ring with a peak value of 1000 V. The rise time is 10 μsec and the half-value decay time is 1000 μsec. This test should be conducted with the primary protection at the main distributing frame removed!

The final surge test involves stresses which are caused by the delay in the breakdown of arrestors. In this test, a waveform with a rising slope of 100 V/μsec is applied with the arrestors removed. The peak voltage applied is equal to three times the standard deviation in arrestor breakdown voltage. The half-value decay time is at least equal to the average turn-on time of the arrestor.

Electrical components used to protect the analog termination and the dielectric strength of insulators in the analog termination should be such that operating specifications are met after the five tests described in this section have been conducted. This simulates a real world situation where the system must operate properly after overvoltage stresses.

3.5.   Customer Loop (Access Line) Design

The customer loop is the means to connect the telephone to the digital switch. The analog line termination of a digital switch must provide the required interface to existing customer loops which have been designed using many techniques.[8] Some of these techniques include resistance design, pair gain systems, and loop extenders. These customer loop design techniques are discussed in this section since they influence the requirements for the analog termination.

Resistance design involves the selection of wire gauges and loop lengths to provide adequate transmission and signaling from the telephone to the switching system. The maximum allowable transmission attenuation in the customer loop is on the order of 8 dB as shown in Fig. 6. The gauge of wire is selected to meet the objective. For example, the attenuation of 26 and 19 gauge cable at 1 kHz is 2.8 dB and 1.3 dB per mile, respectively. Short loops might only use 26 gauge cable where long loops might use 26 gauge near the office and successively lower gauges in sections along the loop.

Inductors are added in series with the tip and ring at various points along long loops to prevent excessive attenuation at the high-frequency end of the audio spectrum. This is called "loading".[9] The frequency response of loaded and nonloaded 26 gauge cable with a 12 kf length is shown in Fig. 14. Loading changes the impedance of the customer loop as has been shown in Fig. 7. Load coils are generally applied on loops which are 18,000 feet or longer. Coils with an inductance of 88 mH are placed every 6,000 ft (H88 loading) after an initial 3,000-ft section adjacent to the central office.

The resistance of the customer loop increases with loop length and therefore the loop current decreases with length. This makes loop signaling difficult to detect on long loops. The signaling limit of the switch is established by the sensitivity of the current detector in the analog termination. This detector must be sensitive enough to detect an off-hook condition but must not respond to loop leakage or to current drawn by some types of pair gain systems. Most public digital switching systems can detect signaling from a 1900-Ω loop (including the telephone) with 25 kΩ of leakage resistance. The ac impedance, dc resistance, and leakage of the cable can

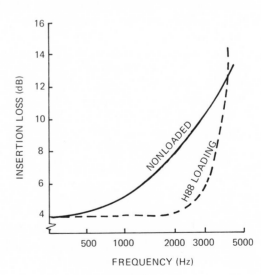

Fig. 14. High-frequency attenuation reduction due to loading.

vary substantially not only with the length of the cable but also with temperature and moisture present in the cable.

Additional measures must be taken to provide for adequate transmission and signaling for extremely long customer loops. Loop extenders are installed between the switch termination and the loop to provide audio amplification, battery boosting, and signaling detection for ranges out to 4500 Ω (about 10 miles). The input impedance of the analog termination must be carefully controlled to allow negative impedance amplifiers to function properly. A single centrally located switch can serve an area with a radius of 10 miles using loop extenders. Larger areas can be served using pair gain technology, which is discussed below.

Studies have shown that a customer loop serving a single party line is occupied about 3% of the time. Multiparty lines improve loop utilization but degrade service levels since the parties must contend for use of the loop. Pair gain systems have been designed to improve loop utilization through the use of analog or digital multiplexing or by switching many subscribers onto a smaller number of links which connect the concentrator to the central office. A demultiplexer or switching expander is located at the central office to interface with the local switch. The pair gain system central office terminal presents a separate termination to the switching system for each customer and, in many cases, the switching system analog interface serves an identical function whether or not the pair gain system is present. The customer loop is then connected to the pair gain system remote terminal. Some pair gain systems derive their dc power from the switching system analog termination. Therefore, care must be taken to ensure that the termination functions properly in the presence of the pair gain system. Overall network cost savings can be obtained if the pair gain system is integrated with the digital switching system as described in Chapter 10 of this volume.

mouth and ear are unidirectional anatomical sensors. Therefore, it is possible to connect the telephone to the digital switching system over a 4-wire circuit without the use of hybrids. However, this would require twice the amount of copper and the savings in eliminating the hybrids in the telephone and in the analog termination might not offset the cost of additional cable.

3.6. Testing

Customer loops traverse long distances and are subject to many types of faults including moisture ingress, power line crosses, open splices, and cable cuts. Automated testing systems have been developed to periodically monitor customer loops to detect these faults before the customer is inconvenienced. These systems require analog access to loops so that measurements can be made. The analog termination of a digital switch must provide this access.

Test systems have been designed to automatically cycle through all customer loops in an office during off-peak periods and detect fault conditions. These systems can also be used to test specific lines at any time when a customer complains. In an analog switching system, test access is provided at trunk circuits which access the customer loop through the analog switching fabric. In a digital switching system, the switching fabric is digital and trunks do not have metallic access to the loop for measuring purposes. Therefore, a means must be provided to test customer loops at the analog termination.

If the analog termination contains a large number of electronic components, the termination failure rate might lead to an unacceptable system availability for a given customer. It is therefore desirable to provide an automatic testing capability to detect failures in line associated equipment before a customer complains. A testing function is therefore required in the analog termination to provide both for testing the customer loop and the electronic circuitry associated with the termination.

3.7. BORSHT

The requirements for the digital switching system analog termination have been presented in Section 3. These requirements can be summarized by the acronym BORSHT. BORSHT gives a convenient summary of the functions required in the analog termination:

Battery feed
Overvoltage protection
Ringing
Signaling
Hybrid
Test

Sometimes the analog termination includes a codec function, and we then have BORSCHT, which also spells the delicious beet soup.

Before leaving the subject of analog termination requirements, two additional requirements should be explored: reliability and energy consumption. A digital switching system can have a large number of electronic components associated with each customer, whose failure might deny all switching system services to the customer until the fault is cleared. Therefore, the termination reliability goal might be based on a customer complaint rate objective. Switching system maintenance requirements might be another approach in establishing the analog termination reliability goal since per line failure rates are multiplied by a large number in most digital switching systems.

A customer complaint rate of 3 per 100 telephones per month might be a reasonable overall office goal. These complaints might be due to defective telephones, customer loop faults, or switching system faults. It is reasonable to allocate 10% of these complaints to the digital switching system. If analog termination failures cause 75% of the overall switching system failures affecting customer availability, the failure rate of the line termination should be no more than 0.23 failures per 100 lines per month (assuming single party lines with 1 telephone per line). This corresponds to a termination failure rate of 3194 failures in 10^9 hours. This calculation assumes that automatic testing systems will not catch the problem and allow it to be cleared before the customer complains. Also, it assumes that there is no line termination redundancy. For this failure rate, a 10,000 line office will have a line termination failure approximately once each day. Thus, it seems that 3194 failures in 10^9 hours might be too generous based on maintainability. A line termination failure rate goal of 600 failures in 10^9 hours is more reasonable.

Power consumption per line is also an important system requirement. Energy, environmental control, and standby battery costs are fixed by power consumption. The overall system power consumption is largely established by the analog termination. A system goal of 1 to 2 W per line is reasonable.

4. Digital Representation of Speech

Digital switching requires the conversion of analog signals such as speech into a digital form. The goal of the speech conversion process is to create a digital bit stream which can be switched by the digital switch and then reproduced in a way that a listener can understand what is being said and who said it. The requirements for the transmission of speech through a digital switching system have been discussed in Section 3.3. Techniques for speech digitization are discussed in this section. Various digitization techniques are summarized and then pulse code modulation (PCM) is described. The section concludes with a description of differential PCM, delta modulation, and vocoders.

4.1. Voice Digitization Techniques

There are two broad classes of speech digitization techniques: waveform coders and source coders. Waveform coders strive to accurately reproduce a signal waveform in amplitude and phase. Waveform coders are essentially signal source independent and can digitize a wide variety of signals such as speech, music, tones, and voice-band data. The waveform is sampled, quantized, coded, and transmitted in digital form to the receiver. At the receiver, the digitized waveform is converted back into analog and an approximation of the original waveform is obtained. This reconstruction can be very accurate and the digitization process frequently cannot be detected by the average listener.

Source coders rely on a knowledge of how the signal is generated at the source. Vocoders (voice coders) are a class of source coders which digitize human speech. A vocoder establishes a mathematical model for the physical speech generating process. The parameters which are used to cause the model to synthesize speech are detected at the source and transmitted in digital form to the decoder. Vocoder methods make no attempt to preserve the original waveform. Vocoders can be used to digitize speech at a substantially lower bit rate for the same level of quality as a waveform coder. However, the vocoder is only suitable for voice digitization and cannot be used for music, tones, or voice-band data. A vocoder can only reproduce sounds which can be produced by a human vocal tract.

A comparison between waveform coders and source coders is shown in Fig. 15. Various types of coders have been invented to provide a given degree of subjective quality at the lowest possible transmission bit rate. Quality levels ranging from broadcast to synthetic are illustrated in Fig. 15. Waveform coders provide the highest fidelity but they similarly have the highest bit rate requirements. Vocoders provide the lowest transmission bit rate by sacrificing speech quality and service flexibility.

The basic process of waveform coding is illustrated in Fig. 16a. An analog waveform is applied to an analog-to-digital converter or coder. The coder converts the waveform into a binary bit stream which can be transmitted, switched, processed, or placed in digital storage. The digital-to-analog converter receives the binary bit stream, decodes the bits, and creates an approximation of the original signal.

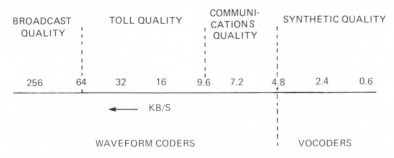

Fig. 15.   Quality levels and required bit rates for various voice digitization techniques.

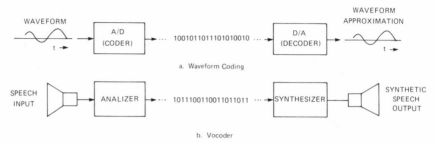

Fig. 16. Waveform and source coding techniques.

Pulse code modulation is a waveform coding technique invented by Reeves in 1939. This was the first technique used to digitize voice, and PCM continues to find the widest use today. Other waveform coding techniques include differential PCM, delta modulation, transform coders, subband coders; and nearly instantaneous companding.

The basic vocoder process is illustrated in Fig. 16b. This process assumes that the sound generating mechanism (human vocal tract) is linearly separable from the intelligence which modulates the vocal tract. The analyzer detects and digitizes the intelligence in the source. A binary bit stream is then transmitted to the synthesizer which reconstructs the original speech. Vocoders use many techniques including the channel vocoder, cepstrum vocoder, formant vocoder, voice excited vocoder, and linear predictive vocoder.[10]

Because of its widespread use, PCM will now be discussed. Summary descriptions of other waveform and vocoder digitization techniques will follow.

4.2. Pulse Code Modulation

Pulse code modulation is the waveform coding technique illustrated in Fig. 17. An input signal is band limited and then sampled at a rate at least twice as high as the highest significant frequency established by the band limiting filter. The individual samples are applied to a coder where the amplitude of the samples are quantized and PCM code words are established. The PCM words pass through the digital switching medium and are applied to a decoder which creates analog samples whose height are proportional to the PCM code words. The output signal is obtained by passing the samples through a low-pass filter which reconstructs the original analog waveform. The basic steps in pulse code modulation are prefiltering, sampling, quantizing, coding, decoding, and reconstruction. Each of these steps will now be described.

A sample is a pulse whose width is theoretically zero and whose

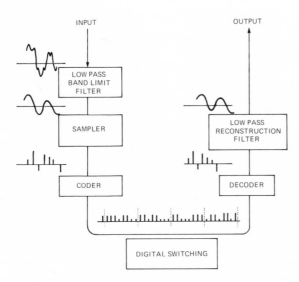

Fig. 17.   Principles of pulse code modulation.

height is equal to the original waveform voltage or current at the time of the sample. Samples of the waveform are taken at a rate dictated by the highest significant frequency contained in the signal waveform. The sampling rate is established by the sampling theorem stated in Chapter 5 of this volume.

The input low-pass filter must restrict the band of frequencies applied to the sampler to satisfy the sampling theorem. If signal energy exists above one-half the sampling rate, foldover distortion will occur as illustrated in Fig. 18. Foldover distortion is sometimes called aliasing distortion. The frequency spectrum of the input signal is shown in Fig. 18a along with the sampling frequency f_s. Foldover distortion is caused by inadequate low-pass filtering of the signal spectrum. Inadequate filtering is shown in Fig. 18b and the corresponding frequency spectrum of the sampler output is shown in Fig 18c. Note that the initial band limited spectrum is present but there are also sum and difference frequencies between the sampling frequency and the band limited spectrum and their harmonics. Foldover distortion at the output of a low-pass reconstruction filter is shown in Fig. 18d. Note that the foldover distortion will disappear if the low-pass input filter has a sharper cutoff characteristic.

The quantizing and coding process is illustrated in Fig. 19. The amplitude of an analog waveform is shown vs. time. Sampling times are shown at 1, 2, etc. The range of possible amplitudes is divided into discrete levels called quantization levels. Code words then define each quantization level. The distance between quantization levels is established by the number of

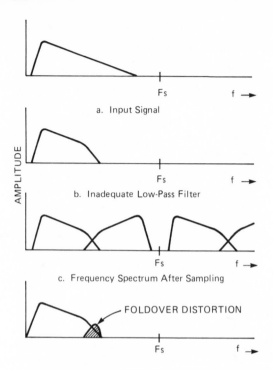

a. Input Signal

b. Inadequate Low-Pass Filter

c. Frequency Spectrum After Sampling

FOLDOVER DISTORTION

d. Frequency Spectrum After Reconstruction

Fig. 18.   Distortion caused by inadequate input filtering.

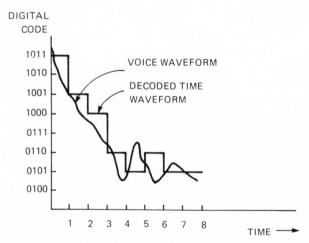

Fig. 19.   Quantizing and coding process in PCM.

bits contained in each code word. At time 1, the amplitude of the wave-form is sampled and the nearest quantization level is found. The digital code word for this quantization level is used to represent the amplitude of that sample. The code word is then transmitted through the digital switch and is applied to a decoder as shown in Fig. 17. The decoder converts the code word into an analog sample which, when combined with other sam-ples, produces a waveform which approximates the original signal. Another digital code word is established at 2 and 3, etc. The amplitude of the original signal changes continuously but the digital code changes only in discrete steps. Therefore, there is an error associated with this process called quantizing error. This error can be made arbitrarily small by increasing the number of bits in the code word.

There are many types of circuits which can create PCM code words. A circuit which accomplishes quantizing and coding using the successive approximation technique is shown in Fig. 20. The signal sample amplitude is held constant for the duration of the coding process. A current I_s, pro-portional to the signal amplitude, is applied to a comparator circuit. The digital-to-analog converter creates a reference current I_{ref} which is com-pared with I_s. Transistor switches S_1 through S_8 are controlled by the successive approximation register and determine the value of I_{ref}. I_{ref} is the sum of the currents through the resistors in the digital-to-analog converter. Each current is related by a factor of 2 and thus there are 2^8 uniformly spaced reference currents which can be compared with I_s.

The coding process operates as follows. Initially, I_s is applied to the comparator and all switches S are open. S_1 is first closed. If I_s is smaller than I_{ref}, S_1 is opened. If I_s is larger than I_{ref}, S_1 is left closed for the duration of the coding process. This establishes the most significant PCM bit. Next, S_2 is closed and the comparator output is tested. If I_s is less than I_{ref}, S_2 is opened; if not, S_2 is closed for the remainder of the process. This establishes the next PCM bit. The process repeats for all switches. At the conclusion of the conversion, I_{ref} will equal I_s within one half of a PCM code step. The PCM code word is taken from the status of the switches stored in the successive approximation register. The number of trials (successive approximations) for this converter is equal to the number of bits in the PCM code word.

The decoder, illustrated in Fig. 17, can employ the same type of digital-to-analog converter as illustrated in Fig. 20. The received PCM code words control the switches S_1 through S_8 and the analog output corre-sponding to the code word for that sample is I_{ref}. The decoder does not use a comparator or successive approximation register. The decoder output is a pulse whose amplitude is established by the code word and whose width is theoretically zero.

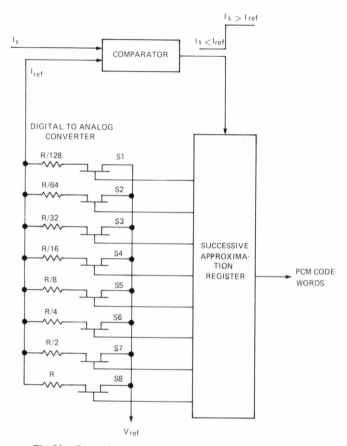

Fig. 20.   Successive approximation digital-to-analog converter.

Reconstruction of the original waveform is accomplished by passing the decoder output pulses through a rectangular shaped low-pass filter with a cutoff frequency equal to one-half of the sampling frequency. The reconstruction process is illustrated in Fig. 21. Pulses from the decoder occur at the sampling rate as shown in Fig. 21a. The height of each pulse is established by the PCM code word. Each pulse causes the filter to respond with its impulse response which has a $(\sin x)/x$ shape as shown in Fig. 21b for the sample at time 3. The composite output voltage of the low-pass filter is the sum of the individual impulse responses of the pulses applied to the filter. The envelope of this sum of the impulse responses is the reconstructed output waveform shown in Fig. 21c.

The principles of PCM have now been described. For speech applications, the sampling rate is set by the highest frequency in speech. As discussed in Section 3.3, speech can be band limited to 3.4 kHz without a serious degradation in quality. Therefore, the sampling rate must be at least 2 × 3.4 kHz or 6.8 kHz. The sampling rate must be higher than 6.8 kHz because of practical antialiasing input filter rejection characteristics. The sampling rate for PCM has therefore been internationally standardized at 8 kHz.

The number of bits required for the PCM code word is established by the dynamic range of the speech signals and the allowable quantizing distortion. Talker volume levels have been described in Section 3.3. Signals are

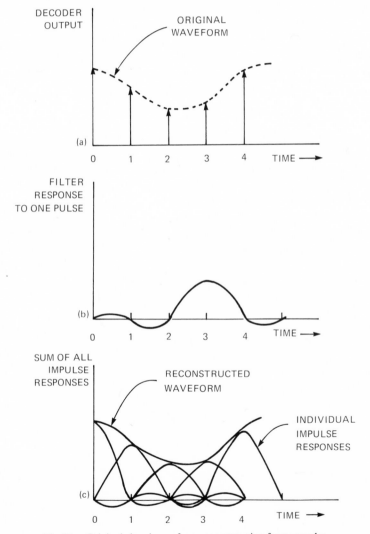

Fig. 21.   Original signal waveform reconstruction from samples.

normally distributed with an average ranging from −16 dBm to −25 dBm and a peak to average ratio of 19 dB. Low-volume talkers can be another 10 dB below the average. A theoretical signal-to-quantizing distortion on the order of 40 dB is typically required for long-distance telephony purposes. Therefore, the dynamic range required for a digital codec is 78 dB (+3 dBm to −75 dBm). This requires a linear PCM code word of 13 bits (80 dB dynamic range). With 8-kHz sampling and 13 bits per sample, we have a PCM code word bit rate of 104 kbit/sec.

The cost of a digital transmission or switching system is influenced by the PCM code word bit rate. The bit rate can be reduced through information compression and expansion (*companding*) without degradation in the required signal to quantizing distortion of 40 dB.

The inefficiency in using a linear PCM code will now be demonstrated. We require that the signal-to-quantizing distortion be at least 40 dB for signal levels as low as −35 dBm and the overload point must be at least +3 dBm. Signal-to-quantizing distortion is plotted versus input level for a 13-bit linear code with an overload level at +3 dBm in Fig. 22. The signal to quantizing distortion at −35 dBm input is 42 dB which slightly exceeds the 40-dB goal. But the goal is greatly exceeded for higher signal levels. This "waste" is paid for in a channel bit rate which is higher than necessary to meet the 40-dB minimum signal-to-quantizing distortion goal for a wide range of inputs. It is desirable, therefore, to find a technique which can reduce the bit rate while meeting the minimum signal-to-quantizing distortion goal. These desirable objectives are achieved through companding.

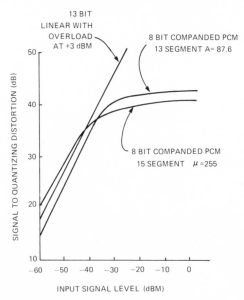

Fig. 22.   Quantizing distortion for linear and companded PCM.

Companding gives a fairly constant signal-to-quantizing distortion over a broad range of signal inputs as shown in Fig. 22. Two companding laws which have received international recognition[11] are illustrated for 8-bit PCM: μ-law and A-law. Note that both companding laws produce approximately a 40-dB signal-to-quantizing noise at an input level of -35 dBm. Also, both techniques only require 8-bit code words rather than 13 bits! The channel bit rate is reduced through companding by 38% and the minimum signal-to-quantizing goal is met.

The transfer function of a coder which produces the μ-law characteristic is shown in Fig. 23. Analog input voltages are shown on the abscissa and 8-bit code words are shown on the ordinate. The transfer function is divided into 15 segments (the segment through the origin is continuous). The most significant bit is used to establish the polarity of the input signal. The next 3 bits are used to define the segment number. The last 4 bits

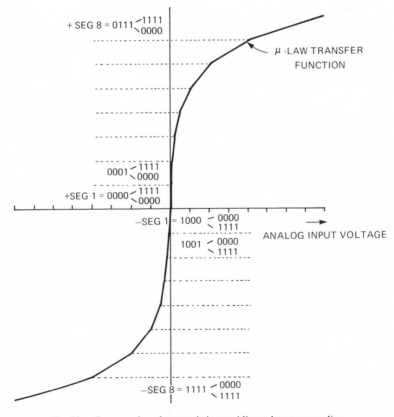

Fig. 23.   Compression characteristic providing μ-law companding.

denote the voltage within a segment. This transfer function approximates the μ companding law given by

$$F(x) = \text{sgn}(x) \frac{\ln(1 + \mu|x|)}{\ln(1 + \mu)} \qquad -1 \le x \le 1 \qquad (2)$$

Figure 23 illustrates how compression occurs. The slope of the transfer function is steep for low-level signals. This provides for low quantizing distortion. As the signal level increases, the slope is less. This produces more absolute quantizing distortion but gives a constant percentage quantizing distortion which is the compandor goal. The expandor must use identically the same transfer function as the compressor.

Signal-to-quantizing distortion for A-law compandors is also shown in Fig. 22. The A-law achieves the goal of providing an adequate signal-to-quantizing distortion with 8-bit PCM. The companding formula for the A-law is given by

$$F(x) = \text{sgn}(x) \frac{1 + \ln A|x|}{1 + \ln A} \qquad \frac{1}{A} \le |x| \le 1 \qquad (3)$$

$$F(x) = \text{sgn}(x) \frac{A|x|}{1 + \ln A} \qquad 0 \le |x| \le \frac{1}{A} \qquad (4)$$

There are small differences in the μ-law and the A-law. First, as shown in Fig. 22, the A-law provides slightly higher signal-to-quantizing distortion at high input levels. However, the signal to distortion falls off more quickly for lower-level input signals. The common approximations for the two companding laws also differ near the origin. A-law compandors have a quantizing step at zero input volts where μ-law compandors are continuous at the origin. This might cause a slightly higher idle channel noise for an A-law codec since the slightest noise will cause the least significant bit to change.

4.3. Other Digitization Techniques

Speech digitization techniques fall into two categories as shown in Fig. 15: waveform coders and vocoders. The PCM waveform coder has been presented in detail in the previous section. A separate section has been devoted to PCM because of its international standardization and widespread use. Other voice coding schemes which have a lower bit rate than PCM will now be described. The price paid for this lower bit rate is a restriction in the type of message traffic which the channel can carry. Differential PCM, delta modulation, and channel vocoders will be discussed.

PCM codes each waveform sample independently of all others. In a band-limited situation, the average amplitude change from one sample to the next is small compared with the maximum amplitude range of the system. When two adjacent samples have the same or nearly the same amplitude, it is redundant to transmit both absolute values. It would be more efficient to transmit only incremental changes rather than absolute values. Differential PCM provides this step towards redundancy reduction since fewer bits are needed per sample to provide speech quality equivalent to PCM. Rather than coding the actual difference between waveform samples, a differential PCM coder provides a code word which is the difference between the current sample and a predicted amplitude which is estimated from past samples as shown in Fig. 24. The input signal is filtered to prevent aliasing and then sampled. The sample X_k is held until the next sample.

The difference between X_k and the predicted amplitude Y_k is quantized and coded for transmission. The estimator uses past samples which are weighted to minimize the average energy in the difference signal. The predictor is updated by adding the current estimates Y_k to the current difference D_k. Predictor weights are calculated based on the statistics of speech. Once the weights are selected they remain fixed for a given differential PCM system. Adaptive differential PCM is a coding scheme where the prediction weights are not fixed and are continuously updated. Code words are received and decided using the estimator shown in Fig. 24.

A differential PCM converter employing prediction based on the past 3 samples can eliminate two bits per sample over PCM and provide equivalent speech quality. This means that bit rates might be reduced from 64 kbit/sec to 48 kbit/sec. Adaptive differential PCM can provide PCM quality speech with bit rates on the order of 20 kbit/sec. However, voice band data at rates exceeding 2400 Baud will be severely distorted by this coder.

Delta modulation is another speech-digitizing technique in the class of waveform coders. A delta modulation codec is shown in Fig. 25. The delta

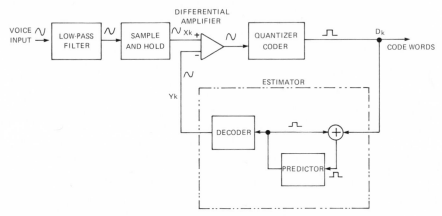

Fig. 24.   Differential PCM coder.

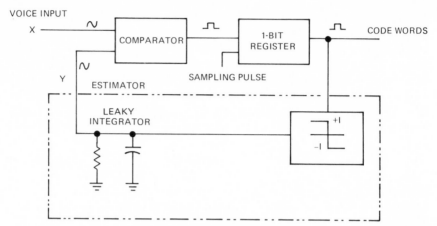

Fig. 25.   Delta modulation coder.

modulation coder is very much like a closed loop servo system where the feedback voltage Y is adjusted to be equal to the input voltage X.

Referring to Fig. 25, the input voltage X is continuously compared with the feedback voltage Y. X will always be greater than or less than Y and this is represented by the binary output of the comparator. The comparator output is sampled and the state at that instant becomes the coder output. The binary code word (1 bit) controls a positive or negative current source in the feedback loop which is integrated to create Y. The integration is leaky to provide for a slight imbalance in the current sources. Code word decoding simply employs the estimator.

Sampling in a delta modulation coder is placed inside the feedback loop as shown, instead of outside the loop as in a PCM system. When the input waveform rate of change exceeds the rate which the feedback voltage can follow, the delta modulation coder experiences slope overload. This limits the use of delta modulation coders to voice band data of 2400 Baud or less. Methods have been suggested to change the estimator current magnitude to minimize slope overload. Coders using these methods are called adaptive delta modulation coders. Adaptive delta modulation techniques typically require 20 kbit/sec for satisfactory speech reproduction.

Vocoders give the lowest bit rate of all speech digitization techniques but have not been used in digital switching because of their cost and poor speech quality. However, this could possibly change in the future since vocoders are being considered for packet switching. Therefore, the technique will be described. Unlike waveform coders which attempt to preserve the amplitude and phase of the voice waveform, vocoders do not try to preserve the original waveform. The goal, instead, is to synthesize a sound at the receiver which simulates the original speech. The vocoder system, shown in Fig. 16b, analyzes the speech waveform and transmits significant parameters which are used by the receiver to synthesize sound from a mathematical model of the human voice tract. Since waveforms are not preserved, the vocoder cannot transmit music, signaling, or voice-band data. The output of the vocoder is often talker dependent and the speech has a synthetic quality. These factors limit the performance levels that vocoders can achieve. Since the vocoder models the human vocal tract, a vocoder system cannot pass information which cannot be originated by the vocal tract.

The vocoder must extract the intelligence from the speech input and then transmit the intelligence in digital form to the reproduction means. Vocoders analyze the input waveform and compute parameters that provide the information required in the speech reproduction mechanism. Vocoder models assume that speech sounds are either voiced or unvoiced. Voiced sounds occur when vocal cords vibrate with a variable pitch (highness or lowness of sound). The vocal cords control the flow of air from the lungs into the resonant structure of the vocal tract formed by the throat, mouth, and nasal cavities. The voice pitch is talker dependent and is typically 50–200 Hz for men and 100–400 Hz for women. Unvoiced (voiceless) sounds are produced by turbulent air flow which excites the vocal tract.

The analyzer portion of the vocoder models the resonant structure of the vocal tract and estimates the pitch of speech. The analyzer also decides whether a speech segment is voiced or unvoiced. The analyzer output is digitized and transmitted through the digital switch to the synthesizer.

The synthesizer reconstructs a time waveform which approximates the original speech. The source for voiced sounds is a periodic pulse generator whose frequency is established by pitch. The source for unvoiced sounds is a random noise generator. The synthesizer receives a signal which indicates the presence of voiced or unvoiced sounds which are considered mutually exclusive. The sound sources are then passed through a vocal tract filter to create the analyzer output.

There are many vocoder techniques which differ in the means for extracting the information from the original speech and in the means for reconstructing the original speech approximation. A channel vocoder is shown in Fig. 26. The analyzer contains a number of bandpass filters which are used to provide an estimate of the power-spectral density in the speech waveform using square law detectors and integrators. Independent of this spectral analysis, a circuit determines the voice pitch and a voicing detector detects the voiced or unvoiced state. The signals in digital form are multiplexed onto the transmission system.

The synthesizer reconstructs the original speech using the spectrum estimates and the pitch and voicing information. During voicing intervals, the synthesizer energy source is the pulse generator whose frequency is

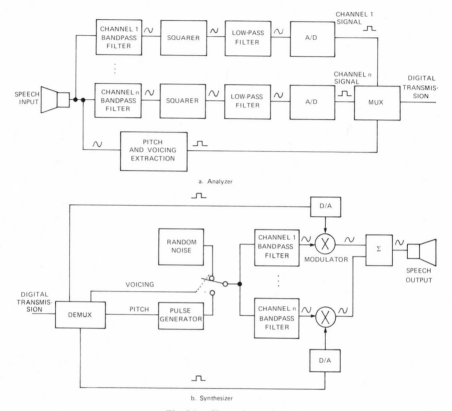

a. Analyzer

b. Synthesizer

Fig. 26.   Channel vocoder.

established by the pitch information. These pulses excite the filters whose output is adjusted by the frequency spectrum estimates to match the original information. A random noise source is used for unvoiced sounds.

Channel vocoders typically use 16 bandpass filters each with a 20-Hz low-pass filter which is sampled every 20 msec. Channel vocoders operating between 2400 and 4800 bit/sec can produce speech with high intelligibility; however, there are noticeable degradations in naturalness and in speaker recognizability.

In summary, there are many techniques to convert speech into a digital format at the analog termination. Waveform coders can provide toll quality speech at rates down to 16 kbit/sec and vocoders have not found broad acceptance for commercial telephone applications. However, vocoders have many special communication applications where the cost of the transmission facility dictates a sacrifice in voice quality to achieve a very low bit rate. The principle of digital switching accommodates any of these digitizing schemes.

5. Line Circuit Description

Requirements for the analog termination of a digital switching system are discussed in Section 3. These requirements include the need to interface existing telephone instruments and trunks. Transmission and overvoltage requirements have also been discussed and the requirements for the line circuit are summarized by the acronym BORSHT.

Design approaches which meet the requirements for the digital switch analog termination are discussed in this section. Architectural approaches for the location of the various BORSHT elements are first presented and then the technology for realizing each of the elements is described.

5.1. BORSHT Element Location

A block diagram for a local digital switching system is shown in Fig. 27. Analog signals are applied to the switch, the input traffic is concentrated, and the signals are routed to their destination.

The first commercial local digital switching system[12] used relay crosspoints for the concentration stage and digital switching for the routing stage. Portions of the BORSHT circuit were located at point A and other portions were located at point B. For example, off-hook signaling and overvoltage protection were located at A and battery feed, ringing, on-hook signaling, hybrid, testing, and coding were at location B. The relay crosspoints provided high-voltage isolation so that ringing could be accomplished through the concentrator. This approach has also been used where the analog crosspoints are realized using high-voltage semiconductors.[13] In these designs, the concentration stage is a 2-wire network.

The BORSHT circuit functions can be arbitrarily partitioned between locations A and B. Some designers have chosen to locate the overvoltage protection, battery feed, ringing, signaling, hybrid, and test at location A and use a 4-wire analog concentration stage with low-voltage semiconductor components.[14] Codecs are at location B. Other designers have

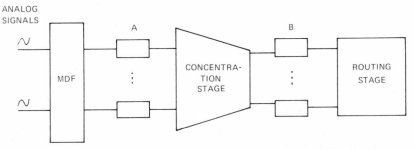

Fig. 27.   Digital switching system with possible BORSHT locations identified.

chosen to provide the BORSHT and codec functions at location A and realize the concentration stage using digital switching techniques.[15]

The choice for the location of the BORSHT functions is established by many factors including manufacturing cost, system reliability, power consumption, and the technology available to the manufacturer. Since the cost of the analog termination including the first concentration stage can be as high as 80% of the overall system manufacturing cost, selection of the BORSHT location is critical. Further, since the BORSHT location depends on available semiconductor technology, the optimum location will change through time as semiconductors improve.

The amount of concentration possible in the concentration stage decreases as the line traffic increases. The relative economic advantages of concentrating the BORSHT functions decline as this concentration ratio decreases. However, even for busy offices, a concentration ratio of 4 : 1 is possible. Therefore, the per line cost of expensive parts located at point B are 1/4 the cost of equivalent parts located at point A. The net saving is somewhat less due to the cost of the analog crosspoints.

If the cost of semiconductor components continues to decline with time, the location of all BORSHT functions will migrate to location A and the concentration stage will be digital. A block diagram for such an analog termination for a Model 500 telephone is shown in Fig. 28. The tip and ring from the customer loop interfaces the line circuit through the main distributing frame (MDF) where primary overvoltage protection is located. The tip and ring are then connected to two relays: one to allow analog testing of the customer loop and the line circuit and the other to apply high-voltage ringing. Secondary protection is applied at the input to the subscriber (customer) line interface circuit (SLIC). The SLIC performs the functions of battery feed, signaling detection and 2- to 4-wire conversion.

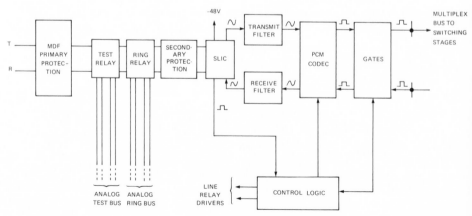

Fig. 28.   Line circuit.

The originating analog signal is filtered to prevent aliasing and applied to the PCM codec. The codec output is gated onto a multiplex bus which forms the input to the digital concentrator. Signaling is detected by the SLIC and stored in the control logic. Time slots on the multiplex bus send polling commands to the control logic and signaling is gated onto the multiplex bus during the proper time slots. The multiplex bus has separate time slots for information and control. The polling command could be the line circuit address which is recognized by the control logic. Control information is sent to the line circuit via time slots on the multiplex bus to cause the test relay or ring relay to be energized. Digital speech from the multiplex bus is applied to the gates and then to the PCM decoder and output filter. Finally, the received speech information is applied across the tip and ring through the hybrid in the SLIC. The SLIC also supplies dc current to energize the transmitter in the telephone. The control logic gives a power down signal to the line circuit components during the idle state to minimize power consumption.

The operation of the line circuit can best be understood by tracing a call from a Model 500 telephone through the line circuit. When the calling customer goes off-hook, a dc path is established between the tip and ring via the telephone and current flows. This current is detected in the SLIC and the off-hook signal is sent to the control logic. The line circuit is periodically scanned over the multiplex bus from a central control. When the line circuit control recognizes its address, an off-hook message is returned through the gates and the multiplex bus. The switching system interprets this off-hook as a request for service and causes dial tone to be digitally synthesized and placed on the multiplex bus. A message is sent to the line circuit control to identify the message channel transmit and receive time slots on the multiplex bus. The control logic powers up the codec and filters and dial tone is gated off the multiplex bus to the customer.

As the customer dials a number, the current in the loop is interrupted a number of times corresponding to the dialed digit. This current interruption is detected in the SLIC and sent to the control logic. The control logic passes these makes and breaks to the multiplex bus signaling time slot. The switching system accumulates the dialed number and, assuming an intraoffice call, a command is sent to the called party line circuit to close the ringing relay. This causes the called party telephone to ring and a digitally synthesized ringback tone is heard by the calling party. Ringing normally has a cadence of 2 sec on and 4 sec off. Ring trip during ringing can be detected on the ring bus. Ring trip during the idle period is detected by the SLIC and sent through the control logic and gates to the multiplex bus. When the called party answers, a 4-wire path is established through the switching network to allow conversation. Calling or called party disconnect is detected by the SLIC and sent to the switching system control to remove the connection and restore both line circuits to the idle state.

5.2. Line Circuit Technology

Techniques for physically realizing the various BORSHT elements are described in this section. It is shown that semiconductor technology plays a vital role in element design.

5.2.1. Subscriber Line Interface Circuit (SLIC)

The SLIC must provide battery feed, signaling detection, and 2- to 4-wire conversion. In addition, it must have good longitudinal balance, high rejection of large longitudinal voltages, and the ability to survive overvoltage faults. A traditional SLIC using transformer technology is shown in Fig. 29.

Referring to Fig. 29, a single transformer with four windings of n turns each is illustrated. The dots on the transformer windings indicate polarity. The customer loop and station instrument have been replaced by a Thévenin equivalent circuit with open circuit voltage e_t and impedance Z_L. The capacitor connecting the two primary windings is assumed to pass the lowest speech frequency but be open to dial pulses. If $R \gg R_1$, the current through the loop is given by

$$I_L \cong \frac{48}{2R_1 + Z_L} \tag{5}$$

Normal Model 500 telephone current needs will be satisfied if $2R_1 = 400 \ \Omega$. A resistance bridge is formed by resistors R to detect signaling. The threshold circuit input voltage is given by

$$e_s = \frac{e_1 + e_2}{2} \tag{6}$$

Since e_s is proportional to the sum of the voltage across the two

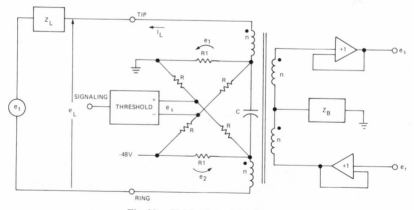

Fig. 29.   SLIC using a transformer.

resistors R_1, a threshold can be set to determine off-hook and differentiate against cable leakage. The threshold device is used to detect off-hook, on-hook, and dial pulses and contains a low-pass filter to discriminate against line noise.

The ac transfer functions for the circuit are given by equations (7)–(9) assuming a large C and an ideal transformer:

$$\left.\frac{e_s}{e_t}\right|_{e_r=0} = \frac{4Z_B}{Z_L + 4Z_B} \tag{7}$$

$$\left.\frac{e_L}{e_r}\right|_{e_s=0} = \frac{2Z_L}{Z_L + 4Z_B} \tag{8}$$

$$\left.\frac{e_s}{e_r}\right|_{e_t=0} = \frac{4Z_B - Z_L}{4Z_B + Z_L} \tag{9}$$

This SLIC realization has many disadvantages including the size and weight of the transformer required to pass the maximum loop current of approximately 80 mA and maintain transmission at 200 Hz. The transformer must also be carefully shielded to minimize crosstalk due to low-frequency magnetic coupling from adjacent circuits.

However, the transformer has many advantages. The transformer is a robust device which is hard to destroy. It also has energy limiting properties for circuits attached to its secondary. It can also withstand large longitudinal voltages and has good longitudinal balance. Because of these valuable characteristics, many design innovations have been made to minimize the size and weight of the transformer.[16]

The battery feed scheme shown in Fig. 29 has the disadvantage of generating heat for short loops or when ring-to-ground shorts occur. But, it is undesirable to provide a current source feed since this would defeat the telephone's self-equalizing transmission properties illustrated in Fig. 5. Modified current source schemes have been proposed to satisfy the telephone transmitter power requirements and to minimize the maximum line circuit dissipation.[17]

Other technologies have been proposed which realize the SLIC using optical or operational amplifier techniques. A SLIC which does not require a transformer is shown in Fig. 30.[18] Relays (not shown) are required to apply ringing and test signals to the loop. Battery current is supplied through two 450-Ω resistors. Signals from the telephone e_t are applied to a differential amplifier which also provides good longitudinal balance.

The differential loop voltage e_L is converted into an unbalanced voltage e_3. The hybrid transmit signal e_s is proportional to e_3. Current through the 450-Ω resistors caused by e_L flows into the two power supplies. The dc component in e_3 is used to detect signaling.

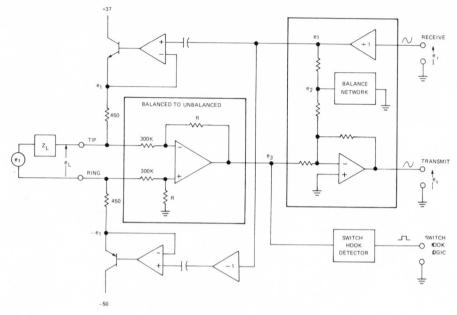

Fig. 30.   SLIC without a transformer.

The received voltage e_r is equal to e_1 and is differentially applied to the loop through the 450-Ω resistors. This causes a loop voltage

$$\left.\frac{e_L}{e_r}\right|_{e_t=0} = \frac{Z_L}{450 + Z_L} \tag{10}$$

But this also causes a voltage at e_3 and a proportional current flows into the transmit operational amplifier. The hybrid function must provide high loss between the transmit and receive ports. Therefore, an equal and opposite current must be applied to the transmit operational amplifier from e_2.

The SLIC in Fig. 30 can be realized using discrete semiconductor devices or the complete circuit can be integrated and placed on a single silicon die. A photograph of a monolithic silicon SLIC with a roughly similar circuit design is shown in Fig. 31.[19] This circuit is realized using 80-V dielectric isolation technology and provides the following functions: battery feed with loop current limiting, supervision, ringing control, and 2- to 4-wire conversion. There are over 300 components on this single die which measures 0.124 × 0.237 in.

Referring to Fig. 31, the tip and ring connect to a transversal (metallic component) current sense amplifier which performs a balanced-to-unbalanced transmission function. Line amplifiers with large power tran-

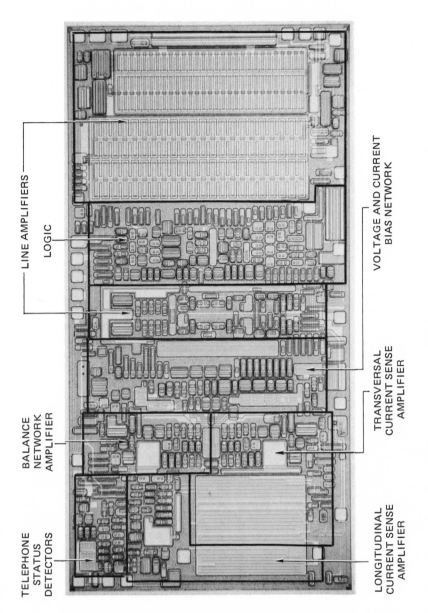

TELEPHONE
STATUS
DETECTORS

BALANCE
NETWORK
AMPLIFIER

LINE AMPLIFIERS

LOGIC

VOLTAGE AND CURRENT
BIAS NETWORK

TRANSVERSAL
CURRENT SENSE
AMPLIFIER

LONGITUDINAL
CURRENT SENSE
AMPLIFIER

Fig. 31.   Photomicrograph of the Harris Corporation HC-5501 monolithic SLIC.

sistors supply dc and signal current to the tip and ring through external 300-Ω resistors and a − 48-V source. The balance network amplifier with external components provides current cancellation to realize the hybrid function. Telephone status detectors in combination with the longitudinal current sense amplifier provide supervision by detecting telephone hook switch status (including ring trip) and a grounded ring. The logic section provides power denial, supervision output, and control for an external ringing relay.

5.2.2. Echo Control

Analog termination transmission requirements have been summarized in Section 3.3. These requirements describe the need for echo control due to the 4-wire path required by the digital switch. Weighted echo path loss (WEPL) is an important measure for specifying echo performance. Techniques for minimizing echo and thereby meeting WEPL objectives are discussed in this section.

There are two common techniques for echo control: adding loss in the echo path and adjusting the hybrid termination impedance to increase transhybrid loss. Adding loss to the echo path cannot be employed if it is desirable to have zero cross-office loss. However, some administrations have permitted a loss of 2 dB or more and this has effectively controlled echo. A 2-dB cross-office loss improves the WEPL by 4 dB over the lossless case. Loss is often inserted by a digital attenuator whose value is changed under stored program control. This allows the switching system to operate with one cross-office loss for intraoffice calls (maybe 2 dB) and another for interoffice calls (maybe 0 dB). Switching digital attenuators to control loss is discussed in more detail in Chapter 10 of this volume.

A second means for controlling echo is suggested by Fig. 7. The input impedance of telephone loops varies substantially from one loop to the next and it is difficult to find one complex impedance Z_B which, when substituted in equation (9) provides adequate transhybrid loss to meet WEPL objectives. But Fig. 7 shows that loop impedance Z_L generally fits one of two models: one Z_L for loops which are unloaded and another for loops which are loaded. It has been shown[20] that adequate WEPL can be obtained without adding loss to the echo path for intraoffice calls if one of two values of Z_B are applied to the hybrid: one for loaded loops and one for nonloaded loops. The impedance of nonloaded loops can be approximated by 800 Ω in parallel with 0.05 μF where the loaded loop approximation of 1650 Ω in parallel with 5 nF.

If two separate hybrid terminating impedances are used to meet WEPL objectives, a means must be provided to select the proper network according to the loaded or nonloaded loop criteria. One method is to manually select the impedance value at the switching system line card based on telephone company administration records. Another method has been suggested where each loop is automatically measured during low-traffic hours to determine the loaded or nonloaded condition. This information is stored in the switching system memory and a control signal is sent to the line circuit to select one of two hybrid balance networks.

Both of these schemes have effectively controlled echo in digital local switching systems. In the future, adaptive techniques[21] or echo cancellors might be used to further improve echo performance. The quality of the entire communications network will be greatly improved when these devices are available.

5.2.3. Filter and Codec

Techniques for digitizing speech have been presented in Section 4. Since international standards have been established for PCM, most telephone administrations have specified this coding scheme for public network applications. PCM standardization has given the semiconductor industry the necessary volume to economically produce standard integrated circuits.

The technology for realizing PCM filters and codecs has rapidly evolved. The first single-chip integrated circuit codecs were introduced in 1976. Single-chip filters appeared in 1977 and a single-chip filter/codec was announced in 1978.

A photograph of a NMOS single-chip PCM filter/codec die is shown in Fig. 32. The transmit and receive filters, coder, decoder, reference voltages, and control logic are all contained on a single chip. Switched capacitor technology[22] is used to realize the transmit and receive low-pass filters and the digital-to-analog converters use a weighted capacitor array.

Referring to Fig. 32, analog input signals are buffered (transmit input amplifier), prefiltered to prevent aliasing due to the switched-capacitor low-pass filter (transmit antialias filter) and band-pass filtered prior to encoding (transmit low-pass core antialias filter and 60-Hz hi-pass filter). The coder includes the voltage references, digital-to-analog converter (encoder segment A and B and step capacitor arrays), comparator, and a successive approximation register (encoder logic).

The decoder receives a digital bit stream and converts the digital PCM words into analog levels (decoder capacitor array). The analog levels are applied to a reconstruction low-pass filter (receive core filter) and receive power amplifier. There are approximately 4000 devices on this chip which measures 0.262×0.145 in.

New circuit techniques have the potential to reduce power consumption and chip cost. One new codec technique samples the analog waveform at a high frequency to minimize the complexity of the antialiasing filter. Then, digital processing techniques are used to filter the signal and convert

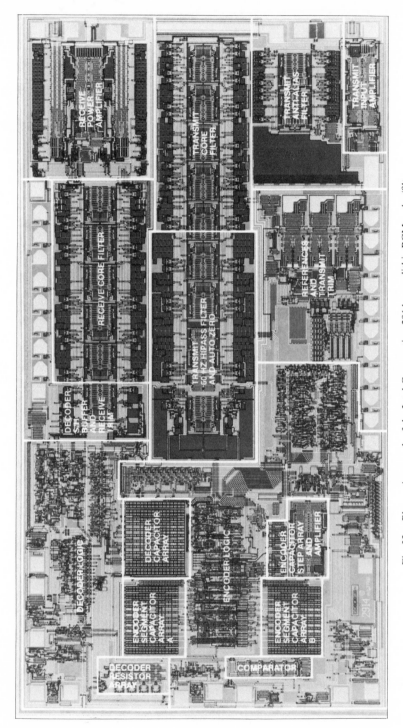

Fig. 32.   Photomicrograph of the Intel Corporation 2914 monolithic PCM codec/filter.

the high-speed bit stream into standard 64 kbit/sec PCM. The terminal performance of the filter/codec using this technology will be identical to the switched capacitor approach but the cost could be lower due to fewer analog circuits and reduced die size.

The complexity of integrated circuits has historically doubled every year. The analog termination now relies on integrated circuits for its major functions and it is not unreasonable to forecast that all of the functions shown in Fig. 28 will some day be contained on a single silicon chip.

5.2.4. Overvoltage Protection

The analog termination must meet the overvoltage stress requirements described in Section 3.4. Overvoltage protection usually consists of primary and secondary protection. Primary protection is located at the main distributing frame and secondary protection is located on the line card. Two types of circuit devices have been used to provide primary protection: carbon blocks and gas discharge tubes. Gas tubes have less variability in breakdown voltage compared with carbon blocks. However, the carbon block is adequate for many primary protection applications.

Two carbon blocks are usually used for primary protection: one between the tip and ground and the other between the ring and ground. Since one block will most likely fire a short time before the other, a large longitudinal voltage will be converted into a metallic voltage when the first block fires and then arrested when the second block fires. This problem is eliminated by the 3-element gas tube where the tip, ring, and ground electrodes are all contained within the same glass envelope. When one anode fires, the other follows because of gas ionization. This minimizes the metallic voltage created by large longitudinal surges.

Secondary protection usually consists of power resistors, varistors (variable resistors), and zener diodes. The location of the secondary protection components is a function of the circuit design

The line circuit must operate normally in the presence of large longitudinal potentials described in Fig. 9. These requirements are especially difficult to meet with an electronic SLIC circuit.

5.3. Redundancy

There are a large number of semiconductor devices per line in many digital switch designs. These devices cause the line card to have a high failure rate which can potentially exceed the objectives for satisfactory service described in Section 3.7.

Full redundancy at the line circuit level is obviously impractical. However, a 1-for-n protection scheme can be employed where one spare line circuit is used to protect *n* active line circuits. The test bus can be used to give the spare line circuit access to *n* lines. The tip and ring of a customer line associated with the defective line circuit is switched onto the test bus and the spare is activated. When the protection line card is switched into service, the test bus cannot be used for normal testing functions. Therefore, line card sparing might be accomplished at the rack level rather than at the system level so the test bus for only one rack is occupied during the protection interval.

Switching to the spare line circuit can be automatically accomplished. Line card failures can be detected by automatic routines during off-peak hours. The testing system can inform the switch of the failure and thereby cause the redundancy to be applied. If the digital switching system is located in an unattended office, such a redundancy scheme might prevent a customer outage.

Thus, redundancy can be applied at the line circuit level to maintain high system availability. To minimize cost, the redundancy scheme must be simple and must rely on a small number of protection circuits. The reliability of the individual line circuits must be sufficient to allow simple redundancy to be effective.

6. Conclusions

Analog terminations for a digital switching system have been presented in this chapter. These terminations provide the interface between a digital switching system and analog customer loops, trunks, and service circuits. The digital termination is described in Chapter 8 of this volume.

The analog termination is an extremely important element of a digital switching system since it establishes many system parameters including cost, power consumption, size, and transmission quality. Requirements for customer loop and trunk terminations have been described in this chapter. It has been shown that customer loop termination design is established by the type of telephone instrument. As telephone instruments continue to evolve, substantial changes will be needed in the analog termination. Future use of low-power transmitters and tone ringers in telephones will substantially ease the design difficulty of the line circuit.

This chapter has placed emphasis on pulse code modulation as a means for digitizing analog signals. This modulation scheme provides a highly transparent channel for voice and high-speed data. Other speech digitization techniques have been presented and it is possible that one or more of these techniques will find increasing use in the future. This could result from network designs where data are segregated from voice at the customer's premises. In this case, the transmission channel for voice need not also accommodate data. This would give the system designer additional flexibility in selecting the voice coding technique. The future Integrated Services Digital Network described in Chapter 10 might conserve bandwidth by using voice-coding techniques which have bit rates substantially less than 64 kbit/sec.

PCM has also been selected in the past to prevent degradation in signal to noise in the presence of many tandem analog-to-digital and digital-to-analog conversions which are required when analog switching is used. The number of these conversions will be substantially reduced in the all-digital network.

The chapter has concluded with a description of the cost-sensitive line circuit. Typical functions have been described along with line circuit technology. Advances in large-scale integrated circuits will be the key to future line circuit architecture, cost, reliability, power consumption, and size. Improvements in semiconductor technology will pace advances in the line circuit.

Questions

1. Discuss the various terminations for a digital switching system.
2. The line circuit represents a large percentage of the total manufacturing cost of a local digital switching system. Estimate the number of printed circuit boards in a local digital switching system. In terms of printed circuit boards, estimate the percentage of the total boards in the system which are line circuits for systems of the following sizes: (a) 1000 lines; (b) 10,000 lines; (c) 50,000 lines.
3. Explain the difference between 2-wire circuits and 4-wire circuits. If a subscriber loop contains a single wire and current is returned to ground, is this a 2-wire or a 1-wire circuit? In a 4-wire digital switching network with a common ground, is the network 2-wire, 3-wire, or 4-wire? When are four physical wires required to make a 4-wire circuit?
4. Why must a digital switching system be compatible with existing telephone instruments?
5. Explain the purpose of the battery feed portion of the BORSHT circuit. Why is it important to keep the voltage on the subscriber loop negative with respect to ground?
6. Why is a hybrid required both in the telephone instrument and in the BORSHT circuit of a digital switch. Discuss techniques which can be used to eliminate both hybrids.
7. Discuss the benefits of side tone. Experiment with your telephone by blocking the receiver and talking into the transmitter. What did you find?
8. Discuss the advantages and disadvantages of multiparty telephone service. Suggest techniques to provide selective ringing and proper billing identification for multiparty lines.
9. Describe the special functions required to interface a coin telephone to a local digital switching system.

10. What is the difference between bridged, divided, and superimposed ringing?

11. A digital switching system can detect signaling on loops which can have a dc resistance of as much as 1900 ohms. How long can this loop be in the following circumstances: (a) 26-gauge wire; (b) 24-gauge wire; (c) 19-gauge wire; (d) an equal mixture of 26-, 24-, and 19-gauge wire?

12. To prevent excessive dissipation in a digital switching system line circuit, it is desirable to limit the current supplied to the customer loop. Discuss the advantages and disadvantages of such a loop current limiting scheme and reasonable values for any limit. Is a constant current feed a good idea?

13. Discuss the voltages which can exist at the line interface tip and ring of a digital switching system.

14. Suggest values for the line circuit hybrid compromise network for loaded and nonloaded subscriber loops. Why is it desirable to load loops? Explain the loading technique.

15. Discuss the difference between customer loops and trunks. Why are customer loops usually 2-wire? Why are long-distance trunks 4-wire?

16. What is the difference between one-way trunks and two-way trunks? Discuss the concept of glare.

17. In an E&M trunk circuit, discuss the functions of the E&M leads. If a digital switch trunk circuit had leads called E&M and a carrier system also had E&M leads, would the corresponding E&M leads be connected or cross-connected to establish proper system operation? In Fig. 8, why are the signaling leads called Sig. 1 and Sig. 2?

18. What are the fundamental requirements for the transmission quality of the codecs used in a digital switching system.

19. Discuss trade-offs in the voice quality and bit rate in a digital switching system and in a digital transmission system.

20. Discuss the importance of longitudinal balance in the line circuit of a digital switching system.

21. Discuss the differences between talker and listener echo. Make some long distance calls and listen for echo. Rate the quality of these circuits.

22. Define singing margin and discuss the impact that circuit delay has on the echo grade of service. Why is WEPL used to specify the quality of a circuit?

23. Discuss the vulnerability of the line circuit to high-voltage sources for various types of digital switching systems, public and private.

24. If the subscriber loop maximum transmission loss goal is 8 dB, and the maximum signaling sensitivity is 1900 ohms, which parameter first limits the maximum subscriber loop length for the following cases: (a) 19-gauge wire; (b) 26-gauge wire; (c) equal distances of 19- and 26-gauge wire.

25. Discuss the various technologies for connecting a residential telephone to a digital class-5 central office. What is the traffic occupancy for wire pairs used for this connection under the different techniques described.

26. Why is the testing function required in the line circuit of a digital switching system? Discuss the various techniques which might be used to perform subscriber loop testing in a digital switching system.

27. What is a reasonable failure rate for a digital switching system line circuit? Why?

28. The energy cost for a particular location is $0.2 per kilowatt hour. Assume that

the line circuit consumes two watts per line and the balance of the system consumes 0.5 watts per line. What is the energy bill per month for a system with the following sizes: (a) 1000 lines; (b) 10,000 lines; (c) 50,000 lines?

29. Discuss the advantages and disadvantages of the two classes of speech digitization techniques.

30. Can digital switching only use PCM? Discuss.

31. Explain the process of pulse code modulation.

32. What is fold-over distortion? Describe two techniques to minimize its amplitude?

33. What is the percentage peak-to-peak quantizing error for a linear PCM codec with a 4-bit code, an 8-bit code, and a 10-bit code?

34. Using a successive questioning technique, what is the maximum number of trials required to guess any number between 0 and 100? Between 0 and 1000?

35. In a PCM system, what happens if the sampling interval varies from sample to sample. Explain your answer with the use of Fig. 21.

36. Discuss the reasons why 8 kHz has been established as the international sampling rate for PCM?

37. Describe the process of companding and its benefits. Derive the number of bits required in a linear PCM code word to provide an 80 dB dynamic range.

38. What are the differences between A-law and μ-law companders?

39. Discuss the differences between PCM, differential PCM, and adaptive differential PCM.

40. Discuss the use of various waveform and source coders for both private and public digital switching systems.

41. Referring to Fig. 27, discuss the relative advantages of providing the BORSCHT circuit functions at locations A and B.

42. Describe the functions of the line circuit illustrated in Fig. 28.

43. Derive the equations for the transfer functions of the transformer shown in Fig. 29.

44. Using the basic circuit shown in Fig. 29, suggest some alternate techniques for detecting customer signaling.

45. What would be the advantages and disadvantages of using battery feed from a transformer or an active SLIC?

46. Discuss techniques which can be used to minimize echo in line circuit designs.

47. Discuss the need for line circuit redundancy and suggest techniques to accomplish this redundancy.

References

1. N. J. Skaperda, "Some Architectural Alternatives in the Design of a Digital Switch," *IEEE Trans. Commun.*, vol. COM-27 (7), p. 961, July 1979.

2. A. F. Bennett, "An Improved Circuit for the Telephone Set," *Bell Syst. Tech. J.*, vol. 32, May 1953.

3. Bell Telephone Laboratories, Inc., *Transmission Systems for Communications*, Chap. 3, 1970.

4. J. C. McDonald, "Techniques for Digital Switching, *IEEE Commun. Mag.*, July, 1978.

5. R. L. Bunker, F. J. Scida, and R. P. McCabe, "Line Matching Networks to Support Zero Loss Operation in Digital Class 5 Offices," *Intl. Symp. on Subscriber Loops and Services Record*, 1978.

6. J. L. Neigh, "Transmission Planning for an Evolving Local Switched Digital Network," *IEEE Trans. Commun.*, vol. COM 27, July, 1979.

7. United States Department of Agriculture Rural Electrification Administration, "General Specification for Digital, Stored Program Controlled Central Office Equipment," June 1978.

8. M. N. Evans, "Telephone Company Planning for the Integration of Electronics in the Local Network," *Intl. Symp. on Subscriber Loops and Services Record*, 1976.

9. J. O. Bergholm, J. G. Eckert, and P. A. Gresh, "Evolving Designs for Bell System Urban-Suburban Loop Plant," *Intl. Symp. on Subscriber Loops and Services Record*, 1974.

10. J. L. Flanagan, M. R. Schroeder, B. S. Atal, R. E. Crochiere, N. S. Jayant, and J. M. Tribolet, "Speech Coding," *IEEE Trans. Commun.*, vol. COM-27, April 1979.

11. CCITT, Recommendation Series G700, Geneva, 1972.

12. P. Fritz, "Citedis Production PCM Public Telephone Switching System," *IEEE Trans. Commun.*, September, 1974.

13. F. T. Andrews, Jr. and W. B. Smith, "No. 5 ESS—Overview," *Intl. Switching Symp.*, September, 1981.

14. H. Sueyoshi, N. Shimasaki, A. Kitamura, and T. Yamaguchi, "System Design of Digital Telephone Switching System—NEAX 61," *IEEE Trans. Commun.*, vol. COM-27, July, 1979.

15. N. J. Skaperda, "Generic Digital Switching System," *Intl. Switching Symp.*, October, 1976.

16. V. K. Korsky, "Telepone Line Circuit with Differential Loop Current Sensing and Compensation," U.S. Patent 4,103,112.

17. H. Mussman *et al.*, "Design Techniques Which Reduce the Size and Power of the Subscriber Interface to a Local Exchange," *Zurich Conference on Digital Communications*, 1978.

18. J. R. Sergo, "DSS Quad Line Circuit," *Intl. Symp. on Subscriber Loops and Services*, 1978.

19. N. Mokhoff, "Communication ICs," *IEEE Spectrum*, January, 1982.

20. J. L. Neigh, "Transmission Planning for an Evolving Local Switched Digital Network," *IEEE Trans. Commun.*, vol. COM-27, July 1979.

21. D. G. Messerschmitt, "An Electronic Hybrid with Adaptive Balancing for Telephony," *IEEE Trans. Commun.*, vol. COM-28, August 1980.

22. Y. P. Tsividis, P. R. Gray, D. Hodges, and J. Chacko, Jr. "A Segmented μ-255 Law PCM Voice Encoder Utilizing NMOS Technology," *IEEE J. Solid-State Circuits*, December, 1976.

8

Digital Terminations and Digital Signal Processing

David G. Messerschmitt

1. Introduction

An important aspect of digital switching is that the distinction between where the digital switch ends and digital transmission begins is very blurred (hence the term "integrated transmission and switching"). Many functions which were once thought to reside in the transmission world are now included in the switching system. The purpose of this Chapter is to describe many of these transmission functions, including the interface to digital transmission facilities in both the trunk and customer loop plant. These interfaces are the digital counterparts to the analog terminations described in Chapter 7 of this volume. Other transmission functions such as tone generation and detection, echo suppression, echo cancellation, and digital filtering, which are advantageously implemented in the context of a digital switch, are also discussed in this chapter.

In Section 2 the interface to the digital transmission world is described; In Section 3 the relatively new field of digital transmission on the customer loop is briefly outlined, and in Section 4 transmission functions which can be implemented in the digital switch using digital signal processing techniques are reviewed.

David G. Messerschmitt ● Department of Electrical Engineering and Computer Sciences, University of California, Berkeley, California 94720

2. Interface to Digital Transmission Facilities

One of the major economies of digital switching lies in a common signal representation in the transmission and switching worlds. Namely, the time-division multiplexed PCM bit stream used within the switch is the same as that prevalent in much of the transmission world. The result is that the interface between the switch and digital transmission facilities is relatively simple and inexpensive. Not only does this save interface expense, but it also results in a zero-mile prove-in distance for digital trunk transmission, resulting in indirect savings in transmission costs (as described in Chapter 10 of this volume). The foregoing savings also apply to the customer loop transmission plant.

In the trunk plant, the collection of digital transmission facilities are known as the digital hierarchy. This hierarchy consists of transmission systems at various bit rates, as well as multiplexes which time-division multiplex lower-rate bit streams into higher-rate bit streams. The details of what bit rates are accommodated in the hierarchy vary from country to country. In the United States, the digital transmission line equipment is known as T-carrier. The most prevalent system is the T1, which carries bidirectional bit streams with rate 1.544 Mbit/sec over separate pairs of wires utilizing regenerative repeaters spaced at approximately one mile intervals. There are higher-rate T-carrier facilities, such as T1C, T2, T3, and T4, which transmit groups of 1.544 Mbit/sec bit streams time-division multiplexed together. Since the basic rate is at 1.544 Mbit/sec, this is the rate at which most digital switch designs interface the digital transmission world. In Europe, on the other hand, the basic bit rate at which the digital switches interface the transmission world is 2.048 Mbit/sec.

Before proceeding, it is important to make one distinction. A digital transmission facility carries a bit stream without interpreting what the bits themselves mean. However, the transmission terminals or digital switches at the two ends of the facility must have a common understanding as to the interpretation of the bits within the bit stream. Thus, there are two types of requirements which relate to the interface between a digital terminal or switch and a digital transmission facility:

1. *Electrical requirements*, such as voltage, pulse shape, impedance, bit rate, etc., which apply to the interface between transmission facility and switch or terminal.

2. *Requirements relating to meaning of the bits*, such as whether they represent voice or data, framing format, signaling format, maintenance data, etc. With few exceptions, these requirements have nothing to do with the transmission facility itself (some exceptions will be seen later).

These two sets of requirements together completely specify the signal which passes through the transmission facility. For example, the most common interface between a digital switch and the digital transmission world in the United States is the so-called DS1, which stands for "digital signal one." It specifies electrical requirements consistent with transmission over a T1 transmission facility, as well as specifying that the bit stream itself contains 24 channels (voice or data) together with a certain framing format and maintenance protocols which will be specified later. Thus digital channel banks, such as the D1D, D2, D3, and D4, which meet the DS1 specification can be connected together over a transmission facility and will be compatible. Similarly, digital switches which interface digital trunk facilities meet the DS1 or similar interface specifications and are therefore compatible with channel banks and with other digital switches. However, not all T1 transmission facilities will carry DS1 compatible information. For example, the D1 channel bank is not DS1 compatible (signaling and framing protocols differ).

The foregoing applies to the trunk transmission plant. With respect to the customer loop, there are basically three digital transmission options:

1. Pair-gain or customer-loop multiplex systems, which utilize digital transmission facilities to reduce the number of copper pairs required in the loop plant. The differences between pair-gain systems and trunk carrier systems lie in the terminals; that is, pair gain systems must perform functions such as ringing the telephone not required in the trunk plant. In the case of a local digital switch, the pair-gain central office terminal which otherwise might be collocated with the switch, can essentially be eliminated. The pair gain system might use a T1 repeatered line for transmission between the remote terminal and the digital switch but the interface might not be DS1 compatible. The T1 bit stream might carry additional signaling and maintenance information required for the remote terminal. However, many aspects of the design of this interface (particularly those relating to the transmission facility itself) are identical to the DS1 interface.

2. Remote switching unit, wherein concentration and some switching functions of a local digital switch are located remotely from the host switch and are connected to the host switch again by a digital transmission facility. In this case the interface is also not precisely DS1 compatible, but it is similar enough to use nearly identical hardware.

3. Customer loop transmission, in which the transmission between a local switch (analog or digital) and the customer instrument is digital. Since the bit rate is usually only about 80 kbit/sec (as compared to 1.544 Mbit/sec for T-carrier) and the transmission medium is one pair of wires (as compared to two wire-pairs for T-carrier), the interface in this case is quite different from T-carrier. This option will be covered in Section 3.

The remainder of this section will cover the interface to a DS1 in some detail. As we have seen, this interface can be used with little or no modification for trunk, customer loop pair-gain, and remote switching unit connections via T-carrier or other digital transmission facilities.

2.1. Digital Termination Requirements

The digital termination provides the interface between digital transmission facilities and the digital switch. Countries using the μ companding law also have standardized on a 24-channel 1.544 Mbit/sec multiplexing format. In the United States, the standard interface is the DS1 signal referred to earlier. While other countries use a different multiplexing format, the basic principles discussed in connection with interfacing a DS1 apply to other formats as well. Thus, in this section, the interface to a DS1 will be described in detail as an example of the requirements for a general digital transmission termination.

Although we have left the impression that the DS1 interface specification applies to both the standard channel banks as well as digital switches, there is one crucial distinction. While channel banks usually do not attempt to synchronize the bit rate of incoming and outgoing bit streams (although some the newer channel banks do have this capability, which is called "loop timing" as discussed in Chapter 10 of this volume), all bit streams arriving at a digital switch are assumed to be synchronous with each other and with the internal switch clock. By synchronous, we mean that they have the same *average* bit rate (there are many mechanisms, such as jitter on the transmission facility and propagation delay variations due to seasonal temperature variations, which can vary the relative phase of the bits of the bit streams without changing their average rate). The incoming bit streams will only be synchronous if (a) channel banks connected to the digital switch are loop timed, and (b) all digital switches connected together via digital transmission facilities have their internal clocks synchronized together. This latter requirement is accomplished by "network synchronization" as discussed in Chapter 10 of this volume.

The remaining DS1 specifications are the same for digital switches and channel banks.[1–5] They are divided, as previously mentioned, into parts relating to the electrical interface and the contents of the bit stream itself.

Relative to the electrical interface, one interesting requirement is that the bit stream is transmitted in a bipolar format (sometimes called AMI, or "alternate mark inversion"). This three-level, or ternary, format consists of no pulse for a 0 bit, and alternating positive and negative pulses for 1 bits (this ensures that the transmitted signal has no dc content).

The remaining requirements relate to the contents of the bit stream itself:

1. In order to maintain an adequate ones-density for timing extraction on the T-carrier facility, the bit stream must average at least 12.5% ones and have no more than 15 consecutive zeros. This is usually accomplished at the analog-to-digital converter by ensuring that each eight-bit channel sample have at least a single one (the all-zero word is prohibited). In data transmission the all-zero word prohibition is undesirable and to achieve 64 kbit/sec data transmission in place of a voice channel the DS1 interface must be modified, using bipolar violations, to allow long streams of zeros in the data stream while still meeting the digital transmission system restrictions mentioned above.

2. In μ-law countries, the bit stream is composed of *frames* of 193 bits each. Each frame consists of 24 eight-bit samples from each of 24 channels, preceded by a single framing bit. The purpose of the framing bit is to identify to the receiving terminal or switch the location of the individual samples as well as the signaling bits mentioned below.

3. In μ-law countries, the signaling state (off-hook, on-hook, or other states) of each channel is included in the multiplexed bit stream by robbing the least-significant bit of each channel every sixth frame. The information samples in these frames are only seven bits. The locations of these signaling bits are identified to the receiving terminal by a code contained in the framing bit position. Bit robbing can cease when common channel signaling is used.

It remains to specify the precise sequence of framing bits, which repeat in a twelve-frame sequence. The sequence is (100011011100). The purpose of this choice is better understood when it is noted that it consists of the sequence (101010) interleaved with (001110). The first sequence is simply an alternating 0–1 pattern which repeats in the bit stream every 386 bits and can be used by the receiving terminal to identify the beginning of every second frame (it is extremely unlikely that this pattern will occur in any other of the 385 bit positions). Bits in the second pattern also occur every 386 bits at a position which is easily identified by the receiving terminal once the first sequence has been identified. The second pattern repeats every 2316 bits and identifies the 12-frame *superframe*. The location of the robbed signaling bits is summarized in Table 1. There are actually two signaling channels, the A-Channel and the B-channel, for each of the 24 channels. The meaning of these A-bits and B-bits, which are each transmitted at a 666.667-Hz rate, depends on the type of signaling in use on the particular trunk (for example, E and M or revertive pulse).

The foregoing specifies the DS1 requirements, but there are other functions which the digital switch must typically perform:

1. A carefully chosen *idle channel code* should be put out on all idle

Table 1. DS1 Superframe Bit Assignment and Robbed
Signaling Bits

Frame No.	Superframe bit	Signaling bit	Signaling channel
1	1		
2	0		
3	0		
4	0		
5	1		
6	1	8th bit of each channel	A
7	0		
8	1		
9	1		
10	1		
11	0		
12	0	8th bit of each channel	B

trunks. This code should meet the ones-density requirements and decode to nearly zero volts dc. The common choice is the repetitive 8-bit code (01111111).[5]

2. To ensure that the all-zero 8-bit code can never be transmitted, it is common to perform *zero substitution* at the DS1 interface. Specifically, if the (00000000) code occurs, it is replaced by (00000010). This ensures that at least a single one is transmitted in each 8-bit word, even in frames where bit robbing occurs. Note that bit-robbing together with zero-substitution imply that if a channel is used for data transmission, only 6-bits per channel, or 48 kbits/sec, are available. It appears certain that this will be increased to 64 kbits/sec at some future time, requiring that the capability exist to disable both bit-robbing and zero-substitution. A new DS1 specification is forthcoming in the United States to provide this 64 kbit/sec capability.

3. It has been mentioned that even though the incoming bit streams are synchronous, they will have no fixed phase relationship relative to one another. The digital switch, on the other hand, expects that all the samples from channel one in the various incoming DS1's will appear at the input to the switch network simultaneously in order for it to perform its switching function as described in Chapter 5 of this volume. Thus, the DS1 interface must provide delay in the individual bit streams so that they have the proper phase relationship prior to the switching function. This is the function of the elastic store to be described later.

4. The DS1 interface will typically provide maintenance and alarm reports indicating marginal or failed transmission facilities.

With respect to the last item, it is best illustrated by examining the maintenance actions of the No. 4 ESS DS1 interface (which is part of the Digroup Terminal).[3] These are summarized in Table 2. The Digroup Terminal generates "line reports," indicating marginal or failed facilities, whenever there are excessive bipolar violations (violations of the alternating pulse polarity constraints indicating a transmission error occurred), excessive reframes (loss of frame and subsequent reacquisition of frame due to transmission errors), or excessive slips (overflow or underflow of the elastic store indicating an absence of the required synchronization). Both reframes and slips will be further discussed later. The actual rates of anomalies are specified in Table 2 for both maintenance limits (indicating a marginal facility) and out-of-service limits (indicating a failed facility).

In addition to the line reports, the Digroup Terminal generates the standard alarms also provided by channel banks. A failure of the incoming facility, as indicated by the inability to find frame, generates a "local alarm" (sometimes called "carrier group alarm"). One means to signal this alarm to the remote terminal or switch, is to set to zero ("digit two zero") the next to the most significant bit of each eight-bit word during a local alarm. The local alarm is removed when frame is acquired and retained. The failure of an outgoing facility is indicated by a local alarm in the remote terminal or switch, and generates a "remote alarm". This is recognized by an incoming "digit two zero" being persistent for some time. The incoming signaling states are all set to on-hook during both a remote and local alarm to ensure that all calls through the failed facility are disconnected. Since the switch is not able to signal through the facility, this also ensures that no additional calls are connected through the facility.

Table 2. Digroup Terminal Maintenance Actions for No. 4 ESS

A. DS1 line reports

Degradation	Maintenance limit	Out-of-service limit
Slip	4 per 24 hr	255
Framing loss	17 per 24 hr	511
Bipolar violations	1 violation/10^6 bits	10^3 bits

B. Alarms

Local alarm (LCA)
    Out-of-frame for 2.43 sec
    Action: Digit two to zero on all outgoing channels
        All incoming signaling states on-hook
    Removal: in-frame for 9.73 sec

Remote alarm (RMA)
    Digit two zero for 464 msec
    Action: All incoming signaling states on-hook
    Removal: Digit two forcing removed for 464 msec

2.2. Typical Digital Termination

A block diagram illustrating the functions of a typical DS1 interface is shown in Fig. 1. On the receive side, the bit-rate timing is first recovered in the same fashion as in a T1 repeater. The data stream is then sampled and sliced according to the derived timing, and then converted to binary by turning positive and negative sliced values to one-bits. Bipolar violations (two positive or two negative sliced values in a row) are noted for the maintenance reports. The framing recovery circuit detects an out-of-frame condition, notes that condition for maintenance reports, and searches systematically each bit portion for the expected framing pattern.

The purpose of the elastic store is to absorb any phase jitter on the incoming bit streams and line up channel one samples from each DS1 termination at the input to the switch network by providing a variable delay in the bit stream. It consists of a memory into which the speech samples are written according to the recovered timing, and from which they are read according to the internal switch clock. The slip detection circuit monitors those two clocks for an overflow or underflow of that memory, and notes these slips for maintenance reports. Finally, the signaling bits are stripped off for eventual transmission to the switch processor. This signaling function of the DS1 interface is not used when common-channel signaling is engaged. Both the framing recovery and elastic store circuits will be described in more detail in Section 2.3.

On the transmit side, the switch provides the 8-bit words from each channel time-division multiplexed together, as well as the signaling state of each channel. The digital interface then substitutes (robs) the least significant bit of each channel in every sixth frame to provide the signaling state.

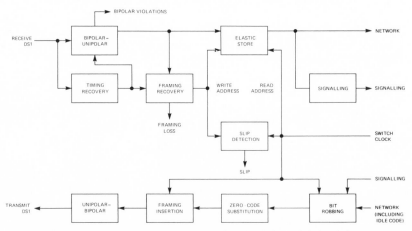

Fig. 1. Digital transmission termination circuit for a digital switch.

The resulting 8-bit samples are examined for the all-zero code, for which (00000010) is substituted. The known framing pattern is then inserted into the bit stream prior to the most significant bit of channel one, and conversion to bipolar completes the generation of the bit stream.

2.3. Detailed Digital Termination Design Considerations

In this section several interesting aspects of the design of the DS1 interface, including framing recovery, the elastic store, and the transmission impact of bit robbing, will receive further consideration.

2.3.1. Framing Recovery

A framing recovery circuit has two basic states, as shown in Fig. 2. When the known framing pattern is being observed in the expected framing position, the state is "in-frame." When some specified number of violations of the known pattern are observed (more than one to avoid reframes due to a single transmission error), the circuit goes into the "out-of-frame" state. In this state the circuit systematically searches the possible bit positions (every 193 bits) for the known framing pattern. Once it observes this pattern for some number of frames (usually more than ten to avoid declaring in-frame erroneously), it goes back to the in-frame state.

There are two measures usually applied to gauge the effectiveness of a framing strategy. First, the effectiveness of the out-of-frame detection strategy can by gauged by the rate of *misframes*, which are unnecessary reframes (because the circuit is actually in frame) caused by transmission errors. Second, the effectiveness of a reframe strategy can be measured by the *maximum average reframe time*, which is the average time to reframe when starting from the worst-case position. The reframe time can only be expressed as an average because the search time depends on the number of bits which are examined during the reframe, most of which are not framing bits and are therefore random.

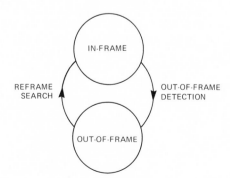

Fig. 2.   States of a digital termination framing circuit.

Calculations of the rate of misframes are necessarily based on ideal-ized transmission error generation models, such as independent errors. Since errors are not usually independent, the calculations are almost mea-ningless in terms of predicting actual misframe rates. We will therefore refrain from any further consideration of misframe rate here.

Calculation of maximum average reframe time is much more informa-tive and meaningful, so an illustrative example will be given. To make the example simple, consider the following frame format, which is simpler than the DS1 (and is actually what was used in the earliest D1 digital channel bank): Let the frame length be 193 bits, with an alternating 101010 . . . framing pattern (and hence no superframe structure). The reframe strategy is to examine only one bit position at a time looking for the alternating pattern. When a single violation of that pattern is observed (00 or 11), the circuit moves on to the next bit position. When the alternating pattern is observed in one position for ten successive frames, the circuit declares itself to be in-frame.

In calculating the reframe time for this situation, the worst case is clearly when the circuit starts its search in the bit position immediately following the actual framing bit, so that it has to observe 192 random data positions before it reaches the actual frame position. Although the out-of-frame detection time is usually included in the reframe time, it is usually an insignificant component (on the order of 1–2 msec) of that time, so it will be ignored. The average number of frames searched during the reframe is therefore 192 times the average number of frames spent in one bit position while observing the alternating pattern in random data (called "hold frames"), plus ten frames in the actual framing bit position.

It remains, then, to calculate the average number of hold frames. At each bit position, the circuit examines the first bit (which does not tell it anything) and then compares the bit 193 bit positions later. If it is the same (which occurs with probability one-half in random data) there was a vio-lation, it moves on to the next bit position, and there was just one hold frame. If the second bit was different (which also has probability one-half), it must examine a third bit one frame later. Proceeding in this manner, it is apparent that n hold frames occur with probability 2^{-n}. The average number of hold frames is thus

$$\sum_{n=1}^{\infty} n2^{-n} = 2 \tag{1}$$

Finally, the total maximum average reframe time is

$$\frac{2 \times 192 + 10}{8000 \text{ Hz}} = 49 \text{ msec} \tag{2}$$

The 8000 Hz in the denominator is the rate at which bit positions are examined (frame rate).

What can we conclude from this example about the reframe time for a DS1 format? If the same reframe strategy was employed, namely, search one bit position at a time, the reframe time would be four times as great, or about 200 msec. This is because the alternating framing bit occurs every 386 bit positions instead of every 193 bit positions, so that twice as many bit positions must be examined in the worst case. In addition, a given bit position is examined at half the rate, or 4000 Hz. Hence, the factor of 4.

An obvious way to reduce the reframe time is to examine more than one bit position at a time. Thus, one can envision the following strategy: Have a sliding window of N consecutive bit positions, each of which is being examined for the expected framing pattern. Each time one or more framing pattern violations are observed, the N-bit window is slid along the frame as far as possible. When the actual framing bit appears in the window, the circuit will acquire frame by eventually observing violations in all the other bit positions, and by recognizing the known framing pattern in the actual framing bit position for the required number of frames in a row. Clearly, the fastest reframe corresponds to a window the same size as the frame, $N = 386$ for a DS1. This is the smallest number of bits which is always guaranteed to include the known framing pattern.

The calculation of reframe time for this more complicated strategy is very detailed, and will not be considered here. Suffice it to say that a 50-msec maximum average reframe time can be achieved with $N = 8$.

What factors go into the choice of a misframe rate and reframe time objective? The most serious consequence of a reframe is the loss of the signaling information during a reframe. When dial-pulse signaling is in use, a reframe can result in the misdirection of a call (this is the source of the misframe objective of one per two days). A less serious problem will be a hit on a voiceband data call. On particularly long reframes a carrier group alarm (reframe lasting longer than 2.4 sec) will be generated (this is the source of the 50-msec objective). Finally, the most minor consequence of a reframe is a pop or click on a voice call.

2.3.2. Elastic Stores and Synchronization

An excellent thought model for an elastic store is the commutator model of Fig. 3. The elastic store has a number of storage cells (in this case eight) each capable of storing one bit. There are two commutators, a write commutator and a read commutator, the positions of which are determined by the write clock and read clock, respectively. Successive input bits are written in successive storage cells by the write commutator, and later read out by the read commutator. The store occupancy, which is defined to be

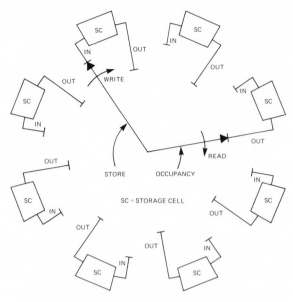

Fig. 3.   Commutator model of an elastic store.

the number of bits of delay imparted to the bit stream by the elastic store, is given by the relative positions of the write and read commutators. Note that since there is no reason why writes and reads must occur simultaneously, the store occupancy need not be an integer number of bits. For example, if reads occur midway between writes, the occupancy will be an integer plus one-half a bit. This illustrates that the term "occupancy" is somewhat misleading, since it only approximately represents the number of bits actually stored in the elastic store (which must of course be an integer).

The mechanism for a slip can now be clearly seen. If the write commutator is moving faster than the read commutator (the incoming bit stream is at a higher rate than the outgoing bit stream), the store occupancy is increasing with time. Eventually, the write commutator overtakes the read commutator, and the store occupancy suddenly changes from N bits (where N is the number of storage cells) to zero. This is an overflow, which is one of the two possible types of slips. The external effect is to delete N bits from the bit stream, since N bits which were written into the store are never read (this loss of bits is an inevitable consequence of reducing the read rate relative to the write rate). Conversely, when the read commutator is faster than the write, an underflow occurs, and N bits are read from the store twice resulting in a repetition of N bits in the output bit stream. A slip is easily noted by monitoring the store occupancy vs. time (which is related to the relative phase of the read and write clocks).

If the read and write clocks have the same average rates, but there is some relative phase jitter between them, there is a problem when the two commutators are close to being lined up on the average. This is because multiple slips will occur as the two commutators pass each other as the phase changes. For this reason, it is common to slip by only half the number of storage cells by forcing an $N/2$ change in the phase of the read or write clock when a slip is detected. There are then two possible relative positions of the read and write commutators, and one of them is always guaranteed to be far from a slip position.

In the case of a digital switch DS1 interface, it is convenient to slip by exactly one frame, or 193 bits, so that the concurrence of the channel-one sample at the elastic store output and the time it is needed at the switch network input can be easily maintained even immediately following a slip. It would be common, then, to build an elastic store with twice that number of storage cells, or 386. The elastic store can be implemented using a random-access memory with two address counters, one for writing and one for reading.

Now that the operation of the elastic store is understood, it is simple to predict the interval between slips for a given offset between the average rates of the read and write clocks. Consider the simple situation of Fig. 4a,

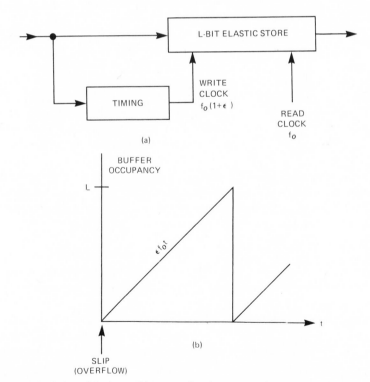

Fig. 4. Calculation of the interval between slips for constant frequency read and write clocks with (a) configuration of the elastic store, (b) store occupancy over one slip interval.

where an N-bit elastic store has an input bit stream with rate (as derived by timing recovery circuit) of $f_0(1 + \epsilon)$, where ϵ is the (small) fractional offset. The read clock, derived from the internal switch clock, has bit rate f_0. The net rate at which bits are accumulating in the store is $f_0 \epsilon$, and thus the occupancy of the store increases with slope $f_0 \epsilon$ as shown in Fig. 4b. An overflow occurs when $f_0 \epsilon t = N$, or at

$$t = \frac{N}{f_0 \epsilon} \tag{3}$$

In order to get a feeling for what this implies about clock accuracy, assume that the slip is by $N = 193$ bits, and that f_0 is the DS1 rate, 1.544 Mbit/sec. Then the ϵ required to keep the slips one day apart is $\epsilon = 1.45 \times 10^{-9}$. Since $\epsilon \approx 10^{-12}$ is achievable with an atomic clock, this negligible slip rate could be maintained without any attempt to synchronize digital switches together. However, the cost of an atomic clock at every switch would be prohibitive, and since it is desirable to eliminate slips altogether (in the absence of hardware or facility failures), in practice the internal clocks are phase-locked to a network reference standard. This is the function of network synchronization, which is discussed in Chapter 10 of this volume.

The objective for slips in the United States telephone network is a maximum of one slip per 20 hr ($\epsilon = 1.7 \times 10^{-9}$) during failure conditions. Since it is economical to provide atomic standards on a national basis, and since countries are loath to use the standard of another country as a reference, there is at present no attempt to synchronize across national boundaries.

2.3.3. Effect of Bit Robbing

Signalling in μ-law countries is accomplished by stealing the least significant bit every six frames for all channels. In A-law countries, signaling is sent over a common channel without need for bit robbing. The effect of bit robbing on transmission quality (quantization distortion in particular) is examined in this section.

The effect of bit robbing for signaling is to provide only 7-bit quantization precision, rather than 8-bit, in frames in which bit robbing takes place. There is no attempt to line up the 12-frame superframes between incoming and outgoing DS1's in a toll digital switch (this would require 12-frame elastic stores, resulting in an unacceptable transmission delay). Thus, bit robbing can occur in different frames for a given channel on an incoming and outgoing DS1. The worst case in a given connection is that bit robbing would occur in every frame (this would require a minimum of five digital switches in the connection).

It is easily shown that if L out of every six frames have 7-bit quantization, then the penalty in signal-to-quantization ratio (relative to eight-bit quantization) is approximately

$$\text{Penalty (dB)} = 10 \log_{10}(1 + L/2) \tag{4}$$

Thus, the penalty ranges from 1.8 dB for $L = 1$ to 6 dB for $L = 6$. This penalty is of little consequence, since it is largest for connections with the greatest preponderance of digital transmission, where there is the greatest margin of performance (8-bit quantization is provided primarily for margin against multiple analog-to-digital conversions). An additional factor is that it will gradually be eliminated as common-channel signaling also eliminates the need for bit-robbing signaling.

3. Digital Customer Loop Transmission

After the introduction of digital technology into the trunk network, and digital toll and local switches, the next logical application for digital transmission is between the digital local switch and the customer instrument. This application is motivated primarily by the ability to provide enhanced services (such as alternate voice-data, slow scan television, etc.) at lower incremental cost because of the availability of a relatively high-speed full-duplex data stream all the way to the customer premises. The digital customer loop can be provided as an option for those customers desiring these services and willing to pay the compensating rates.

The basic concept behind the digital customer loop is to give the customer direct access to the digital bit stream in the digital transmission and switching network. This can be accomplished by moving the low-pass filtering and analog-to-digital conversion to the customer premises and providing an effective full-duplex (two-way) data stream between the central office and the filter-codec. The data steam must be able to at least accommodate the 64-kbit/sec per-channel rate used internally by the digital switch, as well as provide some capacity for signaling information. Some realizations have provided 8 kbit/sec for signaling, as well as 8 kbit/sec for synchronization purposes for a total rate of 80 kbit/sec.

Since an appreciable fraction of the total telephone plant investment is in customer loop cable, it is not considered economical (or in fact necessary) to actually provide a separate wire-pair for each direction of data transmission. Rather, the two-way transmission is actually accomplished on a single wire-pair. Several methods of doing this have been proposed and demonstrated:

1. *"Burst-mode," "ping-pong,"* or *"time-compression multiplexing,"* in which the data are transmitted first in one direction and then the other. The

bits are first accumulated (buffered) in each direction and then transmitted at a rate at least twice as great as the average bit rate desired (in practice 2.25 to 2.5 times the rate).

2. The *hybrid method*, in which the two-wire connection is made into an effective four-wire connection by using a transmission hybrid as shown in Fig. 5. The hybrid of course depends upon knowledge of the impedance of the loop in the frequency range of interest in providing its balance. That impedance is somewhat variable, so the hybrid can provide an imperfect balance at best. The difficulty is compounded by the fact that normal telephony hybrids need only provide balance at voice frequencies, while the digital subscriber loop hybrid must provide a balance over a bandwidth approaching 100 kHz. These problems, coupled with the fact that the local transmitter signal which is leaking through the hybrid is much larger than the signal being received from the far end, implies that an adaptive echo canceller is necessary to cancel the leakage through the hybrid.

3. *Frequency-division multiplex*, in which the data streams passing in the two directions are separated in frequency (one is at baseband and the other is centred at a higher frequency).

The considerations in choosing one method over another relate primarily to circuit complexity (cost) and range. Both burst-mode and frequency-division multiplex offer less circuit complexity than the hybrid method (although this is becoming less important in this age of large-scale integration). The burst-mode approach offers the important advantage over the other two of eliminating near-end crosstalk (which is crosstalk from a high-level local transmitter into a local receiver). The hybrid method offers the advantage over the other two of requiring only half the bandwidth. In view of all these conflicting parameters, the final word is not in yet on which technique will become the most accepted. The greatest effort thus far, however, has been directed at the burst-mode approach.

The most important design parameter is the length of loop which is going to be accommodated (the so-called range). There are two basic factors which limit loop length in a burst-mode modem:

1. The choice of burst length, burst bit rate, and minimum interval

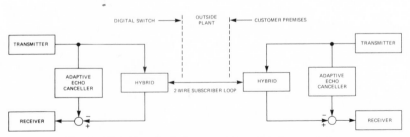

Fig. 5.   Hybrid method of customer loop digital transmission.

between bursts determines the maximum propagation delay which can be accommodated, and this in turn relates directly to the loop length.

2. The maximum attenuation of the loop, which is usually specified at half the transmitted bit rate, is directly related to the maximum loop length. This attenuation value is indicative of the susceptibility of the modem to noise and crosstalk.

Once the maximum half bit-rate loss has been specified on the basis of noise and crosstalk considerations, the maximum length of the loop depends on the gauge of wire. The standard design procedure is to choose the burst length and bit rate to accommodate the greatest distance desired (since propagation delay is dependent primarily on distance), so that the distance is limited only by the loss of the cable.

In the case of frequency-division multiplex and the hybrid method, the range is limited only by cable loss. It would seem that the hybrid method would have the greatest range since the bandwidth is the lowest and the cable loss increases rapidly with frequency; however, this depends on the degree of echo suppression which can be obtained in the hybrid method in the face of many echo-producing irregularities such as bridge taps.

Once a transmission method has been chosen, the impact on a local digital switch is twofold: First, the line interface filter, codec, and hybrid are replaced by a data modem. Thus, the circuitry located at the switch is quite different, as are the requirements on parameters such as longitudinal balance. Second, the signaling technique is radically changed. Instead of ringing the phone with a large ac voltage and providing information signaling by tones of various sorts, the signaling is sent by codes over the bit stream itself. In addition, since the primary purpose of customer loop digital transmission is to provide additional services, many of which are likely to require many more signaling states, the impact on the switch common-control processor software is likely to be profound. The method of signaling over the customer loop will likely be standardized by CCITT to accommodate any manufacturer's equipment.

4. Digital Signal Processing in Digital Switching

As was already mentioned, digital switching is resulting in some fundamental changes in the partitioning of functions between the switching and transmission worlds. Many functions formerly thought to be the exclusive domain of transmission are becoming integrated into the switching office. There are two reasons for this: First, the previously discussed integration of transmission and switching has resulted in the functions of analog-to-digital conversion and time-division multiplexing, formally implemented by channel banks in the transmission plant, to reside at the customer loop interface to the local digital switch. Second, both toll and local digital switches make all the channels passing through them accessible to digital signal processing devices in a standardized time-division multiplexed digital format, regardless of the nature of the transmission facility.

The latter presents opportunities to implement many transmission functions, including echo-control and loss, using time-division multiplexed digital signal-processing hardware at the interface or internal to a digital switch. The advantages of this are primarily economic: First, the initial cost can be lower, because the cost of digital logic implemented via large-scale integration is declining rapidly, and because many channels can be processed simultaneously by time-division multiplexing a single piece of hardware (in the analog world the processing hardware is usually replicated on a per-channel basis). Second, the recurring costs are substantially lower, because digital hardware is much more amenable to automated fault detection and isolation techniques, virtually eliminating scheduled maintenance and substantially reducing the cost of repairs. An additional factor is that the switch common-control processor provides a convenient administrative and control mechanism for that automated maintenance process.

It is beyond the scope of this chapter to discuss the implementation of transmission functions such as echo suppression, echo cancellation, digital speech interpolation, and analog-carrier multiplexing in the context of digital switching offices. The basic analog-to-digital conversion and time-division multiplexing functions are discussed in Chapter 7. Thus this section, after some general discussion about maintenance of digital signal-processing hardware and signal processing in the context of $\mu = 255$ encoding, will illustrate the use of digital signal-processing techniques with two functions which are traditionally associated with switching offices: attenuation and tone generation and detection.

4.1. Automated Maintenance Techniques

A major advantage of implementing signal-processing functions digitally is the relative ease with which automated maintenance can be achieved. There are three basic techniques for detecting faults in digital signal-processing hardware:

1. *Functional test*, such as for example connecting a tone generator to a tone detector and observing for proper operation. This technique applies equally well to analog as well as digital implementations, although the results are much more reproducible (in fact always identically the same in the absence of a fault) in the digital case. This technique has its limitations, however, since such factors as ability to discriminate against noise are difficult to assess in this fashion.

2. The use of *self-checking hardware*, as for example triplicating a

function and cross-matching the outputs to identify a failed unit. This approach is expensive, and most often applied to critical functions such as the common-control processor. A simpler example is the use of parity checks on address and data.

3. Perhaps the most powerful technique for signal-processing units (which perform identical repetitive functions) is to *exercise the unit in a spare time-slot*. This works when the hardware is performing the identical function on many channels time-division multiplexed together, so that a spare maintenance time-slot can easily be provided. A carefully chosen stimulus can be stored in read-only memory, as well as the correct response, with which the output can be compared. In addition, the correct response at many intermediate points in the processing can be compared to the correct response, providing a powerful method of isolating the fault. A 1-for-N protection-switched spare can then be provided for replacing a failed unit. Redundancy schemes are further discussed in Chapter 9 of this volume.

4.2. Signal Processing in a Nonuniform Quantization Environment

Common to all signal processing in the context of digital switching is the need to process signals encoded via the A or μ companding laws. The companding laws themselves have been discussed in Chapter 7 of this volume. Here, the impact of companding, specifically the μ-law, on signal-processing implementation will be reviewed.

To briefly review the $\mu = 255$ law, its eight bits are divided into a sign bit S, three bits which specify one of eight "chords" or "segments" $0 \leq L \leq 7$, and four bits which specify one of 16 equally spaced levels within a chord, $0 \leq V \leq 15$. The analog level X represented by these eight bits, i.e., the analog level which would be generated by a $\mu = 255$ decoder, is given by[6]

$$X = \pm \, | \, 2^L(V + 16.5) - 16.5 \, | \tag{5}$$

The general philosophy of processing signals encoded in $\mu = 255$ is to treat each 8-bit sample as if it represented analog value X. For example, to add two such signals it would be convenient to convert S, L, and V to a binary (fixed point) representation of X, which requires 14 bits (13 plus sign) of precision (the A/D requires 13 bits but the D/A requires 14 bits because the D/A first cord boundary moves by 1.5 steps in μ-law implementations). The two 14-bit binary numbers can then simply be added by ordinary binary arithmetic to form a representation for X of the sum. That X could then be converted back to the $\mu = 255$ L and V representation if desired. The effect of this addition of samples would be precisely the same as if both samples were converted to analog using an ideal $\mu = 255$ decoder, added using an analog pad, and converted to digital with an ideal $\mu = 255$ coder.

In signal processing systems, there are three representations of general interest:

1. *The $\mu = 255$ representation* for interfacing the outside digital transmission and switching world,
2. *A fixed point representation* for adding samples, and
3. One that has not been mentioned, *a floating point representation* for performing multiplications of two sample values or a sample value and a constant.

It is of interest to specify how conversions between these representations can be performed. The $\mu = 255$ to fixed point conversion can be achieved by simply implementing the equation already given. This can be done with arithmetic hardware, or in many applications more economically by a read-only memory which inputs L and V and outputs X (this requires 128 words $\times$ 7 bits = 1664 bits of memory).

Conversion from fixed point back to $\mu = 255$ is a bit more involved. The following simple algorithm, implemented in sequential logic, will suffice: Given an X, choose L such that

$$16 \leq 2^{-L}(X + 16.5) < 32 \tag{6}$$

and for this L, choose V such that

$$V \leq 2^{-L}(X + 16.5) - 16 < V + 1 \tag{7}$$

Implementing this function using a read-only memory requires 8192 words $\times$ 7 bits = 57344 bits of memory, which is perhaps excessive. Thus, the sequential logic method is usually preferred.

The idea of converting a $\mu = 255$ sample to floating point to expedite a subsequent multiplication has been applied in an echo canceller design[12]. Due to the doubling step-size of the $\mu = 255$ coding law, it is already close to a floating point representation. A floating point representation for X can be found by setting it equal to $2^L V'$, where L is the exponent (the same as the segment number in the $\mu = 255$) and V' is the mantissa of the floating point representation. Solving for V',

$$V' = V + 16.5(1 - 2^{-L}) \tag{8}$$

It is straightforward to see that $0 \leq V' < 32$, and that a full precision representation of V' would require 13 bits. However, if only 5 bits are used, the accuracy in V' would be plus or minus 0.5, which would result in an accuracy in X of plus or minus 2^{L-1}. This is exactly half a $\mu = 255$ step size, since on segment L the step size is 2^L. Thus, a 5-bit precision on V' results in a maximum error of half a step-size in the $\mu = 255$ law, and adding bits to V' reduces the error correspondingly. In short, more than five bits of precision for V' is seldom justified.

The actual conversion from V to V' can be effected by simple combinatorial logic. It should also be apparent that conversion from fixed point to floating point would also be simple and advantageous in many instances.

4.3. An Example: Digital Attenuation

The ideas of the preceding section can be illustrated by the example of digital attenuation.[6-9] Transmission considerations dictate that several different losses be provided in local digital switches. One option, and as will be seen momentarily the best option from the point of view of transmission performance (but perhaps not cost), would be to provide a programmable resistive attenuation pad on the customer loop prior to analog-to-digital conversion.

What if it is desired to digitally process the $\mu = 255$ samples to achieve the equivalent of this analog attenuation? Conceptually, the equivalent of Fig. 6 is desired; that is, convert to analog, multiply by a value $A < 1$ which depends on the desired attenuation, and convert back to digital. A more cost-effective alternative would be to convert the $\mu = 255$ sample to a floating point representation, multiply by the constant A using digital hardware, and convert the resulting floating point value to fixed point and subsequently back to $\mu = 255$. An even more cost-effective approach is to recognize that the hardware of Fig. 6 simply generates, for each input 8-bit sample, an output 8-bit sample which can be determined in advance for a given value of A. Why not then simply program a ROM to perform this translation (requiring only 128 words $\times$ 7 bits = 896 bits of memory)? The latter is the simple solution preferred by digital switch manufacturers.

One problem with this approach to attenuation can be seen from the equivalent block diagram of Fig. 6: When the output of the decoder is multiplied by A, the result is not necessarily another allowed decoder output. Thus, there is an additional quantization error introduced by the coder. In fact, digital attenuation introduces an additional quantization error comparable to a tandem analog-to-digital conversion, which is a 3-dB impairment (the impairment is actually greater at low signal levels).[8] This is why analog attenuation prior to conversion to digital would be the preferable approach to obtain optimum transmission performance.

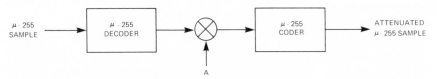

Fig. 6. A method of attenuating a companded digital signal by converting to analog.

4.4. Another Example: Tone Generation and Detection

As a final example of digital signal processing in a digital switching environment, consider tone generation and detection. These operations are required in the following contexts, all relating to signaling:

1. *Alerting signals,* such as tone ringing and receiver-off-hook, as well as *information signals,* such as audible ring, busy, reorder, and dial tone.
2. *Loop address signaling,* and more specifically DTMF (dual-tone multifrequency).
3. *Trunk address signaling,* and specifically MF (multifrequency).

This section will first consider the generation of these tones, and then the detection of DTMF, which is more extensive than MF (especially as the latter is made obsolete by common channel signaling).

4.4.1. Tone Generation

Options for generating the many tones required in a switching office include building an oscillator for each frequency required, or deriving all the frequencies from a single accurate reference. Since a very accurate reference is available in any digital switching office, the second alternative is to be preferred. Alternatives in using the reference include the phase locked loop (PLL) or generating the tones by some direct digital means. In a digital switch, the tones are needed in digital form, so the latter is to be preferred. In fact, tones at any frequency which is a rational multiple of a reference frequency can be easily generated by a read-only memory together with some addressing circuitry.[13,14] The reference frequency in this case is simply the sampling rate (8 kHz)!

The approach is illustrated in Fig. 7. Let f_s be the sampling rate and f_s/N be the lowest common denominator of the frequencies which it is desired to generate (for example, if all frequencies are multiples of 1 Hz, $N = 8000$). Then the circuit of Fig. 7a generates frequency $M(f_s/N)$, the samples of which are given by the relation

$$x_k = \sin\left(\frac{2\pi Mk}{N}\right) \tag{9}$$

The read-only memory is simply programmed with one cycle of frequency f_s/N,

$$y_k = \sin\left(\frac{2\pi k}{N}\right), \qquad 0 \le k < N \tag{10}$$

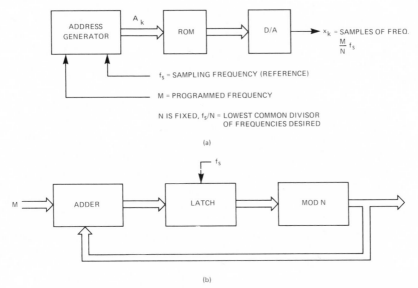

(a)

(b)

Fig. 7.   Generation of a single frequency tone by reading it from a read-only memory (ROM).
(a) The tone generation circuit. (b) Detail of the address generator.

requiring $N \mu = 255$ samples (actually, by symmetry one-quarter cycle will
suffice). It is easy to see that

$$x_k = y_{A(k)} \tag{11}$$

where the address is given by

$$A(k) = Mk \text{ modulo } N \tag{12}$$

This address is easily generated by the address generator of Fig. 7b, recognizing that

$$A(k + 1) = [A(k) + M] \text{ modulo } N \tag{13}$$

The "mod N" block is not needed when N is chosen to be a power of 2,
since $\log_2 N$ bit arithmetic with overflow ignored will accomplish the same
thing.

The foregoing specifies how a single tone can be generated, but how
do we go about generating the superposition of two or more tones (which is
required for many of the signaling methods mentioned earlier)? One approach is to sum the outputs of two generators of the type already described. However, if programmability is not required, a simpler approach is
to program a read-only memory with the sum of the two tones[15,16] (this
works again if both tones have frequencies rationally related to the sampling rate, in which case the number of samples which must be stored is the
least common multiple of the periods of the two sinusoids).

In conclusion, tones are simple and accurate to generate in a digital system. The most economical methods relay on a read-only memory to store a segment of the tone. The frequencies of the resulting tones are as accurate as the basic clock used to address the memory, which is typically quite accurate.

4.4.2. DTMF Detection

A wealth of literature exists on tone detection. That portion of this literature which applies specifically to DTMF detection will be summarized here.[17-24]

The environmental factors which most affect DTMF detection are that the digits are generated manually (which results in very broadly specified timing relationships), the first digit must be detected in the presence of dial-tone, and the detector is never disabled and must therefore not incorrectly declare speech or background noise to be a valid digit (called "digit simulation").

In order to give acceptable performance in this environment, a valid DTMF digit consists of exactly two tones, one in each of a high-band of frequencies and a low-band of frequencies. The frequencies are shown in Table 3 for each digit. These frequencies were carefully chosen to have no low-order harmonics in the signal set in order to minimize the chance of digit simulation.[17] All the frequencies are also chosen in the band between 700 and 1700 Hz, where there is no dial-tone and where delay distortion and attenuation are minimal problems.

The DTMF requirements[20] are listed in Table 4. There are two types of requirements: First, environmental factors such as frequency offsets, timing relationships, and signal power can be used to minimize the chances of digit simulation by noise or speech. Second, the performance require-

Table 3. DTMF Frequency Assignments

	Low band				High band			
	697	770	852	941	1209	1336	1477	1633
697					1	2	3	S
770					4	5	6	S
852					7	8	9	S
941					*	0	#	S
1209	1	4	7	*				
1336	2	5	8	0				
1477	3	6	9	#				
1633	S[a]	S	S	S				

[a] S = spare.

Table 4. DTMF Requirements for Central Office Applications

Frequency offsets	Respond if < 1.5%
	Not respond if > 3.5%
	(Additional 15-Hz
	carrier offset in 403)
Digit interval	≥ 40 msec
Interdigit interval	≥ 40 msec
Cycle time	≥ 85 msec
Power per frequency	−25 to 0^a dBm at 900 Ω
Twist (level skew	High tone +4 to −8 dB
between frequencies)	relative to low tone
Dial tone	0 dBm at 900 Ω total
Error rate	
Gaussian noise	
Impulse noise	
False double digit registration in impulse noise	
echo	20 msec delay, > 10 dB loss
	(40 msec and 14 dB for 403)
Digit simulation by speech	1 in 3000 calls digits 0–9
Input impedance	> 40 kΩ
Longitudinal balance	> 50 dB

^{a} +6 dBm at 900 Ω in electromechanical office.

ments, such as error rate in the presence of noise or speech, specify which detection techniques will yield acceptable performance.

A particularly troublesome requirement is the frequency of digit simulation by speech. The best way of ensuring that this requirement is met is to put a DTMF detector in a central office which is known not to have any DTMF loop address signaling and then observe the number of detected digits (all of which are known to be simulations). Unfortunately, this is too expensive a proposition for most manufacturers. Thus, many measure digit simulation performance using a 30-min test tape provided by one of the manufacturers of tone receivers. This tape includes utterances which caused digit simulation for one particular DTMF receiver design. This tape enables all manufacturers to specify digit simulation performance by a common criterion. However, it also has the undesirable aspect that it is tempting to tune up the performance of a detector design to this tape, which may not relate well to its performance in a central office environment. A modern tone receiver design may have only two or three digit simulations on this tape, which is not enough to be statistically significant.

Based on Tables 3 and 4, the following strategy for avoiding digit simulations can be developed:

1. Look for exactly two of the eight expected frequencies, one in the high-band and one in the low-band, at nearly the same amplitude and within the range of expected amplitudes.

2. Reject signals satisfying (1) which are accompanied by significant energy at other than the expected frequencies.
3. Reject signals satisfying (1) and (2) unless they also satisfy expected timing relationships, i.e., minimum length of a digit, minimum time between digits, etc.

Based on this strategy, the prototype tone detector of Fig. 8 can be developed. A bandpass filter is implemented for each of the expected frequencies (eight in this case). By squaring and low-pass filtering the output of each band-pass filter, the power in the vicinity of each frequency can be estimated. The total signal power is also estimated. A valid digit is indicated when exactly two band-pass output powers are large, about equal, and also sum to near the total power estimate. The "thresholds and timing" box looks for this condition and also checks for the expected timing relationships. No actual tone detectors are constructed in exactly this fashion, but most use these basic principles.

Although many tone detection techniques have been proposed, there are three particularly important ones which have appeared in commercial products and which will therefore be discussed here. They are the classical DTMF receiver,[17] the quadrature detector,[23] and the zero-crossing detector[24].

The classical detector is shown in Fig. 9. It consists of first a high-pass filter which rejects 60 Hz and dial-tone, followed by two band-elimination filters which reject the low-band and high-band, respectively. For a valid digit, the outputs of the band elimination filters should be pure tones. (This is one characteristic of the signal set which leads to inexpensive implementation.)

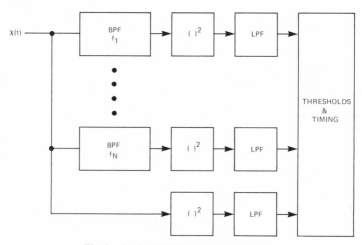

Fig. 8.   Basic principle of the tone detector.

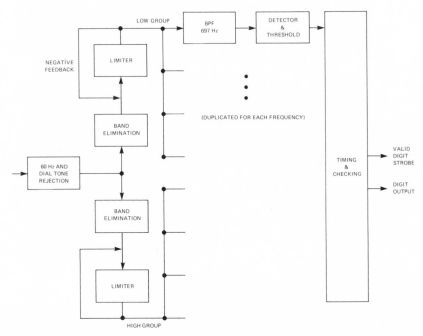

Fig. 9.   A classical DTMF tone receiver.

Deferring discussion of the limiter for a moment, the individual tones are detected by essentially our prototype tone detector, except that the squarers are approximated by simple rectifiers. The purpose of the two limiters is to desensitize the receiver to signals at the output of the band elimination filters which are not pure tones, and also to make the receiver relatively insensitive to signal level. When the signals are pure tones, the limiter outputs are square waves with a precisely known amplitude; thus, the fundamental which is picked out by the band-pass filter is also of known amplitude (independent of the amplitude of the input tone). The thresholds can therefore be set very close to this known amplitude. Now, when the tone at the limiter input is accompanied by other signals, or is not a tone at all (such as speech), the limiter output is no longer a square wave, but is much more complex. Its component within the bandwidth of the band-pass filters is therefore much smaller than if it were a square wave, and the detection threshold is not exceeded. The negative feedback around the limiter serves to desensitize the receiver to very low amplitude inputs.

The classical DTMF receiver is most amenable to analog realization (including switched capacitor filter realization). When a digital implementation is desired, as in a time-division multiplexed tone detector for a digital switch, then the quadrature tone detection technique is an attractive alternative. This detector, which is equally valid for MF or DTMF detection, is

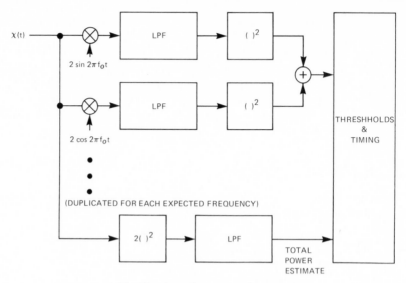

Fig. 10.   A quadrature tone detector.

shown in Fig. 10. It is actually the prototype tone detector in disguise, for the band-pass filters have been replaced by equivalent multipliers and low-pass filters. The advantage of this realization for digital implementation is that the low-pass filters are all identical, and hence can be replaced by a single time-division multiplexed filter. The effective center frequencies of the equivalent band-pass filters are determined by the quadrature multiplications by the center frequencies, and as has been previously shown these frequencies are easily generated digitally by addressing a read-only memory.

The operation of this tone detector can be illustrated by a simple example: If the input is

$$x(t) = \sin(2\pi f_1 t + \theta) \tag{14}$$

then

$$2x(t)\sin(2\pi f_0 t) = \cos[2\pi(f_1 - f_0)t + \theta] - \cos[2\pi(f_1 + f_0)t + \theta] \tag{15}$$

$$2x(t)\cos(2\pi f_0 t) = \sin[2\pi(f_1 - f_0)t + \theta] + \sin[2\pi(f_1 + f_0)t + \theta] \tag{16}$$

$$2x^2(t) = 1 - \cos(4\pi f_1 t + 2\theta) \tag{17}$$

Thus, if $(f_1 - f_0)$ is within the bandwidth of the low-pass filter, the input to the threshold circuitry is

$$\cos^2[2\pi(f_1 - f_0)t + \theta] + \sin^2[2\pi(f_1 - f_0)t + \theta] = 1 \tag{18}$$

independent of the angle θ and the total power estimate is also 1. Thus, the single tone is correctly detected independent of the phase angle θ.

The third tone detector mentioned, the zero crossing detector, is based on the following observation: In the classical DTMF detector, after band separation and limiting, the frequency of the square wave can be gauged accurately and simply by counting the number of zero-crossings of the waveform during a known interval. This is illustrated in Fig. 11a, where a sinusoid of frequency f is shown in an interval of length τ. The unknown phase of the sinusoid is represented by τ_0, which is the time to the first zero-crossing. It is simple to show that exactly N zero-crossings will occur if

$$\frac{N - 1 + 2f\tau_0}{2\tau} < f < \frac{N + 2f\tau_0}{2\tau} \tag{19}$$

It follows that, for a range of zero-crossings between N_L and N_U, there are acceptance, rejection, and uncertain regions as shown in Fig. 11b. In the acceptance region, the number of zero-crossings is within the specified range independent of the phase of the sinusoid. In the rejection region, the number is never within the specified range. In the two uncertain regions, each of width $1/2\tau$, the number of zero-crossings may or may not be within the specified range depending on the phase (τ_0). This uncertain region can be narrowed by choosing a longer interval τ.

The problem with a zero-crossing detector as it has been specified thus far is that many signals other than an input sinusoid could have the expected range of zero crossings. The digit simulation performance would

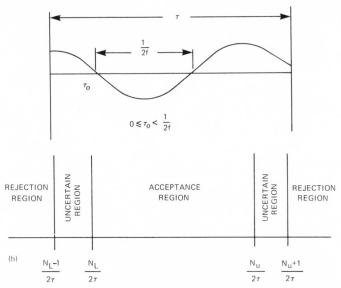

Fig. 11.   Basic principle of a zero-crossing tone detector. (a) Number of periods of a tone in an interval. (b) Frequency ranges for acceptance and rejection.

therefore be very poor. The factor which distinguishes a sinusoid is that the *rate* of zero-crossings is also a constant. Therefore a zero-crossing detector must also implement a criterion which measures the rate of zero crossings. One technique is to divide the long interval into multiple short intervals and require acceptance in a number (but not all) of those short intervals. A more sophisticated technique is to calculate the mean and standard deviation of the interval between zero-crossings. For a tone, the mean will be an estimate of the reciprocal of the frequency and the standard deviation will be very small.

Of the three types of detectors described, the classical and quadrature types have been shown to meet the central office requirements of Table 4. Most of the monolithic detectors which have appeared use zero-crossing techniques, and most do not meet these central office requirements. However, the performances of zero-crossing detectors have been improving rapidly as more sophisticated algorithms have evolved, and it appears that detectors of this type meeting central office requirements are close at hand.

5. Conclusions

This chapter has outlined some considerations in the design of digital transmission terminations and digital signal-processing functions in a digital switching office. Many of the functions described here have traditionally resided in the transmission world, but become a natural part of the digital switching office. The digital transmission termination resides in the digital switching office because of the integration of switching and transmission which occurs when digital switching and digital transmission coexist. The digital switching office is an attractive location to implement signal-processing functions digitally because all trunks are available in a convenient digital format regardless of the form in which they are transmitted.

Questions

1. Qualitatively compare the noise buildup which occurs in a long-distance connection with analog transmission (with periodic repeaters, which are simply amplifiers) and digital transmission (with regenerative repeaters, which detect the individual bits and generate a new bit stream).
2. It is virtually universal in world telephone systems to have bit rates which are an integral multiple of 8 kbit/s. Why?
3. State some inevitable differences between the 1.544-Mbit/s bit stream in a trunk digital transmission system and a bit stream between a local digital switch and one of its remote switching units.

4. Relate briefly the type of hardware and software which would have to be provided to test subscriber lines connected to a remote switching unit under the control of the base switch central processor.

5. The digital transmission lines terminating on a digital switch are synchronized together. In transmission systems which are not connected to digital switches, there is no attempt to synchronize them, even where they are to be multiplexed together into a higher bit rate. State reason(s) why this is so.

6. The elimination of the all-zeros word by substitution, and the robbing of the least-significant bit of every sixth frame, both result in an increase of quantization distortion if the digital signal is an encoded analog signal. Which will have the greatest effect on the quantization distortion?

7. Once the framing is found, the additional time to find the twelve-frame superframe is insignificant. Why?

8. The choice of a framing pattern is an important consideration in minimizing the probability of false lock on a data bit position rather than the actual framing bit position. State why it would not be a good idea, for example, to choose a framing pattern consisting of all ones.

9. Discuss the effect, if any, of a slip on framing. In particular, is it likely or possible for a slip to cause a reframe?

10. Derive the formula for the penalty in quantization noise due to bit robbing given in Eq. (4). Hint: When a bit is robbed for one channel, the mean-square quantization noise for that channel is increased by a factor of four (6 dB).

11. It was stated that the $\mu = 255$ representation is very similar to the floating point. Discuss the relative merits of $\mu = 255$ and the true floating point for encoding signals in the telephone network.

12. Describe how you might implement a conferencing bridge using digital circuitry operating on a $\mu = 255$ representation. Discuss the related problem of providing extension phones with a digital subscriber loop.

13. Verify Eqs (11) through (13).

14. Verify that the sum of two sinusoids with frequencies Lf/N and Mf/N (where f is the sampling rate) can be generated by reading the samples from a read-only memory repetitively. How many samples need to be stored in the memory?

15. Verify Eq. (19).

References

1. AT&T, "D3 Channel Bank Compatibility Specification," October 1977.
2. AT&T, "DSX-1 Compatibility Specification," October 1977.
3. AT&T, "Digroup Terminal Technical Reference and Compatibility Specification," January 1976.
4. J. F. Boyle, J. R. Colton, C. L. Damnann, B. T. Karafin, and H. Mann, "Transmission/Switching Interfaces and Toll Terminal Equipment," *Bell Syst. Tech. J.*, September 1977.
5. J. E. Abate, L. E. Brandenburg, J. C. Lawson, and W. L. Ross, "The Switched Digital Network Plan," *Bell Syst. Tech. J.*, September 1977.
6. H. Kaneko, "A Unified Formulation of Segment Companding Laws and Synthesis of Codecs and Digital Compandors," *Bell Syst., Tech. J.*, vol. 49, pp. 155–158, September 1970.

7. W. L. Montgomery, "Digitally Linearizable Compandors with Comments on Project for a Digital Telephone Network," *IEEE Trans. Commun. Technol.*, vol. COM-18, pp. 1–4, February 1970.

8. M. R. Aaron and H. Kaneko, "Synthesis of Digital Attenuators for Segment-Companded PCM Codes," *IEEE Trans. Commun. Technol.*, vol. COM-19, pp. 1076–1086, December 1971.

9. W. L. Montgomery, "Six-Decibel Digital Attenuation," *IEEE Trans. Commun. Technol.*, vol. COM-19, pp. 315–319, June 1971.

10. P. W. Osborne, H. Kaneko, and M. R. Aaron, "Synthesis of Code Converters for Segment Companded PCM Codes," Conference on Digital Processing of Signals in Communications, Loughborough, England, April 1972.

11. S. G. Pitroda and B. J. Rekiere, "A Digital Conference Circuit for an Instant Speaker Algorithm," *IEEE Trans. Commun.*, vol. COM-19, p. 1069, 1971.

12. D. L. Duttweiler, "A Twelve-Channel Digital Echo Canceller," *IEEE Trans. Commun.*, vol. COM-26, p. 647, 1978.

13. D. L. Duttweiler, in D. G. Messerschmitt, "Analysis of Digitally Generated Sinusoids with Applications to A/D and D/A Converter Testing," *IEEE Trans. Commun.*, vol. COM-26, p. 669, 1978.

14. D. G. Messrschmitt, "A New PLL Frequency Synthesis Structure," *IEEE Trans. Commun.*, vol. COM-26, p. 1195, 1978.

15. S. G. Pitroda and R. L. Lindsay, "Progress Tones in PCM Switching Environment," *IEEE Trans. Commun.*, vol. COM-21, p. 1431, 1973.

16. N. Tullius, "Selection of Call Progress Tones for Digital Systems," *IEEE Trans. Commun.*, vol. COM-23, p. 301, 1975.

17. R. N. Battista, C. G. Morrison, and D. H. Nash, "Signaling System and Receivers for TOUCH-TONE Calling," *IEEE Trans. Commun. and Elec.*, vol. 82, p. 9, 1963.

18. J. H. Soderberg, R. R. Campbell, F. E. Bates, "The TOUCH-TONE Telephone-Transmission of Digital Information," *IEEE Trans. Commun.*, vol. 15, p. 812, 1967.

19. J. F. O'Neill, "Multiplex Touch-Tone Detection Using Time Speed-Up," *Bell Syst. Tech. J.*, vol. 48, p. 249, 1969.

20. USITA Subcommittee on Network Planning, Meeting May 28, 1975, Issue 4, August 8, 1975, Items 20 and 28–36 Part B, "Touch Tone Calling," and "Touch Tone Receiver."

21. K. Niwa and M. Sato, "Multifrequency Receiver for Pushbutton Signalling Using Digital Processing Techniques," Conference Record, ICC 1974, Minneapolis.

22. "A TOUCH-TONE Receiver-Generator with Digital Channel Filters," *Bell Syst. Tech. J.*, vol. 55, p. 455, 1976.

23. C. R. Baugh, "Design and Performance of a Digital Multifrequency Receiver," *IEEE Trans. Commun.*, vol. COM-25, p. 608, 1977.

24. T. Zebo, "Digital Tone Detector Using Concatenated Detection Intervals," U.S. Patent 3990006, November 2, 1976.

9

Digital Switching System Architectures

John C. McDonald

1. Introduction

Functional elements of digital switching systems have been described in prior chapters. These chapters have presented analog and digital terminations, the switching center network, and system control. In this chapter, the internal structure of complete systems which are composed of these elements will be described. The architecture of a digital switch is studied by summarizing the operation of the individual system elements and by describing the operation of a hypothetical switch. Examples of commercial digital switching systems are then presented.

Since a switching system is a node in an overall communications network, the architecture of the switch is established from the functional requirements of the node. The principles discussed in this chapter apply to all types of circuit-switched nodes both public and private. Integrated circuit and packet switching has been discussed in Chapter 6 of this volume.

Operation of a digital switching system is presented in Section 2. Elements of the system are summarized and digital switching system operation is described by tracing the progress of a call through a hypothetical switch. System synthesis is presented in Section 3. Synthesis is based on a requirements statement and begins with an analysis of architectural alter-

John C. McDonald ● MBX Inc., 54 Comstock Hill Road, New Canaan, Connecticut 06840

natives which satisfy the requirements. Examples of commercial digital
switching systems are presented in Section 4, and the chapter concludes
with a discussion of system design trends in Section 5.

2. Digital Switching System Operation

This section describes the operation of a digital switching system.
First, a short summary of the digital switching system elements which have
been studied in depth in other chapters is presented. Then, the operation of
the digital switch is explained by tracing the progress of a call through a
hypothetical system.

The elements of a circuit switching digital switch are shown in Fig. 1.
Terminations are provided by the switch for both analog and digital signals. Analog signals, described in Chapter 7 of this volume, interface at the
A ports. Analog information is converted to digital and many identical
ports are multiplexed onto a bus connecting the A ports to the switching
center network. Information from the switching center network is demultiplexed and converted from digital to analog for application to the A ports.

Digital signals, described in Chapter 8 of this volume, interface at the
B ports. If the multiplex applied at the B port has a different format from
the switching center network multiplex, translation is required as shown in
the figure.

The switching center network, described in Chapter 5 of this volume,
contains time-divided switching stages which allow information on any
multiplex time slot to be transferred to any other multiplex time slot.

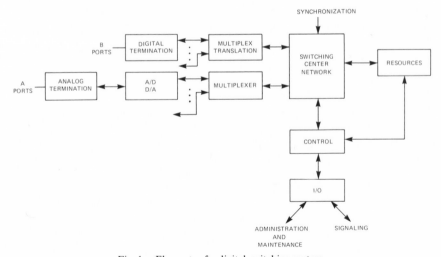

Fig. 1.   Elements of a digital switching system.

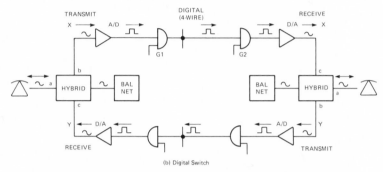

Fig. 2. Transmission through analog and digital switching systems.

Various resources, described in Chapter 8 of this volume, are attached to the switching center network. These include digitally synthesized tones, conference circuits, tone receivers, and other signal-processing devices.

Control of the overall system, described in Chapter 3 of this volume, is provided by a stored program controlled (SPC) processor which has access to various system elements. The control process will be demonstrated later in this chapter by tracing a call through a hypothetical system.

Input/output devices are used to provide a variety of system functions including dial administration, alarm reporting, maintenance access, traffic reporting, automatic message accounting, and common channel signaling.

2.1. Analog Terminations

Analog information from subscriber loops, trunks, or analog service circuits is applied to the switch at the analog termination. Transmission of analog information through both analog and digital switching systems is illustrated in Fig. 2. In the analog switching case, transmission is accomplished most frequently using the 2-wire circuit illustrated in Fig. 2a. Two wires are required to complete the current path to the customer's telephone and information can flow in either direction along the pair. In the early days of telephony, one wire was provided to the telephone and current returned to the switch through the earth. This scheme gave poor noise performance since ground noise appears in series with telephony signals. Now, the customer connection is most frequently provided by two wires forming a current loop which can be used to reject ground noise. These two wires are called the customer loop or access line.

Transmission through a digital switch is shown in Fig. 2b. Since digital conversion can only occur in one direction, transmission through a digital switch is more complex than its analog counterpart. Hybrids, described in Chapter 7 of this volume, are required to convert the 2-wire circuit of the customer loop into the 4-wire circuit required for digital switching. The name "4-wire" comes from the nature of the transmission through the switch. A separate path for transmission is required in each direction due to the unidirectional nature of the digital conversion process. Two wires are required for one direction of transmission and two wires for the other. In practice, a common wire is shared in the switch and we really need only three wires. But, the connection retains the name of a 4-wire circuit.

Analog signals originating at the telephone appear at hybrid port a. There is low transmission loss between hybrid ports a and b and the analog signal appears at the A/D converter. The signal, once in digital form, is switched through the switching center network, represented by gates G1 and G2.

The digital signal is converted back to analog and applied at hybrid port c. There is low loss between hybrid ports c and a, and thus, the analog signal is applied to the customer loop and appears at the distant telephone. Transmission in the opposite direction follows an identical process.

Since the 4-wire circuit forms a closed feedback loop, there is the potential for oscillation. Therefore, transmission loss between hybrid ports c and b must be high to minimize closed loop gain. Techniques for maintaining the desired hybrid loss are described in Chapter 7 in this volume.

In practice, some signal energy will be transmitted across the hybrid from port c to port b and this will cause talker and listener echo. The amount of circuit quality degradation due to echo is influenced by the delay around the 4-wire circuit, as discussed in Chapter 7 in this volume. Delay is introduced by antialiasing and reconstruction filters, the switching center network, digital terminations, propagation time, and sometimes by codecs.

Only basic transmission functions are illustrated in Fig. 2. Other analog termination functions are included in the acronym BORSHT defined in Chapter 7 in this volume.

2.2. Digital Terminations

Digital information from customer loops, trunks, or service circuits is applied to the switch at the digital termination. A single circuit or a multiplex of circuits can be applied at the digital termination. Digital termination

Table 1.   Worldwide PCM Standards

Standard	μ-Law standard	A-Law standard
Sampling rate	8 kHz	8 kHz
Modulation	8 bit PCM	8 bit PCM
Companding	μ 255	A 87.6
Frame	24 time slots	32 time slots (30 information
	+ 1 framing bit	+ 1 signaling + 1 framing)
Signaling	Bit robbing	1 dedicated channel
Bit rate	1.544 Mb	2.048 Mb

design is heavily influenced by the two standards which have been established for digital PCM carrier systems,[1] shown in Table 1.

Functions performed by a digital termination illustrated in Fig. 3 have been described in Chapter 8 in this volume. The incoming bit stream is applied to a clock recovery circuit and the incoming waveform is converted from bipolar to standard unipolar logic levels. In a bipolar waveform, a binary 1 is sent by the presence of a pulse. A 0 is sent by the absence of a pulse. The polarity of the pulse alternates from positive going to negative going (bipolar) on the transmission of successive ones. This prevents a dc component from developing in the bit stream. A unipolar signal only has two states, one for a one and the other for a zero.

Information arriving at the switch is read into a frame alignment buffer by the rederived clock. The buffer output, in frame synchronism with the switch, is set by the switch clock. Frame alignment is required since each multiplex arrives at the digital switch in bit but not frame synchronism. Frame synchronism is required for all bit streams reaching the switching center network as described in Chapter 5 in this volume. Alarm detection and signaling extraction can also be a function of the digital termination.

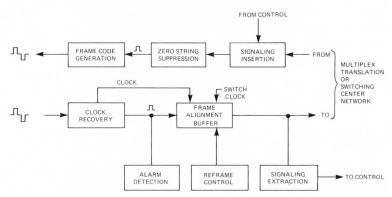

Fig. 3.   Digital switch interface to a digital carrier system.

Information leaving the switching center network is combined with signaling and a multiplex frame code to form the outgoing multiplex. Long strings of binary zeros in the information stream must be supressed to keep carrier repeaters "alive."[2] Signaling insertion and extraction functions are eliminated when common channel signaling is used. Common channel signaling[3] is a technique whereby signaling for groups of trunks is sent over a single common channel rather than signaling where the trunk which carries conversations also carries signaling. Common channel signaling is described in Chapter 10 in this volume.

The analog termination is described by its BORSHT functions. Another delicious soup comes to mind when describing the digital termination— GAZPACHO:

*G*eneration of frame code
*A*lignment of frames
*Z*ero string suppression
*P*olar conversion
*A*larm processing
*C*lock recovery
*H*unt during reframe
*O*ffice signaling

Delay is introduced at the digital termination due to the frame alignment process illustrated in Fig. 4. Information X appearing at the time slot 1 might be delayed until time slot 24 before it is applied to the switching center network. When two digital terminations are connected back to back, the loop delay is given by:

$$\text{loop delay} = \overbrace{\text{incoming frame alignment} + \text{outgoing delay}}^{\text{switch}}$$
$$+ \overbrace{\text{incoming frame alignment} + \text{outgoing delay}}^{\text{remote device}}$$

$$= 125 \ \mu\text{sec (max)} + 0 + 0 + 0 \qquad \text{(for } D \text{ channel bank)}$$

$$= \frac{125}{24} \ \mu\text{sec} \times n + 0 + \frac{125}{24} \ \mu\text{sec} \ (24 - n) + 0 \qquad \text{(for remote digital switch)}$$

$$\tag{1}$$

where n is the number of time slots of delay.

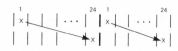

Fig. 4.   An illustration of the frame alignment process.

Note that if the remote device is a *D* channel bank, the delay is variable from 0 to 125 μsec. If the remote device is another digital termination, the delay is constant at 125 μsec irrespective of the phase of the relative frames between the two switching systems.

2.3.   Multiplexing

The process of multiplexing is illustrated in Fig. 5a. Information from many analog terminations, shown in the figure, is converted to digital and the digital information is time multiplexed onto a single bus called the transmit multiplex. Analog information at termination 1 is converted to digital and transmitted on the transmit multiplex at time slot 1. Similarly, analog information on terminations 2 through 8 are converted to digital and transmitted at corresponding time slots. The analog-to-digital converter in this example could be PCM, differential PCM, delta modulation, or any conversion technique.

The demultiplexer follows the process shown in Fig. 5b. Digital information in time slot 1 is converted to analog and appears at termination 1. Similarly, digital information at time slots 2 through 8 is demultiplexed, converted to analog, and appears on terminations 2 through 8.

It is common to have more than one level of multiplexing in a digital switching system. Two levels are shown in Fig. 6. The primary multiplex is established by the process shown in Fig. 5. Then, many primary multiplex sources are combined to form a synchronous secondary multiplex. The multiplexer places more information into a given frame but does not alter the information contained in each time slot. The secondary multiplex has a

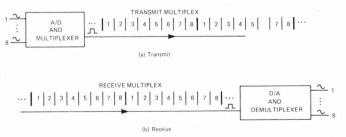

Fig. 5.   The digital multiplexing and demultiplexing process.

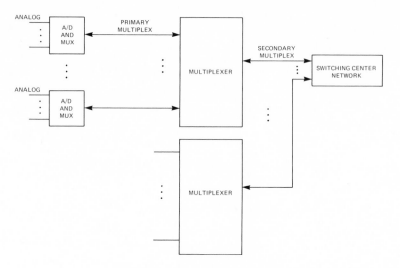

Fig. 6.   Two levels of multiplexing.

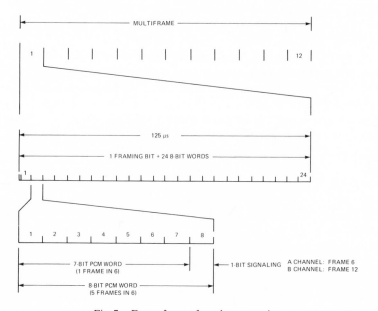

Fig. 7.   Frame format for μ-law countries.

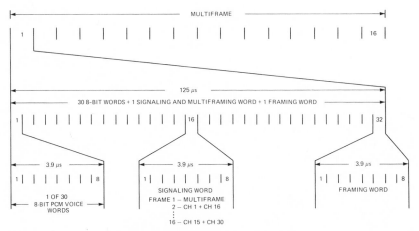

Fig. 8. Frame format for A-law countries.

higher bit rate and thereby reduces the hardware required in the switching center network since logic gates, wires, connector pins, and other components are time shared over many channels.

Time slot assignments for the two multiplexing standards of Table 1. are shown in Figs 7 and 8. It is common to adopt one of these standards as the primary multiplex for a digital switching system.

2.4. Switching Center Network

A simple switching center network is shown in Fig. 9a. A full duplex circuit can be illustrated by a switching connection between the two telephones. The A/D and multiplexer and D/A and demultiplexer obey the rules defined in Fig. 5.

Analog information at transmit termination 1 is converted to digital and multiplexed onto the transmit multiplex at time slot 1. For information X, originating at the upper telephone, to appear in the receiver of the lower telephone, it is necessary to have X appear at time slot 4 in the receive multiplex. Similarly, information Y, originating at the lower telephone, appears at transmit termination 4 and will occur on the transmit multiplex at time slot 4. To have Y appear in the receiver of the upper telephone, it is necessary for Y to appear on the receive multiplex at time slot 1.

The time slot interchanger is the system element which accomplishes the desired switching function. The time slot interchanger causes X to be delayed and moved from time slot 1 in the transmit multiplex to time slot 4 in the receive multiplex as shown in Fig. 9b. Y is similarly delayed from time slot 4 to time slot 1. A digital switching function is thus realized by

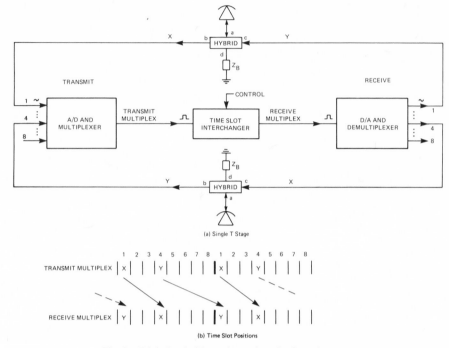

(a) Single T Stage

(b) Time Slot Positions

Fig. 9.   Digital switching using a time slot interchanger.

information storage, delay, and gating onto the receive multiplex. A two-way message channel is thereby established between the two telephones.

The loop delay through this system, assuming no A/D or D/A delay, and a 125-μsec frame is

$$\text{loop delay} = \text{delay from terminal 1 to 4}$$

$$+ \text{ delay from terminal 4 to 1}$$

$$= \frac{125 \ \mu\text{sec}}{8} \times n + \frac{125 \ \mu\text{sec}}{8} (8 - n) \qquad (2)$$

where n is the number of time slots of delay.

Note that the loop delay through this simple time slot interchanger is constant at 125 μsec and is independent of n.

2.5.   Control

The control elements of a digital switch provide the artificial intelligence to properly interpret customer requests for service and to cause that service to be provided. In addition, the control elements provide for overall

Table 2.   Basic Control Operations

Analog line termination	Switching center network	I/O
Off-hook detection	Path setup	Dial administration
Tip party detection	Path test	Maintenance
Makes and breaks detection	Path release	Traffic reports
Coin in hopper		Charging
Ringing	*Resources*	
Test	MF senders	
Coin collect	MF receivers	
	DTMF receivers	
	Tone synthesizers	

system self-testing and for the maintenance and administration functions. Shown in Fig. 1, system control must interface many system elements.

Basic control operations are given in Table 2. Since control is required at many locations in the switching system, it is often convenient to have a control structure which is distributed and hierarchical in nature. Control can then be located at the point where it is needed. Such a control structure with three levels is shown in Fig. 10. Functions such as line scanning and line circuit control are performed at the lowest hierarchical level. Next, digits might be formed from the makes and breaks of the customer loop current. Finally, the highest control level might be used to receive digits and process calls. Many control structure variations have been suggested as described in Chapter 4 in this volume.

The control of a switching system must react to offered load in the manner illustrated in Fig. 11. As the offered load increases, the processed load should also increase until the control capacity is reached. At this point the processed load should stay constant as the offered load continues to increase. The dashed line in Fig. 11 shows the undesired possibility that the

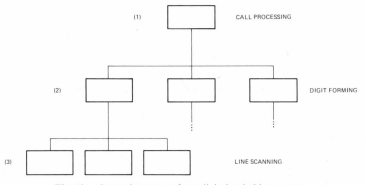

Fig. 10.   Control structure for a digital switching system.

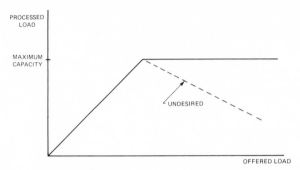

Fig. 11.   Control characteristic for a stored program switching system.

processed load might decline as the offered load increases past the point of maximum capacity.

Control of a digital switching system can be understood by tracing the progress of a call through the hypothetical switch shown in Fig. 12. Control of the switch will be described and then a call will be traced.

The hypothetical switch has three levels of control: a system controller, preprocessors, and control at the line concentrator. Analog signals interface at BORSHT circuits, are converted to digital, and are switched onto time slots in the primary multiplex. There are more analog terminations than primary multiplex time slots and therefore a first stage of concentration occurs. This concentration can range from 2:1 to 10:1 depend-

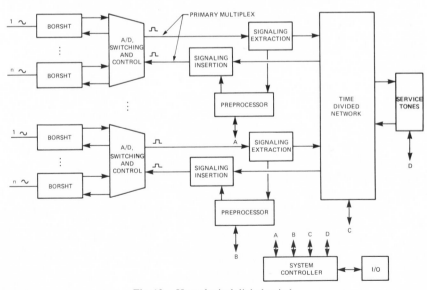

Fig. 12.   Hypothetical digital switch.

ing on line traffic. The primary multiplex contains a dedicated common channel for signaling. The primary multiplex can be realized using the form of either Fig. 7 or Fig. 8. Systems using the multiplexing format of Fig. 8 send control words in time slot 16. Systems using the format of Fig. 7 send control words using either the A or B signaling channels,[4] a channel derived from the framing bit positions,[5] or one of the 24 channels in the multiplex.[6]

A request for service is detected by the "S" circuit in the BORSHT interface and is stored in a microprocessor common to many lines. The common signaling channel in the primary multiplex is used to transmit messages between the line microprocessor and the preprocessor. Messages reach the preprocessor from signaling extraction circuits which monitor the primary multiplex. The preprocessor communicates with the system controller over a dedicated I/O port. If the multiplex in Fig. 8 is used or if one of the 24 channels of the multiplex in Fig. 7 is used for signaling, the control bytes can be semipermanently switched through the switching center network to a preprocessor termination.

The overall control function will now be illustrated by tracing the progress of a call through the switching system of Fig. 12. A customer goes off-hook and the BORSHT circuit detects loop current. A line scanning microprocessor serially accesses all BORSHT circuits and detects the off-hook. The microprocessor formulates an off-hook message which is sent over the signaling channel in the primary multiplex to its associated preprocessor. The preprocessor receives the off-hook message and starts a timer to digitally integrate the off-hook interval and discriminate against noise hits.

When the preprocessor detects a solid off-hook, it interrupts the system controller with a message that the particular termination has gone off-hook. The controller then begins the call-processing algorithm by examining the subscriber's class mark in memory to determine the type of service which should be allowed. Assuming the subscriber successfully passes the criteria for service, the controller prepares to provide dial tone. Memory is searched to find an available time slot in the primary multiplex serving the calling customer. Assuming a time slot is available, the controller causes the switching center network to connect the service tone generator to the desired primary multiplex time slot. The controller then commands the service tone generator to place a digitally synthesized dial tone at its output. The controller then sends a message to the line scanning microprocessor via the preprocessor and primary multiplex to cause the customer's voice path to be connected to the desired primary multiplex time slot. Dial tone is then heard by the customer and a timer is started in the controller awaiting the first dialed digit.

Assuming a rotary dial telephone, the customer rotates his dial off-normal and as the dial restores to normal, the current in the customer loop is interrupted corresponding to the dialed digit. This current interruption is detected by the BORSHT circuit and the makes and breaks are sent over the signaling channel to the preprocessor. The preprocessor times and counts the makes and breaks to determine the dialed digit. When an interdigital pause is detected, the preprocessor interrupts the controller with the dialed digit. The controller recognizes the first digit and causes dial tone to be removed and idle code is applied. A timer is started awaiting the second digit.

This process continues until a complete number is dialed. Assuming an intraoffice call, the controller examines its memory to determine if the called number is idle and if a time slot in his primary multiplex is available. The controller then causes ring-back tone from the service tone generator to be returned to the calling customer and a message is sent via the preprocessor and primary multiplex to the line microprocessor associated with the called customer to cause ringing to be applied via the BORSHT circuit. The controller reserves the idle primary multiplex time slot to the called customer for the potential conversation.

When the called customer answers, the BORSHT circuit detects the off-hook and the line microprocessor sends a message to the controller via the primary multiplex and preprocessor. The controller sends a message back to trip ringing, to connect the called subscriber to the reserved primary multiplex time slot, and ringback tone to the calling party is removed. Conversation can begin when the controller establishes a path through the switching center network connecting the desired primary multiplex time slots.

During the conversation state, the preprocessor and the system controller have no additional work. The line microprocessors and switching center network hold the call. The line microprocessors also continue to scan the lines to detect when a party goes on-hook. When this occurs, the line microprocessor informs the controller via the primary multiplex and preprocessor and the switch is restored to normal.

2.6. Remote Units

Digital switching systems provide many customer services in addition to basic telephone service. These services include direct distance dialing, push-button telephone signaling, custom calling, local message metering, and services provided via common channel signaling. The cost of providing software and hardware for these additional services is substantial.

The cost per customer for these additional services in a small office is substantially higher than the cost in a large office since a minimum set of the required equipment can usually serve many subscribers. In addition, the cost of common equipment for providing basic telephone service is substantially higher per customer in a small office compared with a larger office.

This has led many operating administrations to consider replacing an older office with a remote switching unit[7] which is controlled from a nearby digital central office rather than using a stand-alone switching system. Such a remote unit is easily implemented using digital technology since the primary multiplex of Fig. 12 can be easily extended for long distances using standard digital carrier systems. This is especially easy if the primary multiplex has the same format as a PCM carrier system.

Thus, a low-cost remote unit can be created where the BORSHT circuits, digital conversion, first switching stage, and line microprocessor are remotely located from the balance of the switch. The preprocessors, switching center network, and system controller can be shared over many remote units. In addition, maintenance and administration functions are centralized for more efficient personnel deployment. Remote units thereby provide the possibility of reducing the cost of providing customer services in small central offices.

One problem with remote units lies in their reliance on the host for basic telephone service. If the cable connecting the remote and host is cut or if the host fails or is destroyed, basic telephone service at the remote is not available. Therefore, it is desirable to provide additional capabilities in the remote units for basic telephone service in such an emergency situation. Special services might be denied during the emergency. Emergency service is provided by the addition of capabilities at the remote to allow intraremote call processing, switching, service tone generation, and push-button telephone detection. Number translation tables can be automatically loaded into the remote from the host over the digital connecting facility during dial administration procedures. The remote unit with emergency protection can remain cost effective when compared to a complete switching system.

2.7. Pair Gain Systems

The cost of providing the customer loop using copper wires continues to rise. At the same time, the cost of electronic devices is falling. Therefore, it can be cost effective to connect the customer's telephone to the switching system by an electronic multiplexing or switching means where many customers are served over a fewer number of wire pairs. These systems are called pair gain systems.[8] The pair gain of a given system is

$$\text{pair gain} = \text{equivalent pairs provided} - \text{metallic pairs required} \quad (3)$$

Pair gain systems can be implemented using digital switching technology. The remote unit described in Section 2.6 can be placed in the customer plant to form a pair gain system. In this application, emergency protection is probably unnecessary. Multiplexing systems without switching concentration can be used for pair gain. Traffic varies substantially among customers and it is often desirable to place all concentration functions at the central office where load rebalancing can be easily accomplished. Pure multiplexing avoids any service impairment due to unforeseen peaks in customer traffic.

Portions of the customer interface can be remotely located away from the switch using digital carrier techniques to create pair gain. BORSHT circuits, digital conversion, and multiplexing can be located in an environmentally controlled housing in the customer plant. For example, 24 circuits can be multiplexed and applied to a T1 carrier facility. The pair gain system terminates at the switch on the digital ports shown in Fig. 1. The incremental cost of providing the pair gain system, assuming available pairs, is the cost of the remote housing, the carrier facility, and the digital termination. The BORSHT circuits do not contribute to this incremental cost since they are required with or without the pair gain system.

Pair gain systems are an important element of the digital network. The pair gain interface to a digital switching system must be carefully considered in system design.

3. Digital Switching System Synthesis

Elements of a digital switching system have been described in previous sections. These elements include analog and digital terminations, multiplexers, the switching center network, control, remote units, and pair gain systems. This section describes the synthesis of digital switching systems. System requirements are presented which lead to a consideration of design alternatives and system synthesis.

3.1. Requirements

The structure of a digital switching system is influenced by its functional requirements. No two designs are precisely alike because each is optimized for its particular application. Digital switching systems in small or large sizes can be tailored for public or private applications.

Many agencies around the world have established digital switching system specifications.[9–13] These specifications are the product of international consulting bodies, local operating administrations, and government agencies.

System requirements influence the design selection process in the synthesis of a digital switching system. A partial list of system requirement categories is shown in Table 3.

Table 3.   Key Digital Switching Architectural Requirements

Capacity	Features	Availability	Compatibility
Terminations	Transmission	MTBF	Loss/noise/echo
TDN traffic	specifications	MTTR	Customer loop
Processor traffic	Call processing	Self diagnostics	Trunk plant
	Network integration	Redundancy	SDN
Maintainability			
MTBF	Planning	Administration	
Self diagnostics	Size	Dial	
Documentation	Power	Program generics	
TAC	Environment	Reports	
		Local/remote	

3.2.   System Capacity

There are three independent parameters which determine the capacity of a switching system: number of terminations, termination traffic, and processor call rate. System terminations provide line and trunk access to the switching center network. The number of lines plus the number of trunks which a switching system can terminate set one capacity limit.

The amount of traffic which the switching system can provide with a prescribed grade of service sets another capacity limit. This traffic limit, measured in units of erlangs or hundred call seconds (CCS), summed over all terminations specifies the ability of the switching system to allow information to flow between terminations with a prescribed blocking probability.

The processors in the switching system detect requests for service and provide that service. The number of requests for service (attempts) which the processor can successfully provide per unit time is another capacity limit. Processor capacity is reached by the process illustrated in Fig. 11. As the offered load increases, the processors successfully provide service until the capacity limit is reached. As offered load increases further, the processors continue at their capacity limit.

The limiting capacity of a given switching system will be set by any one of these three parameters. For example, a switch might have a low processor capacity and this capacity might be reached before all available terminations are occupied. On the other hand, the processors might be quite powerful and the switch might become termination limited. If the holding time per termination is high, the switch capacity might be set by the switching network. Fewer terminations than the maximum number might be used to serve the high occupancy terminations with an acceptable grade of service. Thus, three parameters independently set the switching system capacity.

Table 4. Typical Traffic Statistics in the United States
(ABSBH)

	Rural	Suburban	Urban
Originating plus incoming CCS:	2.7	3.1	3.0
Originating plus incoming calls:	1.1	1.5	1.7

Typical traffic offered per line in a public switching environment is shown in Table 4. Traffic varies substantially depending on the location of the customers and can also vary substantially within a given office. Multiparty line service will cause calling rates and holding times to be considerably higher than the average. Also, traffic parameters will change from country to country.

The calling rates shown are average busy season busy hour rates. Peak busy hour rates on the busiest day of the year can be 30% above the average rates. Subscribers cause a partial attempt when they change their mind and hang-up after dialing a few digits. A partial attempt also might occur when a telephone is cleaned. It is common to increase the originating traffic high day busy hour calling rate by 20% to account for partial attempts. Finally, a processor might be rated at a maximum of 95% occupancy with 10% reserved for maintenance and administration functions.

Using Table 4, a rural public switch with 5,000 lines and 500 trunks must have the following capacities:

$$\text{terminations} \geq 5,500$$

$$\text{network CCS} \geq 13,500$$

$$\text{peak processor calls} \geq 5,500 \times 1.3$$

$$(\text{at } 80\% \text{ occupancy})$$

3.3. Analog Termination Alternatives

Analog termination design alternatives are discussed in this section. Digital encoding techniques and encoder placement are analyzed.

The choice of the digital encoding technique is a fundamental design decision. Pulse code modulation (PCM), described in Chapter 7 in this volume, is a common modulation technique in trunk carrier systems. However, it has been argued that since lines outnumber trunks by almost 10 to 1 in a local digital switch, the encoding technique for lines should not be dictated by the trunk technique.[14] Modulation conversion at the trunk interface can be employed. Encoding schemes such as delta modulation, adaptive delta modulation, differential PCM, and linear predictive coding, can be considered.

However, there are substantial arguments which favor PCM as the line modulation scheme. PCM is the only internationally standard digital modulation technique. While research continues in other coding schemes, standards are yet to be established. PCM standards are providing the semiconductor industry with the necessary volume to make commercial LSI devices economical. Therefore, PCM should provide a low-cost approach.

But there are additional arguments for PCM. If PCM is not used, conversion devices are required at the trunk interface which add cost and contribute additional quantizing distortion. Further, a common technology between lines and trunks such as PCM will simplify craftsperson training and maintenance. Finally, system control is complicated if modulation conversion devices are located at trunk circuits. These devices must be switched out to provide circuit transparency for end-to-end direct digital service.

Therefore, PCM is highly desirable as the encoding scheme. If PCM is selected, standard companding laws and sampling rates should be used.

Some alternative analog termination locations are shown in Fig. 13. The point of digital conversion could be inside the telephone (a), at the customer's residence interface (b), at a pair gain system interface (c), at the switching system input (d), or after an analog space division switching stage (e).

The analog interface for trunks can be placed in analogous locations. This interface would not be required, however, if two digital switches are connected by digital trunk facilities. Because of the location similarity between line and trunk terminations, it is possible to mix lines and trunks

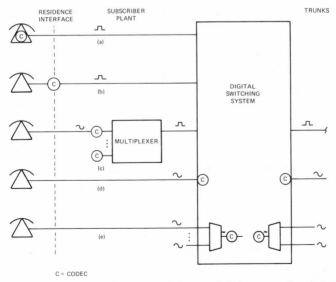

Fig. 13. Alternatives for the location of the analog-to-digital converter in a digital switch.

within one interface shelf. However, it might be desirable to segregate line and trunk terminations since the average traffic carried on each varies considerably. Trunk traffic usually exceeds line traffic by substantial margins. It is possible to provide nonblocking in the switching center network and therefore trunks can interface at nonblocking terminations. Office rebalancing in this case would never be required in the event of a change in trunk traffic patterns.

Each analog-to-digital conversion location shown in Fig. 13 has advantages and disadvantages. If the converter is located on a customer's premises either at the telephone or at the residence interface, it is possible to allow customer access to the digital bit stream. It is also possible to supply nontelephony services. Customer data could access the bit stream without need for a modem. Burglar alarm status monitoring, utility meter reading, and energy load shedding could be accomplished. Techniques for providing a digital customer loop which is required for this location are described in Chapter 8 in this volume.

It might be desirable to locate the analog interface in the outside customer plant and multiplex many customers onto two pairs of wires. This is the pair gain application described in Section 2.7.

Interfaces collocated with the digital switching system are shown in Figs. 13d and 13e. In Fig. 13d, the codec is located at the input to the switch. The analog-to-digital conversion function can be accomplished on a per line basis or a high-speed codec can be shared over many customer lines. In Fig. 13e, the BORSHT circuit and codec appear after concentration and the cost of this analog interface is shared over many customer lines. This scheme has the potential for low cost; however, the analog space division concentrator ahead of the analog interface must have very low crosstalk and must be able to withstand high voltage. Other analog concentration techniques can be used where only portions of the BORSHT circuit are concentrated.

The technique selected for providing the analog termination is a challenging design problem. The cost of the analog termination can be 50%–80% of the total system cost.[15] Therefore, this area of digital switching system design must be carefully considered.

3.4. Switching Center Network Alternatives

The switching center network provides connectivity between all terminations on a digital switch. Shown in Fig. 1, the switching center network interfaces terminations which have been previously multiplexed. The switching center network employs the two techniques described in Chapter 5 in this volume to provide the required connectivity: time slot interchanging (T) and time-shared space switching (S). These two techniques are illustrated in Fig. 14.

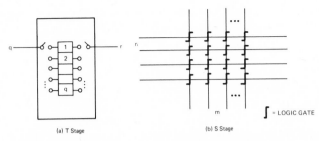

Fig. 14. Time and space switching stages in the digital switch.

A time slot interchanger (TSI) is shown in Fig. 14a. A multiplex with q time slots is shown coming into the time slot interchanger. A multiplex with r time slots leaves the time slot interchanger. This structure is nonblocking if $r \geq q$.

There are q memory cells in the time slot interchanger. Information is read into the cells and after the appropriate delay to accomplish the time slot interchanging function, the information is read onto the r multiplex. In the case of a multistage network, many T and S stages are used and it is common for r to be greater than q to minimize overall network blocking.

A time-shared space switching stage is shown in Fig. 14b. There are n horizontals and m verticals in this network. Each horizontal and each vertical contains a multiplex with t time slots. The crosspoint closure configuration of the overall network is changed each time slot. This is, of course, different from the well-known analog space division network where the crosspoint configuration remains time invarient until a new call is set up or an old call is removed. Thus, each crosspoint in the S stage can be open or closed at each time slot.

The S stage contains no memory and information from the horizontals is passed without delay to the verticals. While a single stage network is shown in Fig. 14b, the time-shared space stage can be implemented as a multistage time-shared space network. This network can be designed with or without blocking.

The switching center network can be synthesized using a combination of T and S stages. The simplest network is a pure T network shown in Fig. 9. For larger systems, several T and S switching stages are used. Various combinations of T and S stages are shown below:

$$
\begin{array}{ll}
T & S \\
TS & ST \\
TST & STS \\
\cdot & \cdot \\
\cdot & \cdot \\
\cdot & \cdot
\end{array}
$$

As an illustration of the design of a switching center network, consider the following problem:

Design a switching center network for a 10,000 line, 1,000 trunk digital central office. Blocking probability is unspecified.

Solution 1. Single-Stage T Network. A single-stage nonblocking *T* network which satisfies the requirements of the problem is shown in Fig. 15a. If the switch uses 64 kbit/sec PCM, the bit rate into the TSI is

$$\text{bit rate} = 11,000 \times 64 \text{ kbit/sec}$$

$$= 704 \text{ mbit/sec} \tag{4}$$

Memories in the TSI would have to have an access time of

$$\text{memory access} = \frac{1}{2} \times \frac{1}{704 \times 10^6}$$

$$= 0.71 \text{ nsec} \tag{5}$$

Access time requirements can be eased if the serial PCM bit stream is changed to 8 bit parallel. In this case, memory requirements are

$$\text{memory access} = 0.71 \times 8 \text{ nsec}$$

$$= 5.7 \text{ nsec} \tag{6}$$

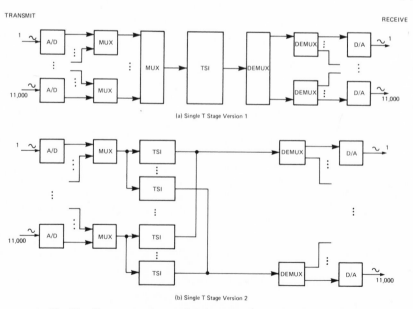

Fig. 15. Two approaches to digital switching using a single *T*-stage.

Clearly, a different solution to the problem is required since memories which provide this access time are not readily available. Unfortunately, it is difficult to introduce blocking into a single-stage T network so adding blocking does not help us.

Another pure T network solution is shown in Fig. 15b. Information from each primary multiplex is stored in a number of parallel time slot interchangers corresponding to each outgoing multiplex. The outgoing multiplex connected to the receive terminations is derived by selecting data from the desired time slot interchangers. If the switch is nonblocking and the multiplex contains 30 channels, there must be 367 TSIs per multiplex and 134,689 TSIs per system to give 11,000 terminations. The memory access time would be a reasonable 260 nsec for serial operation. In this example, lower memory access time is obtained at the expense of more memories.

Solution 2. A Two-Stage Network—TS or ST. A two-stage TS solution to our problem is shown in Fig. 16. A transmit multiplex with 120 time slots is created and applied to a T stage. Then, the S stage provides connectivity between the multiplexes. Memory requirements are given by

$$\text{memory access} = \frac{1}{2} \times \frac{1}{120 \times 64 \text{ kbit/sec}}$$

$$= 65.1 \text{ nsec} \quad \text{(serial)}$$

$$521 \text{ nsec} \quad \text{(parallel)} \quad (7)$$

In this case, memory requirements are reasonable; however, blocking has been introduced into the switching center network. Note that crosspoints A and B or C and D cannot be simultaneously closed. Similarly A and C or B and D cannot be simultaneously closed. Therefore, blocking is

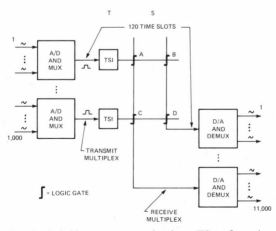

Fig. 16. Switching center network using a TS configuration.

introduced since the number of time slots in the S stage is equal to the number of time slots in the transmit multiplex. Nonblocking could be realized by increasing the number of time slots in the receive multiplex. But then, the transmit and receive multiplex time slots would be unequal and this is impractical. The ST network suffers from the same deficiencies.

Solution 3. A Three-Stage Network—TST or STS. Two additional solutions are shown in Fig. 17 using TST and STS networks. The number of time slots entering each T stage is identical with Solution 2 and therefore the memory requirements are identical.

The advantage of the three-stage structure is that it can provide nonblocking with the same number of time slots in the transmit and receive multiplex. The three-stage network is quite significant since it allows memories to be used which have reasonable access times for a large switch and it can be nonblocking with full availability. Therefore the three-stage network will be examined in more detail.

A digital switching system with a TST switching center network is shown in Fig. 18. Assume that we wish to make a two-way connection between terminations 1 and 12.

To establish the desired connection, information X on transmit termination 1 must be moved to receive termination 12. Similarly, information Y at transmit termination 12 must be moved to receive termination 1. Information on the transmit terminations is converted to digital and 8 terminations are multiplexed together. The multiplex is then sent to a T stage. The A/D and Mux and D/A and Demux follow the rules of Fig. 5. X appears in the transmit multiplex on time slot 1. Y appears on another transmit multiplex at time slot 4. To accomplish the desired switching we must cause Y to appear on the receive multiplex corresponding to TSI 3 at time slot 1. Similarly X must appear at time slot 4 on the receive multiplex corresponding to TSI 4.

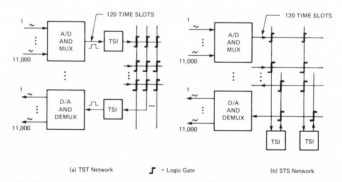

Fig. 17.   Switching center network using a TST and STS configuration.

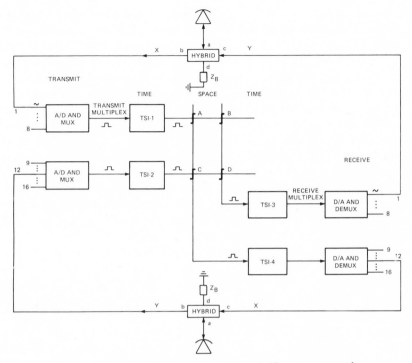

Fig. 18.   Channel establishment for a *TST* switching center network.

A path through the TST network is established as shown in Fig. 19. We know that X appears at time slot 1 at the input to TSI 1. We want X to appear at time slot 4 on the multiplex leaving TSI 4. To accomplish this switching function, crosspoint A must close so that X can be transmitted from TSI 1 to TSI 4.

We must now find an idle time slot in the space stage where A can be closed while B and C are open. We cannot close A and B simultaneously

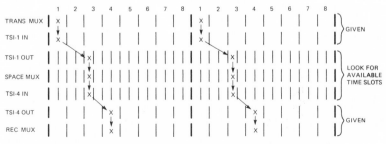

Fig. 19.   Path finding through a *TST* switching center network.

since information from TSI 1 would then be directed to both TSI 3 and TSI 4. Similarly we cannot close crosspoints A and C simultaneously. Time slots in the space stage are also illustrated in Fig. 19. The number of time slots in the space stage is shown equal to twice the number of time slots which are in the input multiplexes. The number of space stage time slots is arbitrarily selected in this example. The consequence of various numbers of space stage time slots is discussed after this example.

An idle time slot in the space stage has been found in Fig. 19 during the first half of time slot 3. The functions of TSI 1 and TSI 4 are therefore defined once an idle space-time slot is found which meets the closure requirements. TSI 1 must accept X during time slot 1 and store it until the first half of time slot 3. Then, X proceeds onto the horizontal of the space stage during the first half of time slot 3 and moves through the space stage without delay to the input of TSI 4. TSI 4 accepts X and stores it until time slot 4. X is then delivered to its desired receive multiplex at time slot 4. X is decoded and appears at termination 12 in analog form. Y proceeds through the network in a similar way.

The number of time slots in the space stage will now be considered. How many time slots must there be in the space stage to guarantee non-blocking? What is the blocking probability for various numbers of space stage time slots?

The general case for a TST network is shown in Fig. 20a. N time slots are at the input to the first T stage. M time slots are in the space stage. We wish to make a connection between TSI 1 and TSI 4. We have already observed that we must close crosspoint A to make this connection. We have

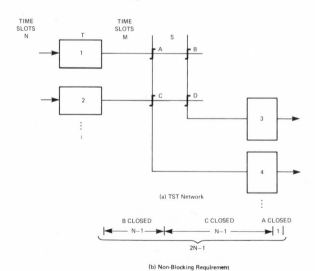

(a) TST Network

(b) Non-Blocking Requirement

Fig. 20.   Demonstration of nonblocking requirement in a TST switching center network.

also observed that we cannot close A and B simultaneously or A and C simultaneously. How many time slots, M, must there be in the space stage to guarantee nonblocking? As shown in Fig. 20b, crosspoint B can be closed for $N - 1$ time slots (the desired information is contained in one of the N time slots). Crosspoint C can be closed for a different $N - 1$ time slots (C cannot be closed during the one desired time slot to TSI 4). To guarantee nonblocking without rearranging the network, the space stage must contain $2N - 1$ time slots as shown in Fig. 20b. If $M = 2N - 1$, we have a strictly nonblocking network. If $N - 2 < M < 2N - 1$, the blocking probability through the network is given by[16]

$$P_B = \frac{[(N-1)!]^2}{M!(2N-2-M)!} \, a^M (2-a)^{(2N-2-M)} \tag{8}$$

where a is the circuit occupancy. Equation (8) applies for a single connection through the network. If two independent routes are established through the network to create a two-way circuit, then equation (8) is almost doubled. Blocking probabilities for various N and M are shown in Table 5. This table illustrates a number of interesting points regarding digital switching center networks. First, a TST network with a small expansion in the number of time slots for the S stage will give a very small blocking probability. Since this probability is small but not zero, these networks are called "essentially" nonblocking. Note, however, that the blocking probability is strongly influenced by the circuit occupancy, a. Thus, it is important to specify the circuit occupancy when describing the blocking probability.

The number of stages used in the switching center network depends on the design requirements for the switch. The following parameters usually determine network selection:

- Ultimate size
- Cost
- Control complexity

Various combinations of T and S stages are ranked in Table 6. The simple T stage is the easiest to control, has the lowest cost for small

Table 5. Blocking Probabilities

		a (Erlang)			
N	M	0.7	0.8	0.9	1.0
105	128	2.8×10^{-11}	3.3×10^{-9}	1.1×10^{-5}	0.0038
240	256	1.3×10^{-15}	1.8×10^{-8}	8.9×10^{-4}	0.3
384	384	1.1×10^{-16}	1.1×10^{-7}	1.7×10^{-2}	0.99
384	386	3.1×10^{-17}	4.7×10^{-8}	1.1×10^{-2}	0.98
480	512	3.3×10^{-30}	5.1×10^{-16}	1.1×10^{-6}	0.1

Table 6.   Time-Divided Network Ranking

Design	Control complexity	Reasonable capacity (time slots)	Cost
T	Low	1,000	Low
STS	Low	5,000	Moderate
TST	Moderate	10,000	Moderate
$TSSST$	Difficult	100,000	High

networks, but can only be reasonably expanded to around 1000 time slots. This could accommodate on the order of 1000 trunks or 4000 lines. A multistage design such as the $TSSST$ is more difficult to control and costs more but it can be expanded to an extremely large number of time slots.

3.5.   System Availability

Benjamin Franklin said "In this world nothing is certain but death and taxes." A corollary to this profound observation is: in an electronic system nothing is certain but the ultimate failure of each component. The consequence of these failures depends on the type of failure and the mission of the system.

In a digital switching system, a failure such as an LED indicator might be insignificant. On the other hand, a memory failure in the system controller could cause a complete system outage. In a PABX, a memory failure might only inconvenience the business. However, in a public switching system, a memory failure might deny a community their access to fire and police protection. Therefore, switching system synthesis must consider the concept of system availability.

System availability is defined as

$$\text{system availability} = \frac{\text{up time}}{\text{up time} + \text{outage time}} \tag{9}$$

A public switching system has rigorous availability requirements since the total system outage time during a 40-yr period must be less than 2 hr. This requires an availability of 0.9999943. Since digital switching systems are quite complex, the only way to realize the public switching availability requirement is through the use of redundancy.

A number of common redundancy schemes are shown in Fig. 21. These diagrams illustrate a communication path between points A and B with various approaches to redundancy. Figure 21a shows a two-plane redundancy scheme with a means for switching between the planes. This

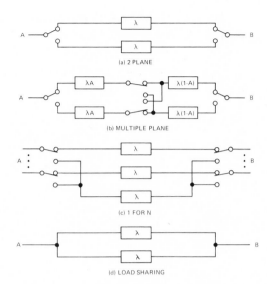

Fig. 21.   Common redundancy
schemes.

common redundancy scheme will be studied in detail and then the other schemes will be explained.

Various system states are shown in Fig. 22. In normal system operation, a two-plane redundancy scheme has an on-line unit operating without fault and a standby unit with identical capabilities ready to assume the load. If the on-line unit fails, automatic detection mechanisms cause a system reconfiguration and the standby unit is brought into operation. The failed unit is then repaired, tested, and brought back on-line. Normal system operation is then restored. Failures in the standby unit must be similarly detected and repaired to ensure its availability when the on-line unit fails.

A vulnerable period exists during the interval between failure and restoral to normal, as shown in Fig. 22. During this time a failure in the standby unit could cause a complete system outage.

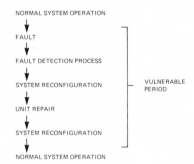

Fig. 22.   Operational states for a switching system.

The unavailability for the redundancy scheme shown in Fig. 21a will now be derived. Design constraints in order to meet a system unavailability of 2 hr in 40 years will be described.

System unavailability is given by

$$\text{unavailability} = 1 - \text{availability} \tag{10}$$

$$= \frac{\text{outage time}}{\text{system life}} \tag{11}$$

The number of vulnerable instances of the type shown in Fig. 22 in a system's life is

$$\text{number of vulnerable instances} = 2\lambda(\text{system life}) \tag{12}$$

where λ is the failure rate of 1 redundancy plane.

The outage time per vulnerable instance is

$$\text{outage time per instance} = P_r(\text{outage during repair}) \, \text{MTTR} \tag{13}$$

where MTTR is the mean time to repair. MTTR includes the total vulnerable period shown in Fig. 22.

One redundancy plane has a probability of survival during an interval t given by

$$P_r(\text{survival during time } t) = e^{-\lambda t} \tag{14}$$

Thus

$$P_r(\text{outage during repair}) = 1 - e^{-\lambda \text{MTTR}} \tag{15}$$

From equations (12), (13), and (15),

$$\text{outage time during life} = (\text{number of vulnerable instances})$$

$$\times (\text{outage time per instance}) \tag{16}$$

$$= 2\lambda(\text{system life})(1 - e^{-\lambda \text{MTTR}})\text{MTTR} \tag{17}$$

If $(\lambda \, \text{MTTR})$ is much less than 1,

$$\text{outage time during life} \simeq 2\lambda(\text{system life})(\lambda \text{MTTR})\text{MTTR} \tag{18}$$

From equation (11), unavailability is therefore

$$\text{unavailability} \simeq 2(\lambda \text{MTTR})^2 \tag{19}$$

Thus, unavailability for the redundancy scheme of Fig. 22a is established by λ and MTTR as given in equation (19).

If the desired unavailability is less than 2 hr in 40 years and the mean time to repair is 0.5 hr, without redundancy λ must be less than or equal to 1.14×10^{-5}.

If λ exceeds this number, the redundancy scheme of Fig. 21a can meet the requirements if $\lambda \leq 0.0034$. If λ exceeds this number, another redundancy scheme such as Fig. 21b might be used. In Fig. 21b, each redundant plane is divided and interplane switching is allowed. If $A = 1/2$ then

$$\text{unavailability} \simeq (\lambda\text{MTTR})^2 \tag{20}$$

A 2-hr in 40-yr unavailability requirement can be met for this case if $\lambda \leq 0.0068$ and MTTR ≤ 0.5 hr.

If the individual parts of the system (e.g. integrated circuits, resistors, connector pins, etc.) have an independent and constant failure rate, the overall failure rate λ is the sum of the individual failure rates.[17] Component failure rates are expressed in the following units: percent per thousand hours, failures per 10^6 hours, or failures per 10^9 hours. The last unit is commonly called a FIT (failure in ten to the 9th).

Two additional redundancy schemes are shown in Fig. 21. Figure 21c shows a 1 for N protection scheme where many on-line units share a common standby unit. If any on-line unit fails, the single standby unit is switched into operation. Of course, no protection is provided if a second on-line unit fails before the first is fixed.

Figure 21d shows a load-sharing redundancy scheme where the system load is processed by both redundancy planes. If one path fails, the other assumes the whole load with no degradation in service. Equation (19) also applies to this scheme.

In most digital switching systems, it is possible to realize the desired system availability without need for triplicated redundancy. For a duplicated system, the following single-point failure criteria must be met:

There will be no single failure (open or short) that will cause a complete system outage.

Single-point failures are often difficult to eliminate in system design. Open connector pins can be particularly troublesome. Power buses can also be single-point failures when shorted. Single-point failures must be automatically detected and redundancy must be automatically applied to reach system availability objectives.

Where failures affect only a portion of the switch, a cost/benefit decision must be made on duplication. For example, should redundancy be provided for single failures which affect only 1 customer? 10 customers? 100 customers? Each operating administration must establish its criteria for the level of redundancy. Techniques such as 1 for N protection can be effectively utilized to provide high availability even for failures which only affect one customer.

3.6. System Maintainability

System availability, described in the previous section, is established by two parameters: system failure rate and system repair time. Given a system failure rate and availability objective, equation (19) specifies the required MTTR for a two-plane redundancy scheme.

System repair time therefore is key to reaching availability objectives. The parameters influencing repair time and ultimately system availability are shown in Fig. 23. Repair time is heavily influenced by the craftsperson who provides the brains and hands to fix a failed system. The craftsperson has many resources available to him or her, including maching diagnostics, fault clearing documentation, special test equipment, spare parts, and a remotely located technical assistance center (TAC) which can provide centralized advice when needed or as a last resort.

When the craftsperson feels the fault is cleared, the system must be retested using a combination of manual and automatic means. The system is then reconfigured into its normal mode.

Availability objectives are finally reached through proper periodic maintenance of fans, magnetic tape recorder heads, and other mechanical devices. Management systems should be developed to record failure rates

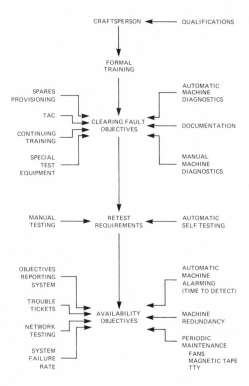

Fig. 23. Factors influencing system availability.

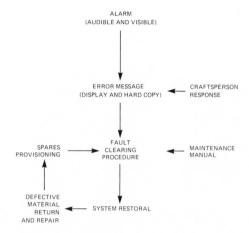

Fig. 24. System fault-clearing procedure.

and repair times in order to ensure that availability objectives are being reached.

A typical fault-clearing procedure is diagrammed in Fig. 24. The switching system automatically detects a fault condition and provides an audible or visible alarm to alert the maintenance force. The craftsperson receives the alarm and often must travel to an unattended office. Printed messages provided by the system are studied and the fault-clearing procedure begins with the aid of the maintenance manual. Spare parts are used to restore the system to normal and the defective material is returned for repair. The spares store is then brought back to normal. Any element of this process which is not kept under strict control could have a major adverse impact on system availability.

The switching system must also provide test access for maintenance of other portions of the network such as trunks and subscriber loops. Many automatic systems have been designed for this purpose.[18] Switching systems must provide the appropriate interface to these systems.

4. Examples of System Architectures

The internal structure of digital switching systems has been described in this chapter. The operation of both the individual switching system elements and the overall system has been presented. Some architectural alternatives in the design of a digital switching system have been discussed. This section presents a method for architecture analysis. This method is then used to analyze commercial digital switching systems. The chapter concludes by presenting a summary of the key architectural design decisions and indicates trends in system design.

4.1. Analysis Method

Laboratory models of experimental digital switching systems have been studied since 1959.[19] Experimental results were published during the 1960s[20] and the first production digital switching system was introduced in 1970.[21] Since that time, commercial digital switching systems have been announced by virtually every major switching supplier in the world. This section presents a method for analyzing digital-switching-system architectures.

A digital-switching-system architecture can be studied by examining the features listed in Table 7. These features identify the key decisions an architect must make in creating a system.

First, the architect must set the maximum system capacity. This decision is influenced by the intended system application. The system could be a key telephone system with ten lines or a toll tandem switch with 100,000 trunks. Architects strive to establish a system which is cost effective over a broad range of capacities, but this has been an elusive goal. There are three independent capacity limits: terminations, network traffic, and processor "horsepower". System manufacturing cost goals usually set the capacity limit where first cost (the cost of the first termination) and incremental cost (the cost as terminations are added) are the deciding factors. Technologies available in the designer's organization also set capacity limits. For example, a processor with a capacity of 100,000 ABSBHC is a formidable design task and is beyond the capabilities of many organizations.

The type and location of the analog to digital converters must be decided by the architect. Should the system use delta-modulation, PCM, ADPCM, etc.? Where should the codecs be located? Per termination? Concentrated? Time shared?

Multiplexing is a key technology in digital switching systems. The architect must decide the bit rate and frame structure of the primary and secondary multiplexes. In addition, the signaling means must be set.

The type and location of the terminations must be established. Will there be customer loop as well as trunk terminations? Will these two termi-

Table 7. Architectural Parameters

Capacity	Termination structure
Terminations	Switching center network
Network traffic	Structure
Processor	Blocking
Codec type and location	Availability
Primary multiplex	Control
Secondary multiplex	Redundancy
Maintenance and administration	

nation types be concentrated together or segregated? What type of digital terminations will be provided: trunks, pair gain systems, or remote switching units?

Next, the architect must select the structure of the switching center network. This decision is usually made on the basis of maximum desired capacity, control ease, and cost. Blocking and availability in the switching structure must also be established.

Control is a major architectural decision. All new systems use stored program control but there are a number of possible innovative multiprocessing schemes. The structure of the software must be established and the programming language chosen.

Finally, the architect must establish the redundancy scheme for his system. Also the maintenance and administration plan must be developed.

The architectural features listed in Table 7 will be used to examine commercial digital switching systems in the following sections.

4.2. E10

The E10[21] is a medium sized digital switching system which provides both local and transit switching functions. Designed in France, the E10 was placed in service in 1970 at Lannion, France and became the first commercial digital switching system in the world. The early E10 systems were called E10A. The E10A was subsequently modified and became the E10B. Because of its historical significance, the E10A will be described.

The E10A can terminate 3600 trunks or 16,000 lines. The switching center network can switch 1600 Erlang and the processors can accommodate 50,400 BHCA.

The E10A architecture is shown in Fig. 25. Customer loops interface the system at local or remote analog concentrators designated A. Up to 512 loops are concentrated using pulse amplitude modulation switching technology onto 60 links connecting the concentrator to digital channel banks. Codecs employ 8-bit PCM with A-law companding and 8-kHz sampling.

Analog trunks terminate at digital channel banks accommodating 30 trunks each. Sync units provide a standard 2.048 mHz interface where signaling is removed and sent to the system control. Digital trunks similarly interface at the Sync unit.

The switching center network employs a T structure which is nonblocking. This network can terminate 128 2.048-mHz multiplexes, but eight are reserved for tone signaling. Blocking is only introduced at concentrators A.

The primary multiplex contains 32 time slots with 30 message channels. One time slot is reserved for signaling and another provides frame synchronization as shown in Fig. 8. No secondary multiplex is used.

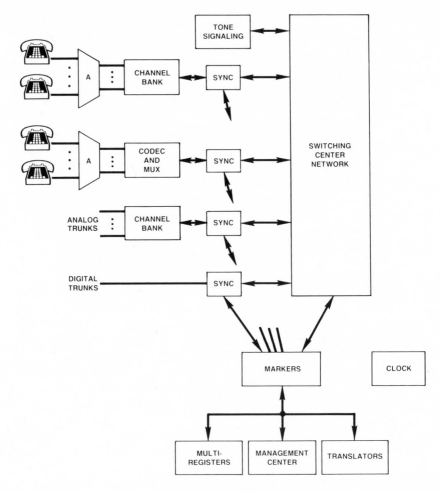

Fig. 25.   E10A architecture.

System control employs markers, multiregisters, and translators. Two markers provide information transfer to as many as eight multiregisters. This early E10A system did not employ stored program control.

The redundancy scheme is $n + 1$ for the multiregisters. The markers and translators are duplicated.

The E10A was one of the first systems to allow remote maintenance and administration from a management center. Subsequent systems have adopted versions of this architecture.

The E10B has the same architectural concept as the E10A but provides twice as many terminations with a *TST* switching center network. In addition, the processors use *SPC* technology and the line concentrators use analog *CMOS* crosspoints.

4.3. No. 4 ESS

The No. 4 ESS[22] is a large digital tandem switching system designed at Bell Laboratories. First placed in service at Chicago, Illinois in 1976, the No. 4 ESS can terminate 107,000 trunks and can switch 47,000 Erlang. The processors can accommodate 550,000 busy hour calls. The No. 4 ESS was the first public digital switching system in North America.

As shown in Fig. 26, the No. 4 ESS terminates analog trunks at the voice frequency terminal. These trunks can be either metallic or carrier derived. Digital trunks terminate at the digroup terminal. The No. 4 ESS is not designed to interface customer loops.

High-speed codecs are time shared over many trunks and employ 8-bit $\mu 255$ companded PCM sampled at 8 kHz. This choice was made to provide compatibility with D-channel banks.

The primary multiplex contains 120 channels on 128 time slots as shown. This multiplex operates at 8.192 mbit/s. A secondary multiplex contains 105 channels in the same 128 time slots operating at 8.192 mbit/s. This

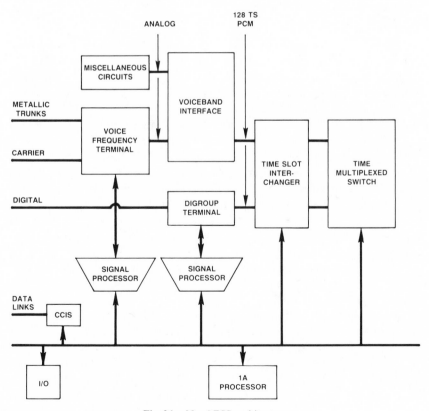

Fig. 26. No. 4 ESS architecture.

provides time expansion between the T and S stages to reduce the probability of blocking.

The switching center network employs a $TSSSST$ structure. Blocking is introduced between the T and S stages since the S stages do not contain at least 209 time slots. In addition, the four-stage time-multiplexed switch has a small blocking probability.

Control in the No. 4 ESS is hierarchical and distributed in architecture. The 1A processor provides the highest level of control and signal processors preprocess signaling and control information from the trunks. This information is extracted from the trunks, preprocessed by the signal processors, and sent to the 1A processor. The 1A processor also provides maintenance and administration data through $I/0$ ports and supports common channel interoffice signaling (CCIS).

Redundancy is provided by duplication and one-for-N protection. Duplication is used in the 1A processors, switching center network, and signal processors. One-for-N protection is employed in the voice frequency terminal.

4.4. ITS 4/5

The ITS 4/5[23] is a rural digital switching system which provides both tandem and local switching functions. It was designed by an American team and was placed in service at Ridgecrest, California in 1976. It became the first system in North America to directly interface digital trunks and digital switching. The ITS 4/5 can terminate 3072 trunks or 12,768 lines with 9% trunking. The switching center network can switch 1536 Erlang and the processors can accommodate 20,000 average busy season busy hour calls.

The ITS 4/5 architecture is shown in Fig. 27. Customer loops interface the *ITS* at three locations: the *local* subscriber *switch* (LSS), the *remote* subscriber *switch* (RSS) and the *subscriber* carrier *terminal* (SCT). Analog trunks terminate at voice banks (VB3) or at D-channel banks.

The base switch provides up to 128 $DS1$-terminations. The time divided network in the base switch is an STS structure which is strictly nonblocking.

The codecs are located at the LSS, RSS or VB3, and use 8-bit PCM with $\mu 255$ companding sampled at 8 kHz. Codecs are time shared with one codec serving twelve customer lines.

The primary multiplex contains 24 time slots operating at 1.544 mbit/s. A secondary multiplex uses 384 channels and 386 time slots at 3.088 mbit/s. The serial 8-bit samples in the primary multiplex are converted to 8-bit parallel (plus parity) in the secondary multiplex.

The LSS and RSS contain a T stage, and up to 336 customer loops can access 48 time slots. For customer loop connections, the switching

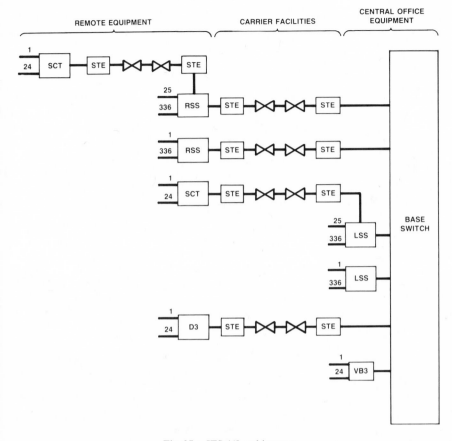

Fig. 27.   ITS 4/5 architecture.

network structure is $TSTST$; for trunks, the structure is STS. Blocking is only introduced in the LSS or RSS. All trunk switching is nonblocking.

Processors employ microprocessor technology at the LSS, RSS, and in the base switch. The base switch processor structure is similar to the No. 4 ESS.

Redundancy is provided using duplication and load sharing techniques. $DS1$ interfaces and processors are duplicated. The switching center network employs load-sharing redundancy.

4.5.   NEAX 61

The NEAX 61[24] is a large combined local–toll digital switching system designed in Japan. The first system was placed in service in 1979 at Manteca, California. The NEAX 61 can terminate 60,000 trunks or 100,000

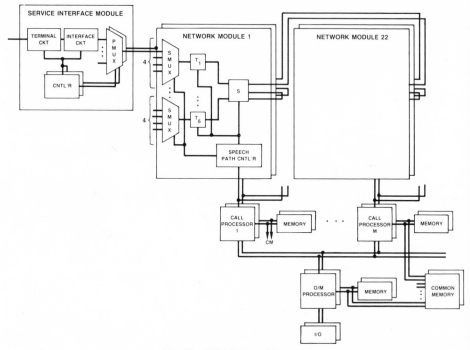

Fig. 28.   NEAX 61 architecture.

lines. The switching center network can switch 22,000 Erlang, and the processors can accommodate 700,000 BHCA.

The architecture of the NEAX 61 is shown in Fig. 28. Customer loops interface the system at the service interface module. There are several types of service interface modules: analog line modules, digital line modules, remote switch interface modules, analog trunk modules, digital trunk modules, and operator position interface modules. The analog line module employs 4-wire switching to concentrate from 60 to 240 loops onto 39 outlets. *CMOS* crosspoints are used to provide this analog switching function.

The PMUX is identical in each module and contains 128 channels for five 1.544-mbit/s or four 2.048-mbit/s multiplexes. The primary multiplex operates at 8.192 mbit/s. A SMUX employs 480 channels in 512 time slots at 32.768 mbit/s.

The switching center network uses a *TSST* structure, which is essentially nonblocking.

Codecs use 8-bit PCM sampled at 8 kHz. Companding is available for both the μ-law and A-law standards.

The control structure of the NEAX 61 consists of a processor group of M call processors, operations and maintenance processors, speech path controllers, and service interface module controllers. The M call processors operate in the load-sharing mode but each call processor is dedicated to a portion of the switch. The operations and maintenance processors are functionally independent except for very small systems where these functions are accomplished in the call processor.

Redundancy is provided by full duplication as shown in Fig. 28.

4.6. AXE 10

The AXE 10[25] is a large digital switching system which provides both local and transit switching functions. Designed in Sweden, the AXE 10 initially employed an analog switching center network but this network was upgraded to digital with first service in Finland in 1978. The AXE 10 can terminate 65,000 trunks or 200,000 lines. The switching center network can switch 30,000 Erlang and the processors can accommodate 1,000,000 BHCA.

The AXE 10 architecture is shown in Fig. 29. Customer loops interface at the subscriber switching subsystem (SSS). Analog loops initially interfaced at an analog concentrator employing reed relays. A subsequent concentrator uses digital switching. Remote concentrators can be used to provide pair gain. Up to 2048 customer lines can interface at the SSS in modules of 128. There can be 480 PCM channels providing links from the SSS to the group selector subsystem (GSS).

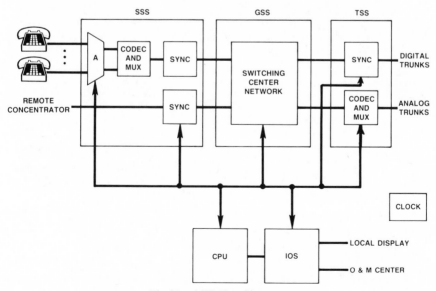

Fig. 29. AXE 10 architecture.

Analog and digital trunks interface the switch at the *trunk* and *signal-ing* subsystem (TSS). The AXE 10 employs 8-bit PCM sampled at 8 kHz. Either μ-law or A-law versions are provided.

The GSS is a *TST* structure which is essentially nonblocking. The primary multiplex has 32 time slots operating at 2.048 mbit/s. A secondary multiplex has 512 time slots with 10-bit parallel words at 4.096 mbit/s.

The CPU employs multiprocessing where a single processor can provide 150,000 BHCA. Eight processors will give 1,000,000 BHCA.

Duplication of the GSS and CPU provide the required redundancy.

4.7. DMS 100

The DMS 100[26] is a large combined local–toll digital switching system designed in Canada. It was first placed in service in 1979 in Canada. An earlier, small Canadian system, the DMS 10[27] was placed in service in 1977. The DMS 100 can terminate 100,000 lines; the toll tandem version, the DMS 200, can terminate 61,440 trunks. The processors can accommodate 350,000 ABSBHC, and the switching center network can switch 39,000 Erlang.

The DMS 100 architecture is shown in Fig. 30. Customer loops interface the system at the line module. Up to 1280 customer loops are digitally concentrated onto 240 digital links to the switching network. The line module employs a *TS* digital concentrator. The DMS 100 supports a number of pair gain system types.

Analog trunks interface the DMS 100 at the analog trunk module. There is no concentration of trunk traffic on digital links to the switching network. Digital trunks interface at the digital carrier module where five *DS*1 channels interface with four switching network ports.

The switching network provides 2048 32-channel multiplexes and employs four stages of time switching which is essentially nonblocking.

Codecs employ 8-bit PCM sampled at 8 kHz. Initial installations have used μ255 companding.

The primary multiplex contains 32 time slots operating at 2.048 mHz. A secondary multiplex also operates at 2.048 mHz, but employs parallel rather than serial words.

Blocking is only introduced in the line modules or in pair gain systems. All trunk switching is essentially nonblocking.

Central control consists of a synchronized pair of central processing units (CPU). Each CPU has a dedicated program and data store. Access to and from peripheral units is via the message controller.

Redundancy is provided using duplication in the switching network, message controller, and CPU. Load sharing redundancy is employed in the line module.

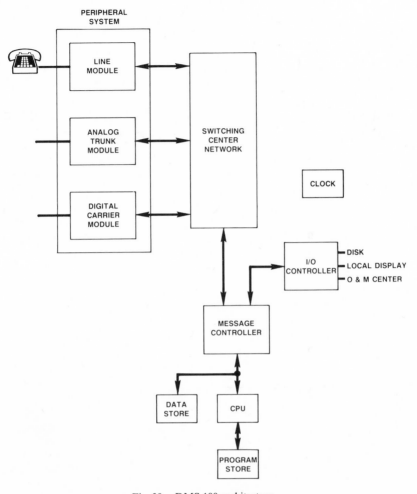

Fig. 30. DMS 100 architecture.

4.8. EWSD

The EWSD[28] is a large combined local–transit digital switching system designed in West Germany. The first system was placed in service in South Africa in 1980. The EWSD can terminate 60,000 trunks or 100,000 lines. The switching center network can switch 30,000 Erlang and the processors can accommodate 800,000 BHCA.

The EWSD architecture is shown in Fig. 31. Customer loops interface the digital concentrator (DIC) or at remote pair gain devices. The DIC interfaces 256 customer loops and concentrates them onto 120 digital links

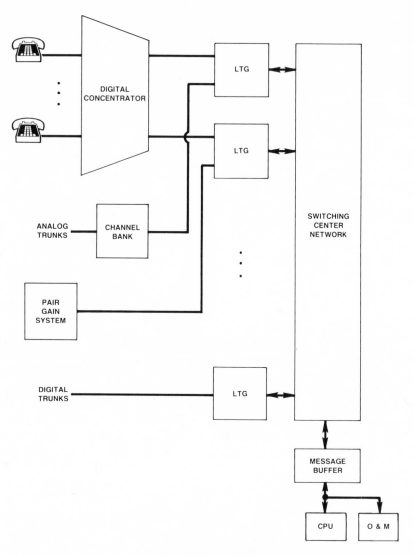

Fig. 31. EWSD architecture.

to the switching network. Analog trunks interface at channel banks, and are applied to digital links without concentration. The switching network is a *TST* structure.

The primary multiplex contains either 30 or 24 time slots, depending on national standards. The secondary multiplex contains 128 time slots operating at 8.192 mbit/s.

Codecs use 8-bit PCM sampled at 8 kHz. Either *A*-law or *μ*-law companders are used.

The EWSD features a highly decentralized control. Microprocessors in each LTG perform control and signaling functions including necessary receivers and senders. The switching network also has a dedicated controller for setting up and releasing network paths. Control time slots in the primary multiplex are switched through the switching network on a semi-permanent basis. The message buffer relieves the CPU from providing the communication protocol over the 64-kbit/s channels to the LTGs.

The CPU performs overall system coordination, the centralized portions of call processing, and all operations and maintenance functions. Software is written in the *CCITT* high-level language CHILL. LTGs can communicate directly with each other via the message buffer.

All vital parts of the EWSD are duplicated, and calls are handled simultaneously in both switching networks. The LTGs are not redundant since they only serve a limited number of terminations. Traffic from the DIC is routed to two independent LTGs to provide load sharing redundancy.

4.9. System 12

System 12 is a family of medium–large digital switching systems. The 1210[29] is a medium-sized combined local–toll digital switching system designed by an American team. The 1240[30] is a large digital switching system designed by a multinational team. It provides both local and tandem switching functions. The 1210 was first placed in service in the United States in 1978 and the 1240 was placed in service in Belgium in 1982.

The 1240 can terminate 60,000 trunks or 100,000 lines. The switching center network can switch 25,000 Erlang and the processors can accommodate 750,000 BHCA.

The 1240 architecture is shown in Fig. 32. This architecture is based on a grouping of terminal circuits which are equipped with their own microprocessor. Each group can access a pool of additional processing resources through the same 64 kbit/s-switched paths used by the voice channels. The control of the 1240 is therefore fully distributed and grows as the switching system grows.

As shown in Fig. 32, there is a microprocessor for every 60 lines (LC) or 30 trunks (TC). Up to 480 lines are concentrated onto 120 time slots. The terminal interface (TI) provides the primary multiplex interface for signaling and message channels. There is no centralized path control of the switching center network. Instead, each microprocessor, through its associated TI, controls the establishment of paths by sending a 16-bit message which identifies the special route for the connection to the switch element (SE). The switch element then selects the outgoing channel time slot. When the path reaches the called terminal, the called microprocessor establishes a

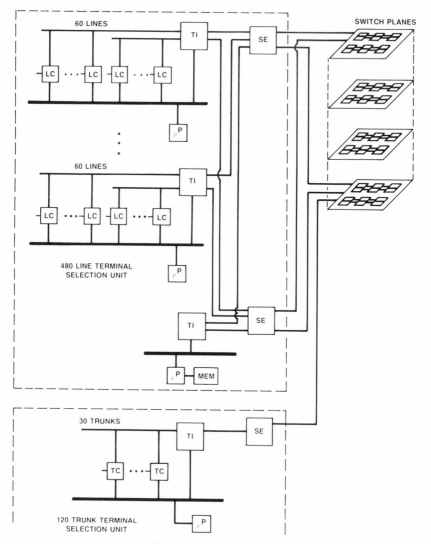

Fig. 32.　1240 architecture.

path in the opposite direction to complete the full duplex circuit. Each switch plane contains many SEs.

The primary multiplex contains 32 time slots and operates at 4.096 mHz. The time slot words are 16 bits long. Each SE contains both time and space switching with eight multiplex inputs and eight outputs. There are seven switching elements in tandem for a connection in a large system causing a $TSTSTSTSTSTS$ connection. A secondary multiplex with 256 time slots is contained within each SE.

The 1240 employs 8-bit PCM sampled at 8 kHz. Both *A*- and μ-law companders are provided.

Redundancy is provided using duplication and load sharing techniques. Two switch planes are used in small systems.

4.10. System *X*

System *X*[31] is a family of combined local–transit digital switches designed in the United Kingdom. It was first placed in service in London in

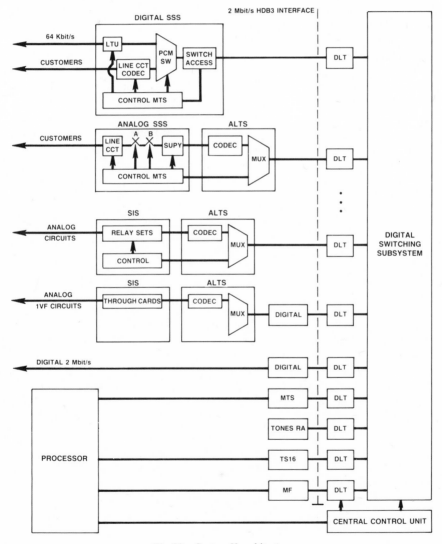

Fig. 33.   System X architecture.

1980. System X has been configured in three sizes to reach a range of switching applications. The maximum capacity is 450,000 BHCA, 20,000 Erlang and 3072 32-channel multiplexes. The next smaller capacity is 75,000 BHCA and 1000 Erlang. The smallest is 40 Erlang and 30,000 BHCA.

The System X architecture is shown in Fig. 33. Up to 250 customer loops interface the digital or analog subscriber switching subsystem (SSS). The SSS detects calls, concentrates traffic, and provides call supervision. The analog SSS employs reed relays for concentration. Connection between the SSS and digital switching subsystem (DSS) is by duplicated 32-channel 2.048 mbit/s multiplexes. The DSS is a single T stage for small systems and is TST for the maximum size. Semipermanent switching paths are provided between different subsystems.

The codecs are 8-bit PCM sampled at 8 kHz. A-law companding is employed.

The primary multiplex has 32 channels operating at 2.048 mHz. A secondary multiplex contains 512 time slots with parallel 8-bit words, plus parity.

The signaling interworking subsystem (SIS) provides analog terminations for trunks. Digital trunks interface directly at DSS HDB3 terminations.

System X can have up to 12 active processors. This multiprocessing configuration has limited private memory and each CPU has access to a common mainframe store for programs and data.

Redundancy is provided using duplication and load sharing techniques.

4.11. GTD-5 EAX

The GTD-5 EAX[32] is a medium–large digital switching system with combined local–toll capabilities. It was designed by an American engineering team, and was first placed in service at Banning, California in 1982. The GTD-5 EAX can terminate as many as 150,000 lines or 49,000 trunks. The switching center network can switch 36,000 Erlang and the processors can accommodate 360,000 BHCA.

The GTD-5 EAX architecture is shown in Fig. 34. Customer loops interface at the base unit or at remote equipment. The facility interface unit provides customer loop terminations for up to 768 loops. These loops are concentrated onto 192 PCM links to the network. Remote customer loops interface at a multiplexer (MUX), a remote line unit, or a remote switch unit. These systems provide pair gain functions. Analog trunks interface at a facility interface unit in groups of 192. Digital trunks or links interface at a facility interface unit in groups of 192 PCM channels.

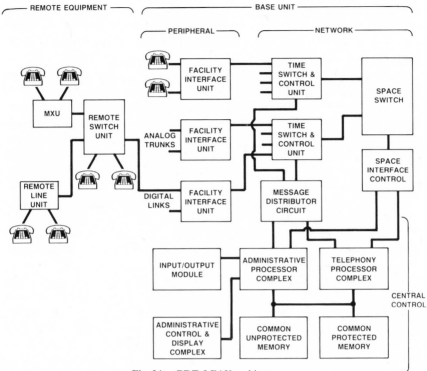

Fig. 34.   GDT-5 EAX architecture.

The network can interface 49,152 PCM channels in a *TST* configuration and is essentially nonblocking. The network switches 12 parallel bits in each 64-kbit/s channel.

The codecs use 8-bit PCM sampled at 8 kHz. Companding for the initial configuration is $\mu255$.

The primary multiplex contains 192 time slots and operates at 1.544 mbit/s. A secondary multiplex is employed in the space stage of the *TST* network. This multiplex contains 384 time slots and operates at 3.088 mbit/s.

Control in the GTD-5 EAX is distributed throughout the system. A message distributor circuit routes messages to and from the central control, the facility interface units, and the network. The central control consists of an administrative processor complex and up to seven telephone processor complexes.

Redundancy is provided using duplication in the network, primary multiplex, and central control equipment.

5. Summary and Trends

Representative production digital switching systems have been presented in the previous sections. There are many additional production systems from design teams around the world.[33-40]

The architecture of future digital switching systems will be influenced by expanding services and by progress in semiconductor and software technology. The time has now passed where a switching system can be considered as a separate economic entity without consideration for the cost of the overall network. Design trends toward the integration of transmission and switching to minimize overall network costs, as described in Chapter 10 in this volume, are firmly established. As data services grow, there will be a trend toward switching systems which can provide both voice and data services using combinations of circuit, packet, and message switching as described in Chapter 6 of this volume.

The integration of transmission and switching is a solid future trend. Use of remote units to rehome small central offices and pair gain systems to minimize the cost of the customer plant are essential parts of a digital switching system. Other digital network oriented system elements such as a direct digital interface to digital trunk carrier systems, network synchronization, and common channel signaling are important parts of a digital switching system.

Semiconductor technology will have the greatest impact on the design of the future customer interface and on the control structure. In larger switching systems, the cost of the customer interface can represent up to 80% of the total system cost. In addition, the customer interface must be compatible with the hostile outside plant environment. Many alternatives for the location of the customer interface are shown in Fig. 13 of Chapter 7. There are two apparent design trends: provide the complete customer interface on a per line basis and, alternatively, minimize the system cost of the customer circuit by concentrating its functions behind an analog switching stage. Crosspoints used in this approach must be able to withstand voltages of between 300 and 500 V. In addition, they should have very low crosstalk. The concentrator approach was applied to the first digital switching systems before LSI codecs were available. The crosspoints used were reed relays. These relays are no longer cost competitive. However, new semiconductor crosspoint technology is not out of reach.[41] In applications where the complete customer line interface is provided on a per line basis, the trend is to provide many customer lines per board so that LSI control devices can be shared over many lines. This trend also provides for high line density and for lowering the per line cost of connectors and printed circuit boards. Up to eight customer interfaces per board have been used.

Digital customer loops and digital telephones will become an important part of future networks. This will allow customers to have access to either voice or a variety of low- and high-speed data services on an efficient basis. Transmission technologies to provide the digital customer loop have been described in Chapter 8. Since 8-bit PCM with 8-kHz sampling is now a world standard, the 64 kbit/sec channel will become a standard service offering. In μ-law countries, bit robbing must be eliminated in order to establish a clear channel 64 kbit/sec capability. Common channel signaling in these countries is an absolute requirement to eliminate bit robbing. While 64 kbit/sec has become a network standard, subrate and superate multiplexing will also be used to provide a variety of new services. Future switching systems should therefore accommodate variable bit rate services.

Signaling standards have been developed for the trunk network. These standards have allowed information to be transmitted between nations and between switching systems from different manufacturers within a nation. Such standards in the local plant have not been established except for the standard telephones. Pair gain systems, remote switching systems, and digital customer loops will most likely have unique signaling techniques to their digital switch host. It is unlikely that standards will be established to allow interchangeability between customer loop equipment from various manufacturers. Standards will be set at the interface between the customer instrument or terminal and the customer loop equipment. This means that there will most likely be an incompatibility between remote switching units, pair gain systems, and digital customer loop systems between manufacturers unless national administrations force standardization.

The switching center network represents between 5% and 10% of the cost of the overall system. Because of this relatively low cost, designers have been influenced by expandability and control ease rather than manufacturing cost. In some cases, custom LSI semiconductor devices have been designed to implement a particularly unique switching center network structure.[30,37,40] There is a trend in switching center network design, however, toward the time–space–time or time–multiple space–time structures.

Hardware and software for control functions in future digital switching systems will be heavily influenced by progress in the computer and semiconductor industry. Microprocessor technology and semiconductor memory have been vital technologies in the progress of digital switching system control design. In the past, hardware architectures and manufacturing cost have been the major factors influencing control design. Indeed, some designers have proposed that memory should be considered to have zero cost and used at any point in the system. However, software development and maintenance costs have now become significant and this cost must be amortized over the systems to be produced. This cost can be a significant individual system cost and should be considered along with hardware manufacturing cost in selecting a control design approach. Therefore, there is a trend to select control architectures which minimize both hardware and software costs. High-level languages, feature modularity, and structured programming are now used to minimize software development, maintenance, and feature addition costs as described in Chapter 5 in this volume.

There is a trend toward providing a hierarchical form of distributed control as shown in Fig. 10. This will ease the real time requirements on the processors so that high-level programming languages can be used at the expense of real time performance. There is a trend toward providing more functional capability at lower levels in the processor hierarchy as microprocessors become more powerful. A process of downloading software through the hierarchy will provide flexibility in effecting program changes at low hierarchical levels without the need to change hardware (ROMs). Modularity in control combined with switching center networks which can grow from small to large sizes will give switching systems which are economical over broad size ranges.

In the area of maintenance and administration for digital switching systems, there is a trend toward centralization which will allow craftspersons to efficiently administer and maintain groups of switching systems. The goal is to lower overall network maintenance and administration cost through centralization. Digital switching systems must provide the necessary interface capabilities to support these remote functions. Since the failure rate is low in digital switching systems, a craftsperson soon forgets much of what he or she learned in training school. A centralized staff of maintenance experts can be established to assist the local craftsperson in fault clearing. The centralized staff provides a valuable resource to the local craftsperson since they have more troubleshooting experience and they can be at higher pay scales. The trend in self diagnostics for digital switching systems is toward system-generated fault identification and printout showing the location of the defective printed circuit board. This location includes the frame and shelf number and the defective board slot.

The trends in redundancy in digital switching systems varies with the portion of the switch. In the switching center network, the trend is toward complete duplication rather than load sharing due to the low cost of the time-divided network and the ease in fault isolation and testing provided by duplication. Duplication also provides a higher grade of customer service since failures do not affect calls in progress or increase the blocking probability. In the area of system control redundancy, there is a trend toward decentralization where control failures affect fewer lines. Load sharing or on-line/standby schemes are used in the hierarchy. At the top of the hierarchy where failures affect the whole system, there is also a trend toward on-line/standby redundancy or load sharing rather than synchronous/parallel processors. If sufficient call processing is accomplished down in the hierarchy, the on-line/standby scheme at the top does not cause a loss in transient call data when a failure occurs. Since software faults now dominate over hardware faults, control schemes which simplify software will provide the most reliable systems. At the line circuit level, there is a trend to provide redundancy when one spare line circuit can be shared over a number of lines.

In summary, advances in semiconductor components and in software technology will allow continued progress in the design of digital switching systems. Future systems will offer more services with higher system availability and will have a broader range in economic size.

Questions

1. Referring to Fig. 1, a 24-channel multiplex operating at 1.544 mbit/s is applied to a *B* port digital termination. The multiplex which interfaces the switching center network contains 32 channels and operates at 2.048 mbit/s. Discuss the multiplex translation function. Suggest techniques for converting one multiplex format to the other. What is the impact of sampling rate? What is the impact of companding law? What is the impact of voice encoding technique?

2. The control function in Fig. 1 shows interfaces to administration, maintenance and signaling. Discuss the benefits of remote administration and maintenance. Discuss the interface between the switching system and a common channel signaling system.

3. Describe the analog termination of a digital switch. How does this termination differ for customer loops and trunks?

4. Describe the digital termination of a digital switch.

5. Discuss the length of the digital termination frame alignment buffer. What is the loop delay caused by this buffer? Discuss the loop delay caused by two frame alignment buffers in tandem in separate digital switching systems.

6. Most digital switching systems have primary and secondary multiplexing functions. Discuss the secondary multiplex. What are its advantages and disadvantages? Suggest formats for the primary multiplex?

7. What are the functions of a time slot interchanger? Explain with a timing diagram. Why is the loop delay through a time slot interchanger constant and independent of the particular time slots which are interchanged?

8. What are the benefits of the hierarchy of control illustrated in Fig. 10? Discuss the impact of microprocessors on such an architecture.

9. Processors in a digital switch have a maximum capacity. As the offered load exceeds this maximum capacity, what is the desired characteristic of processed versus offered load? The hypothetical switch shown in Fig. 12 is described in the text with a particular partitioning of control. Discuss the partitioning of control and suggest other partitioning schemes. Include their advantages and disadvantages.

10. What are the economic advantages of a remote unit? What are the limitations of remote units? Draw a system block diagram which includes a remote unit, a digital transmission facility, and a digital host switch. Describe the progress of a

call between two customers in the same remote unit. Describe the performance of your remote unit in the presence of various types of faults.

11. What are the benefits of pair gain systems? What amount of concentration should be allowed in a remote terminal?

12. Discuss the importance of including remote switching and pair gain systems in a digital switching system architecture.

13. System capacity is established by three independent parameters. Discuss these parameters and explain why they are independent.

14. Determine the capacity of an urban switching system required to serve 20,000 customer loops and 3000 trunks.

15. If you were designing a digital switch, what type of digital encoding technique would you use and why? Would you use companding? What sampling rate would you use? Where would you place the codec in your architecture?

16. What are the differences between a time multiplexed space stage used in a digital switch and an analog space division network in an analog switch?

17. While it might be common to have a switching center network of a digital switch with a single T stage, would it be equally common to have a single S stage? Why?

18. Design a switching center network for a 30,000 termination digital switch. Assume you have memories with an access time of 100 ns.

19. Can a TS or ST switching center network be nonblocking? Why?

20. Discuss the differences between TST and STS networks.

21. You have decided to use a TST network in a digital switch and the secondary multiplex contains 120 time slots. How many time slots would you include in the time multiplexed space stage for nonblocking operation? What would be the blocking probability if the time multiplexed space stage contained 120 time slots, 150 time slots, 200 time slots? Assume channel occupancies of $0.6E$ and $0.9E$.

22. A system has a nonredundant failure rate of 20,000 FITS. Suggest a redundancy scheme to provide a system unavailability of less than 2 hours in 40 years assuming a mean time to repair of 0.5 hours. Discuss the requirements which must be met in order to reach this availability objective.

23. Single point failures can occur at many locations in a switching system. Identify sources of single point failures and suggest a redundancy strategy.

24. What level of redundancy would you suggest for a public local switching system? Should a single failure only affect one subscriber, ten subscribers, 100 subscribers?

25. Describe the benefits of a tactical assistance center.

References

1. CCITT, *Recommendation Series G 700*, Geneva, 1972.
2. D. F. Hoth,"The T1 Carrier System," *Bell Labs Rec.*, November 1962, pp. 358–364.
3. C. A. Dahlbom, "Common Channel Signaling—A New Flexible Interoffice Signaling Technique," *Int. Switching Symp. Rec.*, p. 421, 1972.
4. J. C. McDonald, "Field Experience with a Combined Local and Toll Digital Switch," *Intl. Switching Symp. Rec.*, p. 295, 1979.
5. N. J. Skaperda, "Generic Digital Switching System," *Int. Switching Symp. Rec.*, p. 223, 1976.

6. M. H. Esperseth and D. A. Mnichowicz, "GTD-5 EAX—A Family of Digital Switches," *Int. Switching Symp. Rec.,* 1979.

7. J. C. McDonald, "An Integrated Subscriber Carrier and Local Digital Switching System," *Int. Symp. Subscriber Loops and Services Rec.,* p. 172, 1978.

8. R. D. Guenther and T. A. Daugherty, "Introduction of Subscriber Pair Gain Systems," *Int. Symp. on Subscriber Loops and Services Rec.,* p. 4.4.1, 1974.

9. Staff, "Digital Central Office Switching Specification," Continental Telephone Corporation, 1980.

10. J. Ryan, "The Role of the ITU and CCITT in Telecommunications," *Int. Switching Symp. Rec.,* 1974.

11. Rural Electrification Administration, "General Specification for Digital, Stored Program Controlled Central Office Equipment," *REA Form 522,* September 1977.

12. Purchased Products Division, "Class 5 Switching Systems 1978 Study-CDD," American Telephone and Telegraph, 1978.

13. Staff, "Central Office System Requirements and Specifications," United Telecommunications, 1980.

14. H. S. McDonald, "An Experimental Digital Local System," *Int. Switching Symp. Rec.,* p. 212, 1974.

15. N. J. Skaperda, "Some Architectural Alternatives in the Design of a Digital Switch," *IEEE Trans. Commun.,* vol. COM-27(7), p. 961, July 1979.

16. M. Karnaugh, "Design Considerations for a Digital Switch," *Int. Switching Symp. Rec.,* p. 212, 1976.

17. Department of Defense, "Reliability Stress and Failure Rate Data for Electronic Equipment," MIL Handbook 217A December, 1965.

18. Technical Staff, "Engineering and Operations in the Bell System," Western Electric Company, 1978.

19. H. Vaughn, "Research Model for Time-Separation Integrated Communication," *Bell Syst. Tech. J.,* vol. 38, No. 4, pp. 909–932, July 1959.

20. K. Hanawa, S. Yoshida, and P. Yamato, "An Exploratory PCM Switching System DEX-T1," *Rev. Electr. Commun. Lab.,* vol. 16, pp. 253–256, March–April 1968.

21. P. Fritz, "Citedis Production PCM Public Telephone Switching System," *IEEE Trans. Commun.,* vol. COM-22(4), pp. 1264–1268, September, 1974.

22. H. Vaughn, "An Introduction to No. 4 ESS," *Intl. Switching Symposium Record,* pp. 19–25, June, 1972.

23. J. McDonald and J. Baichtal, "A New Integrated Digital Switching System," *Nat. Telecommun. Conf. Rec.,* November, 1976.

24. H. Sueyoshi, N. Shimasaki, A. Kitamura, and T. Yanaguchi, "System Design of Digital Telephone Switching System NEAX 61," *IEEE Trans. Commun.,* vol. COM-27(7), pp. 993–1001, July, 1979.

25. M. Eklund, C. Larson, and K. Sörme, "AXE 10—System Description," *Ericsson Rev.,* No. 2, pp. 70–89, February, 1976.

26. J. Terry, D. Younge, and R. Matsunaga, "A Subscriber Line Interface for the DMS-100 Digital Switch," *Nat. Telecommun. Conf. Rec.,* pp. 28.3.1–28.3.6, 1979.

27. B. Wathinson and B. Voss, "The DMS 10 Digital Switching System, *Nat. Telecommun. Conf. Rec.,* December, 1977.

28. H. Suckfull, "Architecture of a New Line of Digital Switches," *Int. Switching Symp. Rec.,* pp. 221–228, May, 1979.

29. C. Svala, "DSS 1, A Digital Local Switching System with Remote Line Switches," *Nat. Telecommun. Conf. Rec.,* pp. 39: 5-1–39: 5-7, 1977.

30. J. Cox, D. Lawson, J. Deneberg, and F. Van der Brande, "A Digital Switch for Wide Range of Applications," *Int. Commun. Conf. Rec.,* June, 1980.

31. L. Harris, "Introduction to System X," *Int. Switching Symp. Rec.,* pp. 19–25, June, 1972.

32. S. Puccini and R. Wolff, "Architecture of GTD-5 EAX Digital Family," *Int. Commun. Conf. Rec.*, p. 18.2, June, 1980.
33. D. Hinshaw, "Digital Switching Techniques in System Century, DCO," *Nat. Telecommun. Conf. Rec.*, December, 1977.
34. T. Nakajo, M. Hashimoto, and A. Moridera, "Development of a Digital Switching System for Central Office," *Int. Switching Symp. Rec.*, May, 1979.
35. P. Charransol, A. Regnier, and J. Trelut, "Presentation and General Principles of the MT Time Division System," *Int. Switching Symp. Rec.*, May, 1979.
36. K. Kok and S. Liem, "The PRXD Switching System," *Int. Switching Symp. Rec.*, pp. 213–220, May, 1979.
37. P. Charransol, J. Hauri, C. Athenes, and D. Hardy, "A Development of a Time Division Switching Network Usable in a Very Large Range of Capacities," *IEEE Trans. Commun.*, pp. 982–988, July, 1979.
38. J. Bagley, "The No. 3 EAX Digital Switching System," *Electronics and Aerospace Systems Convention Record*, pp. 11-2A–11-2E, September, 1977.
39. F. Andrews and W. Smith, "No. 5 ESS-Overview," *Int. Switching Symp. Rec.*, pp. 31A1–31A1-6, 1981.
40. S. Dal Monte and J. Israel, "Proteo System—UT 10/3: A Combined Local and Toll Exchange," *Int. Switching Symp. Rec.*, pp. 32A2-1–32A2-7, 1981.
41. P. Shackle, A. Hartman, T. Riley, J. North, and J. Berthold, "A 500 V Monolithic Bidirectional 2 × 2 Crosspoint Array," *Int. Sold State Cir. Conf.*, January, 1980.

10

Digital Networks

John C. McDonald

1. Introduction

A digital switching system rarely stands alone and performs its functions for a closed community. Most frequently, the system operates as a node in a network of switching systems. Such networks are formed by design procedures which trade-off transmission and switching cost to minimize overall network cost. When communications services are to be provided over a large geographic area, these procedures yield minimum cost solutions which involve a multiplicity of switching systems. While previous chapters have described the elements and operation of digital switching systems in their own context, this chapter will describe networks of interconnected digital switching systems.

Digital networks provide a unique capability to deliver a wide variety of services to network customers. This capability is particularly important as demand for nonvoice services begins to grow and the deficiencies in the analog network become apparent. This chapter begins with a description of the evolution of telecommunications networks from an all-analog network to an all-digital network. Requirements for digital networks are presented and digital network design is described. Important economies resulting from the integration of digital transmission and digital switching are also described. Separate sections are included on transmission loss plans, synchronization, signaling, and centralized maintenance.

John C. McDonald • MBX Inc., 54 Comstock Hill Road, New Canaan, Connecticut 06840

2. Digital Network Evolution

A network is a means to deliver communications services to customers. The network consists of customer terminal apparatus, transmission means, switching means, maintenance and administration means, and artificial intelligence to properly interpret customer requests for service and cause that service to be provided.

The number of services provided by public networks is growing rapidly as shown in Fig. 1. For over a century, the telephone network has provided simple voice services over analog facilities. Speech has been converted into electrical signals by an analog telephone and these signals have been carried over analog transmission and analog switching facilities to a far end telephone. This network might be called the *integrated analog network* (IAN).

Digital transmission technology, introduced in 1962,[1] was the first departure from the IAN. In 1970, digital local and toll switching was introduced and caused a further departure from the IAN.[2]

In the early 1970s, the needs of communication users began to rapidly expand and these needs continue to grow. By 1981, the trend toward the use of digital transmission and digital switching was very strong and small *integrated digital networks* (IDN) had been formed. With the increased use of digital technology, network planners have tried to maximize the usefulness of their investment by providing both voice and data services over the same facilities. This will lead to the *integrated services digital network* (ISDN).[3]

This section will describe the evolution in communication networks from the IAN to the IDN and then to the ISDN.

2.1. Integrated Analog Network

The integrated analog network (IAN) is

> a switched network providing voice or voice simulated services where cost is minimized through the synergistic application of analog transmission and analog switching technology.

The IAN began with the invention of the telephone in 1876. Analog sonic voice energy was converted into analog electrical energy by Bell's invention. Analog transmission facilities, copper wires, connected two of Bell's telephones. As the demand for voice services expanded, means for analog switching were developed. The analog network grew as new means for analog transmission and analog switching were devised and placed in-service.

Network transmission plans were based on subjective human testing

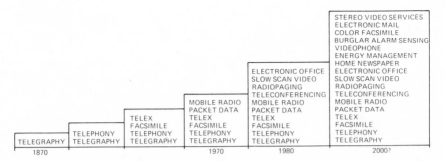

Fig. 1.   Explosive growth in communications services.

relating to the primary IAN service, voice. Information frequency and phase response was optimized for voice. Nonvoice services were provided over voice grade circuits using conversion devices. For example, data are transmitted through the voice network using modems which cause data to "simulate" voice. Modems have also been used to transmit facsimile and other nonvoice information over the voice network.

The IAN has continued to expand and efficiently provide voice services. The trend in this expansion changed in 1962 when digital carrier began to successfully compete with analog carrier. This was the beginning of the integrated digital network.

2.2. Integrated Digital Network

The integrated digital network (IDN) is

a switched network providing voice or voice simulated services where cost is minimized through the synergistic application of digital transmission and digital switching technology.

The IDN began in 1970 when digital switching was introduced in Europe and integrated with digital transmission. Since that time, small IDN islands have been formed around the world. IDN islands, shown in Fig. 2, are growing in size and are becoming contiguous. The services provided by the IDN are identical to the IAN.

An IDN can begin with the introduction of a digital trunk transmission system, a digital pair gain system, or a digital switching system. Interactive economies between digital transmission and digital switching technologies cause the equipment using digital to be less costly than equivalent analog technologies. The "I" in IDN stands for the integration of transmission and switching. Therefore, there is a synergy between digital transmission and digital switching. This synergy is analyzed in more detail in Section 3.2.

Fig. 2.   Locations of digital islands.

A new technology can only be slowly introduced into a communications network because of the substantial investment required. Situations where the new technology can be applied involve new growth or old technology replacement. During the transition period, which lasts for decades, there is a mixture of old and new technology which must cohabit in the network in a compatible fashion. This compatability is discussed in Section 3.1.

In the IAN, data is required to simulate voice for transmission and switching. In the IDN, voice is required to simulate data. Coders and decoders (codecs) are required to convert analog voice into digital and back to analog. But this process is very efficient since new LSI semiconductor technology is available for this purpose.

2.3.   Integrated Services Digital Network

The integrated services digital network (ISDN) is

a switched network providing end-to-end digital transparency where voice and data services are provided using common transmission and switching facilities.

The ISDN is a logical extension of the IDN. The "I" in IDN stands for the integration of transmission and switching whereas the "I" in ISDN stands for the integration of services.

Since the IDN is designed to transmit and switch information in binary form, data can be directly placed on the network bit stream. The IDN can be converted to an ISDN if the customer is given access to this bit stream and the stream flows through the network without modification.

Three significant technologies must be added to the IDN to create an ISDN: digital customer loops, digital long-haul carrier, and common channel signaling. Digital customer loops are required to deliver the bit stream to the customer and digital long-haul carrier is required to interconnect ISDN islands and provide end-to-end digital connectivity. Common channel signaling is required to remove signaling information from the customer channel in μ-law countries and allow the customer to have access to all bits. In addition, common channel signaling is needed to provide additional signaling capability for new services.

The ISDN will evolve from the IDN. The ISDN will have localized IDN beginnings where digital subscriber loops will be added to the IDN and digital long-haul facilities will be installed to connect IDN islands. New services will be defined and we will have an ISDN. New signaling must be provided in the ISDN to switch out digital loss pads and other devices which would prevent digital bit stream transparency.

During the transition interval when the IAN, IDN, and ISDN cohabit, there will be digital overlays to the analog network. Such overlays will include separate packet-switched networks (see Chapter 6 in this volume) and integrated circuit- and packet-switched local switching offices.

Additional modifications must be made to the IDN to create the ISDN. Not only digital customer loops, long-haul digital carrier, and common channel signaling, but also new digital carrier interfaces must be added. Digital carrier over paired cables use regenerative repeaters which require a minimum density of transmitted binary ones. In the United States, the T1 repeater cannot see more than 15 zeros in a row and maintain synchronization. Since data can have an arbitrary information content, new techniques must be implemented to satisfy the ones density requirement. Techniques are used to insert bit errors in the 7th bit position to prevent long strings of zeros. A new DS1 format[4] has been introduced to satisfy the ones density requirement without inserting errors. This new format allows full customer access to the bit stream with no information limitations. In μ-law countries, common channel signaling must be introduced to eliminate bit robbing for signaling and thereby allow a 64 kbit/sec clear channel capability where the new DS1 format is also available.

Thus, an evolution will occur in communications networks from the IAN to the IDN and then to the ISDN. The ISDN will provide end-to-end digital connectivity which will allow the customer to have direct access to a digital bit stream. Many services can be provided over this bit stream including voice, image, data, text, and special residential services. These special residential services could include burglar alarm sensing, utility load shedding, and utility meter reading. While the IAN provides for services integration (data are made to simulate voice), data services will grow more quickly with the ISDN and digital technology will become more efficient than analog for offering a multiplicity of services. This efficiency comes from the simplicity in time division multiplexing. Indeed, some services such as 64 kbit/sec data will only be possible through the use of digital technology.

In the ISDN, a typical customer loop might contain a two-way 80 kbit/sec multiplex: 64 kbit/sec for one information channel, 8 kbit/sec for a second information channel, and 8 kbit/sec for signaling and framing. The 64 kbit/sec channel can be used for high-speed services such as voice, high-speed data, slow scan video, or text transmission. The low-speed channel can be used for keyboard interactive entry and response, utility meter reading, power load shedding, or similar slow-speed information requirements. Thus, the key to services integration lies in the end-to-end digital connectivity provided by the ISDN.

3. Digital Network Design

Network design is the process of establishing the means for delivering the required customer services at the lowest cost consistent with prescribed grades of service. Design of digital networks requires a consideration of many factors including service requirements, revenues, and an economic selection between competing technologies to deliver the services. Design considerations for digital networks will be presented in this section. First, service requirements will be summarized. Then, the network integration concepts of the IDN (integrated transmission and switching) and the ISDN (integrated services) will be discussed. Transmission loss, synchronization, and signaling plans will be presented. The section concludes with a discussion of network maintenance.

3.1. Service Requirements

Networks must provide the means for communication between customers at prescribed grades of service. These service requirements include speed of response, routing errors, blocking, distortion, and a host of others.[5] The network must respond to a customer's request for service within a prescribed time. In the United States, dial tone must be provided within 3 sec on 98.5% of the calls during the average busy season busy hour. Delays beyond 3 sec are allowed for peak busy hours. To guarantee the availability of dial tone, the network must have a high degree of reliability. Switching systems are designed for a down time of less than 2 hr in 40 years.

The network must interpret customer dialing and properly route the call with a minimum of delay to the called customer. Routing errors for intraoffice calls should be less than 2 in 10,000. Network blocking due to traffic congestion should also meet national standards. Different standards are usually set depending on the distance to the called party. For intraoffice calls, the standard might be 1 blocked call in 200. For interoffice calls, the standard might be 1 blocked call in 100 during the busy hour.

The network might be required to have operators for directory assistance or special billing. The network also might be required to provide automatic billing for customer usage.

Various types of communication services might be provided. The most common is voice, but data-related services are growing. Other services might be video, text, burglar alarm sensing, utility load shedding, or utility meter reading.

Customer information must be carried through the network with a minimum of distortion. The sensitivity of customer information to various transmission impairments varies with the type of information. Voice information is particularly sensitive to transmission loss, noise, and echo. Data information is particularly sensitive to bit errors, reframes, and slips. A reframe or a slip only causes a short noise burst which is barely noticeable in a voice conversation. Slips in a facsimile system can cause a permanently distorted reproduction since one portion of a page might be offset from the other. While transmission loss and noise cannot be ignored in data transmission, the impact of these impairments on data is substantially less than their impact on voice.

Both voice and data are sensitive to delay. Delay causes echo to be more objectionable in voice transmission. In data transmission, delay can limit channel throughput due to the means for providing error control. For example, the automatic retransmission request protocol can be used to control network-originated errors. In this protocol, information is transmitted along with an added check word derived from the information. At the far end, a new check word is created from the information and compared against the transmitted check word to detect errors. If an error is detected, a message is sent to the originating end to retransmit the information. With a given bit error rate, delay reduces the effective network throughput. Digital network impairments and their effect on voice and data traffic are summarized in Table 1.

Information bits must pass through a digital network without alteration. This bit stream integrity is important for both voice and data traffic.

Table 1. Digital Network Impairments

	Information Sensitivity	
Impairment	Voice	Data
Transmission loss	High	Medium
Noise	High	Medium
Echo	High	Low
Delay	High	High
Bit errors	Low	High
Reframes	Low	High
Slips	Low	High
Bit/stream integrity	High	High

However, three types of bit stream information manipulators are likely to appear in digital networks: code conversion manipulators (e.g., A- to μ-law), digital loss manipulators (e.g., 2 dB, 3 dB, 6 dB attenuators), and digital echo cancelers.[6] It is unlikely that code conversion would be required within a given network; however, such conversions are obviously required between countries using different voice companding laws. Code conversion can be accomplished in the digital domain or by converting from digital to analog and back to digital. The latter process breaks the end-to-end digital network connectivity and such a converter must be switched out for data calls which directly use the digital bit stream. Network signaling must cause the companding conversion devices to be bypassed for data services.

The μ-law multiplex introduces an additional impairment which harms bit stream integrity. This multiplex uses bit robbing to provide a signaling channel as described in Chapter 7 in this volume. If a means is provided outside the information channel to satisfy repeater requirements for a minimum ones density, the maximum data rate is 56 kbit/sec. This rate increases to 64 kbit/sec when common channel signaling is used and bit robbing is thereby eliminated.

Digital loss pads are inserted in a voice connection to control echo. Clearly these pads must be switched out to prevent distortion for data services which directly access the bit stream. Digital loss should only be placed in the receive side at the far end of a 4-wire connection to simplify control and administration of loss.

Voice services are most sensitive to loss, noise, and echo; digital network standards for these parameters are set by voice requirements. Data services are more sensitive to bit errors, reframes, and slips and, therefore, data services establish the requirements for these parameters. Transmission impairments affecting voice and data services are discussed in the next two sections.

3.1.1 Voice Transmission Requirements

Voice services are particularly sensistive to loss, noise, and echo. Digital network design parameters for loss, noise, and echo are therefore established by the requirements of voice services. These requirements are discussed in this section.

The relationship between network loss and noise has been subjectively established through a series of controlled experiments. Results of these studies[7] are shown in Fig. 3. Subjective ratings of network quality for various levels of loss and noise are given. The noise unit, dBrnC, defines a level of filtered noise (using a "C" frequency response weighting) which is referenced to 90 dB below 1 mW. For example, 15 dBrnC refers to a "C" filtered noise which is 75 dB below a reference at 1 mW. Participants in the test were asked to rate a test circuit as excellent, good, fair, poor, or unsatisfactory and the results are shown. For low values of noise, it can be seen that there is an optimum acoustic loss of approximately 7 dB. Customers would prefer less loss if the connection loss exceeds 7 dB. Similarly, they would desire more loss if the connection loss is less than 7 dB. In this case, voice levels are too loud for human comfort.

It is interesting to study Fig. 3 by holding the noise level constant and examining the effect of changing acoustic loss and then by holding acoustic loss constant and examining the effect of increasing noise. For a constant loss of 7 dB, the circuit rating decreases rapidly once the noise exceeds 35

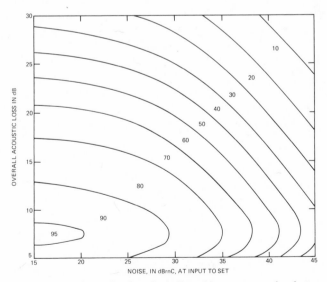

Fig. 3. Loss noise grade of service indicated in percent good or better.

dBrnC. Therefore, the idle channel noise requirement for a digital network might be set at 23 dBrnC. If the noise level is held constant at 23 dBrnC, the circuit rating decreases rapidly when the acoustic loss reaches 15 dB (8 dB more loss than optimum). Thus, network requirements for signal level and noise can be established from Fig. 3.

Crosstalk requirements for the digital network might be set by examining the susceptibility of PCM code words to crosstalk. In 8 bit μ-law PCM, a least significant bit change will cause a signal whose level is -73 dBm. Therefore, crosstalk whose level is less than -73 dBm will not be reproduced in the PCM code except through quantizer enhancement. Therefore, network requirements for crosstalk in μ-law countries might be set at -75 dBm.

Echo is created in a network at the point where hybrid circuits are introduced as shown in Fig. 4. Hybrids are used to create a 4-wire circuit which is required for carrier systems or digital switching. Information from telephone to telephone travels over the primary signal path shown. However, some signal energy will traverse the hybrid from port c to port b. This causes two forms of echo as shown: talker echo and listener echo. Echo creates a voice distortion which can be very objectionable. Echo can make the circuit sound like the speaker is inside a rain barrel. The sound reverberates and is objectionable. In the limit, the 4-wire circuit will oscillate (sing) if the loop gain exceeds unity. However, objectionable echo is created well before the circuit oscillates. The hybrid loss between ports c and b, the transhybrid loss, combined with additional circuit gains and losses must be adequate to minimize echo.

Subjective tests under controlled conditions have been conducted to determine the impact of echo on a voice connection.[8] The results of such

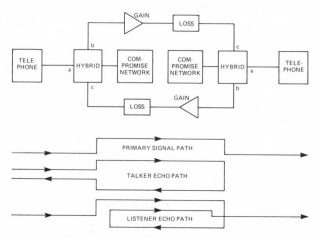

Fig. 4.   Echo generation in a 4-wire office.

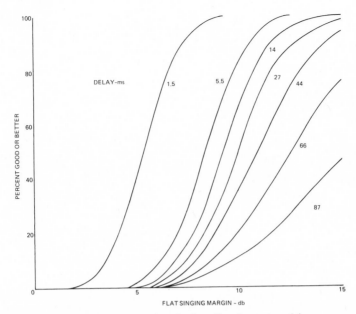

Fig. 5.   Echo grade of service from listening test models.

tests are shown in Fig. 5. Listener opinions using the same measures as before are plotted against singing margins for various 4-wire circuit loop delays. Singing margin is the amount of gain which, when inserted into the 4-wire circuit, would cause unity loop gain. Since transhybrid loss is difficult to control, as discussed in Chapter 7 in this volume, singing margin must be maintained by placing loss in the 4-wire circuit as illustrated in Fig. 4. Placing 1 dB of loss in each leg of the 4-wire circuit will cause a signal loss of 1 dB but will improve the singing margin by 2 dB.

Transmission system propagation delay is primarily a function of the number of tandem low-pass filters and the circuit distance. If the delay is 20 μsec per loop mile and no filters are present, a circuit 500 miles long end to end will have a loop delay of 10 msec. To obtain a circuit rating of 90% good or better, the singing margin must be 11 dB (from Fig. 5). A circuit with a loop delay of 20 msec requires a singing margin of 12.5 dB for the same echo grade of service. Therefore, longer circuits require more loss to maintain an adequate echo grade of service.

But adding loss to control echo also attenuates the signal and there is clearly a conflict between the loss-noise grade of service and the echo grade of service. This conflict has been subjectively studied for circuits of various lengths.[9] For a given circuit length (delay), loss is added which causes the echo grade of service to be improved at the expense of the loss-noise grade of service. Loss is continually added and the two grades of

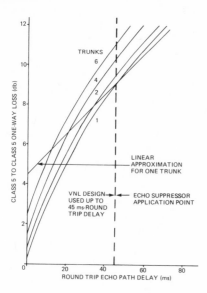

Fig. 6.   Optimum connection loss vs. echo path delay.

service are measured. Finally, an optimum loss is established for a given circuit delay. If the loss exceeds this optimum, the echo grade of service is improved but the loss-noise grade dominates the circuit impairments. If the loss is less than this optimum, the loss-noise grade of service is improved, but then echo is the dominant impairment.

Therefore, there is an optimum loss for each circuit length (delay). Points of optimum loss are plotted against round trip echo path delay in Fig. 6. This curve will be used in Section 3.4 to suggest the design of various network loss plans.

3.1.2.   Data Transmission Requirements

Data services are particularly sensitive to bit errors, slips, and misframes. While these services are also affected by loss, noise, and echo, they are not as sensitive to these parameters as voice services. Thus, voice services set network design parameters for loss, noise, and echo and data services set requirements for bit errors, slips, and misframes. This section discusses these data requirements.

Typical transmission requirements for data in a public telecommunications network are shown in Table 2. The bit error rate objective is less than 1 error in 10^6 bits transmitted on 95% of the calls. Bit errors in a digital network are primarily caused by transmission facilities since the bit error rate through a digital switching system is extremely low. Misframes are created when noise in the transmission facilities becomes sufficiently high to cause a large number of bit errors and the digital switching termination or the digital transmission channel bank loses frame synchronism.

Table 2. Typical Network Requirements for Data

Error rate:
Overall: 10^{-6} on 95% of calls
Trunk allocation (percent of time worse than 10^{-6}):
Toll connecting trunk: 1.5%
Intertoll trunk: 1.0%
Long-haul trunks (percent of time worse than 10^{-6}):
Long-haul facility: 0.5%
Feeder facility: 0.25%

Misframe rate:
Overall: 17 misframes per day
Allocation per trunk: 4 per day

Slip rate:
Overall: one slip per 5 hr
Allocation per trunk: one slip per 20 hr

Reframing techniques must then be applied to hunt for the proper frame as discussed in Chapter 8 in this volume. Slips between digital switching system frames are caused when the clocks establishing the bit rates transmitted between the systems operate at slightly different frequencies. The process by which slips are created has been discussed in Chapter 8 in this volume and is summarized below.

Slips between switching systems are created by the process illustrated in Fig. 7. An incoming data stream buffer is shown which is part of the digital termination of the digital switch. This buffer is used to align the frames between the incoming multiplex and the switching system. A clock is recovered from the incoming multiplex and is used to load data into the buffer register. Data are read out of the buffer by the switching system clock. A serial shift register buffer is illustrated.

If the frequency of the switching system clock is different from the frequency of the clock derived from the incoming multiplex, the point along the buffer where readout occurs will move. If the switching system clock frequency is greater than the incoming multiplex clock, the point along the buffer where readout occurs will advance toward the incoming data port as illustrated. Once the beginning of the register is reached, the readout point

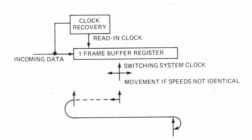

Fig. 7. Generation of slips at a digital termination.

must move to the far end of the register to continue an unbroken stream of bits. A slip thereby occurs and if the buffer is 1 frame long, a frame is repeated.

If the frequency of the switching system clock is less than the frequency of the incoming multiplex clock, the point along the buffer where data are read out will move away from the beginning of the register. When the end of the register is reached, the readout point jumps to the beginning of the register and a slip occurs. In this case an entire frame of data is deleted.

The requirements in Table 2 state that there can be no more than 1 slip in 20 hr for a given trunk. If the buffer register is one frame long, the relative accuracy of the clocks between the two switching systems must be

$$\text{relative clock accuracy} = \frac{125 \ \mu\text{sec}}{(20 \ \text{hr}) \times (36 \times 10^8 \ \mu\text{sec/hr})}$$

$$= 1.74 \times 10^{-9} \qquad (1)$$

Thus, if two digital switching systems are connected together and each has a free-running clock, the difference in frequency between the two clocks must not exceed $1.74 \times 10^{-9} \times$ (clock frequency) to meet the slip rate objective. Techniques for synchronizing the clocks in various switching systems will be discussed in Section 3.5.

3.2. Integrated Transmission and Switching

Overall network cost is reduced in the IDN through the synergistic application of digital transmission and digital switching. The interactive economies of digital transmission and digital switching are so substantial that most telephone administrations have reorganized their design staff to ensure that network designers take advantage of the resulting savings. Analog transmission and analog switching systems compete against their digital counterparts during an economic selection study performed by network designers. If either a digital transmission or switching system is already in place at the start of the study, the interactive economies of digital will favor the digital over the analog alternative in most cases.

Hypothetical network design examples are presented in this section to illustrate the interactive economies of digital transmission and digital switching.

3.2.1. Digital Trunk Transmission

As network traffic grows, new trunks are required between switching systems to reinforce the old trunks and provide the necessary circuits to maintain the desired grade of service. This section will study the cost of providing new trunks using two alternative technologies: digital multiplexing on existing cable and new physical cable pairs. The selection of either multiplexing or new cable will be considered for three switching environments: (1) analog switching at both ends, (2) digital switching at one end and analog at the other, and (3) digital switching at both ends.

The cost of providing digital trunks between two analog switching systems using an existing cable is compared against the cost of providing the new trunks by a new cable in Fig. 8. The cost of providing digital carrier is

$$\text{cost} = 2 \times (\text{analog switching termination})$$

$$+ 2 \times D\text{-banks} + \text{repeatered line} \qquad (2)$$

The T1 repeatered line cost increases with distance since repeaters must be added approximately every 6 kf. Half section spans are required adjacent to each office.

The cost of providing equivalent circuits on new cable is

$$\text{cost} = 2 \times (\text{analog switch termination}) + \text{cable} \qquad (3)$$

This alternative does not require the electronics of D channel banks and repeaters but does require the cost of a new cable, which increases with distance as shown.

As can be seen from Fig. 8, the distance where digital carrier on existing cable has a lower cost than new cable (prove-in distance) is about 5 miles. Therefore, a network designer would select cable if the distance between the offices was less than 5 miles and digital carrier for a distance exceeding 5 miles.

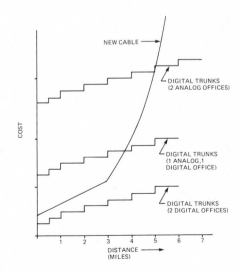

Fig. 8.   Cost comparison between digital carrier on existing pairs to the cost of new pairs.

The second switching environment for comparing the two alternatives is where the trunks are to be reinforced between an analog office at one end and a digital office at the other. In this case, the cost of the digital trunks is given by

$$\text{cost} = 1 \times (\text{digital switch digital termination})$$
$$+ 1 \times (\text{analog switch termination})$$
$$+ 1 \times (D\text{-bank}) + \text{repeatered line} \qquad (4)$$

The cost of the facilities on new cable is

$$\text{cost} = 1 \times (\text{digital switch analog termination})$$
$$+ \text{cable} + 1 \times (\text{analog switch termination}) \qquad (5)$$

In this case, the cost of providing analog trunks, equation (5), is approximately equal to the previous case, equation (3), assuming the cost of the digital switch analog termination is approximately the same as an analog switch termination. The cost of providing digital trunks, equation (4), is less than the previous case, equation (2), since the cost of 1 D-bank is eliminated and the digital switch digital termination has lower cost than the analog switch termination in the prior case. The prove-in distance is now about 3.7 miles, also shown in Fig. 8.

The final case is where the required trunks are between two digital switching offices. In this case, the cost of providing digital carrier on the existing cable is

$$\text{cost} = 2 \times (\text{digital switch digital termination}) + \text{repeatered line} \qquad (6)$$

The cost of providing analog trunks is

$$\text{cost} = 2 \times (\text{digital switch analog termination}) + \text{cable} \qquad (7)$$

The analog trunk cost is approximately the same as that given by equations (3) and (5). The digital alternative now requires no D-channel banks and the digital switch digital termination is lower in cost than the analog switch termination. As can be seen, the digital alternative is always lower in cost than the new cable alternative and the prove-in distance is zero.

Figure 8 illustrates the interactive economies between digital transmission and digital switching. Digital transmission facilities can be provided at substantially lower cost in the presence of digital switching than in the presence of analog switching.

3.2.2 Digital Toll Switching

The selection between transmission technologies to provide trunk reinforcement in the presence of analog and digital switching has been analyzed in the previous section. Results show that digital transmission technology is heavily favored in the presence of digital switching. The interactive economies of digital transmission and digital switching will be illustrated in this section by comparing the cost of analog and digital toll switching systems in the presence of various quantities of digital carrier.

Digital transmission systems have found extensive use as a short-haul carrier system. There are many locations today where analog switching systems are surrounded by a substantial number of trunks using digital technology. When the analog switching office reaches the end of its service life, the selection between analog and digital switching technology for the replacement office is influenced by the penetration of digital carrier. The cost of these two alternatives is analyzed below.

The cost of the analog switch is

$$\text{cost} = \text{analog switching network} + \text{analog terminations} + \text{control} \quad (8)$$

The cost of a digital switch is

$$\text{cost} = \text{digital switching network}$$
$$+ \text{ digital terminations}$$
$$+ \text{ analog terminations} + \text{control} \quad (9)$$

Figure 9 illustrates the digital switching case. The cost of a digital switching system decreases with an increasing percentage of already present digital trunks. This is true since digital terminations for the digital trunks cost less than analog terminations for analog trunks. There is an additional bonus in the digital switching alternative if the D-banks which are no longer needed for interfacing the digital repeatered line to the switch can be reused at another location.

The analog switch cost is constant irrespective of the number of digital trunks in place.

In an environment where there are no digital trunks, the cost of a digital switch might exceed the cost of an analog switch since analog terminations on the digital switch cost more than the same terminations on an analog switch. As the percentage of digital trunks increases, however, the digital switch cost will decline while the cost of the analog switch will stay

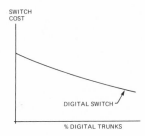

Fig. 9.   Cost of a toll switching system in the presence of various quantities of digital trunks.

constant. In a given situation, the cost of the two systems will depend on many factors including the number of trunks, available building space, and future planned services.

This further illustrates the interactive economics of digital transmission and digital switching.

3.2.3.   Digital Pair Gain

As the number of customers on the network grows, new facilities must be added to connect the customers to the local switching office. Pair gain systems, described in Chapter 9 in this volume, are an important technology for minimizing the cost of providing this growth. The cost of pair gain systems in the presence of both analog and digital switching is presented in this section.

Two cases will be considered: digital pair gain with analog local switching and digital pair gain with digital local switching. In each case, the cost of the pair gain system using existing cable is compared against the cost of new cable.

First consider the analog switching case. The cost of providing the new facilities is

$$\text{cost} = \text{analog switch termination}$$
$$+ \text{ pair gain central office terminal}$$
$$+ \text{ repeatered line} + \text{remote terminal} \qquad (10)$$

The cost of the new facilities using new cable is

$$\text{cost} = \text{analog switch termination} + \text{cable} \qquad (11)$$

Both costs are plotted in Fig. 10.

The cost of cable increases with distance at a nonlinear rate since the wire gauge must be increased at various distances to minimize transmission loss. A network goal might be to keep the customer loop loss below 8 dB. The distance where the digital pair gain system on existing pairs equals the cost of new cable in an analog switching environment is about 4.3 miles.

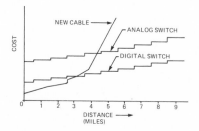

Fig. 10.   Cost comparison between providing customer loops using pair gain systems on existing pairs vs. new cable pairs.

The second case illustrates the use of digital pair gain systems with digital local switching. In this case, the cost of the new facilities is given by

$$\text{cost} = \text{digital switch digital termination}$$

$$+ \text{ repeatered line} + \text{remote terminal} \qquad (12)$$

This cost is also plotted in Fig. 10. The cost of the new cable alternative is approximately the same as given by equation (11). Since the cost of the digital termination on the digital switch is substantially less than the cost of the analog switch termination plus the pair gain central office terminal, the cost of a digital pair gain system in the presence of digital local switching is substantially less as shown. The distance where the pair gain system equals the cost of new cable is reduced to about 3.2 miles. While the difference in prove-in distance between the two cases might not seem consequential, the digital case can reach 2 to 3 times more customers than in the analog case.[10] This further illustrates the interactive economies of digital transmission and digital switching and their impact on network cost.

In summary, this section has illustrated how the integration of digital transmission and digital switching can reduce network cost. The IDN will be formed as network designers recognize the importance of integrating transmission and switching and find that digital transmission and digital switching provide substantial savings over equivalent analog technology. Network design studies[11] have shown that savings using digital technology in the IDN can be as high as 50% over analog technology in the IAN. While these massive savings might not be possible in all network applications, the importance of the IDN cannot be overlooked.

3.3. Integrated Services

Network evolution from the IAN to the ISDN has been presented in Section 2. In summary, the IAN provides voice or voice-simulated services using analog transmission and analog switching technologies. Interactive economies of digital transmission and digital switching cause the IDN to be formed. The services provided by the IDN are the same as the IAN. In both networks, digital data must be transformed and made to appear like voice for transmission over the network. The ISDN is created by adding digital customer loops, digital long-haul carrier facilities, and common channel signaling to the IAN or IDN. Then end-to-end digital connectivity is provided.

The ISDN of the future might resemble the network shown in Fig. 11. Customers satisfied with simple voice services will be served by analog customer loops provided directly from the central office or from digital pair gain systems. If these customers wish to send data, they must use a modem

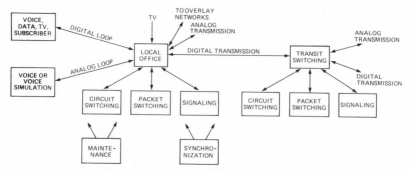

Fig. 11.   Hypothetical integrated services digital network structure.

to simulate voice over the analog loop. Customers desiring high-speed data and other new services will be connected to the central office by a digital customer loop. The digital loop might provide new functions such as utility power load shedding, burglar alarm sensing, or utility meter reading. Variable bit rate services might be provided with charging based on bit rate (bandwidth). The customer might wish to have circuit-switched or packet-switched data depending on his or her particular requirements. Voice must be converted into a digital form to be compatible with the digital transmission facility. This is an interesting turnabout from the IAN where data must be converted into a voice format.

The local switch must provide the artificial intelligence to properly interpret the customer's request for service and properly deliver the requested service. The switch shown in Fig. 11 provides both circuit and packet switching as described in Chapter 6 in this volume. Both types of switching can have access to the same digital trunks.

Signaling between the customer and the local switch and between the local switch and transit switching systems is accomplished using common channel signaling. Transit switching systems also provide both circuit- and packet-switching functions. Existing analog carrier systems or analog switching systems of the IAN might interface the ISDN using analog transmission facilities. Analog local switching systems might be converted to ISDN nodes by applying digital customer loops through junctor circuits with digital trunk interfaces.[12]

Other digital or analog transmission facilities might be provided to separate overlay networks which may operate in parallel with a primary network. Each network might be customized to serve specific functions such as facsimile, packet data, voice, or video. Information requiring high bandwidth such as television might bypass the switch and be directly applied to the customer loop. Television signals might also be directly transmitted to homes via satellites.

Thus, the integration of services over common facilities might evolve into the ISDN. As the ISDN develops, it is possible that separate long-haul networks might be used to deliver a wide variety of services[13] and facilities integration might only occur at the customer loop. The prime reason for the evolution to the ISDN is to provide important new services to satisfy an increasing demand for communications at low cost.

3.4. Transmission Loss and Level Plans

Network requirements for voice transmission have been presented in Section 3.1. It has been shown that there is a conflict between the loss noise grade of service and the echo grade of service. Further, it was stated that voice is more sensitive to loss and noise than is data and therefore the overall network requirements for these parameters are set by voice services.

Transmission loss and level plans are presented in this section. These plans are used to control the loss-noise and echo grades of service. Loss plans for analog and digital networks are first presented. Then, level plans for digital networks are presented and examples are given.

It is desirable to have zero loss through a digital switch for intraoffice calls to maintain high levels of transmission. But, it is necessary to insert loss on interoffice calls to control echo. Inserting loss in the IAN is relatively easy since loss can be added in each trunk circuit between offices. Loss then becomes additive as information travels along via each trunk route in the connection. This plan is called the via net loss (VNL) plan[14] and is used extensively in the United States.

In a digital network, loss is more difficult to add at each trunk in the network since quantizing distortion would be added at each loss point. It is therefore desirable to have digital loss inserted only at one point, the receive end of a digital connection. Since loss is only located at one place in the network and this loss is constant irrespective of the number of tandem trunks in the circuit, this plan is called the fixed loss plan.[15]

Design rules for the via net loss plan can be obtained from a linear approximation to the curves in Fig. 6 which give the optimum loss for a given path delay. This linear approximation for one trunk is

$$\text{loss} = 4.4 \text{ dB} + 0.1 \text{ dB/msec} \tag{13}$$

Each additional trunk adds about 0.4 dB of additional needed loss. Equation (13) is implemented in the via net loss plan shown in Fig. 12a. Local switches have no loss and 2.5 dB of loss + VNL is allocated to toll connecting trunks, where

$$\text{VNL} = 0.4 \text{ dB} + 0.1 \text{ dB/msec} \tag{14}$$

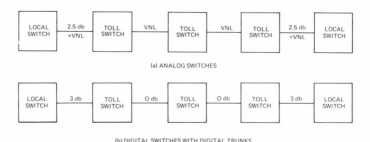

Fig. 12.   Loss plan to maintain an adequate echo grade of service.

Intertoll trunks have a loss established by the VNL formula. The end-to-end loss for toll calls is therefore 5.0 dB + VNL.

When the round-trip delay of a trunk exceeds 45 msec, about 1600 miles, the loss required to provide an adequate echo grade of service yields an unacceptable loss-noise grade of service. Rather than continuing to add loss in such cases, other means of echo control are used such as echo suppressors or echo cancellers.

The echo supressor[16] breaks the 4-wire loop in one direction to eliminate echo. The suppressor detects the presence of speech and opens the circuit in the reverse direction. Speech detection must rapidly occur to prevent impairment of the normal two-way communication process. Of course, two people cannot be simultaneously heard in the presence of an echo suppressor.

Echo cancellers[17] provide a means for controlling echo by estimation and subtraction. Customer information estimates are subtracted from echo path information to minimize the echo component. The process rapidly converges to provide an adequate echo grade of service. Two speakers can be simultaneously heard in the presence of echo cancellers. Digital echo cancellers must be bypassed when end-to-end digital connectivity is required.

It is undesirable to implement the VNL plan in an all digital network as previously described. The fixed loss plan has therefore been established. The fixed loss plan for the United States is illustrated in Fig. 12b. Local switches have no loss and toll connecting trunks have 3 dB loss. Toll switches and intertoll trunks have no loss. Some national networks have used a fixed loss plan rather than VNL for the all-analog network. In these cases, the loss is identical for intra- and interoffice calling.

As digital switching and digital transmission is introduced into an analog network, design rules must be established to control echo with this mixture of analog and digital technology. Such a typical set of design rules are shown in Fig. 13. Figure 13a shows a loss rule for analog intertoll trunks between a digital and an analog toll switch. As shown, echo should

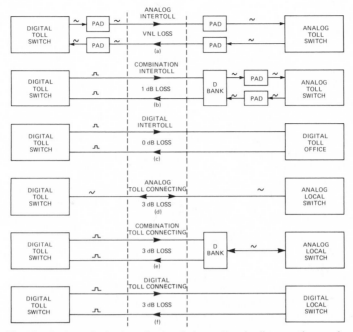

Fig. 13. Design rules for inserting loss in intertoll and toll connecting trunks.

be controlled by inserting loss using VNL rules. Figure 13b shows a digital toll switch connected with an analog toll switch over a "combination" intertoll trunk where a digital channel bank is co-located with the analog toll switch. This trunk is designed with a 1 dB loss.

Figure 13c illustrates a digital intertoll trunk between two digital toll switches. This trunk should have 0 dB loss. Figure 13d illustrates an analog toll connecting trunk between a digital toll switch and an analog local switch. This trunk should have 3 dB loss. Figure 13e illustrates a "combination" toll connecting trunk between a digital toll switch and an analog local switch. In this case, a digital channel bank is co-located with the analog local switch. This trunk should have a 3 dB loss. Figure 13f illustrates a digital toll connecting trunk between a digital toll switch and a digital local switch. This trunk should have a 3 dB loss.

The rules illustrated in Fig. 13 provide for an orderly transition between the IAN and the IDN or ISDN. These rules provide an optimum compromise between the loss-noise grade of service and the echo grade of service.

Performance of a network designed under the VNL and fixed loss rules is shown in Fig. 14.[18] Loss-noise and echo grades of service under both loss design schemes are shown. Figure 14a shows that VNL rules cause the loss-noise grade of service to rapidly deteriorate for calls covering

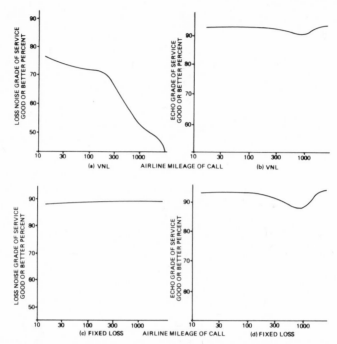

Fig. 14.   Comparison of loss noise and echo grade of service for digital and analog networks.

a long distance. The echo grade of service under VNL rules is quite good, as shown in Fig. 14b.

Under fixed loss rules, a smaller loss is inserted in circuits operating over long distances compared with the loss specified by VNL. Therefore one can expect a better loss-noise grade of service but a slightly degraded echo grade of service as shown in Figs 14c and 14d.

The IDN or ISDN should therefore provide for higher-quality voice service than the IAN due to a substantially improved loss-noise grade of service at the sacrifice of a minor degradation in the echo grade of service.

3.4.1.   Digital Code Levels

Analog voice signals must be converted into digital for transmission through a digital network. If 8-bit PCM is used, there are 256 possible code words. For compatible operation between switching systems from different manufacturers it is necessary for the code words to have agreed upon signal levels.

The PCM words by themselves do not set equivalent analog levels. For example, the code of 11111111 can arbitrarily represent 1 mV, 1 V, or 1,000,000 V. A standard level must be established between an analog signal

Table 3. Digital Milliwatt Definition

(i)	00011110	(iii)	00001011	(v)	10011110	(vii)	10001011
(ii)	00001011	(iv)	00011110	(vi)	10001011	(viii)	10011110

and its equivalent digital code. Such a standard is shown in Table 3 where a series of PCM words are defined and represent a digital milliwatt tone. These 8 PCM words are repeated to provide a sinusoidal digital milliwatt signal at 1 kHz. Once the digital milliwatt is defined, all PCM code words correspond to exact analog levels for given companding law.

Digital network levels are standardized by the digital milliwatt definition and by specifying the analog signal at any digital switch or carrier system termination which is required to produce the digital milliwatt. This analog level is called the encode level point. At the decoder, the analog signal which is produced by the digital milliwatt is called the decode level point.

By defining the encode level point, decode level point, digital milliwatt, and companding law, exact correspondency between analog levels and digital codes are established in the digital network. These definitions allow compatibility between switching and transmission systems from various manufacturers and between networks of various administrations.

3.4.2. Digital Loss Design Examples

Loss must be inserted in a digital network to control echo. The fixed loss and via net loss plans have been discussed and design rules have been presented for a network with a mixture of analog and digital technology. Application of these design rules to a hypothetical network is illustrated in this section. Loss measurement techniques are first discussed and then design examples are presented.

A network connection consists of a series of transmission elements including cable, switching systems, and carrier systems, each of which produce gains and losses in transmission levels. It is necessary to define the signal magnitude at any point in the network relative to a fixed datum which is called the transmission level point (TLP). The Class 5 office in the United States is a 0 dB reference and is defined as a 0 TLP office.

A typical transmission loss measuring configuration is shown in Fig. 15. Two offices are shown with transmission test apparatus. Each office has a defined TLP value and an attenuator equal to the TLP value is inserted between an analog power source and the office and between an analog power measuring meter and the office. In a digital office, the TLP is equal to the encode level point (or the decode level point which has the same value).

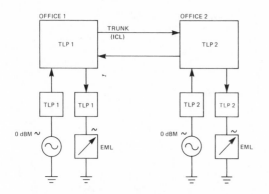

Fig. 15. Measurement procedure for determining network signal levels.

The expected measured loss (EML) is the loss measured according to Fig. 15 when a 1-mW analog sinusoid at 1004 Hz is applied as shown. The frequency differs slightly from 1 kHz to prevent a low-frequency meter reading fluctuation caused by quantizing noise which creates amplitude modulation whose frequency is proportional to the difference between harmonics of the test frequency and the sampling frequency.

The expected measured loss between the two offices is

$$\text{EML (dB)} = -\text{TLP 1 (dB)} + \text{ICL (dB)} - \text{TLP 2 (dB)} \qquad (15)$$

where ICL is the trunk insertion connection loss required to obtain VNL or fixed loss objectives. Examples of loss design using this measurement technique will now be given.

Figure 16 shows a hypothetical network consisting of one digital switching system, one digital remote unit, two analog switching systems, three digital carrier systems, and one analog carrier system. Digital Office *A*

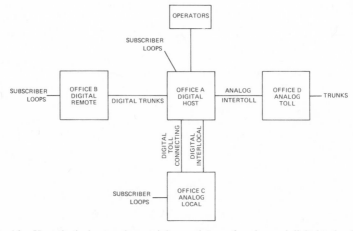

Fig. 16.   Hypothetical network containing a mixture of analog and digital technology.

Table 4. Services and Levels Provided on Trunks between Office *A* and Office *B*

Local to	ICL (dB)	Digital pad (dB)
Local	0	0
Toll connecting	3	6
Intertoll	3	6
Interlocal	3	3
Switchboard	3	6
Recorded ann.	3	6
Busy verify	6	6
Maintenance panel	3	6
Transponder	0	0

provides for a combination of switching functions: local, toll tandem, and interlocal tandem. It also provides host functions for Digital Remote Office *B*.

Each digital trunk connecting Office *A* with Office *B* can provide for a number of services as shown in Table 4. The ICL for each of these services is also shown. Since various values of ICL are necessary to satisfy the requirements defined in Fig. 13, a means must be provided to switch loss depending on the service. For this example we will assume that loss is provided by switchable digital attenuators (pads) which are controlled by the system controller in Office *A* and are selected on the basis of the number dialed.

Consider an intraoffice call originating in Office *B*. The desired ICL is 0 dB and since a local office is a 0 TLP office, the EML from equation (15) is 0 dB. Referring to Fig. 17, the analog test oscillator at 0 dBm causes the digital milliwatt to occur in the Office *B* PCM bit stream since the encode level point is 0 dB. This bit stream is sent to Office *A*, where it is switched back to Office *B*. The decode level point is 0 dB, and the digital milliwatt causes 0 dB to be measured at the meter. No digital attenuation is applied for this connection. Voltages from customer loops are applied to identical terminations and are therefore treated in an identical way.

Transmission loss for a circuit between Offices *B* and *D* will now be illustrated. In this example, the trunk connecting Offices *A* and *B* is toll connecting and the trunk between Offices *A* and *D* is intertoll. From Fig.

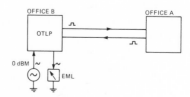

Fig. 17.   Transmission levels between Office *A* and Office *B* for the network of Fig. 16.

13, the ICL between Offices A and B is 3 dB and the ICL between Offices A and D is VNL.

Transmission measurements for this case are illustrated in Fig. 18. First consider the toll connecting trunks between Offices A and B. Office B is a 0 TLP office and Office A is a -3 TLP office. The desired ICL is 3 dB. From equation (15)

$$\text{EML } (A \text{ to } B) = 0 + 3 \text{ dB} + 3 \text{ dB}$$

$$= 6 \text{ dB} \tag{16}$$

Now tracing the signal levels between Offices A and B, the analog milliwatt signal at Office B creates the digital milliwatt since the encode level point is 0 dB. The digital milliwatt is sent to Office A, where the decode level point is -3 dBm. The digital milliwatt from Office B therefore creates a -3-dBm analog signal at the analog output of Office A. This signal is attenuated by an additional 3 dB and the EML is properly measured at 6 dB per equation (16).

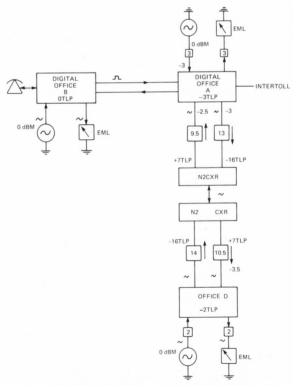

Fig. 18.   Transmission levels between Offices A and B and A and D for the network of Fig. 16.

Since it is desirable for transmission loss through the network to be symmetrical, the EML measured at Office B should also be 6 dB. The analog milliwatt source at Office A is attenuated by 3 dB and applied to an Office A termination. The encode level point for Office A is -3 dBm and therefore the digital milliwatt bit stream is created. If no attenuation was applied in Office B, the meter at Office B would read 0 dB. However, we want an EML of 6 dB. Therefore, a 6-dB digital attenuator is inserted in the receive direction only for this connection and the EML is measured at 6 dB per equation (16). The stored program control in Office A causes this attenuation to be switched in.

Transmission between Office A and Office D is also illustrated in Fig. 18. The ICL for this trunk group is designed using VNL which is 0.5 dB for this case. The EML for this trunk from equation (15) is

$$\text{EML } (A \text{ to } D) = 3 + 2 + 0.5$$

$$= 5.5 \text{ dB} \qquad (17)$$

Figure 18 shows that the analog trunks between Offices A and D are derived using N2 analog multiplex carrier facilities. The various transmission levels for this connection will now be illustrated. The analog milliwatt source at Office A produces a level of 0 dBm. This signal is applied through a 3-dB attenuator to a digital switch termination. The encode level point is -3 dBm at Office A and the digital milliwatt bit stream is created in Office A. Since we have an analog trunk facility, the digital milliwatt in Office A is converted back to a -3 dBm analog signal (decode level point is -3 dBm) for application to the analog carrier system.

The analog carrier system test level points are -16 dBm on transmit and $+7$ dBm on receive. Full scale analog modulation will be caused by an analog signal of -16 dBm applied at the transmit termination. This -16 dBm signal will be reproduced at the far end at $+7$ dBm. Therefore, an attenuation of 13 dB must be inserted between the carrier system input and Office A.

The carrier system delivers an output signal of $+7$ dBm which is attenuated by 10.5 dB and applied at Office D. This signal must be attenuated by 10.5 dB before it is applied to a termination at the analog toll switch to produce the desired EML. Since Office D is lossless, the -3.5 dBm signal level also appears at the switch output. This signal is attenuated by an additional 2 dB and the EML is measured at 5.5 dB as required by equation (17).

In the other transmission direction, the analog milliwatt source at Office D is attenuated by 2 dB and applied to the switch at a level of -2 dBm. The output of the switch is attenuated by 14 dB to cause the desired full-scale carrier system modulation. The carrier system output, $+7$ dBm, is attenuated by 9.5 dB to provide a -2.5-dBm signal at Office A which is required to produce the desired EML. The -2.5-dBm signal produces a digital signal which is 0.5 dB above the digital milliwatt in Office A. Typically the overload point for an analog-to-digital converter is $+3$ dBm and therefore this $+0.5$-dBm signal does not cause overload. The $+0.5$-dB digital signal is decoded at -2.5 dBm and is attenuated by 3 dB to give the desired EML of 5.5 dB.

This example illustrates a typical loss and level transmission plan in a network which combines analog and digital switching and carrier technologies. It also illustrates the need for switchable loss pads when a single digital circuit can carry information to destinations requiring different values of loss. Loss can be inserted using either analog or digital techniques. Digital attenuators must be switched out when end-to-end digital transparency is required. Appropriate network signaling must be provided to control these attenuators.

3.5. Synchronization

Synchronization must be provided in a digital network to prevent slips as described in Section 3.1.2. Slip requirements for a typical network are given in Table 2. Techniques for providing the required digital network synchronization are presented in this section. Synchronization between digital transmission and digital switching systems is first discussed and then synchronization between the switching systems is presented.

3.5.1 Synchronizing Digital Transmission and Digital Switching

Two digital transmission systems are shown in Fig. 19a. Each system consists of two back-to-back digital channel banks with a corresponding repeatered span line. The transmit side of each channel bank has its own oscillator to create timing. The receive side at the far end of the span line derives its timing from the received pulse stream. Therefore, there are four separate oscillators in the example. The transmit and receive sides of a given channel bank operate asynchronously. The transmission system shown operates satisfactorily since the receive sides are synchronized with the far end transmit side.

Terminations at the channel banks are permanently connected to each other through the digitally derived circuit. Channel 1 is always connected to the far end channel 1, 2 to 2, and so forth. The configuration of Fig. 19a can be given more flexibility if a digital switching system is inserted in the middle of the span lines as shown in Fig. 19b. Then any termination can be connected to any other termination under control of the digital switch. Synchronization in this new configuration will now be examined.

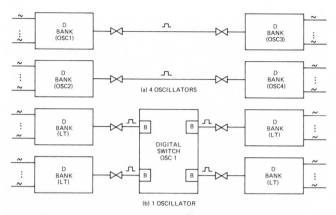

(a) 4 OSCILLATORS

(b) 1 OSCILLATOR

Fig. 19.   Synchronization requirements for digital systems.

Since the digital bit streams from each channel bank arrive at the digital switch in arbitrary frame phase, a buffer (B) must be added to the digital switch to cause frame alignment within the switch. This buffer is discussed in Chapter 9 in this volume. The oscillators in each digital channel bank have a frequency which can differ from each other by as much as 1 part in 3×10^{-5} (normal D-bank stability). If we assume that the digital switch has an oscillator with the same stability and the buffer is 125 μsec long, the average time between slips is

$$\text{slip time} = \frac{125 \ \mu\text{sec}}{3 \times 10^{-5}}$$

$$= 4.2 \text{ sec} \tag{18}$$

The network requirement in Table 2 specifies that slips should not occur more frequently than 1 every 20 hr. Therefore, synchronization of the channel banks to the digital switch is required. This is accomplished by operating the channel banks in the "loop timed" (LT) mode. In this mode, the transmit oscillators in each channel bank are locked to the received bit stream whose frequency originates from the digital switch oscillator. No slips will occur in this mode. The channel banks operate in bit synchronism with the switch but not in frame synchronism. The buffer at the switch input establishes frame synchronization. Thus, slip requirements are met by loop timing in the D channel banks in Fig. 19b.

In μ-law countries, frame periodicity is 12 frames to accommodate signaling. To preserve master frame synchronization, the buffer, B, must be 12 frames long. This would result in a possible 1.5-msec buffer delay which would cause an unacceptable echo impairment. The buffer is therefore only 1 frame long for most designs and therefore signaling on the outgoing bit stream most likely occurs during a different frame than signaling on the incoming frame. This is true since the digital switch frame counter establishes the time for outgoing frames 6 and 12 which are most likely different from the times that incoming frames 6 and 12 occur. Therefore, additional least significant bits are lost as the PCM words traverse the switch due to the bit robbing signaling technique. Ultimately, all least significant bits are lost as the signal traverses many digital switching systems in tandem. The effects of this bit robbing are further described in Chapter 8 in this volume.

When common channel signaling is introduced, bit robbing to accomplish signaling will be stopped and this impairment will disappear. To obtain a clear channel 64-kbit/sec capability, additional changes must be made to keep repeaters alive and remove maintenance information from the bit stream as described in Section 2.2.

3.5.2. Synchronizing Digital Switching Systems

Synchronization between switching systems in a network is required to prevent slips. The clocks in each system can be synchronized by the techniques shown in Fig. 20 or slips can be minimized by plesiochronous operation. In the synchronous case, the frequency of the clock at each switching system is externally controlled so that all switches operate at identical frequencies. In the plesiochronous case, the switching system clocks are independent but their frequencies are accurately controlled within narrow limits.

Slips might be controlled between nations using the plesiochronous mode. This would avoid the international politics of master–slave relations.

(a) MASTER SLAVE

(b) HIERARCHIAL MASTER SLAV

(c) MUTUAL

(d) CENTRALIZED REFERENCE

Fig. 20. Techniques for synchronizing systems in a digital network.

National atomic standards could tightly control the frequency of switching systems within national boundaries and slips would be infrequent. National networks then can use any of the synchronization schemes shown in Fig. 20.

A master–slave scheme is illustrated in Fig. 21. Various clock accuracies are required depending on the network configuration. In Fig. 21a, the master switch sets the frequency of a slave switch and a number of digital channel banks. The digital channel banks operate in the loop-timed mode where their transmit clock is derived from their associated digital switch. The clock of the slave switch is frequency or phase locked to the master and timing is derived from the bit stream on the connecting digital trunk. In this simple example, the frequency accuracy of the master oscillator need only be sufficient to keep the repeatered line alive.

A more complex network is shown in Fig. 21b. The clock in the master again need only have sufficient accuracy to keep the repeatered lines alive. If the network of Fig. 21b is slightly modified to include a digital trunk between the slave switches, a more complex synchronization situation exists. Shown in Fig. 21c, all three digital switching systems in this network now require high stability clocks to meet the network slip rate objectives in the presence of a fault. If synchronization is lost between the master and one slave, the two slaves will operate in a plesiochronous mode and the

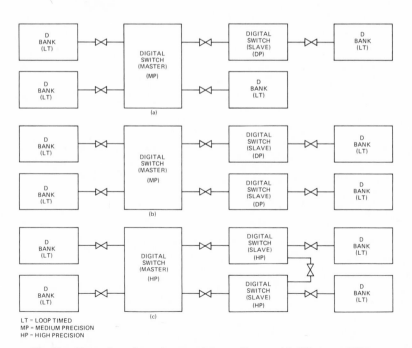

LT = LOOP TIMED
MP = MEDIUM PRECISION
HP = HIGH PRECISION

Fig. 21.   Network configurations requiring oscillators with different stabilities.

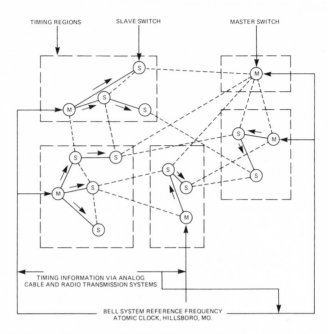

Fig. 22.   Synchronization plan for the United States Public Telecommunications Network.

network slip objectives must be met. This requires a relative clock accuracy of at least 1.7×10^{-9}. One slave could derive its timing from the other but this would require a synchronization switching scheme which would be difficult to administer as the network grows.

The synchronization plan for the United States Telephone Network[19] is shown in Fig. 22. This is a hierarchical master/slave approach with an atomic standard providing the national reference. Timing regions have been established across the country and master switching systems receive the atomic standard via analog cable and radio transmission systems. Slave switching systems receive their timing from the 8-kHz framing pulses on digital trunks from the master. Solid lines indicate the flow of synchronization. Dotted lines indicate trunks which are not used for synchronization.

Table 5. USA Network Synchronization

Clock stratum	Type of clock	Clock accuracy
1	Atomic standard	$< 1 \times 10^{-11}$
2	Master	$< 1.7 \times 10^{-9}$
3	Slave	$< 3.7 \times 10^{-7}$
4	D bank	$< 5.0 \times 10^{-5}$

3.6. Signaling

Signaling is the means whereby switching systems communicate with each other. Signaling is required to seize trunks, transmit customer dialed information, return answer supervision, and release trunks. Signaling channels are also used to provide many new customer services.

In the integrated analog network, signaling is accomplished using tones within the voice spectrum to represent digits. The process of sending a dialed number using multifrequency tones takes a few seconds per office and, for a long-distance connection, the signaling interval could lie between 15 and 20 sec. Signaling in the IAN is usually sent over the same trunk which would subsequently be used for the conversation. Special protocols have been established to allow switching systems to communicate.[20]

Stored program controlled networks can signal more efficiently using digital messages which are sent over dedicated signaling circuits. These circuits connect switching system processors either directly or by tandem signal transfer points (STP). Signaling is not sent through the trunk which will also carry the conversation. This is called common channel signaling since signaling for many trunks is sent over one common signaling channel. Common channel signaling has many advantages over in-band signaling including the following:

- Reduces call setup time;
- Eliminates false customer simulated in-band signaling;
- Provides for more signaling information;
- Reduces trunk holding times;
- Eliminates the need for multifrequency senders, receivers, and single frequency units;
- Provides for many new services;
- Eliminates bit robbing in the μ-law multiplex.

For these reasons, most national networks are planning to use common channel signaling.

International standards have been set for common channel signaling systems by CCITT[21,22] called signaling systems No. 6 and No. 7.

The common channel signaling approach for the United States telephone network is shown in Fig. 23.[23] The nation has been divided into 10 regions and each region contains at least two signal transfer points (STP). One region is shown in the figure. The STP performs a transit switching function for signaling information. Stored program controlled switching offices in the region have circuits to each regional STP called A links. The two primary STPs in each region have direct signaling links to every other STP in the national network over B links. The two STPs per region are used for redundancy and each switching office can reach either STP. STPs

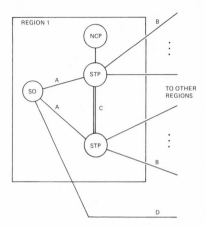

Fig. 23. Common channel signaling network including signaling routes, signaling switching points, and network data bases.

within a region communicate over C links. If a switching office has a high usage trunk route to a switching office in another region, a signaling route can be established which bypasses the STPs called a *D* link. Since *D* links travel along the same route as the conversation trunks, they are called associated signaling links. *A* links are not associated with the trunk route since signaling is accomplished via the STP.

When an interoffice call is detected in the switching office (SO), a series of messages containing the called party and desired trunk is sent to the STP. The STP forwards this information to the destination office and the talking path is established. The STPs provide a more economical signaling path for small trunk groups than the associated signaling approach.

Common channel signaling can also be used to access large data bases located at network control points (NCP). This data base can be used for such services as unassisted credit card calling and national number calling. Many of the potential services associated with the ISDN require the flexibility provided by the common channel signaling network.

3.7. Maintenance

Communications networks consist of complex transmission and switching systems which employ a variety of technologies from the most modern to those which are decades old. These networks are designed to provide a prescribed level of availability to the network customers. Availability objectives are only met when failures in network elements are rapidly detected and repaired. Maintenance of such networks is therefore a vital factor in establishing network availability.

Communications networks are maintained by trained craftspeople who generally have secondary educations but come to the operating administration with no previous technical training. Candidates are sent to maintenance school to study the specific equipment to which they will be assigned. As communications systems have grown and become complex, operating administrations have relied heavily on automatic system self-testing combined with centralized surveillance and trouble shooting to reach availability objectives. Minicomputer-based systems have brought an important new technology to the field of communications network maintenance.

Electronic systems present a new challenge to craftspeople who are only familiar with electromechanical equipment. The new electronic equipment is much more complex and therefore more difficult to troubleshoot than electromechanical equipment. The craftsperson can neither hear nor see improper operation.

Finally, modern electronic equipment has an extremely low failure rate and the maintenance procedures which have been taught in the training school are often forgotten before they can be practically applied.

Because of the different requirements of electromechanical and electronic equipment, new concepts in maintenance are now being implemented. A major new concept is the centralization of many testing and troubleshooting functions which have been previously accomplished at the site of the equipment.

Faults in the network can be detected either through local self-test or centralized routine tests. When the fault is detected, a local craftsperson can attempt to clear the fault. In electronic systems, this is generally accomplished through circuit board substitution and system testing. Most systems have a high degree of built-in self testing. The absence of system-generated alarms gives the craftsperson a high degree of confidence when the trouble is cleared.

However, subtle problems can be difficult to isolate. A centralized tactical assistance center is a maintenance strategy which can be used to assist the local craftsperson. Through the use of remote displays and keyboards, centralized personnel, who are highly trained and have broad exposure to a larger variety of system problems than the local personnel, assist the local craftspeople in isolating and clearing faults. This approach provides a more effective use of personnel since the highly trained (and paid) people are given the difficult, hard-to-clear problems and are a centralized resource which can serve a large geographic area. The local personnel need not have these high skills but must be able to respond to direction which is provided from the tactical assistance center. The centralized people often provide the brains and the local people provide the hands in this new form of fault-clearing teamwork.

Centralized maintenance also provides for administration ease. Customer loop testing systems can be used to rapidly respond to customer complaints. Centralized traffic reports can isolate permanently seized trunks and can provide other indications of faults. Centralized automatic message accounting eliminates the need to transport magnetic tapes from the switching location to the revenue accounting center. Centralized dial administration can eliminate trips to an unattended office.

Thus, maintenance in communication networks is evolving towards a centralization of activities. The functions at this maintenance center will expand due to the power of computer technology.

4. Conclusions

Digital networks have been presented in this chapter. The evolution of networks from the integrated analog network to the integrated digital network and then to the integrated services digital network has been described. Requirements for digital networks which have been established by voice and data services have been presented. Network design subjects have been presented which economically provide these services including the integration of transmission and switching, loss and level plans, synchronization, and signaling. The chapter has concluded with the important subject of network maintenance.

A new network concept is developing as shown in Fig. 24. Four network planes are shown in order to provide the required service to customers. The first plane contains the information transfer from customer to customer. The second plane includes the common channel signaling network. The third represents the means to provide overall network synchronization; and the fourth is the maintenance and administration plane. Digital networks of the future will develop along these lines. The desired services will not be satisfactorily provided without proper attention to each of the areas represented by a separate plane.

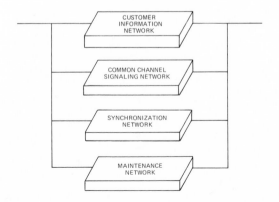

Fig. 24. Four distinct areas of network evolution.

Questions

1. Consider the United States. We wish to establish a new telephone network composed of transmission and switching systems across the country. Discuss the trade-off between transmission and switching. Assume switching costs of $300 per line, and $500 per trunk. Assume a transmission cost of $300 per circuit mile. Is a hierarchy of switching systems desirable? Why? Consider France. Discuss the trade-offs between transmission and switching.

2. What are the causes of the evolution from the IAN to the IDN and the ISDN?

3. Explain the use of the word "integrated" in IDN and ISDN.

4. Network transition from an IAN to an IDN and the ISDN will occur over decades. Explain why this evolution cannot occur more quickly.

5. In the IAN, data must be modulated by modems to simulate voice. In the IDN voice must be converted by codecs to simulate data. Discuss the relative advantages of the IAN and IDN for transmitting voice and data.

6. Why is common channel signaling required in the 1.544-mbit/s multiplex to provide a 64-kilobit/sec data channel to the customer?

7. We wish to transmit digital data over T-carrier facilities. What must be done to the data in order to satisfy the zero density requirement?

8. Suggest quantitative specifications for a communications network: (1) for data, (2) for voice.

9. Transparency must exist in a network for digital data transmission. What types of devices might occur in a network to prevent this transparency?

10. Discuss the methodology whereby network quantitative specifications for idle channel noise, transmission loss, and crosstalk might be established.

11. What are the sources of echo? What are the impacts of satellites on echo? How is echo controlled? What are the advantages and disadvantages of echo cancellors and echo suppressors? At what loop echo delay should echo suppressors be applied? Suggest a method for locating echo suppressors.

12. Figure 6 is a plot of optimum loss versus round-trip echo path delay. Discuss the concept of optimum loss and the conflicting parameters which give an optimum.

13. What factors establish the bit error rate requirements for data transmission? What bit error rate should be set as a minimum acceptable level. Why? In a binary transmission system, how is the bit error rate effected by Gaussian noise?

14. What are slips and how are they caused? How often would a slip occur if the average frequency difference between clocks in two digital systems was 10 Hz and the digital termination buffer frame was 125 microseconds long? How does the slip rate change with buffer length.

15. The prove-in point of a digital transmission system is a function of the switching technology employed at both ends of the transmission facility. Discuss how this prove-in point changes with analog and digital switching environments. Explain why digital transmission can prove-in at zero distance.

16. Explain why the cost of a digital tandem switch declines as the percentage of digital trunks it terminates increases. What is the impact of a digital channel bank reuse program on the economic analysis?

17. Discuss the interactive economies of digital pair gain systems in the presence of analog and digital switching.

18. What portions of a communications network might be integrated to provide an ISDN? What portions might be separately allocated to specific services? What type of interface device is required between integrated and nonintegrated facilities?

19. Explain the VNL plan. Derive the VNL formula.

20. Explain the differences between the fixed loss plan and VNL. What are the advantages and disadvantages of one loss for an entire network for both inter- and intra-office calling?

21. Define encode level point and decode level point. What is the importance of defining the correspondency between an analog voltage and a digital code word? Could the digital milliwatt be defined at any phase of a 1-kHz sinusoid with identical results? How does sampling and quantizing effect the digital milliwatt code?

22. Consider the network in Fig. 16. Assume that the desired intra-office loss in office B is 2 dB. Discuss the need for a 2 dB switchable pad at office B in this network. Draw a transmission measurement diagram including test sources and voltage measurements for an intra-office call at office B. Label the transmission levels for a call between office B and office D using the design rules of Fig. 13. What would be the value of the loss pads at office B if the VNL between office A and office D is 2 dB? What would be the value of the pad at office A in this case?

23. Referring to Fig. 19, why are four oscillators required in part a? Explain the function of loop timing and the reason that it is required. Discuss the length of the buffer B in Fig. 19b. What happens to slip rates and bit robbing if the buffer is one frame long? Is 12 frames long? What would be the circuit delay caused by a buffer which is one frame long? 12 frames long?

24. Explain the difference between master–slave and plesiochronous synchronization schemes. How can network slip rate objectives be met in either case?

25. Explain why the slave switches in Fig. 21c must have a high precision clock whereas the slave switches in Fig. 21b do not.

26. Explain the differences between inband signaling and common channel signaling.

27. Discuss the benefits of centralized maintenance and administration in a communications network.

References

1. D. F. Hoth, "The T1 Carrier System," *Bell Labs Rec.*, November 1962.
2. P. Fritz, "Citedis Production PCM Public Telephone Switching System," *IEEE Trans. Commun.*, pp. 1264–1268, September 1974.
3. I. Dorros, "ISDN," *IEEE Commun. Mag.*, March 1981.
4. "Clear Channel Capability," *Technical Advisory No. 69*, American Telephone and Telegraph Co., April 1981.
5. *Engineering and Operations in the Bell System*, Bell Telephone Laboratories, 1977.
6. S. Weinstein, "Echo Cancellation in the Telephone Network," *IEEE Commun. Soc. Mag.*, January 1977.
7. *Notes on the Network*, American Telephone and Telegraph Co., 1980.

8. *Agenda and Record of Meeting Held December 9, 1976*, United States Independent Telephone Association Equipment Compatibility Committee and American Telephone and Telegraph Co., December 1976.
9. *Notes on the Network*," American Telephone and Telegraph Co., 1980.
10. J. McDonald, "An Integrated Subscriber Carrier and Local Digital Switching System," *Int. Symp. Subscriber Loops and Services Rec.*, 1978.
11 J. Adams, "1000 Days of Digital," *Int. Conf. Commun. Rec.*, June 1981.
12. S. Johnston and B. Litofsky, "End-to-End 56 kb/s Switched Digital Connections in the Stored Program Controlled Network," *Int. Switching Symp. Rec.*, 1981.
13. B. Ghillibaert, J. Guernin, J. Invernici, and P. Lopez, "Presentation of the Nostradamus System," *Int. Symp. Subscriber Loops and Services Rec.*, 1980.
14. *Transmission Systems for Communications*, Bell Telephone Laboratories, Inc., 1970.
15. J. Abate, L. Brandenburg, J. Lawson, and W. Ross, "The Switched Digital Network Plan," *Bell Syst. Tech. J.*, vol. 56(7), September 1977.
16. R. Gould and G. Herder, "Transmission Delay and Echo Suppression," *IEEE Spectrum*, pp. 47–59, April 1970.
17. D. Duttweiler, "A Twelve Channel Digital Echo Canceler," *IEEE Trans. Commun.*, May 1978.
18. "Transmission Plan for DDD Network with Digital and Analog Switching Systems," *Technical Advisory No. 1*, American Telephone and Telegraph Co., July 15, 1974.
19. J. Abate, C. Cooper, J. Pan, and I. Shapiro, "Synchronization Considerations for the Switched Digital Network," *Int. Commun. Conf. Rec.*, June 1979.
20. J. Ryan, "Potential Impact of CCITT Signaling System No. 6," *Int. Commun. Conf. Rec.*, June 1973.
21. "Signaling System No. 6," *CCITT Green Book*, Volume VI, Part XIV, 1973.
22. "Signaling System No. 7," *CCITT Recommendations Q.701–Q.707; Q.721–Q.725*, Yellow Book, vol. VI, 7.
23. R. Nance and B. Kaskey, "Initial Implementation of Common Channel Interoffice Signaling," *Int. Switching Symp. Rec.*, 1976.

Glossary

This glossary has been compiled from CCITT recommendations and from common usage. CCITT recommendations are indicated by a (C).

A-law: A logarithmic compression function where $A = 87.6$ in the CEPT standard.

Access line: A means of providing a communications customer access to a switching system.

Algorithm: A prescribed finite set of well-defined rules or processes for the solution of a problem in a finite number of steps. (C)

Alternate routing: The process of selecting an alternate trunk group to the same ultimate destination when all trunks in the preferred route are busy.

Analog information: Information represented by a voltage, current, or other physical phenomenon whose amplitude is a continuous set of values in proportion to the information.

Analog switch: A means to interconnect two or more circuits whose information is represented in analog form using a network which may or may not be time divided and may or may not consist of linear elements.

Assembly language: A low level language whose instructions are usually in one-to-one correspondence with computer instructions and that may provide facilities such as the use of macroinstructions. (C)

Associated signaling: The mode where messages for a signaling relation involving two adjacent signaling points are conveyed over a directly interconnecting signaling link. (C)

Automatic call distributor: A switching system used to evenly distribute a number of incoming trunks onto a larger number of operator positions.

Automatic number identification: A means to identify a calling station without operator intervention.

Availability: The ability of trunks in a group to be accessed by a particular line.

Average busy season busy hour: The hour which has the highest average traffic for the three highest months, not necessarily consecutive. The busy hour traffic averaged across the busy season is termed the average busy season busy hour traffic.

Battery feed: The means to supply current from the switching system to a telephone.

Bipolar signal: A pseudo-ternary signal, conveying binary digits, in which successive "marks" are normally of alternating positive and negative polarity, but equal in amplitude, and in which "space" is of zero amplitude. (C)

Blocked calls cleared system: A system where calls which find all servers busy leave the system and have no effect upon it. (The calls encountering congestion are immediately cleared from the system.)

Blocked calls delayed system: A system where calls which find all servers busy form a queue and wait as long as necessary for service.

Blocked calls held system: A system where calls spend an amount of time T in the system. At the end of that time the call leaves the system irrespective of whether it is still waiting for service in queue or is being served.

Blocking: The inability of a calling customer to be connected to a service port or to the called customer either because all paths are busy or because all idle paths cannot be accessed.

BORSHT: An acronym for *b*attery, *o*vervoltage, *r*inging, *s*upervision, *h*ybrid, and *t*est. Sometimes called BORSCHT to include coding.

Burst mode: A digital modulation technique whereby a 4-wire circuit is established over two wires by alternately transmitting pulses in one direction and then the other.

Call: In an automatic system, the action performed by a calling party in order to obtain the called party and, by extension, the operations necessary in making a call. (C)

CCIS: Common *c*hannel *i*nteroffice *s*ignaling. A U.S. Bell System version of CCITT No. 6 signaling.

CCITT MML: The man–machine language (MML) for stored-program controlled switching systems developed by the International Telegraph and Telephone Consultative Committee (CCITT). (C)

CEPT: Conference of European postal and telecommunications administrations.

Channel associated signaling: A signaling method in which the signals necessary for the traffic carried by a single channel are transmitted in the channel itself or in a signaling channel permanently dedicated to it. (C)

CHILL: A high-level programming language for programming SPC telephone exchanges, developed by CCITT, and fully described in Recommendation Z.200. (C)

Circuit: A means of both-way communication between two points, comprising associated "go" and "return" channels. (C)

Circuit switching: The switching of circuits for the exclusive use of the connection for the duration of a call. (C)

C-message weighting: A filter characteristic which approximates the acoustic frequency response of a circuit between two telephones.

Codec: A contraction of encoder–decoder. The term may be used when the encoder and decoder are associated in the same equipment. (C)

Common channel signaling: A signaling technique in which signaling information relating to a multiplicity of circuits, and other information such as that used for network management, is conveyed over a single channel by addressed messages. (C)

Companding: A modulation technique to increase the signal-to-noise ratio in the presence of quantizing or additive noise.

Compelled signaling: A signaling method in which, after one signal or group of signals has been sent, the sending of any further signals in the same direction is inhibited until the sent signal has been acknowledged in the opposite direction by the receiving terminal, and the acknowledgement has been received. (C)

Compile: To translate a program expressed in a high level language into a program expressed in a computer language. (C)

Concentration: A configuration wherein the number of inlets into the switching stage is larger than the number of outlets. (C)

Connection: An association of channels and other functional units providing means for the transfer of information between two or more terminal points. (C)

Custom calling: A set of calling services provided by a switching system which enhances the value of communications.

Customer loop: Another term for access line.

D bank: A digital (D) channel bank which interfaces analog trunks with T carrier.

dBrnCO: A measurement in dB relative to a reference at -90 dBm which is C-weighted and further referenced to the 0 dB network datum point.

Decode level point: The analog power level caused by a digital milliwatt bit stream.

Delta modulation: A form of DPCM in which the magnitude of the difference between the predicted value and the actual value is encoded by one bit only, i.e., where only the sign of that difference is detected and transmitted. (C)

Differential pulse code modulation: A process in which a signal is sampled, and the difference between the actual value of each sample and its predicted value derived from the previous sample(s) is quantized and converted by encoding to a digital signal. (C)

Digital switching: A process in which connections are established by operations on digital signals without converting them to analog signals (usually in combination with time division multiplexing and digital memories). (C)

Digroup terminal: A terminal in the No. 4 ESS that provides a *DS*1 termination.

Distribution frame: A structure for terminating wires and connecting them together in any desired order. (C)

*DS*1: Digital signal at level 1, a 1.544 Mbit/s stream.

Dual tone multifrequency: A two-tone station signaling scheme.

Electronic switching system: A means to interconnect two or more circuits using a control device with solid state logic.

Encode level point: The analog power level required to produce a digital milliwatt bit stream.

Encoding law: The law defining the relative values of the quantum steps used in quantizing and encoding. (C)

Erlang: A measure of occupancy during a one hour interval e.g., 0.5 *E* equals 30 minutes of occupancy.

Executive program: A program, usually part of an operating system, that controls the execution of other programs and regulates the flow of work in a data processing system. (C)

Field: In a record, a specified area used for a particular category of data. (C)

Firmware: Software committed to read only memories.

Four-wire switching: Switching using a separate path, frequency band, or time interval for each direction of transmission. (C)

Frame: A set of consecutive digit time slots in which the position of each digit time slot can be identified by reference to a frame alignment signal. (C)

Frame alignment: The state in which the frame of the receiving equipment is correctly phased with respect to that of the received signal. (C)

Frequency division: The separation in the frequency domain of a plurality of transmission channels between two points. (C)

Full duplex: Transmission in both directions simultaneously.

GAZPACHO: An acronym for a digital interface: *g*enerating of frame code, *a*lignment of frames, *z*ero suppression, *p*olar conversion, *a*larming, *c*lock recovery, *h*unt during reframe, and *o*ffice signaling.

Glare: Simultaneous seizure of a two-way trunk from both ends.

Half duplex: Transmission in one direction or the other over a communications channel, but not simultaneously.

High day busy hour: The hour of the day that has the highest average traffic on the ten highest days of the busy season.

High level language: A programming language that does not reflect the structure of any given computer or any given class of computers. (C)

Hybrid transformer: A means to convert a two-wire circuit into a four-wire circuit and the reverse.

In-band signaling: A signaling method in which signals are sent over the same transmission channel or circuit as the user's communication and in the same frequency band as that provided for the users. (C)

Incoming response delay: A characteristic that is applicable where channel associated signaling is used. It is defined as the interval from the instant an incoming circuit seizure signal is recognized until a proceed-to-send signal is sent backwards by the exchange. (C)

In-slot signaling (bit robbing): Signaling associated with a channel and transmitted in a digit time slot permanently (or periodically) allocated in the channel time slot. (C)

Integrated digital network: A network in which connections established by digital switching are used for the transmission of digital signals, for a single service; for example telephony. (C)

Integrated services digital network: An integrated digital network in which the same digital switches and digital paths are used to establish connections for different services, for example, telephony, data, etc. (C)

Junctor: A circuit extending between frames of a switching unit and terminating in a switching device on each frame.

Key telephone: A special telephone instrument which includes a switching function by pressing keys.

Link: A communication path of specified character between two points. (C)

Local area network: A communications network connecting data and/or voice terminals within a building or in contiguous buildings.

Longitudinal voltage: A voltage which appears at the tip and ring with equal magnitude and phase.

Loop timing: A synchronization scheme whereby transmit pulses are synchronized to receive pulses.

Machine language: A low level language whose instructions consist only of computer instructions. (C)

Man–machine language: A language designed to facilitate direct user control of a computer. (C)

Master clock: A clock that generates accurate timing signals for the control of other clocks and possibly other equipments. (C)

Merged technology switch: A means to interconnect two or more circuits using a series of analog and digital switching stages.

Message switching: The transfer of stored messages so as to minimize queue and idle times of traffic carrying devices. (C)

μ-law: A logarithmic compression function where $D1$ channel banks use $\mu = 100$, and $D2$ and $D3$ channel banks use $\mu = 255$.

Multiframe: A set of consecutive frames in which the position of each frame can be identified by reference to a multiframe alignment signal. (C)

Multifrequency signaling: A signaling technique where information is transmitted using combinations of frequency.

Nonassociated signaling: The mode where messages for a signaling relation involving two (nonadjacent) signaling points are conveyed between those signaling points over two or more signaling links in tandem, passing through one or more signaling transfer points. (C)

Object program: A program in a target language that has been translated from a source language. (C)

Off-hook: A signaling state of an access line or trunk which is requesting service, is signaling, or is in the conversation mode.

One-way: A qualification applying to traffic which implies that the call set-ups always occur in one direction. (C)

On-hook: A signaling state of an access line or trunk which is idle or is in the midst of signaling.

Operating system: Software that controls the management and the execution of programs. (C)

Out-band signaling: A signaling method in which signals are sent over the same transmission channel or circuit as the user's communication, but in a different frequency band from that provided for the users. (C)

Out-slot signaling: Signaling associated with a channel, but transmitted in one or more separate digit time slots not within the channel time slot. (C)

Overload point: In PCM, the level expressed in dBmO of a sinusoidal signal, the positive and negative peaks of which coincide with the positive and negative virtual decision values of the encoder. (C)

PABX: Private automatic branch exchange. A private switching system with a unique dialing plan which can access private stations, the public network or private trunks.

Packet switching: A switching technique where a message is broken into small segments known as packets and the destination address is added to each packet.

Pair gain: The difference between the number of pairs required without the pair gain system and the number required with the system.

Path: The implementation of a means of transmission. The path includes the channels used for the transmission and the means used for connecting them. (C)

Plesiochronous: Signals are plesiochronous if their corresponding significant-instants occur at nominally the same rate, any variation in rate being constrained within specified limits. (C)

Post dialing delay: Time interval between the end of dialing by the subscriber and the reception by him of the appropriate tone or recorded announcement, or the abandon of the call without tone. (C)

Processor: A device capable of performing systematic execution of operations upon data. (C)

Progress tones: Tones to indicate call progress to a customer (e.g., dial tone, ringback, busy, etc.).

Psophometric weighting: A filter characteristic for noise measurements.

Pulse amplitude modulation: A modulation technique in a sampled system where the height of a pulse whose width is arbitrarily short is proportional to the information amplitude.

Pulse code modulation: A process in which a signal is sampled, and the magnitude of each sample is quantized independently of other samples and converted by encoding to a digital signal. (C)

Pulse stuffing: A process of changing the rate of a digital signal in a controlled manner so that it can accord with a rate different from its own inherent rate, usually without loss of information. (C)

Quantizing: A process in which the magnitude of a sample is classified into one of a number of adjacent intervals. Any sample magnitude falling within a given interval is represented by a single value. (C)

Quantizing distortion: The distortion resulting from the process of quantizing. (C)

Real time: Pertaining to the processing of data by a computer in connection with another process outside the computer according to time requirements imposed by the outside process. (C)

Reframe time: The time that elapses between a valid frame alignment signal being available at the receive terminal equipment and frame alignment being established. (C)

Release: The event which is the end of a busy state. (C)

Remote exchange concentrator: A concentrator located remotely from the exchange that controls it and to which its higher traffic volume circuits are connected. The switching stages comprised normally have no capability to directly interconnect subscriber lines (access lines) terminating in that concentration. (C)

Reverting call: A call between two multiparty customers over the same access line.

Revertive pulsing: A signaling technique where the receiving office outpulses and the sending office sends a stop command when the correct number of pulses are received.

Ringback tone: A tone which indicates that the ringing function is being applied at the called end. (C)

Sample: The value of a particular characteristic of a signal at a chosen instant. (C)

Satellite exchange: A local exchange on a low level of the network hierarchy which is associated to another exchange and with no route switching functions except those towards the associated higher level local exchange. A satellite exchange normally has the capability to locally connect subscribers' lines terminating in it. (C)

Seizure: A successful single attempt to obtain the service of a resource. (C)

Side tone: Transmission from the telephone instrument transmitter to receiver so the caller can hear his own speech.

Signal transfer point: A signaling point with the function of transferring signaling messages from one signaling link to another. (C)

Signaling: The exchange of electrical information (other than by speech) specifically concerned with the establishment and control of connections, and management, in a communication network. (C)

Singing: Self-oscillation of a four-wire circuit.

Slip: The uncontrolled loss or gain of a digit position or a set of consecutive digit positions resulting from an aberration of the timing processes associated with transmission or switching of a digital signal. (C)

Software: Computer programs, procedures, rules, and any associated documentation concerned with the operation of a system. (C)

SLIC: An acronym defining the functions required for a subscriber line interface circuit.

Space division: The separation in the space domain of a plurality of transmission channels between two points. (C)

Space division switching: The switching of inlets to outlets using space division techniques. (C)

Specification and description language: The CCITT language used in the presentation of the functional specification and functional description of the internal logic processes in stored programmed control (SPC) switching systems. (C)

S-stage: A time-multiplexed space stage as in *TST*.

Station: A subscriber terminal to access a communications system.

Store and forward switching: A switching system where a message is received at a switching node and then retransmitted in its entirety.

Subscriber carrier system: A pair gain system in the subscriber plant.

Switching: The establishing, on demand, of an individual connection from a desired inlet to a desired outlet within a set of inlets and outlets for as long as is required for the transfer of information. (C)

Switching center network: The switching stages of a switching system taken collectively.

Synchronization: The process of adjusting the corresponding significant instants of signals to make them synchronous. (C)

Synchronous: Signals are synchronous if their corresponding significant instants have a desired phase relationship with each other. (C)

T-carrier: A series of digital transmission systems using various bit rates (e.g., $T1$, $T2$, $T3$, $T4$).

$T1$ repeater: A regenerative device to reconstruct $T1$ bit streams.

Time division: The separation in the time domain of a plurality of transmission channels between two points. (C)

Time-division multiplexing: Multiplexing in which two or more channels are interleaved in time for transmission over a common channel. (C)

Time-division switching: The switching of inlets to outlets using time division (multiplexing) techniques. (C)

Time slot: Any cyclic time interval that can be recognized and uniquely defined. (C)

Time slot interchange: The transfer of information from one time slot to another between incoming and outgoing time division highways. (C)

TLP: *T*ransmission *l*evel *p*oint. An analog power reference to specify signal levels.

Traffic carried: For systems in statistical equilibrium, the traffic carried is equal to the mean number of busy servers.

Traffic offered: Traffic offered or the offered load is a measure of the demand placed on the system.

Translation: In automatic telephony the retransmission of received trains of impulses after changing the number of impulses in each train and/or changing the number of trains. (C)

Transmission delay through a digital exchange: The sum of the times necessary for an octet to pass in both directions on a connection through a digital exchange due to buffering, frame alignment, and time-slot interchange functions for digital-to-digital connections, and in addition, for analog-to-analog connections, to the A/D conversions. (C)